T0383177

Interlinkages between the Sustainable Development Goals

PROGRESSING THE SUSTAINABLE DEVELOPMENT GOALS SERIES

This timely series offers a multidisciplinary forum for the latest research on critical topics and issues related to the UN's Sustainable Development Goals. Focusing on these global targets and efforts to advance them, books in the series address some of the grand challenges facing society today.

For a full list of Edward Elgar published titles, including the titles in this series, visit our website at www.e-elgar.com.

Interlinkages between the Sustainable Development Goals

Edited by

Ranjula Bali Swain

Research Director and Visiting Professor, Center for Sustainability Research, SIR, Stockholm School of Economics and Professor of Economics, Södertörn University, Stockholm, Sweden

Yongyi Min

Chief, Sustainable Development Goal Monitoring Section, Statistics Division, Department of Economic and Social Affairs, United Nations Secretariat, New York, USA

PROGRESSING THE SUSTAINABLE DEVELOPMENT GOALS SERIES

Cheltenham, UK · Northampton, MA, USA

Published by
Edward Elgar Publishing Limited
The Lypiatts
15 Lansdown Road
Cheltenham
Glos GL50 2JA
UK

Edward Elgar Publishing, Inc.
William Pratt House
9 Dewey Court
Northampton
Massachusetts 01060
USA

A catalogue record for this book
is available from the British Library

Library of Congress Control Number: 2023945196

This book is available electronically in the **Elgar**online
Geography, Planning and Tourism subject collection
http://dx.doi.org/10.4337/9781803924946

Printed on elemental chlorine free (ECF)
recycled paper containing 30% Post-Consumer Waste

ISBN 978 1 80392 493 9 (cased)
ISBN 978 1 80392 494 6 (eBook)

Printed and bound in the USA

Contents

Contributors

Ranjula Bali Swain is Research Director at the Center for Sustainability Research (CSR), SIR, Stockholm School of Economics and Professor of Economics at Södertörn University, Stockholm. She is affiliated with the Center for European Research in Microfinance (CERMi) at the Solvay Brussels School of Economics and Management. Bali Swain has worked at the International Labour Organization, Geneva, and Uppsala University and has been Visiting Professor at the University of California, Berkeley, Stanford University, Tufts University, University of Pretoria, South Africa, and UN Sustainable Development Solutions Network, New York, USA, etc. Her research interests are in sustainable development, the circular economy and development finance.

Jean-Pierre Cling holds a PhD in international economics from Paris Dauphine University and graduated from the Ecole Nationale de la Statistique et de l'Administration Economique (ENSAE), Paris. He currently works at the French National Institute of Statistics and Economic Studies (INSEE). He has authored or co-authored numerous books and scientific articles on international and development economics and especially various articles on SDGs in international journals.

Jonathan H. P. Dawes is a mathematician with research interests in complex systems, machine learning and mathematical biology. He especially enjoys the challenges of interdisciplinary research. He was awarded his PhD in 2001 from the University of Cambridge and held a Royal Society University Research Fellowship from 2007 to 2015.

Clément Delecourt studied at Università La Sapienza of Rome and ENSAI. He holds a European master's degree in official statistics. Currently, he is international relations officer at the French National Institute of Statistics and Economic Studies (INSEE). His research focuses on interlinkages between Sustainable Development Goals.

Sara Duerto Valero is the Regional Advisor on Gender Statistics in the United Nations Women's Regional Office for Asia and the Pacific, where she manages several regional programmes on gender statistics. Sara has extensive experience working on environment statistics, development indicators and gender statistics. She previously worked as a statistician for UN DESA, UN ESCAP and UNESCO. She holds a master's degree in Development Studies from Universite Libre de Bruxelles and a graduate degree in business from Universidad de Zaragoza.

Anja Eliasson obtained her master's degree in environmental science at Mid Sweden University. The Sustainable Development Goals have been a main topic throughout her education and were the focus of her master's thesis. Currently working as an environmental consultant, she is able to implement her knowledge in promoting sustainable communities.

Erik Grönlund is a senior lecturer and researcher in the interdisciplinary research group of Ecotechnology and Environmental Science at Mid Sweden University. He has an interdisciplinary interest and background in systems ecology, ecological engineering, environmental engineering, environmental science, ecophilosophy, journalism and human ecology.

Sneha Kaul is a statistician at the United Nations Women's Regional Office of Asia and the Pacific. She has extensive experience in data for development and is a key contributor to UN Women's statistical analysis and flagship publications. She holds a master's degree in social and cultural psychology from the London School of Economics and has previously worked with UNDP's Human Development Report Office, LSE, IIT Delhi, and Delhi University.

Lin Lerpold is a tenured Associate Professor at the Stockholm School of Economics. She is also Director of the SIR Center for Sustainability Research and Vice Director of the Sustainable Finance Lab. Lin is a member of the board of the Stockholm School of Economics Institute for Research, Vice Chairperson of AP2 and a member of the steering committee of the Alliance for Research on Corporate Sustainability. She was the founding director of the Mistra Center for Sustainable Markets and has been a visiting scholar at the LSE and INSEAD.

Suyu Liu is an expert in sustainable development with specialties in fields such as green growth, the blue economy, inclusive development and poverty alleviation. Dr Suyu Liu has extensive experience in both academia and the United Nations, where he developed solid knowledge of international organizations and the SDGs. Dr Suyu Liu obtained a doctorate degree from the University of Oxford.

Yongyi Min is the Chief of the Sustainable Development Goal Monitoring Section at the Statistics Division of the United Nations Department of Economic and Social Affairs. She is responsible for the programme for the global monitoring of the progress towards the SDGs. She manages and contributes to work on the development and implementation of the global SDG indicator framework and supports the work of the Inter-Agency and Expert Group on SDG Indicators. She is the lead author of the annual global *The Sustainable Development Goals Report* and manages other SDG monitoring outputs at the global level. She holds a PhD in statistics from the University of Florida.

Mustafa Moinuddin works as Deputy Director of Integrated Sustainability Centre of the Institute for Global Environmental Strategies (IGES). With more than 12 years of work experience in the field of international development, he is currently involved in several research activities relating to the Sustainable Development Goals and their interlinkages, the green economy, the hydrogen economy and combatting plastic pollution.

Natalia Alonso Ospina is an economist from Universidad del Rosario, born in Bogota, Colombia, in 1992. She worked for four years at the National Administrative Department of Statistics in the measurement of indicators of the Sustainable Development Goals.

Viveka Palm is the Director of the Department of Sectoral and Regional Statistics at Eurostat, the statistical bureau of the EU. The department produces the EU environmental accounts including the monitoring of the Sustainable Development Goals, as well as statistics on energy, transport and agriculture and regional statistics. Earlier, she worked at Statistics Sweden and as Adjunct Professor in the Department of Sustainable Development, Environmental Science and Engineering (SEED) at the Royal Institute of Technology, KTH, in Stockholm. Palm has been the co-chair of the UN Inter-Agency and Expert Group for the Sustainable Development Goal Indicators (IAEG-SDG) in the group for North America and Northern and Western Europe between the years 2019 and 2021.

Prajal Pradhan was a lead author of the IPCC Special Report on Climate Change and Land. He has experience developing relevant research on climate change, sustainable food systems and sustainable development. His research focuses on urban transformations, climate change impacts and Sustainable Development Goal interactions.

Karen Chavez Quintero holds an MS in economics, with a BA in economics and a BA in finance from Universidad del Rosario, Colombia. She worked in DANE as Senior Advisor and Head of the SDG Indicators Taskteam. Previously, she worked in projects related to public policy as Analyst and as Technical Director.

Sharita Serrao is currently working as a statistician at the Population and Social Statistics Section of UNESCAP. Sharita's main responsibilities centre around statistical development and capacity building, with a focus on gender statistics. Sharita has academic training in economics, mathematics and business administration and is currently pursuing an advanced degree in gender and development studies.

Örjan Sjöberg is Professor of Economic Geography, Department of Marketing and Strategy, Stockholm School of Economics. He is also affiliated with the SIR Center for Sustainability Research. A geographer with an interest in issues at the intersection of migration, labour markets and urban change, these and other concerns are typically approached with an eye on political economy aspects as may apply.

Anne Warchold is a sustainability scientist at the Potsdam Institute for Climate Impact Research. She applies her expertise in sustainable development to guide policy coherence for, for example, the 2030 Agenda. Her recent research interests include the Sustainable Development Goals and their synergies and trade-offs with topics such as inequalities, education, cities and food security. In her current work, she identifies how transitioning towards a bioeconomy can contribute to the achievement of SDGs and vice versa.

Xin Zhou is Research Director of the Integrated Sustainability Centre, Institute for Global Environmental Strategies (IGES). She has over 25 years of experience in environmental policy research. She is devoted to supporting SDG integrated policy making and led the development of the SDG Interlinkages Analysis & Visualisation Tool.

Preface

It is with great pleasure that we introduce this edited volume on exploring the interlinkages in the context of the Sustainable Development Goals (SDGs). The SDGs are an ambitious blueprint for a better, sustainable, and equitable future, and understanding the interlinkages among them is crucial for their successful implementation. This book brings together a collection of seminal research to define, identify, and present conceptual frameworks for interlinkages among the goals and targets, providing readers with a comprehensive understanding of the SDGs' interconnectedness.

This book is aimed at a diverse audience, and we hope it will serve as a valuable reference for those seeking to better understand the interlinkages within the SDG framework. We hope the volume will also provide useful insights and examples of possible applications, implications, and best practices to support the implementation of the SDGs.

We would like to gratefully acknowledge and thank the Edward Elgar Publishing team and the contributing authors who have generously shared their expertise and knowledge, making this volume possible. Their insightful contributions have helped to produce a valuable resource for policy makers, researchers, college students, practitioners, stakeholders in the private and public sectors, and civil society.

In conclusion, we would like to emphasize the importance of understanding the interlinkages among the SDGs for the achievement of sustainable development. We hope this edited volume will contribute to the broader discussion on the SDGs' implementation and their impact. Our aspiration is that it will inspire further research, discussions, and collaborations to support the achievement of the SDGs and a more sustainable future for all.

Ranjula Bali Swain, Stockholm
Yongyi Min, New York

1. Interlinkages and interactions among the Sustainable Development Goals

Ranjula Bali Swain and Yongyi Min

1.1 INTRODUCTION

The 2030 Agenda for Sustainable Development adopted by 193 United Nations Member States in 2015 provides a blueprint to set the world on a path of peace, prosperity and opportunity for all on a healthy planet (United Nations, 2015). The new global development agenda contains 17 Sustainable Development Goals (SDGs) and 169 targets, ranging from ending poverty, hunger and discrimination against women and girls, to providing basic services and education to all, protecting the environment and ensuring peace and security, and global partnership. The 17 goals and the targets do not work in silos. They are deeply interconnected and integrated so that action in one area will affect outcomes in others. The agenda emphasizes that 'the interlinkages and integrated nature of the Sustainable Development Goals are of crucial importance in ensuring that the purpose of the new Agenda is realized'. Therefore, in implementing the 2030 Agenda the interlinkages among the goals and targets must be considered and social, economic and environmental sustainability must be balanced (Bali Swain & Ranganathan, 2021; Bali Swain & Wallentin, 2020; Pradhan et al., 2017; Spaiser et al., 2017; Zhou & Moinuddin, 2017).

By identifying strong synergies and trade-offs across goals and related targets, countries can design integrated and coherent policies and leverage policy efficiency. Moreover, this approach allows countries to prioritize the allocation of scarce resources towards targeted programmes and projects to achieve optimal sustainable development outcomes. At the midpoint of the implementation of the 2030 Agenda, the global community needs to turbocharge its efforts to achieve the SDGs to respond to a perfect storm of crises and achieve meaningful progress for people and the planet by 2030. This edited volume aims to explore, examine and demonstrate the breadth and depth of interlinkages related to the SDGs and identify synergies and trade-offs to accelerate the progress towards the global goals.

1.2   CASCADING GLOBAL CRISES PUT ALL SDGS AT RISK AND DEMONSTRATE THEIR INTERLINKED NATURE

The world is currently grappling with a confluence of crises, primarily driven by the COVID-19 pandemic, climate change and increased conflicts. These crises pose a significant threat to human survival and global development. They are interconnected, with the risks they pose amplifying and multiplying, creating a perfect storm of cascading calamities, including a food and nutrition crisis, an energy crisis, a health crisis, an education crisis, a cost-of-living crisis, a debt crisis and the global economic slowdown. These multifaceted and interrelated crises have exacerbated pre-existing challenges, resulting in significant and far-reaching impacts on all of the Sustainable Development Goals. This clearly proves that the 17 goals and their associated targets are deeply intertwined.

1.2.1   The COVID-19 Crisis

The COVID-19 pandemic originated as a public health crisis. However, the rapid spread of the coronavirus quickly turned a public health crisis into a global economic and social crisis, eventually developing into one of the worst human crises of our lifetime. In a matter of months, the coronavirus had spread to more than 200 countries and territories, affecting all segments of the population and all sectors of the economy. At the peak of global lockdowns to cope with the spread of the virus, the global health system was overwhelmed, businesses and factories were shut down, millions of workers lost their jobs, over 90 per cent of students worldwide were out of school (1.6 billion students in April 2020) and the global supply chain was severely disrupted.

The ongoing COVID-19 pandemic has had a significant impact on the progress towards achieving the SDGs globally. Its duration and end point remain uncertain. The pandemic has caused widespread disruption to development activities and set back years of progress on the SDGs. As per 'The Sustainable Development Report 2022', during the first year of the pandemic, more than four years of progress on extreme poverty eradication was wiped out and close to 100 million additional people were pushed back into extreme poverty in 2020. Additionally, 150 million more people faced hunger in 2021 than in 2019. The pandemic has also disrupted essential health services resulting in a drop in life expectancy. In 2020, more children missed their essential vaccines and immunization coverage dropped for the first time in ten years. Data also show an increase in deaths from tuberculosis and malaria for the first time in more than a decade. An estimated 147 million children missed more than half of their in-person instruction in 2020–1, and 24 million learners, especially girls, are at risk of not returning to school (United Nations, 2021b, 2022a).

The crisis has further exacerbated existing inequalities within and among countries. The rich get richer, and the poor get poorer. The world's ten richest men more than doubled their fortunes from $700 billion to $1.5 trillion during the first two years of the pandemic, while the incomes of 99 per cent of humanity fell and hundreds of millions more people were forced into poverty and hunger (Ahmed et al., 2022). The poorest and the most vulnerable people are also affected disproportionally by the pandemic, including women, children, older persons, people with disabilities, migrants and refugees and informal sector workers. The pandemic has set gender parity back from 99 years to now 132 years (World Economic Forum, 2022).

The COVID-19 pandemic has had particularly negative impacts on children's learning and well-being worldwide. It is estimated that this generation of children could lose a combined total of $17 trillion in lifetime earnings in present value (World Bank, UNESCO, & UNICEF, 2021). School closures affected girls, children from disadvantaged backgrounds, those living in rural areas, children with disabilities and children from ethnic minorities more than their peers. The pandemic has triggered a significant rise in anxiety and depression among children and young people. Economic shocks and school closures caused by COVID-19 have also led to an increase in child labour and child marriage. The latest evidence warns that, globally, 9 million additional children are at risk of being pushed into child labour by the end of 2022, compared to 2020. By 2030, it is estimated that up to 10 million more girls are likely to become child brides, in addition to the 100 million girls who were projected to be at risk before the pandemic.

1.2.2   The Climate Crisis

The globe is increasingly facing a climate crisis as human activity has undeniably caused global temperatures to rise at a rate unprecedented in the last 2000 years. Across the world, billions of people have been affected by the increased frequency of heatwaves, droughts and floods caused by climate change. The warming of the atmosphere, ocean and land has caused severe damage and risks to human and natural systems, causing biodiversity loss and environmental degradation, natural disasters and extreme weather events, food and water insecurity, sea level rise and ocean warming, economic disruption, conflict and terrorism. These devastating consequences of climate change reverberate across the SDGs.

According to the sixth assessment report of the Intergovernmental Panel on Climate Change (IPCC, 2021, 2022a), climate change has caused substantial damage and increasingly irreversible losses in many areas:

- **Sea level rise and ocean warming**: Sea levels have already risen faster than in any preceding century. Since 1993, the rate of sea level rise has more than doubled. Sea levels have risen by nearly 10 mm since January 2020, reaching a new high in 2022 (WMO, 2022). If greenhouse gas emissions continue unabated, sea levels will rise between 60 and 110 centimetres by 2010. Even if greenhouse gas emissions are sharply reduced and global warming is limited to well below 2°C above pre-industrial levels, sea levels still could rise 30–60 centimetres (IPCC, 2019). This trend will lead to more frequent and severe coastal flooding and erosion. Ocean warming will continue with increasingly intense and frequent marine heatwaves, ocean acidification and reduced oxygen. Even if global warming is limited to 2°C, 99 per cent of coral reefs will probably disappear, destroying the habitats of over one-quarter of all marine life.
- **Food and water insecurity**: Climate change has increasingly put pressure on food production and water resources and has led to an increased risk to food security through more frequent droughts, floods and heatwaves, increasing temperatures and changing precipitation patterns. Millions of people have been exposed to acute food insecurity and reduced water security. For example, as many as 20 million people in the Horn of Africa region could go hungry in 2022 as delayed rains worsen extreme drought. By 2030, an estimated 700 million people will be at risk of displacement by drought alone. It is projected that about one-third of global land areas will suffer at least moderate drought by 2100.
- **Declining ecosystems and biodiversity loss**: Climate change has already caused substantial damage and increasingly irreversible losses in terrestrial, freshwater and coastal and open ocean marine ecosystems. Near-term risks for biodiversity loss are moderate to high in forest ecosystems and kelp and seagrass ecosystems and high to very high in Arctic sea-ice and terrestrial ecosystems and warm-water coral reefs (IPCC, 2022a). Many natural systems are near the hard limits of their natural adaptation capacity, and additional systems will reach limits with increasing global warming.
- **Increased climate-related disasters**: As a result of climate change, the number of weather, climate and water extremes is increasing, and climate-related disasters are becoming more frequent and severe in many parts of the world. Medium to large disaster events could see a 40 per cent increase between 2015 and 2030 due to climate change exacerbating disaster risk. Children today are expected to experience a nearly four-fold increase in extreme events by 2100 under a 1.5°C scenario and a five-fold increase under a 3°C scenario.
- **Impacting the health and livelihoods of billions of people**: Approximately 3.3 to 3.6 billion people live in contexts that are highly

vulnerable to climate change, many of whom are already facing high levels of poverty, limited basic services, violent conflict and governance challenges. The World Health Organization estimates that climate change is expected to cause approximately 250 000 additional deaths per year between 2030 and 2050 due to malnutrition, malaria, diarrhoea and heat stress. The direct health damage costs are estimated to be between $2 billion and $4 billion per year by 2030 (WHO, 2021).

- **Increased conflicts**: Climate-related events such as droughts and floods threaten access to and availability of resources like food and water, increase competition for natural resources and create civil unrest. Climate change increases the risk of conflict by exacerbating existing social, economic and environmental factors. Intensifying climate change will likely increase the future risk of violent armed conflict within countries. Researchers have estimated that climate change or climate variability has influenced between 3 per cent and 20 per cent of armed conflict risk over the past century (Mach et al., 2019).

1.2.3   The Ukraine Crisis

While the world is still reeling from the social and economic consequences of COVID-19, the Russian invasion of Ukraine in February 2022 poses a new global threat, causing a humanitarian crisis and economic shock. The ongoing conflict in Ukraine has affected many aspects of the global sustainable development agenda, pushing the world's progress back further.

The most significant and immediate consequence of the war is the millions of shattered lives in Ukraine. Overnight, Ukrainians' lives were turned upside down and their families were ripped apart. Millions of refugees fled Ukraine into neighbouring countries seeking protection, the vast majority of them being women and children. Many more have been forced to move inside the country.

Russia and Ukraine are large producers and exporters of key food items, fertilizer, minerals and energy. These two countries represent more than half of the world's supply of sunflower oil and about 30 per cent of the world's wheat. At least 50 countries import at least 30 per cent of their wheat from Ukraine or Russia, with 36 importing at least 50 per cent, and most of them are African and least developed countries (United Nations, 2022b).

The conflict has caused food, fuel and fertilizer prices to skyrocket, disrupted supply chains and global trade and caused distress in financial markets. Together with the refugee crisis, the impacts of the conflict may lead to a global food crisis and deal a significant blow to SDG progress on many fronts. It is estimated that the war could cut global economic growth by 0.9 percentage points in 2022 (United Nations, 2022c).

1.3   SOLUTIONS FOR ACHIEVING THE SDGS ARE ALSO INTERLINKED

The current global crises highlight the interdependency and the interconnectedness of the various dimensions of sustainability – from health and well-being to socio-economic prosperity, climate, ecosystems and peace. In the light of the many challenges encountered, it is more important than ever to develop coherent, coordinated and comprehensive responses from the multilateral system. Just as the impacts and risks of multiple crises are amplified when they are linked, so are the solutions. To address the vulnerabilities exposed by crises, the international community can make structural transformations and develop common solutions guided by the SDGs. Some of these key interventions that can facilitate the achievement of multiple goals include the following.

1.3.1   Strengthening Social Protection Systems

Social protection systems are essential for preventing and reducing poverty and inequality at every stage of people's lives, making societies more inclusive and stable. Different population groups face different challenges to sustainability and have varying levels of resilience. Social protection systems can help to equalize opportunities and ensure no one is left behind. However, the human right to social security is not yet a reality for the majority of people in the world. By 2020, only 47 per cent of the global population was effectively covered by at least one social protection cash benefit. This means that 4.1 billion people in the world are unprotected, lacking access to a pension, unemployment benefits, health insurance and income guarantees. The pandemic has taught us that social protection systems help the poor and the most vulnerable people cope with crises and shocks. In response to the COVID-19 crisis, 211 countries and territories announced nearly 1900 social protection measures. However, 92 per cent of these measures were short term (United Nations, 2022a). Social protection is a primary development priority. Governments and partners need to work together to develop a comprehensive strategy to achieve universal social protection.

1.3.2   Providing Public Services for All

To understand the priority areas of different vulnerable population groups and to ensure that marginalized groups are counted, the Inter-Agency and Expert Group on SDG Indicators (IAEG-SDGs) asked major groups and international organizations to hold consultations to identify a minimum set of policy priorities. The policy priorities identified by different vulnerable groups have many commonalities: access to health care, education, safe transport, water and sanitation, electricity or other forms of energy and affordable housing (IAEG-SDGs, 2019). Economic growth, social inclusion, poverty reduction and equality all go hand in hand with the provision of these basic public services.

Despite significant strides made in improving the quality of and access to basic services around the world, in many countries, the poor and most vulnerable have been left behind. In 2020, 2 billion people still lacked safely managed drinking water services, 3.6 billion lacked safely managed sanitation services, and one in four people worldwide still lacked basic handwashing facilities with soap and water at home. Around 2.4 billion people, mostly women and children, are still cooking with polluting fuel and inefficient stoves, adversely affecting their health and well-being. Improving the lives of the poor and most vulnerable requires significant investments in quality basic services.

1.3.3   Harnessing Science, Technology and Innovation

The COVID-19 pandemic has demonstrated the importance of science, technology and innovation in building back better and achieving the SDGs. In 2021, most industries using medium and high levels of technology had already returned to pre-pandemic production levels. In comparison, lower-tech industries remain below their pre-pandemic levels. Higher-technology industries have proven to be far more resilient in crises than their lower-tech counterparts. The world's ability to develop the COVID-19 vaccines so quickly has shown how science and technology can be lifesaving, and they are one of the key enablers for the achievement of the SDGs. In the last two years, the number of Internet users has increased by 782 million. The pandemic has sped up the digital transformation of governments and businesses, profoundly altering the ways in which we interact, learn and work. It has also resulted in the acceptance of innovative approaches. The global crises can serve as catalysts for adopting innovations, harnessing the power of science and technology and forcing new ways of thinking.

1.3.4   Investing in Data

Data are strategic assets for responding to crises, rebuilding better and accelerating SDG implementation. Timely and high-quality data are needed to guide COVID-19 decision-making throughout the process, from response to recovery and the implementation of the SDGs. However, in many developing countries, even basic health, social and economic data are still lacking. In addition, the most vulnerable populations who need help the most remain invisible, such as older persons, persons with disabilities and refugees.

Mobilizing international and domestic resources to increase investments in national data and information systems will be critical for recovering from crises and accelerating SDG implementation. In addition, new partnerships to increase the use of new data sources and technologies will need to be forged, including between public producers of data and the private sector, academia and civil society. The integration of geospatial information and statistical data is also particularly important.

1.3.5   Taking a Green Economy Approach and Investing in Clean Energy and Industry

To ensure a sustainable economic recovery and combat climate change, the world must seize the opportunity provided by the recovery to take a green approach to improve resource efficiency, reduce waste and pollution and shape a new circular economy. A green economy approach can help reduce carbon emissions, conserve natural resources, transform our food systems and create better jobs. However, international public financing for renewable energy has slowed despite the growing urgency of climate change. Achieving energy and climate goals will require continued policy support and a massive mobilization of public and private capital for clean and renewable energy, especially in developing countries.

1.3.6   Transforming Global Financial and Debt Architecture and Creating Fiscal Space

Vulnerable countries, including least developed countries, small island developing states and countries in a fragile situation, are hit hardest by the multiple global crises due to their weak economic growth, limited financial and other resources, vulnerability to external shocks and unsustainable debt. To recover from the pandemic and rescue the SDGs, a full-scale transformation of the international financial and debt architecture is also required. Concrete and coordinated actions are needed to provide countries with adequate fiscal space and liquidity. Secretary-General António Guterres of the United Nations proposed a three-phased approach to address debt burdens: a debt standstill, targeted debt relief for the most vulnerable and a reform of the international debt architecture. International financial institutions, multinational and national development banks and other partners need to work together to take urgent action to complement existing instruments with more effective debt crisis resolution mechanisms (United Nations, 2021a).

1.4   ABOUT THIS EDITED VOLUME

The goal of this edited volume is to explore the interlinkages in the context of the Sustainable Development Goals. It seeks to investigate the interlinkages at the thematic, regional and country levels and provide examples of possible applications, implications and best practices. The volume is aimed at a diverse audience, including policy makers, researchers, college students, practitioners, stakeholders in the private and public sectors and civil society.

This book brings together seminal research to define, identify and present conceptual frameworks for interlinkages among the goals and targets. The volume analyses and compares the Sustainable Development Goals, targets and indicators to identify possible interlinkages. It identifies areas, tools, frameworks and data collection that can facilitate the quantification and analysis of SDG interlinkages. Integrated analyses that have been tested at a national or international level are discussed. The chapters also propose strategies that use the identified interlinkages to facilitate SDG implementation and produce evidence that may be employed by policy makers to make integrated and coherent decisions in the area of sustainable development.

In Chapter 2, authors Lerpold and Sjöberg focus on the underlying conceptual issues to explore the interdependence and trade-offs between the goals and suggest that decoupling must have a more prominent focus. Climate, environment and social sustainability are often theorized and empirically depicted as separate challenges. This is not the case since the SDGs focusing on social goals are correlated with SDG 8 in a positive way. At the same time, increased climate emissions and ecological footprint are negatively correlated with economic growth and SDG 8. If the social goals are to be met, economic growth must continue but without increasing the planetary footprint of humankind in the natural world. They conclude that the evidence of such decoupling continues to be patchy at best and discuss redistribution as a possible solution.

Research on the interactions between different dimensions of the same goal target or within an SDG indicator is relatively limited. Liu explores this in Chapter 3 by using the example of SDG Indicator 14.7.1 to explore the interactions between the economic and environmental dimensions of using marine resources for sustainable development. It is observed that while this indicator partially meets the 'Specific-Measurable-Achievable-Realistic-Time bounded' (SMART) standard, the interactions between the economic and the environmental dimensions of SDG Indicator 14.7.1 lead to ambiguity in defining, understanding and using this indicator. Several practical implications are generated based on the most recent data for SDG Indicator 14.7.1 from selected countries. For example, a better understanding of the country's context would be helpful to reduce the ambiguity caused by the interactions between the economic and environmental dimensions of SDG Indicator 14.7.1.

Monitoring Sustainable Development Goals at the national level shows distinct patterns of policies that seem to create a good basis for development. For most goals, countries have policies that address a subset of issues and vary in terms of their focus. Furthermore, some policies have side effects that are unintended but still make it difficult to reach other goals within the SDG framework. Policy design can also depend on the historical set-up and local possibilities within the country. Therefore, both the generality of policies and policy coherence are central to the SDG outcomes. Palm explores how society may find paths to sustainability. Categorizing policy choices within a model of the generality of values, which looks at individual, hierarchical, egalitarian and fatalistic values, Palm discusses if these may explain some of the differences between the policies chosen.

Recent research on Sustainable Development Goals synergies and trade-offs has generated a plethora of empirical evidence. These studies employ qualitative methods consisting of literature reviews, expert elicitation or soliciting stakeholder perspectives (Hernández-Orozco et al., 2022; Pham-Truffert et al., 2020; Weitz et al., 2018) and quantitative analysis methods (Asadikia et al., 2021; Bali Swain & Wallentin, 2020; Hegre et al., 2019; Kroll et al., 2019; Lusseau & Mancini, 2019; Pradhan et al., 2017; Spaiser et al., 2017; Warchold et al., 2020; Xu et al., 2022). A few studies have applied mixed methods (Mainali et al., 2018; Smith et al., 2021; Zhou & Moinuddin, 2017). Others have used network analysis (Bali Swain & Ranganathan, 2021; Fariña García et al., 2021; Ospina-Forero et al., 2022; Weitz et al., 2018; Zhou & Moinuddin, 2017; Dawes, 2022), built models (Allen et al., 2019; Anderson et al., 2022; Collste et al., 2017; Dawes, 2020; Pedercini et al., 2019) and created multi-criteria frameworks (Allen, 2019; Plag & Jules-Plag, 2020; Reyers et al., 2017).

To track Agenda 2030 and understand the complex SDG interactions, several methods have been used. Pradhan and Warchold provide an overview of the quantitative studies on SDG interactions, including a diverse SDG data landscape. They provide their insights into selected studies on SDG interactions, data, applied methods and obtained findings. These studies mainly include statistical analysis of SDG interactions based on longitudinal and cross-sectional analyses. Some studies further used obtained results from the statistical analyses to build SDG networks and systems models. Their chapter highlights the need to use quantitative and qualitative methods for a holistic understanding of SDG interactions, including their local- and context-specific mechanisms.

Dawes introduces a few key concepts in network science and applies them to study interactions between the SDGs. The chapter attempts to provide a non-technical overview showing how the overall patterns of co-benefits and trade-offs across the network emerge from the collection of individual interactions between pairs of goals and therefore link individual-scale and system-scale dynamics. Ideas from ecology lead to notions of hierarchy in networks and help in understanding and quantifying the questions of prioritization among the goals. These methods help in conceptually understanding the emergence of system-level behaviour, and they shed light on how one should understand and evaluate policy choices and policy coherence.

Achieving SDGs requires an integrated approach. Existing knowledge on SDG interlinkages remains limited in terms of comprehensiveness (covering all goals and targets), understanding the SDG causality, quantifying the interlinkages and practical applications in supporting SDG decision-making. Zhou and Moinuddin introduce a four-step methodology for identifying and quantifying SDG interlinkages. They present a free online tool to visualize the SDG interlinkages in 27 countries in Asia and Africa. The case studies in Bangladesh and Indonesia demonstrate how the tool can be used to support integrated SDG planning, priority setting and institutional arrangement.

Cling and Delecourt measure interlinkages between SDGs, applying linear dimensionality reduction techniques to a dataset derived from the UN Global SDG Database. Their study finds that SDGs' human (i.e., economic and social) development indicators explain most countries' sustainable development performance. Two other components of sustainable development contribute to the variance of the dataset: the environment and governance. At the global level, they observe strong synergies overall and no trade-offs between SDGs. Hierarchical cluster analysis is used to design three homogeneous country clusters that are empirically differentiated from each other according to their level of gross national income per capita. Nonetheless, relations between development components are found to be similar across groupings. This validates the opportunity for global analysis of interlinkages between SDGs and the objective of universality at the heart of their conception.

To achieve the implementation of the global SDG indicators framework, data is required to monitor the progress of SDG indicators and to establish the interrelationships between them. Considering there are still significant data gaps to overcome by countries, Quintero and Ospina discuss some of the main actions developed in Colombia to boost statistical strengthening processes for widening the availability of SDG data. They recognize that there are remaining challenges to overcome and discuss possible solutions.

Although the gender–environment connections aren't exhaustively understood, largely due to the lack of available data on the topic, increasingly available evidence demonstrates that achieving the SDGs, including meeting the 2030 Agenda's promise of leaving no one behind, will require better mainstreaming of gender into the environment goals. Utilizing examples from the SDG monitoring framework, Duerto Valero and Serrao show that the available data are grossly insufficient to demonstrate and understand gender differences. The chapter also elucidates different examples of ongoing international efforts to generate methodology to address data gaps on the gender–environment nexus. It emphasizes that there is need to step up measures for further methodological development to address data gaps in additional priority areas countries have highlighted, such as environment-related conflict, migration and displacement from a gender angle, among many others.

The 2030 Agenda calls on member states to take action to combat climate change and achieve a sustainable future for all. Existing literature indicates that pre-existing socio-cultural and economic disadvantages are likely to render women and girls especially vulnerable, but empirical evidence on the gender–environment nexus is largely missing. To fill this data gap and explore the gendered effects of climate change, Duerto Valero and Kaul test the association between climate-related factors (drought, humidity, rainfall, flood risk, temperature, proximity to water) and gender outcomes (early marriage and childbirth, intimate partner violence, access to water and clean cooking fuels) across Asia (Bangladesh, Cambodia, Nepal, Philippines, Timor-Leste). A random forest model is applied to identify key climate-related variables of importance in predicting gender-inequality outcomes, and logistic regression analysis is run to measure the strength of the association. Their findings confirm that the associations between key climate variables and gender outcomes are statistically significant and serve as a warning sign that the issues of climate and gender cannot be addressed in isolation. They further illustrate the importance of working towards filling gender–environment data gaps, including SDG monitoring.

Eliasson and Grönlund employ the case of the Swedish region Jämtland Härjedalen to demonstrate how knowledge of synergies and trade-offs may be used to implement Agenda 2030. Identifying interactions between 15 local SDG targets, their methodology follows the SDG interaction framework, and the results are presented in a cross-impact matrix that visualizes the interaction between targets and identifies the targets that have the most and the least positive influence on the network. The analysis shows that most of the interactions are synergistic but a few important trade-offs, between land use and the use of natural resources, exist. Working with the SDGs at a regional level presents challenges related to scale and complexity, but their method is a first step and leads to better-informed decision-making.

REFERENCES

Ahmed, N., Dabi, N., Lawson, M., Lowthers, M., Marriott, A., & Mugehera, L. (2022). Inequality kills: The unparalleled action needed to combat unprecedented inequality in the wake of COVID-19. Oxfam. https://policy-practice.oxfam.org/resources/inequality-kills-the-unparalleled-action-needed-to-combat-unprecedented-inequal-621341/

Allen, C., Metternicht, G., & Wiedmann, T. (2019). Prioritising SDG targets: Assessing baselines, gaps and interlinkages. *Sustainability Science*, 14(2), 421–438. https://doi.org/10.1007/s11625-018-0596-8

Anderson, C. C., Denich, M., Warchold, A., Kropp, J. P., & Pradhan, P. (2022). A systems model of SDG target influence on the 2030 agenda for sustainable development. *Sustainability Science*, 17(4), 1459–1472. https://doi.org/10.1007/s11625-021-01040-8

Asadikia, A., Rajabifard, A., & Kalantari, M. (2021). Systematic prioritisation of SDGs: Machine learning approach. *World Development*, 140, 105269. https://doi .org/10.1016/j.worlddev.2020.105269

Bali Swain, R., & Ranganathan, S. (2021). Modeling interlinkages between sustainable development goals using network analysis. *World Development*, 138, 105136. https://doi.org/10.1016/j.worlddev.2020.105136

Bali Swain, R., & Yang-Wallentin, F. (2020). Achieving sustainable development goals: Predicaments and strategies. *International Journal of Sustainable Development & World Ecology*, 27(2), 96–106. https://doi.org/10.1080/13504509.2019.1692316

Collste, D., Pedercini, M., & Cornell, S. E. (2017). Policy coherence to achieve the SDGs: Using integrated simulation models to assess effective policies. *Sustainability Science*, 12(6), 921–931. https://doi.org/10.1007/s11625-017-0457-x

Dawes, J. H. P. (2020). Are the sustainable development goals self-consistent and mutually achievable? *Sustainable Development*, 28(1), 101–117. https://doi.org/10 .1002/sd.1975

Dawes, J. H. P. (2022). SDG interlinkage networks: Analysis, robustness, sensitivities, and hierarchies. *World Development*, 149, 105693. https://doi.org/10.1016/j.worlddev .2021.105693

Fariña García, M. C., De Nicolás De Nicolás, V. L., Yagüe Blanco, J. L., & Fernández, J. L. (2021). Semantic network analysis of sustainable development goals to quantitatively measure their interactions. *Environmental Development*, 37, 100589. https://doi.org/10.1016/j.envdev.2020.100589

Hegre, H., Petrova, K., & von Uexkull, N. (2019). Synergies and trade-offs in reaching the sustainable development goals. *Sustainability*, 12(20), 8729. https://doi.org/10 .3390/su12208729

Hernández-Orozco, E., Lobos-Alva, I., Cardenas-Vélez, M., Purkey, D., Nilsson, M., & Martin, P. (2022). The application of soft systems thinking in SDG interaction studies: A comparison between SDG interactions at national and subnational levels in Colombia. *Environment, Development and Sustainability*, 24(6), 8930–8964. https://doi.org/10.1007/s10668-021-01808-z

IAEG-SDGs. (2019). Data disaggregation and SDG indicators: Policy priorities and current and future disaggregation plans. https://unstats.un.org/unsd/statcom/50th -session/documents/BG-Item3a-Data-Disaggregation-E.pdf

IPCC. (2019). Special report on the ocean and cryosphere in a changing climate. https://www.ipcc.ch/srocc/

IPCC. (2021). Climate change 2021: The physical science basis. Working group I contribution to the IPCC sixth assessment report. https://www.ipcc.ch/report/sixth -assessment-report-working-group-i/

IPCC. (2022a). Climate change 2022: Impacts, adaptation and vulnerability. Working group II contribution to the IPCC sixth assessment report. https://www.ipcc.ch/ report/ar6/wg2/

IPCC. (2022b). Climate change 2022: Mitigation of climate change. Working group III contribution to the IPCC sixth assessment report. https://www.ipcc.ch/report/sixth -assessment-report-working-group-3/

Kroll, C., Warchold, A., & Pradhan, P. (2019).Sustainable Development Goals (SDGs): Are we successful in turning trade-offs into synergies? *Palgrave Communications*, 5(1), 140. https://doi.org/10.1057/s41599-019-0335-5

Lusseau, D., & Mancini, F. (2019). Income-based variation in sustainable development goal interaction networks. *Nature Sustainability*, 2(3), 242–247. https://doi.org/10 .1038/s41893-019-0231-4

Mach, K., Kraan, C., Adger, W., & Buhaug, H. (2019). Climate as a risk factor for armed conflict. *Nature*. https://www.nature.com/articles/s41586-019-1300-6

Mainali, B., Luukkanen, J., Silveira, S., & Kaivo-oja, J. (2018). Evaluating synergies and trade-offs among Sustainable Development Goals (SDGs): Explorative analyses of development paths in South Asia and Sub-Saharan Africa. *Sustainability*, 10(3), 815. https://doi.org/10.3390/su10030815

Ospina-Forero, L., Castañeda, G., & Guerrero, O. A. (2022). Estimating networks of sustainable development goals. *Information & Management*, 59(5), 103342. https://doi.org/10.1016/j.im.2020.103342

Pedercini, M., Arquitt, S., Collste, D., & Herren, H. (2019). Harvesting synergy from sustainable development goal interactions. *Proceedings of the National Academy of Sciences*, 116(46), 23021–23028. https://doi.org/10.1073/pnas.1817276116

Pham-Truffert, M., Metz, F., Fischer, M., Rueff, H., & Messerli, P. (2020). Interactions among sustainable development goals: Knowledge for identifying multipliers and virtuous cycles. *Sustainable Development*, 28(5), 1236–1250. https://doi.org/10.1002/sd.2073

Plag, H.-P., & Jules-Plag, S.-A. (2020). A goal-based approach to the identification of essential transformation variables in support of the implementation of the 2030 agenda for sustainable development. *International Journal of Digital Earth*, 13(2), 166–187. https://doi.org/10.1080/17538947.2018.1561761

Pradhan, P., Costa, L., Rybski, D., Lucht, W., & Kropp, J. P. (2017). A systematic study of Sustainable Development Goal (SDG) interactions. *Earth's Future*, 5(11), 1169–1179. https://doi.org/10.1002/2017EF000632

Reyers, B., Stafford-Smith, M., Erb, K.-H., Scholes, R. J., & Selomane, O. (2017). Essential variables help to focus sustainable development goals monitoring. *Current Opinion in Environmental Sustainability*, 26–27, 97–105. https://doi.org/10.1016/j.cosust.2017.05.003

Smith, T. B., Vacca, R., Mantegazza, L., & Capua, I. (2021). Natural language processing and network analysis provide novel insights on policy and scientific discourse around sustainable development goals. *Scientific Reports*, 11(1), 22427. https://doi.org/10.1038/s41598-021-01801-6

Spaiser, V., Ranganathan, S., Swain, R. B., & Sumpter, D. J. T. (2017). The sustainable development oxymoron: Quantifying and modelling the incompatibility of sustainable development goals. *International Journal of Sustainable Development and World Ecology*, 24(6), 457–470. https://doi.org/10.1080/13504509.2016.1235624

United Nations. (2015). Transforming our world: The 2030 agenda for sustainable development. United Nations.

United Nations. (2021a). Liquidity and debt solutions to invest in the SDGs: The time to act is now. https://unsdg.un.org/sites/default/files/2021-03/sg-policy-brief-on-liquidity-and-debt-solutions.pdf/

United Nations. (2021b). The sustainable development goals report 2021. https://unstats.un.org/sdgs/report/2021/

United Nations. (2022a). The sustainable development goals report 2022. https://unstats.un.org/sdgs/report/2022/

United Nations. (2022b). Global impact of war in Ukraine on food, energy and finance systems - BRIEF NO.1. https://unsdg.un.org/resources/global-impact-war-ukraine-food-energy-and-finance-systems-brief-no1

United Nations. (2022c). World economic situation and prospects as of mid-2022. https://www.un.org/development/desa/dpad/publication/world-economic-situation-and-prospects-2022/

World Bank, UNESCO, & UNICEF. (2021). The state of the global education crisis. https://www.unicef.org/reports/state-global-education-crisis

Warchold, A., Pradhan, P., & Kropp, J. P. (2020). Variations in sustainable development goal interactions: Population, regional, and income disaggregation. *Sustainable Development*, 29(2), 285–299. https://doi.org/10.1002/sd.2145

Weitz, N., Carlsen, H., Nilsson, M., & Skånberg, K. (2018). Towards systemic and contextual priority setting for implementing the 2030 agenda. *Sustainability Science*, 13(2), 531–548. https://doi.org/10.1007/s11625-017-0470-0

World Economic Forum. (2022). Global gender gap report 2022. https://www.weforum.org/reports/global-gender-gap-report-2022

World Health Organization. (2021). Climate change and health. https://www.who.int/news-room/fact-sheets/detail/climate-change-and-health

World Meteorological Organization. (2022). Provisional state of the global climate in 2022. https://public.wmo.int/en/our-mandate/climate/wmo-statement-state-of-global-climate

Zhou, X., & Moinuddin, M. (2017). *Sustainable Development Goals Interlinkages and Network Analysis: A Practical Tool for SDG Integration and Policy Coherence.* Hayama: Institute for Global Environmental Strategies (IGES). https://doi.org/10.57405/iges-6026

Xu, Z., Chau, S. N., Chen, X., Zhang, J., Li, Y., Dietz, T., Wang, J., Winkler, J. A., Fan, F., Huang, B., Li, S., Wu, S., Herzberger, A., Tang, Y., Hong, D., Li, Y., & Liu, J. (2022). Assessing progress towards sustainable development over space and time. *Nature*, 577(7788), 74–78. https://doi.org/10.1038/s41586-019-1846-3

2. Decoupling and redistribution in realising the Sustainable Development Goals

Lin Lerpold and Örjan Sjöberg

2.1 INTRODUCTION: THE (NOT SO) DISCRETE CHARMS OF SDG 8

The negotiations to form the Sustainable Development Goals (SDGs) based on the 2012 Rio +20 Conference outcome document, "The Future We Want" (UN, 2012), was in many ways a widely inclusive multistakeholder effort that resulted in multilateral consensus around 17 goals with 169 targets. Though the SDGs can be seen as a continuation of the eight Millennium Development Goals (MDGs) that focused more on poverty in developing nations, the SDGs targeted all UN countries and brought in environmental dimensions more squarely, as well as a focus on the interrelated aspects of poverty and marginalisation with the potential to transform the dominant global governance approaches to economic, social and environmental challenges (Sachs, 2015; Stevens & Kanie, 2016).

Since then, in addition to assessing the progress on the goals themselves (cf. Allen et al., 2018), much empirical research has focused on understanding the interlinkages, synergies and trade-offs both between the SDGs and component targets and with other factors such as subjective well-being (De Neve & Sachs, 2020) or inclusive growth (Hay et al., 2022). Though the SDGs were intended to be universal, indivisible and interlinked in the holistic challenge of sustainable development, and though policy makers and corporates have embraced the goals in a way that was less salient for the MDGs, some scholars have questioned the conceptual underpinnings to the goals based in dominant neoliberal economic frameworks (e.g. Carant, 2017; Weber, 2017). Most critical research has been on the impracticability of realising all goals or the (im) possibility of achieving the assumed overall synergies between the natural world and social world goals (Stevance et al., 2015; Barbier & Burgess, 2019; for less pessimistic views see e.g. Bridgewater et al., 2015).

Surprisingly often a main assumption of Agenda 2030 is ignored and this despite it being identified as such early on (Fletcher & Rammelt, 2017): if the SDGs such as no poverty, zero hunger or good health and well-being contextualised in the social world are to be met with a measure of success, economic growth likely must continue but without increasing the climate impact and ecological footprint in the natural world. Known as "decoupling" and explicitly mentioned under SDG 8 that asks signatories to "promote sustained, inclusive and sustainable economic growth, full and productive employment and decent work for all" (UN, 2015: 14), it refers to the process whereby a unit of additional growth does not imply an increased use of planetary resources or increase in greenhouse gases emissions to an equal amount.

Given that the world's population growth is driven by past momentum, the success of lower mortality rates and longer average lifespans, our global population is estimated to reach 8.5 billion by 2030 (UN, 2022a). Since much current resource use and planetary degradation is directly correlated with population growth, affluence and technology development (as simply expressed in Ehrlich and Holden's IPAT equation, 1971) and is already at unsustainable levels, we obviously have a challenging situation. Indeed, even the COVID-19 pandemic and slowdown of global economies did little to decrease global carbon emissions as they reportedly rebounded to the highest ever level in history in 2021 (IEA, 2022) at the same time as millions more of the global population suffered increased food security. However, an interpretation of decoupling that implies an improvement of resource use on the margin – be it in the form of reduced extraction of resources or the reduction of environmental degradation relative to each new unit of GDP produced – needs to be qualified and understood interdependently with the SDGs targeting social goals. To the extent that the planetary boundaries (Rockström et al., 2009; Steffen et al., 2015) are about to be or already have been surpassed, decoupling would imply no further use of such resources at all. In other cases, there might still be room for additional resource extraction while staying within the boundaries of a safe operating space (that is, one that does not threaten a collapse), albeit at a lower rate than has been required or allowed for so far. These two instances can be described as complete and incomplete decoupling, respectively. Only in those cases where truly sustainable resource use, and typically of a fully renewable kind, is to be had might decoupling not be an issue; by definition, it has already been achieved. Yet, to the extent that this is only an expression of weak sustainability – the "ethical premise of keeping the general production capacity of the economy constant" (Hediger, 1999: 1121) – it might not be enough. This is so if the integrity of natural systems is to be preserved, as strong sustainability requires.

The wording in Agenda 2030 resolution does little to clarify this. As Hickel (2019: 875) notes, SDG 8 merely encourages signatories to "endeavour to decouple economic growth from environmental degradation" and it is all couched in terms of a need to "[i]mprove progressively, through 2030, global resource efficiency in consumption and production" (UN 2015: 19). However, this may be too little, too late. The current loss of biodiversity and too high levels of greenhouse gas (GHG) emissions are making the Paris Agreement difficult to achieve (IPCC, 2022), but increasingly, there is also a realisation that the social objectives that are part of Agenda 2030, the most obvious being climate change eroding the possibilities for many to derive a decent livelihood at all, are of more concern. Indeed, COP27 held at the end of 2022 seems to mark a change in focus from *proaction* in the Paris Agreement's "Green Climate Fund" to *reaction* in the COP27's "Loss and damage" fund.

In a situation where decoupling is approached as a desirable goal rather than a compelling imperative, much valuable time might be lost, the cost to future generations therefore being higher than need be. As the Stern Review noted, "[d]elay would entail more climate change and eventually higher costs of tackling the problem" (Stern, 2006: 304). This is made worse by the fact that meeting many of the social SDGs often depends on economic growth taking place, yet unless decoupling is achieved over the longer term this will be self-defeating. If so, decoupling is *sine qua non* for meeting both the environmental and social SDGs. To the extent that it is, decoupling becomes the implicit assumption that permeates Agenda 2030 across all SDGs.

Yet there is little indication that decoupling has been achieved. The two indicators included in the SDGs to capture this, 8.4.1 (material footprint, including per capita and per unit of GDP) and 8.4.2 (domestic material consumption, including per capita and per unit of GDP), have so far failed to provide much evidence of substantial progress and, as Lenzen et al. (2022: 162) report, "widespread near-future absolute decoupling appears unlikely." Thus, we look at the consequences of not achieving the decoupling called for and review the literature on the SDGs focusing specifically on the underlying assumptions and the interlinkages and potential contradictions that may exist. Further, we outline the particulars as regards the trade-offs between the natural world and social goals as approached by Agenda 2030 and make a number of observations. Connecting SDG 8, which assumes economic growth, to the social goals we problematise the underlying assumptions. To the extent that economic growth is a necessary condition for the social objectives to be met, and that decoupling does not appear to be materialising, we identify the compromises that might be inevitable. Extending the literature, which up to now has primarily taken an interest in the real or potential conflict between growth and environmental SDGs (e.g. Hickel, 2019), our focus is on the trade-offs between environmental and social SDGs that will be forced upon us unless decoupling is achieved.

2.2   DILEMMAS, CONTRADICTIONS AND TRADE-OFFS: WHAT THE LITERATURE SUGGESTS

That the implementation of the SDGs requires resources is not in doubt, and it is explicitly claimed "that domestic resources are first and foremost generated by economic growth, supported by an enabling environment at all levels" (UN, 2015: 29). Beyond problematising the conceptual underpinnings to the goals and their targets or the many contextual and measurement issues, many a commentator has pointed out that this makes some SDGs take priority over all others (Niklasson, 2019). Prominently, SDG 8 suggests that "per capita economic growth in accordance with national circumstances" (SDG Target 8.1) is an important part in achieving "sustained, inclusive and sustainable economic growth, full and productive employment and decent work for all" (UN, 2015: 19). To do so, Target 8.1 sets the goal of attaining over the decade and a half from 2015 to 2030 a rate of "at least 7 per cent gross domestic product growth per annum in the least developed countries" (UN, 2015: 19).

In the wake of the COVID-19 pandemic and the invasion of Ukraine, the increased number of extreme poor and growing food security challenges, global economic forecasts (World Bank, 2022) expect a severe slump in economic growth and in many nations even the risk of stagflation. At the same time, carbon emissions increased more than 6% between 2020 and 2021 after the pandemic to their highest levels in history in 2021 (IEA, 2022). The return to normal levels of energy consumption after the pandemic, compounded by adverse weather and energy market conditions leading to a higher volume of coal burnt, illustrates the fact that economic growth and CO_2 emissions are not perfectly correlated; indeed many different factors play a role. Yet over time, it is clear that the goal of high growth in the recent past has translated into an increased environmental footprint (e.g. Wiedmann et al., 2015; Pradhan et al., 2017; Fanning et al., 2022) and continues to do so even as we are half-way through to 2030. The goal of achieving 7 per cent per capita growth per year in low-income countries is unlikely to change that unless decoupling is truly successful. That goal does not just imply a doubling of the least developed economies in a decade but also, or so Hickel (2019: 875) notes, that "this translates into aggregate global GDP growth of 3% per year" if all other countries maintain their growth rate from the early 2010s at 1.85 per cent. Using a rough estimate, if the least developed countries have a population of close to three-quarters of a billion (728 million in 2022) and high-income nations have about a billion and a quarter inhabitants (1.246 million in 2022; UN, 2022b), assuming the largest population group of middle-income countries continue to grow at a rate commensurate with recent (2010s) experience – close to 2 per cent per capita per year – LDC per capita GDP growth at 7 per cent per year logically presumes that high-income countries should have zero economic growth or less. For many reasons this is a political and democratic impossibility for the electorate in the richest countries in the Global North. Indeed, the socioeconomically most fortunate countries where potential degrowth would have to occur are embedded in liberal market economies and social constructions predicated on high or continued growth in most dimensions as measures of success.

There have been numerous attempts to find out to what extent the 17 goals and the 169 targets are connected and whether they are compatible with each other (Le Blanc, 2015; Nilsson et al., 2016; Spaiser et al., 2017; Pradhan et al., 2017; Weitz et al., 2018; Bali Swain & Ranganathan, 2021; Dawes, 2022; Warchold et al., 2022). In parallel, discussions have focused on the need to disaggregate numbers further (Winkler & Satterthwaite, 2017), the impact of the quantitative indicators (that is, those whereby these targets are operationalised) on implementation (Mair et al., 2017) and how to measure them (Bali Swain, 2018). The latter has taken on a practical–technical character, as has much of the research on interlinkages. Thus, Le Blanc (2015: 177) proposes that the SDGs and their targets "can be seen as a network, with links among goals through the target," with SDG 12 being the one connected to the greatest number of other goals (14 out of 17), SDGs 1, 8 and 10 not being far behind. Nilsson et al. (2016; 2018) contend that these links come in different forms – both positive and negative – and suggest a typology of interactions between SDG targets also detailing where context needs to be taken into account. Research by Bali Swain and colleagues (e.g. Spaiser et al., 2017; Bali Swain, 2018) empirically confirms that several of the SDGs are incompatible, that is, in effect, suggesting that many are of the counteracting or cancelling type (Stevance et al., 2015). Even so, Bali Swain and Ranganathan (2021) find that the trade-offs between intra-goal targets are less powerful than are the synergies, a result that stands in contrast to that of Kostetckaia and Hametner (2022). Thus, results must be seen in light of the fact that quite a number of the interlinkages found are between targets underlying individual goals rather than between the goals themselves. Perhaps this is not so surprising as some of the synergies are in effect artifacts or covariates by design rather than genuine cross-SDG spillovers of a positive nature.

Meanwhile, Dawes (2022), setting out to reveal the underlying structure of these interlinkages and how they might favour some goals over others, observes that SDGs 1–3 (all social) stand to gain the most from the presence of the others while environmental SDGs 12–15 are particularly at risk (below water and life on land more so than climate). The latter is in line with the conclusion reached by Dawes (2020) who found SDG 14 to be more vulnerable than the others. Research at Potsdam suggests that for most SDGs, and for most countries, positive correlations (synergies) outweigh negative ones (trade-offs). SDG 1 (no poverty) is found to be the one with most positive interlinkages, while SDG 12 is found at the other end of the spectrum with the most trade-offs (Pradhan et al., 2017). This is further investigated in Warchold et al. (2022) where different datasets are compared, with in many respects diverging results. Irrespective of which, many of the synergies recorded are those across targets under a given SDG, as could be expected. Overall, although the picture is mixed, improvements on social and economic sustainability goals often appear to come at the expense of environmental ones. For while there clearly are synergies between some environmental and social goals and targets, as soon as the social and economic SDGs are positively correlated with SDG 8 the environmental SDGs find themselves at the losing end.

Apart from incompatibilities within the human development and social goals themselves, there has for some time been discussion of the trade-offs between climate and environmental goals as will be discussed in the forest industry; in the quest for more sustainable energy sources, much debate has been on mitigating biodiversity risks in marine ecosystems and the development of offshore wind projects for renewable energy (cf. Gasparatos et al., 2017). Indeed, solving one challenge by creating another is likely not the best option.

As no clear answer is to be had regarding the existence of synergies that might relieve the need for economic growth to achieve the SDGs and their various targets, and since "[t]he combination of quantifiability and non-commitment to planetary boundaries represents not only the maintenance but also the implicit prioritisation of the growth perspective in the SDGs" (Hirai, 2022: 7), the issue of whether decoupling takes place or not is still more acute. If it indeed is a fundamental prerequisite for the SDGs being met, it is of more than mere passing interest to know the extent to which growth can take place without it increasing GHG emissions or threatening other planetary boundaries (such as water, Dalstein & Naqvi, 2022). Given that the terminology is not fully standardised and at times takes on a quality of being persuading rather than persuasive, it is worth noticing that the notions of absolute and relative decoupling are widely accepted. Thus, several studies adopt the definition suggested by the United Nations Environment Programme, namely that "[d]ecoupling is when resource use or some environmental pressure either grows at a slower rate than the economic activity that is causing it (relative decoupling) or declines while the economic activity continues to grow (absolute decoupling)" (Bringezu et al., 2017: 22; cf. Sanyé-Mengual et al., 2019; Lenzen et al., 2022: 160). Partial decoupling has been used as a label for those instances where there is a change in a specific environmental impact, yet where others replace the previous impact (Ward et al., 2016) – both rebound effects and those of boundary drawing may come into play – hence reserving full or complete decoupling for the perhaps utopian instance where no further resource extraction takes place no matter the growth rate. (For an earlier terminology and for its antecedents, see Fischer-Kowalski et al., 2011.)

Turning to the substantive results of research assessing the extent to which decoupling takes place, most of the literature sets its sights on CO_2 emissions rather than other interrelated aspects of the planetary boundaries. Just recently, methane emissions, as the second most important GHG contributor to climate change, have been accorded increased attention, and although biodiversity on land and underwater has of late gained more of a focus, the underlying social dimensions of human behaviour and social processes in sustainable development (Sen, 2013) are investigated to a lesser degree. Furthermore, we note that critics claim that, to the extent to which decoupling happens at all, it tends to be local (e.g. at the regional or national rather than the global level), possibly temporary and of the relative variety, that is, environmental impact merely increases at a slower rate than does economic growth (e.g. Ward et al., 2016; Haberl et al., 2020; Hickel & Kallis, 2020). At the global level, where it really matters the most as the atmosphere is part of the global commons, it is unlikely to happen unless a major break with current production and consumption patterns sees the light of day. If so, it is in keeping with a critique of decoupling as a possible strategy that predates the introduction and evaluation of the SDGs (e.g. Næss & Høyer, 2009; Tienhaara, 2014; Wiedmann et al., 2015), a concern also voiced when the SDGs took form (e.g. Griggs et al., 2014).

Others suggest that relative or weak decoupling is not uncommon (e.g. IEA, 2019). Patterns conforming to the inverted U pattern of the environmental Kuznets curve have been shown to exist, if differentially so for different (classes) of countries, for instance thanks to the increased use of renewable energy (Wang et al., 2022; cf. Kar, 2022). That, however, only implies reduced emissions per unit produced, which, though important, does not necessarily imply a reduction in overall levels. Meanwhile, absolute decoupling – a decline in emissions as growth takes place – can in some cases be observed also when consumption-based measures are used (Sanyé-Mengual et al., 2019, who adopt a life cycle perspective applied to consumption rather than production-based impacts). The latter, however, is rare, and even successful countries "are still adding emissions to the atmosphere thus showing the limits of 'green growth' and the growth paradigm" (Hubacek et al., 2021: 9). Although it is not a long shot to claim that economic growth might make it easier to achieve many of the social objectives of Agenda 2030, as the effects on the environment are likely to be the opposite, there is a need to tread carefully in designing policies that are intended to achieve the various SDGs individually.

2.3   THE PARTICULARS OF EXPLANATION

As noted above, research on interlinkages across the SDGs suggests a positive correlation, implying potential synergies, between SDG 8 and other social and economic SDGs (such as SDG 1, 2, 3, 4, 5 and 12) but also clear trade-offs with the environmental ones (e.g. SDGs 6, 13, 14 and 15). Among the SDGs there are also interlinkages and incompatibilities between the human development-focused and social goals as well as between climate and environmental goals. For instance, Meurs et al. (2019) in their study of Malawi, Uganda and Tanzania explored how healthy a "healthy economy" was and found that the existence of goals focused on GDP growth delayed efforts towards the achievement of the health and well-being goal (SDG 3). Similarly, Ameye and Swinnen (2019) discuss the "gender obesity gap" linking the SDG human development and social goals 3, 5 and 10. Obesity, an important health indicator, changes with income, but in a non-linear way. On average, in low-income countries obesity is concentrated among richer groups where women are more obese than men, and also much more obese in middle-income countries than are men. Beyond gender and income levels, across nations' rural and urban divide, obesity rates continue to increase in all countries, especially in rich countries. In the same vein, there are obvious trade-offs and interlinkages between climate and environmental goals, for instance between carbon sequestration and forest biodiversity much debated in policy and industry in the European Union, also connected to the EU Green Taxonomy (Burrascano et al., 2016; Biber et al., 2020). Though most research has previously focused on comparing one goal with another (e.g. Huston & Marland, 2003), beyond North America and Western Europe, the complexities involving synergies and trade-offs between multiple goals and targets such as climate change, biodiversity loss, land-use, economic, human and social goals are increasingly being studied (e.g. Marques et al., 2019).

2.3.1 Conceptual and Measurement Issues

Understanding the interlinkages, synergies and trade-offs presupposes conceptual clarity and agreement on intention, interpretation and implications, along with the intricacies of how and where boundaries are set for measurement, both in time and space. The term "sustainable development" itself is an unclear concept with different meanings and approaches (Hopwood et al., 2005) along with numerous and diversely related frameworks and tools (Robèrt, 2000). The SDGs and their indicators have been criticised for being at times overlapping, incomplete and unfairly celebratory of regionally clustered nations over emphasising the achievements of developing nations and lower performing goals (Diaz-Sarachaga et al., 2018). This notwithstanding that there is a significant challenge of unavailable data for all indicators, and according to some, data is available for just 19 per cent of what is needed to track real progress across nations and over time (cf. Dang & Serajuddin, 2020).

Time and space are especially important for drawing implications. As indicators are measured over shorter periods, or at a static point in time, the impact of investments for sustainable development is difficult to predict long term. Indeed, counterfactual evidence seems to have little scholarly purchase in sustainable development. Regarding boundaries, the prevalence of methodological nationalism (Wimmer & Glick Schiller, 2002), that is, the arbitrary inclusion and exclusion along nation-state boundaries, renders both the analysis and substantive advancement of global sustainable development problematic. The SDG Index of country development has pitfalls with interpretation and can lead to different and erroneous conclusions about country performance (Dang & Serajuddin, 2020); it also disregards the global interdependence of climate emissions and environmental degradation, production and consumption through trade across nation-state boundaries (Liu, 2017; Hay et al., 2022). Similarly, the concept of sustainable cities suffers from "ontological cityism" (Lerpold & Sjöberg, 2021) whereby gains on sustainability metrics within a narrowly defined boundary may cause negative impacts in adjacent areas to disappear from view (see also Engström et al., 2021).

A problem throughout is that the predominantly quantitative approaches deployed have taken the form of a search for patterns in the data. As such, the results reported say little about causality and hence fall short on delivering an explanation. Although this was pointed out early on (e.g. Hák et al., 2016), efforts to find out how the various SDGs interact with each other, beyond synergies of targets within goals, have continued to be conducted in an inductive fashion with a view of finding instances of correlation and co-variation. Conversely, the studies referred to in the previous section appear to have invested little in stringent conceptualisation, thereby compounding the risk of unwarranted conclusions (an exception being Bali Swain, 2018).

Beyond the data and measurement issues, a key question is whether quantified independent indicators change the way development is conceived, focusing on specific accomplishments rather than transformational or larger structural change (Merry, 2019); as Hirai (2022) argues, quantification implies an implicit prioritisation. GDP can be taken as a case in point. Not only does it not translate into income at the disposal of the average inhabitant – not even GDP/capita does – as a measure it says very little about well-being. As a result, growth takes the upper hand over the welfare of the population or individual. In this connection it has been noted that quantitative indicators also tend to remove contextual information (e.g. Mair et al., 2017), reducing complex issues such as poverty to easily measured dimensions. The pledge of "no one being left behind" in Agenda 2030 (UN, 2015: 3) or the notion of inclusive growth, for instance, though universally hailed as multidimensional and multilateral, requires both context specificity and a deeper reflection on human well-being to make much sense (Hay et al., 2022).

As the choice of indicators and how to measure and process them have consequences for how progress, if any, is assessed (Miola & Schiltz, 2019), policy conclusions will also be based on less than fully solid foundations. A further consequence is that even studies that note the sensitivity to the data availability and choice of dataset to be used (as do Warchold et al., 2022) end up being unable to discriminate between datasets; instead, the standard recipe appears to be to ask for more data. Such a suggestion does little, however, to solve the more acute problem of allowing "the mainstream [supporting weak sustainability] to secure a favourable position in relation to the quantifiability of existing indicators and their incompatibility with the concept of planetary boundaries" (Hirai, 2022: 6).

2.3.2 The Environmental and Social SDG Interlinkages

Although it is generally understood that high-income individuals and nations have a larger negative impact on climate change and that the already poor and vulnerable experience the impacts of climate change more severely, it is also very likely that in any one country climate action (SDG 13) inter- acts with or depend upon other SDGs. For instance, gender inequality (SDG 5) is of relevance to the sources and impacts of climate change. Women's lack of power reduces their ability to contribute important knowledge and insights potentially of significance to adaptation and mitigation; this is par- ticularly true of agricultural production and livelihoods in poorer countries (Demetriades & Esplen, 2010). Also, good health and well-being (SDG 3) and quality education (SDG 4) along with effective anti-corruption regulation and strong national institutions (SDG 16), all of which are more common in the high-income nations, have an impact on the ability of societies to implement climate change mitigation and adaptation strategies, not least of all because of access to the resources needed for climate change investments.

Unfortunately, it cannot be ruled out that causality might work both ways. That climate change threatens to increase the incidence of poverty, with the poor being more vulnerable to adverse changes resulting from increasing tem- peratures, is not in doubt. It is also likely to be the dominant effect, not least because the poor are more likely to be exposed than those enjoying a measure of affluence. As a consequence of climate change, or so a recent report by the World Bank ([2020] 2021: 12) suggests, by 2030 the ranks of the poor will be added to by another 68 million to 132 million people. This adverse outcome, the estimated size of which depends on the "scope and severity" of the pro- cess unfolding, issues directly from the higher temperatures that greenhouse gas emissions generate and from the costs of mitigation and adaptation occa- sioned by climate change. The COVID-19 pandemic and the Russian invasion of Ukraine will also significantly increase the number of poor in the world, as these ill-fated events will likely impact climate mitigation strategies as well as food security.

As these effects are geographically differentiated, the scene is set for increasing inequality across countries (e.g. Taconet et al., 2020).

> Yet there is cause for caution regarding what to make of assessments of climate change impacts, for it is *how* societies respond to climate change impacts, more than these impacts themselves, that determines how aggregate losses are distributed across people and how climate change affects poverty and the well-being of people currently living in poverty.
>
> (Hallegatte et al., 2018: 230)

By way of an example, social inequality impacts within countries (SDG 10) are likely to be of the unfavourable kind. It has been characterised as "a vicious cycle, whereby *initial* inequality makes disadvantaged groups suffer *disproportionately* from the adverse effects of climate change, resulting in greater *subsequent* inequality" (Islam & Winkel 2017: 2; emphasis in the original). This outcome stems from the varied exposure and susceptibility to climate change, to which should be added the differentiated ability to cope with these harmful conditions. All told, from the point of view of poverty reduction there is an acute need to avert climate change and to mitigate the consequences of such change that is already happening or that which cannot be avoided in the future.

But what if poverty forces those vulnerable to both environmental change and social ills to engage in practices that may make matters relatively worse? This question is not as far-fetched as it at first might seem; we do know that in many contexts around the world the poor are more exposed to for instance geomorphological risks (e.g. Satterthwaite, 1997) but also that they at times contribute to a higher incidence of such risks playing out for the simple reason that they are confined to marginal locations the use of which may exacerbate existing or trigger latent risks (e.g. Alcántara-Ayala, 2002). The removal of vegetation cover on steep hillsides in order to eke out a living from marginal lands left by more fortunate peers, thereby adding to processes of erosion and flooding, can serve as an illustration of the challenge. In particular, informal settlements in areas prone to flooding or other geomorphological risks may introduce complications that reach beyond the normal difficulties in introducing disaster prevention and mitigation measures, and this irrespective of whether they give precedence to traditional technical solutions or ecosystems-based ones (e.g. Felson et al., 2013).

It should be noted, of course, that the ecological footprint of the poor is much smaller than that of richer members of society; in terms of per capita carbon footprint the difference is very large indeed (the implementation gap, as Amos and Lydgate (2020) note, is the largest in high-income countries). But can it be the case that the poor contribute more than their typically very low levels of production and consumption would otherwise lead us to believe? Put differently, could it be that helping individuals and households move out of poverty at least initially actually reduces the adverse environmental effects resulting from their perhaps desperate attempts to secure a livelihood? We raise this issue of non-linearity because research has primarily focused on the other side of the coin, that is, the expected effect of moving people out of poverty is rather increased resource use and rising levels of emissions (Hubacek et al., 2017; Malerba, 2019).

Furthermore, similarly to how businesses in the Global North are criticised for short-termism in their assessments of sustainability investments, the economic effects of sustainability standards among smallholder farmers in developing countries are mixed (cf. for a systematic review and meta-analysis, Meemken, 2020). Indeed, studies suggest that environmental standards, depending on context, can keep some farmers in a negative spiral of poor yields, low prices, investments and profits (e.g. Valkila, 2009; Beuchelt & Zeller, 2011, in Fair Trade Organic coffee production in Nicaragua). Not least of all the poverty penalty and its impact on sustainable planetary resource consumption and production are important (Sadler, 2010) as are the consequences of the poor being locked into a poverty trap (on the concept of which, see e.g. Lundahl et al., 2021).

This is all the more unfortunate as it is widely recognised that the environment contributes, or has the capacity to contribute, a wider range of benefits that directly or indirectly impact social sustainability. This includes the potential for biodiversity to contribute to sustainable economic growth, that is SDG 8 (e.g. Blicharska et al., 2019). Even so, the consequences for the environment of realising the social SDG goals through continued economic growth are a persistent and frequently voiced concern. The more successful the global community is in lifting countries or segments thereof out of poverty, the greater the conflict it seems. If so, it is indeed a challenge, one that is compounded by our inability to work out the core causal relationships. At best, the search for interlinkages, be they in the form of positive synergies or negative trade-offs, allows us a glimpse of the net effects of what might be mechanisms that work at cross-purposes.

2.3.3 The Social SDGs and Economic Growth

As breaking out of the vicious cycle identified by Islam and Winkel (2017) is predicated upon resource availability, the redistribution of existing means or economic growth are the two main options for achieving this. The international community, casual observation suggests, would much prefer the latter to the former. To the extent that redistribution is contemplated, it takes the form of richer countries funding poorer countries in their quest to mitigate climate change or to adapt to such changes. In short, it amounts to a measure of redistribution between countries. As such, it is a major issue (not to say bone of contention) in the climate negotiations under the aegis of the United Nations Framework Convention on Climate Change (UNFCCC).

Support for effective measures towards this end would clearly be easier for the rich countries to accept if economic growth can be kept up. Similarly, while the SDGs include a provision for redistribution within countries, it is one that at least implicitly presupposes economic growth. As Target 10.1 under SDG 10 has it, signatories to Agenda 2030 are expected to "progressively achieve and sustain income growth of the bottom 40 per cent of the population at a rate higher than the national average" (UN, 2015: 21). No doubt, there is a pent-up demand for higher levels of consumption among those groups that are to benefit from the implied redistribution; it would be naïve to suggest that the poor should forfeit that possibility should countries prove successful in meeting the targets of SDG 10.

As Bali Swain (2018: 351) concludes, "[t]he pursuit of economic growth and consumption underlies the inconsistencies between the economic and social development and the environmental goals." If so, the ability to measure up to the requirements of SDG 12, responsible consumption and production, becomes critical. Perhaps best seen as a question of stewardship, emphasising the "sustainable management and efficient use of natural resources" (target 12.2; UN, 2015: 22), this is where decoupling is expected to materialise. Other than referring to the 10-Year Framework of Programmes on Sustainable Consumption and Production Patterns (10YFP for short: UN, 2014); however, it says little about how decoupling is to be achieved and what it might entail in terms of resources upfront to achieve it or, for that matter, how big the gains would be if signatories are able to follow through on it. As per the literature already referred to above, all we know is that there is some form of interconnection here, but little is known about the direction of causality, if indeed it amounts to causal links at all and not just random correlations.

The 10YFP set out to "contribute to resource efficiency and decoupling, and thus also to the economic, social and environmental pillars of sustainable development" (UN, 2014: 10), the main vehicle being dedicated programmes on public procurement, consumer information for sustainable consumption and production, sustainable tourism, sustainable lifestyles and education, sustainable buildings and construction and finally sustainable food systems. As such, SDGs 4, 8, 9, 11, 12 and 17 were identified as the most relevant, with SDG 12 being particularly prominent. Incidentally, this also implies that issues of poverty reduction and equality, primarily SDGs 1, 3, 5 and 10, were relegated to secondary roles or left out of sight entirely. Although the programmes were to be conduits of knowledge transfer, a means of scaling up successful initiatives and a source of inspiration, they have turned out to be difficult to evaluate. As the 2022 progress report notes (UN 2022c: 6),

[m]easuring global progress on sustainable consumption and production is fraught, as 7 out of 13 indicators (54 per cent) for Goal 12 are tier II indicators, that is, the indicators are conceptually clear and have an internationally established methodology, and standards are available, but data are not regularly produced by countries. The lack of data for sustainable consumption and production is a gap which requires urgent global attention.

In other words, the evidence for a positive impact of the six programmes under 10YFP is patchy at best. The progress report reflects this: many examples are given, but in a rather *ad hoc* fashion (driven by availability of any information?) or, at best, in quantitative terms such as the number of policies related to SDG target 12.1 that have been reported by member countries. Decoupling? Not mentioned once. Instead, for a more systematic assessment, we are left with the SDG Index as reported in the "Sustainable Development Report," the most recent edition of which notes that not much progress can be seen (Sachs et al., 2021: 28–31). If anything, this seems to give some support to the claim by Gasper et al. (2019: 83) that SDG 12 and "many of its targets were watered down and left vague" and therefore not amenable to stringent implementation or serious follow-up.

In short, both the extent to which decoupling can be accomplished and any positive effects on other SDGs that might materialise remain uncertain. In case SDG 12 is not instrumental in bringing about decoupling, this in turn implies that there is a serious trade-off between the need to protect our planet and the means of achieving other important objectives. The conflict between the environmental and economic sustainability goals has attained some prominence and, unless the decoupling of growth and resource extraction is achieved, we are faced with the need of "rethinking the use of GDP as an indicator of progress – a purpose it was never intended to serve" (Hickel, 2019: 882). Agenda 2030, as noted, pins quite some hope on this happening, yet as neither absolute nor complete decoupling is clearly within reach, we are faced with not just a contradiction between growth and environmental sustainability, but also one where social objectives such as "reduced inequality within and among countries" (as per SDG 10) are likely to run up against the need not to trespass on planetary boundaries. It becomes an issue of either or.

2.4 CONCLUSION

The observation that the SDGs hinge on economic growth continuing is not a novel revelation, nor is the fact that the decoupling called for is not very visible. Decoupling is still "the key fantasy" that Fletcher and Rammelt (2017) early on claimed it was. The problem is rather that the full set of implications that follow from these observations are not clearly spelled out. For, while it is widely recognised that the environmental SDGs may suffer from continued growth and the (often merely implied) focus on weak sustainability, the thought that the social SDGs may likewise suffer is less widely adopted or communicated. One reason for this is that the literature on synergies and trade-offs across the SDGs almost invariably seems to stress the preponderance of the former over the latter, with synergies being particularly prevalent between SDG 8 – the one where the call for growth and for decoupling is the most easily visible – and the other social SDGs. Whether mediated through SDG 12 (sustainable consumption and production) or not, the neglect of the assumption of decoupling being met or not implies that potential trade-offs in the social sphere will be left unaddressed. Also, when decoupling is observed, it is of a variety that does not take absolute limits to human resource extraction into account. As such, it is likely to run up to any planetary boundaries that exist; in the absence of technological advances of a type yet to be seen these are, after all, absolute.

Put differently, if we accept the conclusion by Mair et al. (2017) that the indicators used as part of Agenda 2030 are expressions of political priorities rather than rigorously based on theory and relevant empirical evidence, it becomes clear that due to a lack of coherence across goals and the presence of unrealistic assumptions, attaining all of them is virtually impossible. Without decoupling resource use from economic growth, or if the redistribution of the benefits of economic growth between and within nations is not accomplished, achieving the social SDGs will imply an eroded capacity to meet the environmental ones. And not meeting the environmental ones may well imply that the environment in a sense strikes back, making the future of humankind and the current plight of the poor increasingly bleak.

Specifically, the conceptual underpinnings of all the SDGs are that economic growth is a proxy for not only standards of living and welfare, but also increased resources enabling investments in research and development for new sustainable technologies. As economic growth is thus conceptually understood as a *sine qua non* for the realisation of the SDGs, we are locked into a specific mode of thinking. Not only is GDP growth taken as a proxy for well-being, which it certainly should not be, it conveniently overlooks the observation that infinite growth sits uneasily with finite planetary resources. But precisely because resources are needed to achieve the social SDGs and to fund the development and deployment of green technologies, degrowth strategies do not come across as particularly promising (but see Hickel et al., 2022). At the same time, left to their own devices, markets do not appear to be entirely up to the task of engineering the requisite transformative shift by themselves. This is so if for no other reason than because it might take far too long relative to the time horizons implied by Agenda 2030 and the Paris Agreement. Instead, concerted political action for the purposes of spurring on collective action or more stringent national regulation will have to be relied upon. Should that prove impractical or unattractive, perhaps the suggestion by

Hay et al. (2022) to explore ways of achieving pre- rather than re-distribution might deserve some attention.

ACKNOWLEDGEMENTS

In addition to the useful feedback received at the Interlinkages Workshop held 5–6 April 2022 and from the editors, the authors would like to acknowledge support from Formas (grant 2018-02226) and Sweden's Innovation Agency, Vinnova (grant 2020-04660).

NOTE

REFERENCES

Alcántara-Ayala, I. (2002). Geomorphology, natural hazards, vulnerability and prevention of natural disasters in developing countries. *Geomorphology*, 47(2–4), 107–124.

Allen, C., Metternicht, G., & Wiedmann, T. (2018). Initial progress in implementing the Sustainable Development Goals (SDGs): A review of evidence from countries. *Sustainability Science*, 13(6), 1453–1467.

Ameye, H., & Swinnen, J. (2019). Obesity, income and gender: The changing global relationship. *Global Food Security*, 23, 267–281.

Amos, R., & Lydgate, E. (2020). Trade, transboundary impacts and the implementation of SDG 12. *Sustainability Science*, 15(6), 1699–1710.

Bali Swain, R. (2018). A critical analysis of the sustainable development goals. In W. Leal Filho (Ed.), *Handbook of Sustainability Science and Research* (pp. 341–355). Cham: Springer.

Bali Swain, R., & Ranganathan, S. (2021). Modeling interlinkages between sustainable development goals using network analysis. *World Development*, 138, art. 105136.

Barbier, E. B., & Burgess, J. C. (2019). Sustainable development goal indicators: Analyzing trade-offs and complementarities. *World Development*, 122, 295–305.

Beuchelt, T. D., & Zeller, M. (2011). Profits and poverty: Certification's troubled link for Nicaragua's organic and fairtrade coffee producers. *Ecological Economics*, 70(7), 1316–1324.

Biber, P., Felton, A., Nieuwenhuis, M., Lindbladh, M., Black, K., Bahýl', J., & Bingöl, Ö. et al. (2020). Forest biodiversity, carbon sequestration, and wood production: Modeling synergies and trade-offs for ten forest landscapes across Europe. *Frontiers in Ecology and Evolution*, 8, 103–123.

Blicharska, M., Smithers, R. J., Mikusiński, G., Rönnbäck, P., Harrison, P. A., Nilsson, M., & Sutherland, W. J. (2019). Biodiversity's contributions to sustainable development. *Nature Sustainability*, 2(12), 1083–1093.

Bridgewater, P., Régnier, M., & García, R. C. (2015). Implementing SDG 15: Can large-scale public programs help deliver biodiversity conservation, restoration and management, while assisting human development? *Natural Resources Forum*, 39(3–4), 214–223.

Bringezu, S., Ramaswami, A., Schandl, H., O'Brien, M., Pelton, R., Acquatella, J., Ayuk, E. T., Chiu, A. S. F., Flanegin, R., Fry, J., Giljum, S., Hashimoto, S., Hellweg, S., Hosking, K., Hu, Y., Lenzen, M., Lieber, M., Lutter, S., Miatto, A., Nagpure, A. S., Obersteiner, M., van Oers, L., Pfister, S., Pichler, P.-P., Russell, A., Spini, L., Tanikawa, H., van der Voet, E., Weisz, H., West, J., Wiijkman, A., Zhu, B., & Zivy, R. (2017). *Assessing Global Resource Use: A Systems Approach to Resource Efficiency and Pollution Reduction*. Paris: International Resource Panel, United Nations Environmental Programme.

Burrascano, S., Chytrý, M., Kuemmerle, T., Giarrizzo, E., Luyssaert, S., Sabatini, F. M., & Blasi, C. (2016). Current European policies are unlikely to jointly foster carbon sequestration and protect biodiversity. *Biological Conservation*, 201, 370–376.

Carant, J. B. (2017). Unheard voices: A critical discourse analysis of the Millennium Development Goals' evolution into the sustainable development goals. *Third World Quarterly*, 38(1), 16–41.

Dalstein, F., & Naqvi, A. (2022). 21st Century water withdrawal decoupling: A pathway to a more water-wise world? *Water Resources and Economics*, 38, art 100197.

Dang, H. A. H., & Serajuddin, U. (2020). Tracking the sustainable development goals: Emerging measurement challenges and further reflections. *World Development*, 127, art. 104570.

Dawes, J. H. P. (2020). Are the sustainable development goals self-consistent and mutually achievable? *Sustainable Development*, 28(1), 101–117.

Dawes, J. H. P. (2022). SDG interlinkage networks: Analysis, robustness, sensitivities, and hierarchies. *World Development*, 149, art. 105693.

Demetriades, J., & Esplen, E. (2010). The gender dimensions of poverty and climate change adaptation. In R. Mearns & A. Norton (Eds.), *Social Dimensions of Climate Change: Equity and Vulnerability in a Warming World* (pp. 133–143). Washington, DC: World Bank.

De Neve, J. E., & Sachs, J. D. (2020). The SDGs and human well-being: A global analysis of synergies, trade-offs, and regional differences. *Scientific Reports*, 10, art. 15113.

Diaz-Sarachaga, J. M., Jato-Espino, D., & Castro-Fresno, D. (2018). Is the Sustainable Development Goals (SDG) index an adequate framework to measure the progress of the 2030 Agenda? *Sustainable Development*, 26(6), 663–671.

Ehrlich, P. R., & Holdren, J. P. (1971). Impact of population growth. *Science*, 171(3977), 1212–1217.

Engström, R. E., Collste, D., Cornell, S. E., Johnson, F. X., Carlsen, H., Jaramillo, F., Finnveden, G., Destouni, G., Howells, M., Weitz, N., Palm, V., & Fuso-Nerini, F. (2021). Succeeding at home and abroad: Accounting for the international spillovers of cities' SDG actions. *NPJ Urban Sustainability*, 1, art. 18.

Fanning, A. L., O'Neill, D. W., Hickel, J., & Roux, N. (2022). The social shortfall and ecological overshoot of nations. *Nature Sustainability*, 5(1), 26–36.

Felson, A. J., Oldfield, E. E., & Bradford, M. A. (2013). Involving ecologists in shaping large-scale green infrastructure projects. *BioScience*, 63(11), 882–890.

Fischer-Kowalski, M., Swilling, M., von Weizsäcker, E. U., Ren, Y., Moriguchi, Y., Crane, W., Krausmann, F., Eisenmenger, N., Giljum, S., Hennicke, P., Kemp, R., Romero Lankao, P., Siriban Manalang, A. B., & Sewerin, S. (2011). *Decoupling Natural Resource Use and Environmental Impacts from Economic Growth: A Report of the Working Group on Decoupling to the International Resource Panel.* Paris: United Nations Environment Programme.

Fletcher, R., & Rammelt, C. (2017). Decoupling: A key fantasy of the post-2015 sustainable development agenda. *Globalizations*, 14(3), 450–467.

Gasparatos, A., Doll, C. N. H., Esteban, M., Ahmed, A., & Olang, T. A. (2017). Renewable energy and biodiversity: Implications for transitioning to a Green Economy. *Renewable and Sustainable Energy Reviews*, 70, 161–184.

Gasper, D., Shah, A., & Tankha, S. (2019). The framing of sustainable consumption and production in SDG 12. *Global Policy*, 10(S1), 83–95.

Griggs, D., Smith, M. S., Rockström, J., Öhman, M. C., Gaffney, O., Glaser, G., Glaser, G., Kanie, N., Noble, I., Steffen, W., & Shyamsundar, P. (2014). An integrated framework for sustainable development goals. *Ecology and Society*, 19(4), art. 49.

Hák, T., Janoušková, S., & Moldan, B. (2016). Sustainable development goals: A need for relevant indicators. *Ecological Indicators*, 60, 565–573.

Haberl, H., Wiedenhofer, D., Virág, D., Kalt, G., Plank, B., Brockway, P., Fishman, T., Hausknost, D., Krausmann, F., Leon-Gruchalski, B., Mayer, A., Pichler, M., Schaffartzik, A., Sousa, T., Streeck, J., & Creutzig, F. (2020). A systematic review of the evidence on decoupling of GDP, resource use and GHG emissions, part II: Synthesizing the insights. *Environmental Research Letters*, 15(6), art. 065003.

Hallegatte, S., Fay, M., & Barbier, E. B. (2018). Poverty and climate change: Introduction, *Environment and Development Economics*, 23(3), 217–233.

Hay, C., Hunt, T., & McGregor, J. A. (2022). Inclusive growth: The challenges of multidimensionality and multilateralism. *Cambridge Review of International Affairs*, 35(6), 888–914.

Hediger, W. (1999). Reconciling 'weak' and 'strong' sustainability. *International Journal of Social Economics*, 26(7–9), 1120–1144.

Hickel, J. (2019). The contradiction of the sustainable development goals: Growth versus ecology on a finite planet. *Sustainable Development*, 27(5), 873–884.

Hickel, J., & Kallis, G. (2020). Is green growth possible? *New Political Economy*, 25(4), 469–486.

Hickel, J., Kallis, G., Jackson, T., O'Neill, D. W., Schor, J.B., Steinberger, J. K., Victor, P. A., & Ürge-Vorsatz, D. (2022). Degrowth can work – here's how science can help. *Nature*, 612(7941), 400–403.

Hirai, T. (2022). A balancing act between economic growth and sustainable development: Historical trajectory through the lens of development indicators, *Sustainable Development*, 30(6): 1900–1910.

Hopwood, B., Mellor, M., & O'Brien, G. (2005). Sustainable development: Mapping different approaches. *Sustainable Development*, 13(1), 38–52.

Hubacek, K., Baiocchi, G., Feng, K., & Patwardhan, A. (2017). Poverty eradication in a carbon constrained world. *Nature Communications*, 8, art. 912.

Hubacek, K., Chen, X., Feng, K., Wiedmann, T., & Shan, Y. (2021). Evidence of decoupling consumption-based CO_2 emissions from economic growth. *Advances in Applied Energy*, 4, art. 100074.

Huston, M. A., & Marland, G. (2003). Carbon management and biodiversity. *Journal of Environmental Management*, 67(1), 77–86. https://doi.org/10.1016/S0301-4797(02)00190-1

IEA. (2019). Global energy review: CO_2 emissions in 2018. International Energy Agency, Paris, March.

IEA. (2022). Global energy review: CO_2 emissions in 2021. International Energy Agency, Paris, March.

IPCC. (2022) *Climate Change 2022: Impacts, Adaptation, and Vulnerability.* Contribution of Working Group II to the Sixth Assessment Report of the Intergovernmental Panel on Climate Change [H.-O. Pörtner, D. C. Roberts, M. Tignor, E. S. Poloczanska, K. Mintenbeck, A. Alegría, M. Craig, S. Langsdorf, S. Löschke, V. Möller, A. Okem, B. Rama (Eds.), pp. 3056]. Cambridge, UK and New York, NY, USA: Cambridge University Press. https://doi.org/10.1017/9781009325844

Islam, S. N., & Winkel, J. (2017, October). *Climate change and social inequality.* DESA Working Paper 152, Department of Economic and Social Affairs, United Nations, New York.

Kar, A. K. (2022). Environmental Kuznets curve for CO_2 emissions in Baltic countries: An empirical investigation. *Environmental Science and Pollution Research*, 29(31), 47189–47208.

Kostetckaia, M., & Hametner, M. (2022). How sustainable development goals interlinkages influence European Union countries' progress towards the 2030 Agenda. *Sustainable Development*, 30(5), 916–926.

Le Blanc, D. (2015). Towards integration at last? The sustainable development goals as a network of targets. *Sustainable Development*, 23(3), 176–187.

Lenzen, M., Geschke, A., West, J., Fry, J., Malik, A., Giljum, S., Milà, I., Canals, L., Piñero, P., Lutter, S., Wiedmann, T., Li, M., Sevenster, M., Potočnik, J., Teixeira, I., Van Voore, M., Nansai, K., & Schand, H. (2022). Implementing the material footprint to measure progress towards sustainable development goals 8 and 12. *Nature Sustainability*, 5(2), 157–166.

Lerpold, L., & Sjöberg, Ö. (2021). Urban advantage? Sustainable consumption and ontological cityism across the urban hierarchy. In R. Bali Swain & S. Sweet (Eds.), *Sustainable Consumption and Production, Vol. I: Challenges and Development* (pp. 263–282). Cham: Palgrave Macmillan.

Liu, J. (2017). Integration across a metacoupled world. *Ecology and Society*, 22(4), art. 29.

Lundahl, M., Rauhut, D., & Hatti, N. (Eds.). (2021). *Poverty in Contemporary Economic Thought*. Abingdon: Routledge.

Mair, S., Jones, A., Ward, J., Christie, I., Druckman, A., & Lyon, F. (2017). A critical review of the role of indicators in implementing the sustainable development goals. In W. Leal Filho (Ed.), *Handbook of Sustainability Science and Research* (pp. 41–56). Cham: Springer.

Malerba, D. (2019). Poverty-energy-emissions pathways: Recent trends and future sustainable development goals. *Energy for Sustainable Development*, 49, 109–124.

Marques, A., Martins, I. S., Kastner, T., Plutzar, C., Theurl, M. C., Eisenmenger, N., Huijbregts, M. A. J., et al. (2019). Increasing impacts of land use on biodiversity and carbon sequestration driven by population and economic growth. *Nature Ecology and Evolution*, 3(4), 628–637.

Meemken, E.-M. (2020). Do smallholder farmers benefit from sustainability standards? A systematic review and meta-analysis. *Global Food Security*, 26, art. 100373.

Merry, S. E. (2019). The sustainable development goals confront the infrastructure of measurement. *Global Policy*, 10(S1), 146–148.

Meurs, M., Seidelmann, L., & Koutsoumpa, M. (2019). How healthy is a 'healthy economy'? Incompatibility between current pathways towards SDG3 and SDG8. *Globalization and Health*, 15(1), art. 83.

Miola, A., & Schiltz, F. (2019). Measuring sustainable development goals performance: How to monitor policy action in the 2030 Agenda implementation? *Ecological Economics*, 164, art. 106373.

Næss, P., & Høyer, K. G. (2009). The emperor's green clothes: Growth, decoupling, and capitalism. *Capitalism Nature Socialism*, 20(3), 74–95.

Niklasson, L. (2019). *Improving the Sustainable Development Goals: Strategies and the Governance Challenge*. Abingdon: Routledge.

Nilsson, M., Chisholm, E., Griggs, D., Howden-Chapman, P., McCollum, D., Messerli, P., Neumann, B., Stevance, A.-S., Visbeck, M., & Stafford-Smith, M. (2018). Mapping interactions between the sustainable development goals: Lessons learned and ways forward. *Sustainability Science*, 13(6), 1489–1503.

Nilsson, M., Griggs, D., & Visbeck, M. (2016). Map the interactions between sustainable development goals, *Nature*, 534(7607), 320–322.

Pradhan, P., Costa, L., Rybski, D., Lucht, W., & Kropp, J. P. (2017). A systematic study of Sustainable Development Goal (SDG) interactions. *Earth's Future*, 5(11), 1169–1179.

Robèrt, K.-H. (2000). Tools and concepts for sustainable development, how do they relate to a general framework for sustainable development, and to each other? *Journal of Cleaner Production*, 8(3), 243–254.

Rockström, Johan, Steffen, W., Noone, K., Persson, Å., Chapin III, F. S., Lambin, E., Lenton, T. M., Scheffer, M., Folke, C., Schellnhuber, H. J., Nykvist, B., de Wit, C. A., Hughes, T., van der Leeuw, S., Rodhe, H., Sörlin, S., Snyder, P. K., Costanza, R., Svedin, U., Falkenmark, M., Karlberg, L., Corell, R. W., Fabry, V. J., Hansen, J., Walker, B., Liverman, D., Richardson, K., Crutzen, P., & Foley, J. (2009). Planetary boundaries: Exploring the safe operating space for humanity. *Ecology and Society*, 14(2), art. 32.

Sachs, J. D. (2015). *The Age of Sustainable Development*. New York: Columbia University Press.

Sachs, J., Kroll, C., Lafortune, G., Fuller, G., & Woelm, F. (2021). *Sustainable Development Report 2021: The Decade of Action for the Sustainable Development Goals*. Cambridge: Cambridge University Press.

Sadler, P. (2010). *Sustainable Growth in a Post-Scarcity World: Consumption, Demand, and the Poverty Penalty*. London: Routledge.

Sanyé-Mengual, E., Secchi, M., Corrado, S., Beylot, A., & Sala, S. (2019). Assessing the decoupling of economic growth from environmental impacts in the European Union: A consumption-based approach. *Journal of Cleaner Production*, 236, art. 117535.

Satterthwaite, D. (1997). Sustainable cities or cities that contribute to sustainable development. *Urban Studies*, 34(10), 1667–1691.

Sen, A. (2013). The ends and means of sustainability. *Journal of Human Development and Capabilities*, 14(1), 6–20.

Spaiser, V., Ranganathan, S., Swain, R. B., & Sumpter, D. J. (2017). The sustainable development oxymoron: Quantifying and modelling the incompatibility of sustainable development goals. *International Journal of Sustainable Development and World Ecology*, 24(6), 457–470.

Stern, N. (2006). *The Economics of Climate Change: The Stern Review*. London: HM Treasury.

Steffen, W., Richardson, K., Rockström, J., Cornell, S. E., Fetzer, I., Bennett, E. M., & Biggs, R. (2015). Planetary boundaries: Guiding human development on a changing planet. *Science* 347(6223), art. 1259855.

Stevance, A.-S., Mengel, J., Young, D., Glaser, G., & Symon, C. (Eds.). (2015). *Review of the Sustainable Development Goals: The Science Perspective*. Paris: International Council for Science and International Social Science Council.

Stevens, C., & Kanie, N. (2016). The transformative potential of the Sustainable Development Goals (SDGs). *International Environmental Agreements: Politics, Law and Economics*, 16(3), 393–396.

Taconet, N., Méjean, A., & Guivarch, C. (2020). Influence of climate change impacts and mitigation costs on inequality between countries. *Climatic Change*, 160(1), 15–34.

Tienhaara, K. (2014). Varieties of green capitalism: Economy and environment in the wake of the global financial crisis. *Environmental Politics*, 23(2), 187–204.

UN. (2012). The future we want: Outcome document of the United Nations Conference on Sustainable Development, Rio de Janeiro, Brazil, 20–22 June 2012. United Nations Conference on Sustainable Development, Rio de Janeiro.

UN. (2014). The 10 Year Framework of Programmes on Sustainable Consumption and Production Patterns (10YFP). Interim progress report prepared by the 10YFP Secretariat on behalf of the 10YFP Board for the High-Level Political Forum. High-Level Political Forum on Sustainable Development, United Nations.

UN. (2015). Resolution adopted by the General Assembly on 25 September 2015. A/RES/70/1, General Assembly, United Nations, New York, 21 October.

UN. (2017). Resolution adopted by the General Assembly on 6 July 2017. A/RES/71/313, General Assembly, United Nations, New York, 10 July.

UN. (2022a). *World Population Prospects 2022: Summary of Results*. UN DESA/POP/2022/TR/NO. 3. Population Division, Department of Economic and Social Affairs, United Nations, New York.

UN. (2022b). Total population, as of 1 January (thousands). Population Division, Department of Economic and Social Affairs, United Nations, New York.

UN. (2022c). Progress report on the 10-Year Framework of Programmes on Sustainable Consumption and Production Patterns. E/2022/56, Economic and Social Council, United Nations, 4 May.

Valkila, J. (2009). Fair Trade organic coffee production in Nicaragua – sustainable development or a poverty trap? *Ecological Economics*, 68(12), 3018–3025.

Wang, Q., Zhang, F., Li, R., & Li, L. (2022). The impact of renewable energy on decoupling economic growth from ecological footprint – an empirical analysis of 166 countries. *Journal of Cleaner Production*, 354, art. 131706.

Warchold, A., Pradhan, P., Thapa, P., Putra, M. P. I. F., & Kropp, J. P. (2022). Building a unified sustainability development goal database: Why does sustainable development goal data selection matter? *Sustainable Development*, 30(5), 1278–1293.

Ward, J. D., Sutton, P. C., Werner, A. D., Costanza, R., Mohr, S. H., & Simmons, C. T. (2016). Is decoupling GDP growth from environmental impact possible? *PLoS One*, 11(10), art. e0164733.

Weber, H. (2017). Politics of 'leaving no one behind': Contesting the 2030 sustainable development goals agenda. *Globalizations*, 14(3), 399–414.

Weitz, N., Carlsen, H., Nilsson, M., & Skånberg, K. (2018). Towards systemic and contextual priority setting for implementing the 2030 Agenda. *Sustainability Science*, 13(2), 531–548.

Wiedmann, T. O., Schandl, H., Lenzen, M., Moran, D., Suh, S., West, J., & Kanemoto, K. (2015). The material footprint of nations, *Proceedings of the National Academy of Sciences of the United States of America*, 112(20), 6271–6276.

Wimmer, A., & Schiller, N. G. (2002). Methodological nationalism and the study of migration. *Archives européennes de sociologie*, 43(2), 217–240.

Winkler, I. T., & Satterthwaite, M. L. (2017). Leaving no one behind? Persistent inequalities in the SDGs. *International Journal of Human Rights*, 21(8), 1073–1097.

World Bank. ([2020] 2021). *Poverty and Shared Prosperity 2020: Reversals of Fortune*. Revised version. Washington, DC: World Bank.

World Bank. (2022). *Global Economic Prospects*. Washington, DC: World Bank.

3. Interactions within Sustainable Development Goals (SDGs): the economic and environmental dimensions of SDG Indicator 14.7.1

Suyu Liu

3.1 INTRODUCTION

The 17 Sustainable Development Goals (SDGs) are the core component of the 2030 Sustainable Development Agenda, which was accepted in the United Nations (UN) General Assembly in 2015. By the end of 2021, the 17 SDGs consist of 169 targets and 231 unique indicators. The SDGs, including the targets and indicators, have a wide coverage of different aspects of development, and the interactions between SDGs are gradually observed by researchers and practitioners (for example, Kroll et al., 2019; Liu, 2021). The emerging awareness of the interactions between SDGs contributes to the scientific literature on sustainable development and generates insights for more synthetic policies to support sustainable development (for example, Liu, 2020).

However, in comparison with the increasing knowledge of the interactions between different SDGs, studies on the interactions within the same SDG, especially the same indicator, remain limited. More explorations on the interactions of different dimensions, aspects, and components of the same SDG or the same indicator would not only enrich scientific knowledge, but also boost more science–policy dialogues which could improve the development, data collection, and use of SDG indicators. This would be particularly important for countries with relatively low statistical capacity.

The multi-dimensionality of sustainability and SDGs is a reason for the existence of interactions within the same SDG target or indicator. For example, Gennari and D'Orazio (2020) argue that it is difficult when using only one or two indicators to monitor the full range of complex SDG targets. Therefore, SDG indicators are sometimes multi-dimensional, and trade-offs and/or the synthesis of different dimensions within a single indicator are witnessed. A typical example is SDG Indicator 2.4.1, which sees the difficulty of selecting adequate sub-indicators to reflect the social, environmental, and economic dimensions of sustainable agriculture and the trade-offs and synthesis across dimensions of this indicator (Gennari & Navarro, 2019). SDG Indicator 14.7.1 is another example that reflects the interactions between different aspects within the same indicator.

This chapter uses SDG Indicator 14.7.1 as an entry point to explore the interactions between different dimensions within the same indicator. This chapter analyzes the interactions of economic and environmental dimensions of SDG Indicator 14.7.1 by using the 'Specific-Measurable-Assignable-Realistic-Time related' (SMART) framework (Cormier & Elliott, 2017). The results can generate further academic dialogues and practice-oriented discussions in this field.

The official name of SDG 14 is 'conserve and sustainably use the oceans, seas and marine resources for sustainable development', which is also widely known as 'life below water' in short. It has ten targets which have interactions (Virto, 2018). Each target has a specific indicator to monitor its progress. SDG Indicator 14.7.1 measures 'sustainable fisheries as a percentage of GDP in small island developing States, least developed countries and all countries', which monitors the progress of Target 14.7: 'by 2030, increase the economic benefits to Small Island Developing States and least developed countries from the sustainable use of marine resources, including through sustainable management of fisheries, aquaculture and tourism'. SDG Indicator 14.7.1 is important at both micro and macro levels. For example, in 2010 6.5 percent of the world's population fully relied on fish consumption for protein intake (FAO, 2014: 4). This indicator is also important at country and regional levels, especially for small island developing states, whose national territories consist of a high proportion of oceans. This is a possible reason why, according to the Food and Agriculture Organization's (FAO) definition (FAO, 2021), only marine capture fisheries are included in SDG Indicator 14.7.1.

According to the Inter-agency and Expert Group on SDG Indicators (IAEG-SDGs, 2019), SDG Indicator 14.7.1 has become a Tier One indicator since 2019 because its concept is clear, internationally established methodologies and standards are available, and data is regularly provided with good coverage of countries and populations. In the beginning SDG Indicator 14.7.1 was a Tier Three indicator when internationally established methodologies and standards for this indicator were unavailable (IAEG-SDGs, 2019). The custodian agency of SDG Indicator 14.7.1 is the FAO of the UN.

Based on the concepts and definitions of SDG Indicator 14.7.1 as shown in its metadata (FAO, 2021), this indicator has two core dimensions:

1. The economic dimension, which monitors the value added (VA) of marine capture fisheries and its share in the gross domestic product (GDP).

2. The environmental dimension, which monitors the proportion of marine capture fisheries which are captured in sustainable approaches (reflected by the share of VA of sustainable marine capture fisheries in the VA of total marine capture fisheries).

The VA of marine capture fisheries can be computed by the following equation:

VA of marine capture fisheries = value of fish captured from
marine stocks – intermediate cost (value of goods and
services that are used in the production process on board
or in ocean-based facilities)

SDG Indicator 14.7.1 can be computed by the following equation shown in the metadata (FAO, 2021):

Sustainable marine capture fisheries as a percentage of GDP
= VA of marine capture fisheries × Sustainability multiplier

The sustainability multiplier is 'the average sustainability weighted by the proportion of the quantity of marine capture for each respective fishing area in which the country performs fishing activities' (FAO, 2021: 5). The exact methodology for calculating the sustainability multiplier is not available to the public. Data for SDG Indicator 14.7.1 is released every two years, and the most recent data is for the year 2017 at the time when this chapter was drafted.

The interactions between economic and environmental dimensions of the SDGs have been discussed by existing studies (Selomane et al., 2015; Liu, 2020). However, these studies seldom address the interactions between economic and environmental dimensions within the same SDG, especially within the same SDG indicator. Such a gap increases the difficulty of properly interpreting the relevant SDG indicators and reduces the plausibility of adequately monitoring the progress of sustainable development, especially in countries with relatively lower statistical capacity. It may also lead to more ambiguity and complexity in practice, especially for the design and implementation of more synthetic developmental policies with the guidance of SDGs. Therefore, this chapter explores the interactions between the economic and environmental dimensions within SDG Indicator 14.7.1, with the objectives of enriching scientific knowledge and generating practical implications in the relevant fields.

The remaining parts of the chapter will be arranged as follows. The next section is a review of relevant literature. Section 3.3 analyzes the interactions between the economic and environmental dimensions of SDG Indicator 14.7.1, with country/state level data from the SDG Global Database (UN Statistics Division, 2021). Section 3.4 discusses the results plus the academic and practical implications. Section 3.5 concludes the chapter with the envisaging of future studies and practices.

3.2   LITERATURE REVIEW

As discussed in the previous section, there is a scarcity of previous literature on the interactions of different dimensions within one SDG indicator, especially within SDG Indicator 14.7.1. Nevertheless, this chapter searches and reviews the relevant literature to the best knowledge of the author.

Although the significant improvement in methodologies, principles, and standards related to SDG Indicator 14.7.1 is widely observed and is reflected by the official upgrade from Tier Three to Tier One in the ladder of SDG indicator status (IAEG-SDGs, 2019), some scholars have concerns about the ambiguity of this indicator. For example, Gulseven (2020) argues that the marine sustainability indicators can be ambiguous and confused. This can be somewhat supported by the fact that the exact methodologies to compute the sustainability multiplier, a key component of SDG Indicator 14.7.1, are not available to the public. Kirkfeldt and Santos (2021) introduce the ambiguity of SDG 14, including SDG Indicator 14.7.1, with the perspective that SDG 14 is not adequately connected with marine spatial planning in practice. Therefore, marine spatial planning may not be able to properly balance the economic and environmental objectives, as revealed by SDG Indicator 14.7.1 (Kirkfeldt & Santos, 2021).

Cai et al. (2019) find that the understanding of measuring the fishery sector's contribution to GDP is generally limited and a global consensus on relevant measurement is absent. Since measuring the (marine) fishery sector's contribution to GDP is a key component of SDG Indicator 14.7.1, such limitations may lead to difficulties in the proper use and/or interpretation of this indicator in practice. For example, the fishery sector's VA may be counted as both a direct contribution to GDP and also indirect contributions of other sectors (Cai et al., 2019), and such double counting may generate incorrect estimations of the fishery sector's contribution to GDP. Techniques such as input-output models and demand side analysis (such as measuring industry level final uses) are suggested to reduce these limitations related to the use and interpretation of SDG Indicator 14.7.1 (Cai et al., 2019; Cai & Leung, 2020). However, they may suffer from weaknesses such as low data availability. For example, even though SDG Indicator 14.7.1 has been classified as a Tier One indicator, its global reporting rate between 2017 and 2021 was only 54.1 percent (Bizier et al., 2022), slightly higher than the 50 percent threshold for being a Tier One indicator (IAEG-SDGs, 2019).

Using the SMART framework, Virto (2018) finds that SDG Target 14.7 (including SDG Indicator 14.7.1) is not very precise. This reflects the ambiguity of some SDGs and targets, as well as the difficulty in using one single indicator to capture the full range of a complex SDG target (for example, Gennari & D'Orazio, 2020). This also corresponds to other studies using the SMART framework for analyzing indicators under SDG 14. For example, Cormier and Elliott (2017) argue that the SDG 14 targets and indicators (including SDG Indicator 14.7.1) do not demonstrate specific needs to be measured, which may create difficulties in achieving these targets and indicators in practice.

Such limitations call for more attention to the possible connections between SDG Indicator 14.7.1 and other indicators under SDG 14. For example, FAO (2021) suggests that the sustainability multiplier can be taken from SDG Indicator 14.4.1 'proportion of fish stocks within biologically sustainable levels', although detailed methodologies are not presented. Horan (2020) develops an integrated SDG 14 Index (I-SDG 14) with an analysis of the interlinkages across indicators of SDG 14, including SDG Indicator 14.7.1. The empirical results show that countries with lower scores in I-SDG 14 usually face more challenges on SDG 14 and its implementation. Therefore, studies on SDG Indicator 14.7.1, including this chapter, should pay sufficient attention to the disparities in the country context, especially when using frameworks (such as SMART) to evaluate this indicator.

3.3 DATA AND RESULTS

This chapter uses country/state level data from the SDG Global Database (UN Statistics Division, 2021) to explore the interactions between economic and environmental dimensions of SDG Indicator 14.7.1. The indicator and data will be compared against the SMART framework, which is a widely used tool to examine the validity and effectiveness of indicators, including indicators measuring the progress of sustainable development. Country context will be included in the analysis.

Data for SDG Indicator 14.7.1 is available between 2011 and 2017 on a bi-annual basis. The SDG Global Database, accessed in December 2021, has information on the SDG Indicator of 34 small island developing states (regardless of their UN membership status). The data is presented in Table 3.1.

As shown in Table 3.1, the Marshall Islands has the highest percentage of sustainable fisheries in GDP (12.5 percent in 2013), which is followed by the Federated States of Micronesia (10.26 percent in 2011). Comoros and Sao Tome and Principe are the two immediate runners-up, but they are significantly lower than the top two states (5.35 percent and 3.97 percent respectively in 2015). The Cayman Islands has the lowest percentage of sustainable fisheries in GDP (0.02 percent between 2011 and 2017), slightly lower than Bahrain (0.06–0.07 percent during the same period).

Table 3.1   Sustainable fisheries as a percentage of GDP in selected small island developing states (2011–2017)

Small island developing states	2011	2013	2015	2017
Anguilla	1.12	0.95	N/A	N/A
Antigua and Barbuda	0.60	0.60	N/A	N/A
Bahamas	0.84	0.53	0.57	N/A
Bahrain	0.07	0.06	0.06	0.07
Barbados	0.05	0.10	0.06	0.09
Belize	0.93	1.39	1.20	0.61
Bermuda	0.07	0.05	0.02	0.06
Cabo Verde	0.36	0.46	0.67	0.41
Cayman Islands	0.02	0.02	0.02	0.02
Comoros	4.88	4.50	5.35	N/A
Cook Islands	0.55	0.41	0.22	0.27
Dominica	0.20	0.15	0.27	0.24
Fiji	1.41	1.16	0.66	0.53
French Polynesia	1.13	1.65	1.75	N/A
Grenada	0.73	0.74	0.72	0.68
Guinea-Bissau	1.71	1.91	1.70	1.82
Guyana	1.16	1.02	0.81	0.94
Haiti	0.34	0.31	0.20	0.22
Jamaica	0.18	0.18	0.24	0.23
Maldives	2.78	2.59	2.86	3.03
Marshall Islands	10.14	12.50	8.53	10.01
Micronesia (Federated States of)	10.26	9.06	8.78	9.36
Montserrat	0.18	0.18	0.16	0.14
Palau	1.63	1.45	1.23	1.29
Saint Kitts and Nevis	0.25	0.19	0.20	0.16
Saint Vincent and the Grenadines	0.21	0.22	0.26	0.24
Samoa	1.57	1.64	2.33	2.35
Sao Tome and Principe	2.82	3.20	3.97	3.97
Seychelles	0.68	0.88	0.55	0.51
Suriname	1.61	1.61	2.00	2.14
Tonga	1.99	2.24	1.87	1.72
Trinidad and Tobago	0.02	0.02	0.03	N/A
Turks and Caicos Islands	0.33	0.25	0.28	0.29
Vanuatu	0.53	0.46	0.39	0.42

Note: the unit is percentage, and the figures are rounded up to 2 decimal points

Table 3.2   The SMART framework and its specifications

Specific	The objective(s) to be achieved should be clearly specified and can be interpreted by stakeholders without ambiguity.
Measurable	Objectives and progresses should be measurable in relation to the ecosystems and human societies.
Achievable	Objectives should be able to be achieved and should be consistent with the values and desires of a majority of stakeholders.
Realistic	Objectives should be implementable with the reasonably available resources and should reflect the aspirations of stakeholders to achieve them.
Time-bounded	Clear time scales for meeting objectives should be established.

The chapter uses the SMART framework to further analyze the indicator and data in Table 3.1. The specifications of the SMART framework are shown in Table 3.2 (for example, Cormier & Elliott, 2017: 29).

The interactions between the economic and environmental dimensions of SDG Indicator 14.7.1 affect this indicator's performance under the SMART framework. In terms of 'specific', core components are clearly specified; the co-existence of the economic and environmental dimensions of SDG Indicator 14.7.1 makes it difficult to properly interpret this indicator. In other words, it may lead to ambiguity in understanding what exactly this indicator monitors. The difficulties in the estimation of the fishery sector's VA in GDP and the unavailable information on computing the sustainable multiplier exacerbate such ambiguities.

In terms of 'measureable', although SDG Indicator 14.7.1 is quantifiable in relation to both the ecosystem and human society, the interactions between its economic and environmental dimensions generate confusions in this indicator. More specifically, a core confusion is what this indicator measures exactly, although the indicator is measurable. According to the definition of SDG Indicator 14.7.1, the data for this indicator is the product of the economic dimension (VA of marine fisheries in GDP) and the environmental dimension (sustainability multiplier). However, in practice, the objective of this indicator is unclear. This is because the data for this indicator can reflect either the economic or the environmental dimension or both of them.

For example, sustainable fishery contributed to 1.41 percent of GDP in Fiji in 2011, and this figure dropped to 0.66 percent and 0.53 percent in 2015 and 2017 respectively. This could be a result of a possible reduction in sustainable fisheries but may also be caused by a possible shrinking of the fishery sector in the country. In other words, such a drop of the figure of SDG Indicator 14.7.1 in Fiji is possibly because its fishery sector became less sustainable, or as a result of a drop of the fishery sector in the national economy, or even as the outcome of both of these two possible reasons. Such confusion is expanded when making international comparisons, which is an objective for the development of SDG indicators and collecting data for them at cross-country levels. For example, Trinidad and Tobago had a relatively lower share of sustainable fishery in GDP between 2011 and 2015 than Barbados, also a small island developing state in the Caribbean. However, this is highly likely to be caused by the disparity in economic structures of the two countries. In Barbados, fishery has a relatively strong influence on the economy because fish products are important for tourism (such as restaurants) which has a strong presence in the economy (Mahon et al., 2007). By contrast, Trinidad and Tobago has a more influential oil sector and relies relatively less on fishery and tourism (Hosein, 2021). Therefore, although this indicator is quantifiable, it actually does not identify the exact objectives and progress to be measured. This further reduces its applicability in conducting cross-country comparisons.

It is not possible to evaluate whether SDG Indicator 14.7.1 is achievable and realistic, because the indicator itself does not have any specific target. Instead, it is an indicator measuring SDG Target 14.7. SDG Target 14.7 is achievable and realistic because it does not have a specific requirement or objective. It only requires that by 2030 the economic benefits from the sustainable use of marine resources for small island developing states and least developed countries increase but does not have specific requirements on the amount or percentage of increase. This is possibly due to the difficulty in the collection and computation of data for SDG Indicator 14.7.1 (for example, Cai et al., 2019), including the interactions of the economic and environmental dimensions within this indicator.

Similarly, there is no evidence to decide whether SDG Indicator 14.7.1 is time-bounded as it is only an indicator measuring SDG Target 14.7. However, SDG Target 14.7 is time-bounded as the year 2030 is definitely a time scale, although it is rather general without detailed roadmaps. Nevertheless, there is no time scale to monitor the environmental and economic progress as in SDG Indicator 14.7.1.

A brief summary of SDG Indicator 14.7.1 using the SMART framework can be found in Table 3.3.

3.4   DISCUSSION AND IMPLICATIONS

SDG Indicator 14.7.1 is a Tier One indicator in the SDG framework, which has clear concepts and definitions, plus globally accepted methodologies and standards. Also, it has a wide coverage of countries with high availability of data. For example, as shown in Table 3.1, 34 of 58 small island developing states have data for SDG Indicator 14.7.1, which is a relatively high availability,

Table 3.3   SMART analysis of SDG Indicator 14.7.1

	Result level	Evidence/reasons
Specific	Low level	Ambiguity is caused due to the interactions of the economic and environmental dimensions of this indicator, which may be exacerbated by the difficulties in computing the core components such as the sustainability multiplier.
Measurable	Low level	Although the indicator is quantifiable and has good data coverage and availability (as a Tier One indicator), it is unclear what this indicator exactly measures and monitors, especially in the cross-country and time-series analysis.
Achievable	N/A	This is not an indicator with a clear objective (positive or negative) to achieve.
Realistic	N/A	This is not an indicator with a clear objective to achieve. It is an indicator to monitor the progress of SDG Target 14, which is realistic as it only has an unspecified objective (without an exact amount or percentage of increase).
Time-bounded	Mid-level	It has a clear but general time scale, without more detailed time plans.

especially in consideration of the generally weak statistical capacity of small island developing states (World Bank, 2021a).

However, since environmental and economic dimensions co-exist in SDG Indicator 14.7.1 and it has been demonstrated that these two dimensions interact with each other (Selomane et al., 2015), it is not possible to identify what exactly this indicator measures and monitors. In other words, SDG Indicator 14.7.1 measures the output of the fishery sector's influence in the economy (economic dimension) and the sustainability of fishing (environmental dimension), while the data of this indicator cannot reveal which dimension (and to what extent) contributes to VA of sustainable fishery in GDP. Such ambiguity and confusion may result in difficulties in the interpretation and use of SDG Indicator 14.7.1.

The over-year comparison (time series) of the data for SDG Indicator 14.7.1 is difficult and requires appropriate understanding of the changes in global and national economies. For example, Table 3.1 shows that sustainable fishery's contribution to Fiji's GDP decreased steadily between 2011 and 2017. However, during this period, Fiji's GDP (measured by constant local currency) increased steadily from around 8.2 billion to 10.4 billion Fijian dollars (World Bank, 2021b). Therefore, it is not possible to infer that the sustainability of fishery sector in Fiji declined during this period, and it may not be adequate to conclude that the fishery sector shrunk either. Instead, it may only mean that the growing speed of sustainable fishery in Fiji was slower than the country's GDP growth between 2011 and 2017.

Due to the co-existence and interactions of the economic and environmental dimensions within SDG Indicator 14.7.1, the cross-country comparison and analysis of data for this indicator encounter more challenges and require strong knowledge of the country context. For example, sustainable fishery's contribution to GDP between 2011 and 2017 was significantly higher in the Maldives than Bahrain, as can be noticed in Table 3.1. However, it is widely known that Bahrain's economy relies strongly on the oil sector and banking services instead of fishery, while in the Maldives fishery is one of the most important industries in the economy (Sathiendrakumar & Tisdell, 1986). Therefore, even though Table 3.1 shows that in the Maldives sustainable fishery had a stronger share in GDP than the situation in Bahrain between 2011 and 2017, it is not possible to infer that fishery in Bahrain is less stable than the Maldives.

The practical implementation of SDG Indicator 14.7.1, especially making relevant policies to support sustainable fisheries, may also be affected by the co-existence and interactions of the economic and environmental dimensions of this indicator. Due to the ambiguity of what exactly SDG 14.7.1 measures, it is not possible for researchers and practitioners to decide whether and how to promote sustainable fisheries in the national economy. For example, is it suitable to increase a country's VA of sustainable fishery in GDP, if the fishery sector is very small but very sustainable in that country? If yes, then the solution is to expand the fishery sector at a quicker speed than the country's GDP growth in that country given its fishery is already very sustainable in terms of environment. Such ambiguity caused by the interactions between economic and environmental dimensions of the same indicator partially supports some scholars' arguments that several SDG indicators are largely inspirational and not very useful in practice (Cormier & Elliott, 2017).

A number of practical implications are recommended by this chapter. Firstly, further exploration of measuring and estimating the VA of the fishery sector should be encouraged. This is because it is the core component (economic dimension) of SDG Indicator 14.7.1, while currently there are still difficulties in collecting and computing data for the VA of the fishery sector (Cai et al., 2019). In addition, an international consensus on calculating the VA of the fishery sector has not been established; thus further methodological work is necessary.

Secondly, the further development and sharing of knowledge about sustainable fishery are recommended. Currently, the sustainability of a country's fishery is solely reflected by the sustainability multiplier compiled by the FAO (FAO, 2021). However, the data for the sustainability multiplier, plus the specific methodologies to compute the sustainability multiplier, is not available to the public. Although the metadata of SDG Indicator 14.7.1 introduces the computation of the sustainability multiplier according to arbitrarily divided Fishing Areas and also based on the maximum sustainable yield (FAO, 2021), the methodological details are not available to the public either. Therefore, it is suggested that the data for the sustainability multiplier as well as the methodological details for the computation could be released for publishing by the FAO, the custodian agency of SDG Indicator 14.7.1. Also, FAO is making efforts in compiling country-level estimates of the proportion of fish stocks within biologically sustainable levels (as reflected in SDG Indicator 14.4.1), and its plan is to use such country-level estimates instead of the arbitrarily divided Fishing Areas to compute the sustainability multiplier for each country (FAO, 2021). These efforts should be encouraged and supported as they can better capture the cross-country disparities in the areas and amount of marine fishery and can also reflect the possible interactions between SDG Indicators 14.4.1 and 14.7.1.

Thirdly, the interpretation and use of SDG Indicator 14.7.1 must be consistent with the country context. A high or low contribution from sustainable fishery to a country's GDP does not necessarily reflect the sustainability of that country's fishery sector. Instead, in order to understand the sustainability of a country's fishery sector by using the data for SDG Indicator 14.7.1, it is essential to have adequate knowledge of and influence on the fishery sector in that country. This is particularly important for international comparisons, as the size of fishery industries varies significantly across countries.

Fourthly, more dialogues between science and practice should be supported. The contribution of science–policy interfaces in boosting the understanding of SDG interactions has been demonstrated (Vladimirova & Le Blanc, 2015). More science–policy interfaces on SDG 14.7.1, especially the interactions between economic and environmental dimensions within this indicator, would facilitate the proper integration of scientific knowledge into the policy making process and reduce the 'science–policy gap' in relevant academic and practical fields (Cvitanovic & Hobday, 2018). After all, SDG Indicator 14.7.1 (and also many other goals, targets, and indicators) is interdisciplinary, which requires both scientific and practical expertise for its proper interpretation and use.

3.5   CONCLUSION AND LIMITATIONS

Based on the previous studies on SDG Indicator 14.7.1 and existing literature about interactions between SDGs (including SDG targets and indicators), this chapter explores the co-existence and interactions of the economic and environmental dimensions within SDG Indicator 14.7.1. By using the most recent data from the SDG Global Database, this chapter analyzes SDG Indicator 14.7.1 with the SMART framework. This supplements existing studies which mainly focus on the interlinkages across SDGs and can also support further academic and practical efforts in understanding the multidimensionality of sustainability and SDGs. For example, trade-offs and the synthesis of different dimensions within some other SDG indicators may deserve further attention in future research and practice.

The results demonstrate that, since SDG Indicator 14.7.1 has both economic and environmental dimensions and they interact with each other, it is difficult to specify what exactly this indicator measures and monitors. Although SDG Indicator 14.7.1 is quantifiable, the difficulties in collecting and computing data for both the economic and the environmental dimensions create ambiguity in the interpretation of this indicator. In practice, interactions between economic and environmental dimensions within SDG Indicator 14.7.1 expand the challenges in using this indicator, especially for cross-country and over-year comparisons.

SDG Indicator 14.7.1 only captures one aspect (marine fishery) of SDG Target 14.7, even though fishery is one of the most important marine resources which can be sustainably used for economic benefits. The interactions between the economic and environmental dimensions of SDG Indicator 14.7.1 reduce the measurability of SDG Target 14.7 and increase the difficulty of using this target to monitor the progress of the sustainable use of marine resources.

A number of scientific and practical implications are recommended in this chapter. In particular, the interpretation and use of SDG Indicator 14.7.1 with comprehensive consideration of the country context, especially the influence of the fishery sector in the country's economy, is recommended. Further development and sharing of knowledge about this indicator should be boosted, especially the computation of the sustainability multiplier and the fishery sector's contribution to GDP. In addition, more science–policy interfaces should be encouraged, which would be useful to reduce the widely known gaps between science and policy in the field of sustainable development. Similar implications may also be suitable for some other SDG indicators which witness trade-offs and syntheses between different dimensions of these indicators. More efforts in improving national statistical capacity, especially the statistical capacity of small developing island states and least developed countries, would also be useful to better understand the interactions within SDG indicators including SDG Indicator 14.7.1.

In comparison with the expanding literature about interactions between SDGs, existing studies on the interactions of different dimensions within the same SDG indicator are insufficient. This pioneering research aims to broaden the scientific perspectives on the SDG interactions and generate more insights for the policy making process, which calls for more in-depth studies in this field. There is no doubt that with more efforts from scholars and practitioners, further academic and practical contributions can be generated. For example, it is expected that future studies may further improve the computation and estimation of VA from the fishery sector. More data could be collected to assist the interpretation of SDG Indicator 14.7.1 and the interactions between its economic and environmental dimensions. National agencies' and international organizations' continuous efforts in improving data collection for SDGs including SDG Indicator 14.7.1 would be supportive for further scientific and practical advancement in the relevant fields.

As an initial exploration of the interactions within the same SDG indicator, this chapter is not without limitations. In consideration of the diverse background and expertise of readers, the data and methodology used in this chapter are descriptive and not sophisticated. Therefore, it is not possible to calculate the exact interactions between the economic and environmental dimensions within SDG Indicator 14.7.1. Furthermore, within the limited space in this chapter, the direct connections between the interactions within SDG 14.7.1 and the difficulties in the interpretation and use of this indicator have not been fully demonstrated, which leaves space for future studies. Similar to some scholars' comments on the SDGs and SDG indicators, this chapter may also inspire more research and practice in the relevant fields, rather than providing specific measurements and solutions.

ACKNOWLEDGMENTS

The author appreciates the insights from current and former colleagues at different United Nations departments, organizations, and agencies. Unless otherwise specified, the views expressed in this chapter are the author's and do not reflect any official stance of the United Nations and/or its departments, organizations, and agencies, including the FAO. This study is the author's own research and not the FAO's work/official output. The author would also like to thank their peers, students, and sponsors in academia, including the editors and reviewers.

REFERENCES

Bizier, V., Gennari, P., & Navarro, D. K. (2022). Role of international, regional and country organizations in adapting to statistical standards and regional differences: The case of food and agriculture statistics. *Statistical Journal of the IAOS*, 38, 511–532. https://doi.org/10.3233/SJI-220003

Cai, J., Huang, H., & Leung, P. S. (2019). *Understanding and Measuring the Contribution of Aquaculture and Fisheries to Gross Domestic Product (GDP)*. FAO

Fisheries and Aquaculture Technical Paper 606. https://www.fao.org/documents/card/zh/c/CA3200EN/

Cai, J., & Leung, P. S. (2020). A note on linkage between gross value added and final use at the industry level. *Economic Systems Research*, 32(3), 428–437. https://doi.org/10.1080/09535314.2020.1718617

Cormier, R., & Elliot, M. (2017). SMART marine goals, targets and management – Is SDG 14 operational or aspirational, is 'life below water' sinking or swimming?' *Marine Pollution Bulletin*, 123(1–2), 28–33. https://doi.org/10.1016/j.marpolbul.2017.0e7.060

Cvitanovic, C., & Hobday, A. J. (2018). Building optimism at the environmental science-policy-practice interface through the study of bright spots. *Nature Communication* 9, Article 3466. https://doi.org/10.1038/s41467-018-05977-w

FAO. (2014). *The State of World Fisheries and Aquaculture: Opportunities and Challenges*. Rome: FAO. https://www.fao.org/3/i3720e/i3720e.pdf

FAO. (2021). *SDG Indicator 5.a.1 Metadata*. https://unstats.un.org/sdgs/metadata/files/Metadata-14-07-01.pdf

Gennari, P., & D'Orazio, M. (2020). A statistical approach for assessing progress towards the SDG targets. *Statistical Journal of IAOS*, 36, 1129–1142. https://doi.org/10.3233/SJI-200688

Gennari, P., & Navarro, D. K. (2019). The challenge of measuring agricultural sustainability in all its dimensions. *Journal of Sustainability Research*, 1, e190003. https://doi.org/10.20900/jsr20190013

Gulseven, O. (2020). Measuring achievements towards SDG 14, life below water, in the United Arab Emirates. *Marine Policy*, 117, Article 103972. https://doi.org/10.1016/j.marpol.2020.103972

Horan, D. (2020). National baselines for integrated implementation of an environmental sustainable development goal assessed in a new integrated SDG index. *Sustainability*, 12(17), 6955. https://doi.org/10.3390/su12176955

Hosein, R. (2021). *Oil and Gas in Trinidad and Tobago: Managing the Resource Curse in a Small Petroleum-Exporting Economy*. Cham, Switzerland: Palgrave Macmillan.

IAEG-SDGs. (2019). *Tier Classification for Global SDG Indicators 20 November 2019*. https://unstats.un.org/sdgs/files/Tier_Classification_of_SDG_Indicators_20_November_2019_web.pdf

Kirkfeldt, T. S., & Santos, C. F. (2021). A review of sustainability concepts in marine spatial planning and the potential to supporting the UN sustainable development goal 14. *Frontier Marine Sciences*, 8, Article 713980. https://doi.org/10.3389/fmars.2021.713980

Kroll, C., Warchold, A., & Pradhan, P. (2019). Sustainable Development Goals (SDGs): Are we successful in turning trade-offs into synergies? *Palgrave Communications*, 5, Article 140. https://doi.org/10.1057/s41599-019-0335-5

Liu, S. (2020). Interlinkages between indicators of sustainable development goals: Evidence from seven low income and lower middle-income countries. *Sustainable Development Research*, 2(1), 58–63. http://dx.doi.org/10.30560/sdr.v2n1p58

Liu, S. (2021). Child mortality and water stress under the framework of Sustainable Development Goals (SDGs): Evidence from twenty developing countries. *Present Environment and Sustainable Development*, 15(1), 49–58. https://doi.org/10.15551/pesd2021151004

Mahon, R., Parker, C., Sinckler, T., Willoughby, S., & Johnson, J. (2007). *The Value of Barbados' Fisheries: A Preliminary Assessment*. Barbados Fisheries Management

Plan, Public Information Document No. 2 (FMP-PID-2). https://www.cavehill.uwi
.edu/cermes/docs/publications/barbados_fishery_valuation_2007_08_31.aspx

Sathiendrakumar, R., & Tisdell, C. (1986). Fishery resources and policies in the
Maldives: Trends and issues for an island developing country. *Marine Policy*, 10(4),
279–293. https://doi.org/10.1016/0308-597X(86)90004-7

Selomane, O., Reyers, B., Biggs, R., Tallis, H., & Polasky, S. (2015). Towards
integrated social–ecological sustainability indicators: Exploring the contribution
and gaps in existing global data. *Ecological Economics*, 118, 140–146. http://dx.doi
.org/10.1016/j.ecolecon.2015.07.024

Virto, L. R. (2018). A preliminary assessment of the indicators for Sustainable
Development Goal (SDG) 14 "Conserve and sustainably use the oceans, seas and
marine resources for sustainable development". *Marine Policy*, 98, 47–57. https://
doi.org/10.1016/j.marpol.2018.08.036

Vladimirova, K., & Le Blanc, D. (2015). How well are the links between education and
other sustainable development goals covered in UN flagship reports? A contribution
to the study of the science-policy interface on education in the UN system. *UN
Department of Economic & Social Affairs Working Paper* No. 146, (ST/ESA/2015/
DWP/146). https://www.un.org/esa/desa/papers/2015/wp146_2015.pdf

UN Statistics Division. (2021). *SDG Indicators Database*. https://unstats.un.org/sdgs
/dataportal/database

World Bank. (2021a). *Data on Statistical Capacity*. https://datatopics.worldbank.org/
statisticalcapacity/

World Bank. (2021b). *GDP (Constant LCU) – Fiji*. https://data.worldbank.org/indicator
/NY.GDP.MKTP.KN?end=2020&locations=FJ&start=2009

4. Patterns of sustainability and policy coherence: some lessons learned from Sweden and global SDG follow-up

Viveka Palm

4.1 INTRODUCTION

The statistical follow-up and review of the Sustainable Development Goals is made on many different levels ranging from global to local. Globally there are statistical collaborations within the United Nations (UN) and its many UN agencies and other international organizations. For large regions there are regional statistical offices, for example, Eurostat and the UN regional Commissions such as the United Nations Economic Commission for Europe (UNECE), that collaborate with the countries and with a large number of stakeholders and non-government organizations (NGOs). Through this work, we have had many occasions to reflect on the positive aspects that such a broad statistical framework can bring to cross-sectoral analyses of society and its many goals.

Comparing with earlier sustainability frameworks like Agenda 21 and the Millennium Development Goals, the UN SDG agenda is digging deeper into more topics and uses more indicators in the follow-up and reviews. Interestingly, this wealth of topics has invited a very broad interest from society to take part in the process of monitoring and to draw conclusions from the results. At Statistics Sweden, we were approached by people wishing to understand what their role could be and how they could measure their activities' impact on the goals. For example, we were contacted by small companies wanting to influence their customers to eat sustainable foods, as well as finance actors considering how to include sustainability in their portfolio, and doctors wanting to bring a more holistic view to the health system. This interest is likely to make a difference and keep the sustainability issue in the political realm for many years to come. There is also an ongoing process in Sweden within the government and regionally to react to the follow-up and to consider how to best make all ministries take part in the sustainability agenda.

Some of the policy indicators in the SDG follow-up are also allocated to the ministries that are responsible for the questions. Statistics Sweden regularly reports to a network consisting of the agencies responsible for the themes covered by the indicators.

Working with sustainability follow-up in Sweden means being privileged with a good statistical system, because of a long historical tradition and good administrative records. We could also assume that the country should do reasonably well when it comes to sustainable practices, as this topic has met a lot of enthusiasm over the years and equality and the environment are often highly valued as has been shown in the measurements of the World Value Studies for example. In this respect, the country can also be an interesting special case – when goals are hard to meet in Sweden, it can be assumed they will also be difficult to solve in other countries. Likewise, if there seems to be potential to invest in some areas that look like they are underpinning the other areas, it might be a lesson also for other countries to consider.

This chapter summarizes lessons learned on how the SDGs interact and are monitored, while participating in the work to create the indicator follow-up for the UN SDG agenda. This work meant interacting with colleagues in the international statistical system to investigate how to find the statistics for indicators that can show the progress for the SDG and related targets agreed. From 2015 to 2020, first as a participant and later as a chair for the Inter-Agency Expert Group on SDG Indicators (IAEG-SDGs), I was a representative for the northern part of the European Union while working at Statistics Sweden.

4.2 METHOD

The 17 goals and the indicators that are used to follow up on the targets form a measurable and detailed description of what the countries and policy makers have defined as belonging to sustainable development. The social goals on poverty (1), hunger (2), good health and well-being (3), quality education (4), and inequality between women and men (5) are part of sustainability. Sustainability also requires a society that is built to provide clean water and sanitation (6), affordable and clean energy (7), decent work and a viable economy (8), an innovative society (9), equality (10), and sustainable cities (11), as well as sustainable production and consumption (12). The goals that spell out the need for a functioning environment in the form of a stable climate (13), a healthy water ecosystem (14), and a healthy land ecosystem (15) are part of sustainability together with a functioning law and human rights system and building peace and justice through good governance (16) and the resources to develop this system and the statistical systems to measure the outcomes (17).

In this chapter, we will start by listing typical general policies that are used to counter the problems that need to be overcome to reach the 17 SDGs. If a country is lacking these policies, on for example water management or providing education, then that will be seen in problems in reaching the goals of water or education. In the indicator system some of these types of policies are included as targets or indicators, and in other cases, it is more the outcome of the policies that is measured. We will illustrate how the issues identified as crucial in Sweden are equally relevant on a global scale by using indicator illustrations from the United Nations Statistics Division (UNSD) report on SDGs, (UNSD, 2021). The existence or creation of a policy is the first step of the assessment, but then the way it is being implemented will give certain outcomes, some wanted and some unwanted (Figure 4.1). With the help of the

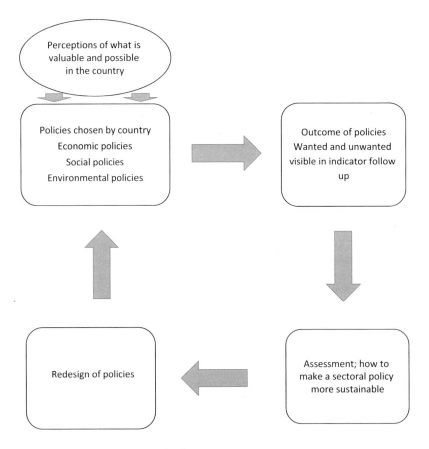

Figure 4.1   Assessment of policies

indicator follow-up, we will reason about how redesigns of the policies can increase sustainability.

Sustainability assessments need to take note of when the responses are not enough or when they are having unwanted side-effects. The reason why interactions between economic, social, and environmental issues are now in focus is because sector-specific policies can have adverse effects on areas that were not considered when they were designed. Short-term economic gain can often be achieved when social or environmental issues are overlooked. For example, the industry selling sugared drinks might grow the economy but will be responsible for an increase in diabetes which can be a side-effect of an increase in consumption and become a problem for the health goal.

Finding policies that provide good results both now and in the future is a core issue in sustainable development, and policy coherence is important. We will consider some of the underlying reasons why policies may be too narrow to be able to deliver a sustainable solution, by investigating how values or perceptions held by decision makers or voters may be shaping economic, social, and environmental policies.

4.3 POLICIES USED TO MOVE TOWARD THE GOALS

Social issues such as poverty and illness have been shown in research studies to be connected to the degree of equality between people in the countries (Marmot, 2015; Wilkinson & Picket, 2019). The degree of equality in turn is dependent on the existence of policies that provide a safety net so that health services, food, education, and safety from violence are available to all members of society (Table 4.1).

The countries that lack the general policies that provide such services have larger vulnerable groups, as inequality will tend to increase without intervening measures (Molander, 2015, 2017). Providing health services and education to all children and families is a good base for a sustainable society as it will give the prerequisite of health and skills to the population at large, increasing the chances of finding employment and a stable income on which to maintain a peaceful society. If policies are designed where groups of people do not have access to health services and education, or are not able to find employment or housing, then this will be apparent in the outcome of the follow-up.

For most of the goals it is possible to pinpoint some specific responses that make a difference for the outcome of each goal. Some of the targets and indicators in the follow-up explicitly measure the availability of such policies and the degree of accessibility to for example education or clean water. The pace of the improvement can sometimes be rather slow, and so it is important to keep analyzing the outcomes of the policies.

Table 4.1   *Sectoral policies to reach the Sustainable Development Goals*

Goal	Policy
1	Social security systems to protect the poor
2	Social security systems to provide access to food for the hungry
3	Health services for all
4	Schools and education available for all
5	Equal rights for women and men, girls and boys
6	Systems to clean drinking water and to treat waste water
7	Systems to harness and distribute energy and to steer away from fossil fuels
8	Stable institutions, workers' rights, rule of law
9	Vocational and adult training, infrastructure, supports for innovation
10	Social security systems, redistribution between groups
11	City and rural planning, good housing, good transportation systems
12	Policies to steer way from fossil fuels and exploitation of ecosystems
13	Policies to decrease greenhouse gas (GHG) emissions, and policies to adapt to a changing climate
14	Laws to safeguard marine nature reserves, to limit exploitation, to maintain good management practices
15	Laws to safeguard terrestrial nature reserves, to limit exploitation, to maintain good management practices
16	Peace, human rights, conflict solving mechanisms, law system, statistics to follow up
17	Development aid, national or international investments, south-south and triangular cooperation

Source: Authors' own assessment of the text and indicators in the UN SDG

By going through the targets in the follow-up of the sustainable development system, it can be seen that country results differ. If policies are in place and are implemented, then that is also visible in the outcome parameters.

Countries that have social security systems that cover most of the population generally have a better outcome. Regions that have committed themselves to implementing environmental protection are in a better position on air and water quality. For every goal, there are typical policies that can be implemented by countries. Depending on political choices, these policies can also be changed and the funding or follow-up provided can differ over time. In most areas there are some international conventions that countries have signed to agree on minimum standards or rights.

In Sweden, there are social security systems and most of the population trust that the state will provide free education and health care. Still, there is homelessness and NGOs that support people that are not covered by safety nets and lack access to important services. There are rules for who is eligible for support in a municipality, and there are rules that can prevent people that are not registered in the region or not able to stay away from drugs from receiving help, for example, in the form of somewhere to sleep. In the 1960s and 1970s you did not see homeless people in the streets of Stockholm, but after a psychiatric reform in 1995, the situation changed. Also, there are sicknesses, criminal behavior, and other circumstances that society is still struggling to come to grips with.

Even if there are official statistics on poverty and illness in Sweden, in the follow-up it was decided to complement these and make a special report to try and capture definitions, and data sources that can show the size of the vulnerable groups in the nation (SCB, 2020). Important data sources came from the agency that is responsible for the follow-up on the Child Convention as children are often not so visible in statistics.

For environmental goals, there are policies and laws that provide for clean drinking water and relatively clean air as compared to many other countries. Nevertheless, the national environmental goals follow-up shows that more policies are needed to arrive at a situation where production and consumption are based on clean energy and adapted to provide a stable climate and restored ecosystems.

4.4 POLICY AREAS THAT SHOW POTENTIAL FOR IMPROVEMENTS IN ALL COUNTRIES: RENEWABLE ENERGY AND EDUCATION FOR ALL

Two broad areas can be seen as important for reaching Swedish goals, and they clearly have potential for all countries and clearly interlink several goals. The first is linked to the phasing out of fossil fuels.

4.4.1 Cleaning Economic Activities by Moving from Fossil Fuels to Renewable Energy

By continuing to invest in renewable energy sources and energy efficiency, the goals on energy (7), sustainable consumption and production (12), and climate (13) and targets on air pollution (3.9 and 11.2) would become much easier to reach.

This is an area where Sweden is strong in policies that have moved the heating of houses to renewables and produce electricity that is virtually carbon free. This has been achieved by policies that encourage the insulation of homes and switching of fuels and energy taxes on fossil fuels as well as investing in combined heat and electricity production and supports for the use of renewables such as wind power, geothermal power, and solar power. Still, there are fossil fuels that need to be phased out of the transportation sector, and work is ongoing to change coal use in steel making to renewable sources via hydrogen. Policies that give incentives to phase out fossil fuels from the transportation sector have not been so prominent. For international transport, the Chicago Convention from the 1930s agreed on keeping fossil fuel prices low, and it would need to be changed for carbon emissions to be properly priced to take their climate change properties into account, but to our knowledge such initiatives have not been taken. There have been subsidies for people living far from their work to be compensated for the fuel purchases of their travels. Now this scheme is being redesigned so that it will not work as an incentive to drive and is planned to start in 2023 (Swedish Government, 2021), although with the new government in 2022 this decision may be retracted. There has also been a gradual movement for the transportation agency to include the national climate goals into some parts of transportation planning although it still has not influenced the core road building activities and is often pursued on a parallel track (Isaksson & Eriksson, 2021). For a long time, the planning for building new roads was done as if increasing traffic was not connected to the level of the national emissions.

Since Sweden is a country that depends on imports and exports, the importance of cleaning up value chains is also being considered, and an environmental goal to decrease the emissions from consumption is part of the environmental quality objectives. Research projects have been investigating scenarios for reaching sustainable consumption and for the monitoring of development (Svenfelt et al., 2019; Palm et al., 2019) and have shown that it is possible for our society to arrive at these goals (Larsson et al., 2022).

Decreasing climate emissions is a goal that all countries have signed up to. In order to contribute to the decrease of emissions, many changes of the fuels in energy systems are necessary. Creating the incentives to make markets speed up this change is important, and several indicators in the follow-up focus on such transformations. Since the climate system is a global ecosystem, the entire energy system needs to undergo changes to decrease the emissions of carbon dioxide and methane from human activities. The system change is time critical as the emission of methane from the natural environment must be avoided, as that would make the change so large that it could not be reversed (Steffen et al., 2018).

It can still be seen that many countries are investing in fossil fuel companies and planning for further extractions, thus using important funding that needs to be used to change the system (SEI, 2021). The International Energy Agency

(IEA) has warned against supporting the fossil fuel economy for many years now, for reasons of climate stability. The discussion on stranded assets, that banks and pension funds investing in fossil fuels are likely to make very bad investments, has also been ongoing for a long time. The prices of fossil fuels are being subsidized in many parts of the world and kept at a level that does not take their damaging properties into account (Figure 4.2). Therefore, they are prolonging the necessary movement to cleaner fuels and more efficient heating and transportation modes. This is a clear example of non-coherent policies, where countries are acting against their stated intentions and putting social, economic, and environmental development in peril. We have to assume that there are more limited rationalities driving these policies, like short-term gains for companies or populist policies to gain votes.

4.4.2   Supporting Vulnerable Groups in Society Which Touches on Most of the Goals

The other major game changer and potential in the SDG framework is to find effective ways to support vulnerable groups. Important vulnerable groups that must be supported as part of achieving the SDGs are vulnerable children,

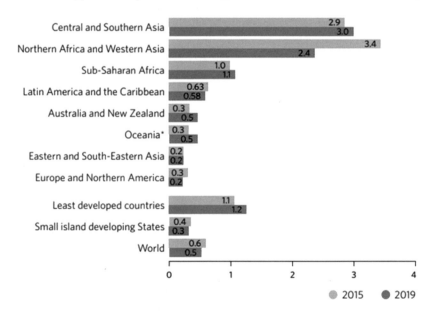

Source: UNSD, 2021

Figure 4.2   *Fossil-fuel subsidies as a proportion of GDP, 2015 and 2019 (percentage)*

youth with problems finishing school and finding gainful employment, and women subjected to violence from their partners.

Sweden is using the Child Convention to find ways to decrease violence against children and make the education system work for everybody. The Swedish Agency for Youth and Civil Society (MUCF) produces and disseminates knowledge on youth policy. They have been tasked with finding out how to strengthen the work on children's rights. A report called '10 Reasons for Dropping Out' (MUCF, 2014) is tightly linked to one of the SDG indicators. How to support families with children that have neuropsychiatric conditions such as ADHD or other vulnerabilities to cope with attaining education is a key area. In Sweden, the Child Convention has sparked investigations into how children's rights are sometimes lacking and need to be improved. This can concern the right to have your say in decisions that concern you, legislation for ventilation and sound levels in pre-schools and schools, and many other areas.

The SDG indicator that shows how many young people are not in education, employment, or training, the so-called NEET indicator, is one of the most important for monitoring this change. In the global follow-up (Figure 4.3) we can see that the youth that may have problems entering society because of a lack of education or employment are a large group in all countries, between 10 and 30 percent, and with large gender disparities.

Note: *Excluding Australia and New Zealand
Source: The-Sustainable-Development-Goals-Report-2021.pdf (un.org) page 45

Figure 4.3   *Proportion of youth not engaged in either education, employment, or training (NEET), by sex, 2019 (percentage)*

In 2019, 22.3 percent of the world's youth were not engaged in either education, employment, or training (NEET), a share that has shown no reduction in over a decade. Moreover, quarterly figures indicate that the NEET rate worsened from the fourth quarter of 2019 to the second quarter of 2020 in 42 out of 49 countries with available data. This is not surprising, as young workers were more severely affected than older workers by employment losses due to the COVID-19 pandemic. Both technical and vocational education and on-the-job training suffered massive disruption, forcing many to quit their studies. Worldwide, young women are twice as likely as young men to be jobless and not engaged in education or training. In 2019, the global NEET rate was 31.1 percent for young women, compared with 14.0 percent for young men. Since more women than men have been pushed out of the labor force during the pandemic, the crisis is likely to worsen the NEET gender gap.

Why do some children stop going to school even when it is obligatory, free, and well equipped? In Sweden, it seems that bullying and sicknesses are important factors. Also, children with special needs are expected to be able to follow the normal curriculum and cope with large classes. Some children may have experience of threats or violence at home or in school; others may just be sensitive or need adaptations to learn. How can bullying be best prevented? Creating a safer environment for children is an important cornerstone of the SDGs with a specific target in 16.2. In Sweden, corporal punishment was forbidden in 1973, but it is still allowed in many countries. The number of countries that have legal systems that protect children against violence in all settings is surprisingly small; only 62 states have full prohibition of corporal punishment, equivalent to around 13 percent of the world's children, with 26 more states committed to reforming their laws.[1]

A legal system is a good starting point, but still there are good reasons to follow up and investigate the situation. In regional schools surveys the children are asked if they have been threatened or experienced violence in school or outside of school, and the results are used in the Swedish national SDG follow-up as part of the education goal. From the government's side, proposals on including more knowledge on developmental difficulties in education for teachers are suggested. At present, there is very little education on how to help children with difficulties. Parental organizations are asking for better support. Specialists and researchers have suggested earlier interventions and more systematic approaches.

That this is still not a top priority, although it would seem to have huge potential, could be due to sectorial organization where some of the responsibilities for schools and for pre-schools lie with the municipalities. The Ministry of Education and Research is responsible for school performance, conditions for teachers, and research policies. Education is an important factor both economically and socially, with goals to do with efficiency and educating to invest in a good workforce but also to prepare a new generation to find employment and life satisfaction. Having a good social network in schools can prevent children from dropping out, but this means that funding is needed to employ personnel that can support it. The funding needed is small compared to the problems that can arise without a good education (Nilsson & Wadeskog, 2009). However, the costs for sicknesses and similar do not fall on the same organizations that pay the school budgets. This can then be seen as an example of a lack of policy coherence.

One key area is finding ways to teach populations at large about the way people mature and how to prevent violence. It is a sad reality that a lot of the problems that can be identified in society are man-made (Figure 4.4). From a brighter perspective, this means that many of the SDGs are possible to reach with available knowledge. In the public debate schools are a hot topic, and the Swedish school system has gone through some drastic changes, both in the sense that private actors are allowed to own and make money from schools, and in the sense that the grading system has changed, asking for a constant follow-up on and rating students in ways that have profoundly changed the learning situation.

Nearly one in three women (736 million) have been subjected to physical and/or sexual violence at least once since the age of 15, usually by an

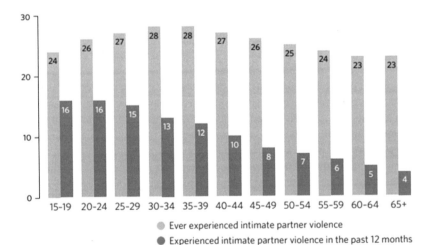

Source: UNSD, 2021

Figure 4.4   *Global prevalence of physical and/or sexual intimate part-*
               ner violence against women, by age group, 2000–2019
               (percentage)

intimate partner. Intimate partner violence starts early. Among girls and women who have ever been married or had a partner, nearly 24 percent of those aged 15 to 19 years have been subjected to such violence, as have 26 percent of those aged 20 to 24. Disparities in intimate partner violence are found across regions, with consistently higher prevalence in low- and lower-middle-income regions compared with high-income regions. In the area of violence against women, 83 percent of countries included budgetary commitments to implement legislation addressing violence against women, but 63 percent lacked rape laws based on the principle of consent. In the area of marriage and family, almost a quarter of countries failed to grant women equal rights with men to enter into marriage and initiate divorce, and three-quarters of countries did not stipulate 18 years as the minimum age of marriage for women and men, with no exceptions (UNSD, 2021).

4.5   MORE OR LESS GENERAL POLICIES CAN DEPEND ON WHAT IS VALUED

What are the reasons for designing limited policies? One model to understand this is to identify the values of the decision makers and discuss the impact on the policies in place. In life cycle assessments (LCA), a method used to model the potential environmental and social impacts from the production of products or services, some archetypes of world views are labeled hierarchist, egalitarian, individualist, and fatalist (Hofstetter et al., 2000).

These labels are then described by their view on nature, a time perspective for what effects to include as consequences of decision making, their view of what is enough knowledge to make an informed decision, what procedures to use, and what criteria to apply.

The hierarchist worldview is characterized by a view of nature as being tolerant to impact, a time perspective of at least an election cycle, considering knowledge to be of importance, using evidence, and trusting that if rules are followed, then the issues are being dealt with while accepting a certain level of risk (Table 4.2).

The egalitarian worldview considers nature to be fragile, plans for a longer time perspective of at least a generation or more, considers holistic knowledge and participation to ensure good decision making, and is risk averse.

The individualist worldview considers nature to be benign, has a short-term time perspective, looks for timely knowledge and experience, and puts trust in successful individuals, being open to taking risk-seeking decisions.

The fatalist worldview is that nature is capricious, that policy is mainly about what happens now, and that knowledge is not to be trusted, and thus does not really seek long-term solutions to today's problems.

Table 4.2   Attributes of world views, attitudes, and management styles of the four archetypes

	Hierarchist	Egalitarian	Individualist	Fatalist
Nature	Perverse/tolerant	Fragile	Benign	Capricious
Time perspective	Balanced	Long term	Short term	Myopic
Knowledge	Near complete and organized	Imperfect but holistic	Sufficient and timely	Irrelevant
Procedures applied	Rules	Ethical standards	Skills	—
Criteria	Evidence	Argument	Experience	—
Trust	Procedures	Participation	Successful individuals	—
Attitude towards risk	Risk-accepting	Risk-aversive	Risk-seeking	—

Source: Selection from Hofstetter et al., 2000

The countries that apply a hierarchist policy set, following international conventions that the country has signed, provide education and medical care to the population, have implemented rules that are risk-accepting, and perceive some groups of people as fragile and in need of support structures (such as children, parents, old people) and nature as rather tolerant. These include countries that have implemented rather broad social policies and that cover some agreed environmental issues in their planning, but where vulnerable groups, future generations, and some environmental issues are only partly covered.

The people that have a more egalitarian value system are described as having a set of values that also include animals and ecosystems and future generations. Since animals, ecosystems, and future generations do not have a voice, these values depend on people working to implement policies to safeguard them. These aspects are not very visible in the SDGs and are typically not covered by international laws or conventions.

The individualist policy setting is mainly interested in systems that can support able individuals and finding moralist arguments for not including all. With such an ethical system, social systems or insurance would cover those that can afford private solutions or have access via their work or family. Those outside of these systems may rely on 'other people that want to do good'.

Last, the fatalist does not see the need for interventions or finds the problems too difficult to overcome.

For the countries that report on the follow-up of SDGs we might think that it would mainly be the hierarchists that could deliver on the social SDG agenda and be willing to work on environmental goals as long as they are agreed on an international level. We might expect that the individualists would have a too narrow coverage of social policies and be less interested in acting on environmental issues, hoping that individual morals would be good enough to handle the situation or wanting to promote the economy and hoping that the environment will be resilient. The political groups that appeal to the egalitarians are likely to be working to include more issues in politics and be successful to the extent that they can bring in new ideas and make them mainstream by either introducing them into law or moving discussions or society towards new ways of thinking. The fatalists on the other hand might argue for the status quo and think that faith or a deity will decide what is to come or that the possibilities of working together are too slim to be considered.

To illustrate the differences in the coverage of social protection systems, we can use an indicator from the UNSD report on the SDGs (Figure 4.5). Before the pandemic, most of the population (85.4 percent) in high-income countries was effectively covered by at least one social protection benefit, compared with just over one-tenth (13.4 percent) in low-income countries. The coverage gap is even greater for those considered vulnerable, only 7.8 percent of whom were covered by social assistance in low-income countries.

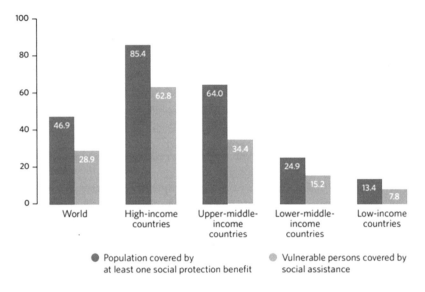

Source: UNSD, 2021

Figure 4.5   *Proportion of total population effectively covered by at least one social protection benefit and vulnerable persons covered by social assistance, by income level of country, 2020 or latest available year (percentage)*

Another example of the lack of substantiated policies put in place to protect biodiversity is the indicator for protecting threatened species (Figure 4.6). Among 134 400 species assessed, 28 percent (more than 37 400 species) are threatened with extinction, including 41 percent of amphibians, 34 percent of conifers, 33 percent of reef-building corals, 26 percent of mammals, and 14 percent of birds. The main drivers of species loss are agricultural and urban development; unsustainable harvesting through hunting, fishing, trapping, and logging; and invasive alien species.

4.6   CONCLUSIONS

A too narrow focus on what is valuable in society is a recipe for policy incoherence. This happens when the systems in place to alleviate poverty or pollution are very narrowly focused and leave large parts of the population or ecosystems outside of the system boundaries. Of paramount importance is investment in school systems that can cater to all children, that build a solid ground for skills needed, and also ideally are a chance to find friends and to understand society.

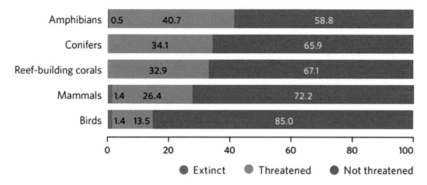

Source: UNSD, 2021

Figure 4.6 *Best estimates of the proportions of species threatened with extinction in the Red List Index, by species group, 2021 (percentage)*

The SDGs show the need for a solid net of social policies that can support children in growing up to reach their full potential. The youngest are normally not that visible in the statistics, but they feature in the follow-up in the educational goal and importantly in target 16.2 (end abuse, exploitation, trafficking, and all forms of violence and torture against children). By increasing the focus on them and decreasing the violence in their environments, the possibilities for preventing many problems are apparent. It is one important way to improve the situation for the most vulnerable groups.

The economic principles that allow for short-term benefits but that damage the social and environmental fabric need to be identified and redirected. The reforming of fossil fuel subsidies is a target in the follow-up and would introduce some better incentives to change the energy system to use energy sources with less impact on the environment.

Sectoral policies that have side-effects because they are too narrow need to be identified. Some economic rules for enterprises shift the responsibility for bad side-effects onto society, for example when the air or water is polluted by economic activities and policies to decrease the pollution lead to companies being able to sue the government for compensation. The rules of the economy make it possible to earn money by increasing activities with grave side-effects. This is clearly seen in the continuation of investments in extracting more fossil fuels, against clear recommendations that such investments need to decrease rapidly to maintain a stable climate. There are other companies whose products or services are avoided by ethical investors but that do not have to take responsibility for the risks of their customers and that are allowed to market products like tobacco or gambling.

The monitoring of the SDGs shows that there are policies that can improve the situation and result in more sustainable development. The lack of important policies or the existence of policies that undermine the efforts to come to terms with the problems identified in the SDGs are clearly relevant and need to be examined. Monitoring itself does not necessarily achieve sustainability as an outcome but can serve to highlight what is working and what is not.

NOTE

1. https://endcorporalpunishment.org/wp-content/uploads/2021/04/Prohibiting-all-corporal-punishment-of-children-laying-the-foundations-for-nonviolent-childhoods.pdf

REFERENCES

Hofstetter, P., Baumgartner, T., & Scholz, R. W. (2000). Modelling the valuesphere and the Ecosphere: Integrating the decision makers' perspectives into LCA. *The International Journal of Life Cycle Assessment*, 5(3) 161–175. https://doi.org/10.1065/lca2000.02.015

Isaksson, K., & Eriksson, I. (2021). Att integrera klimatmål i nationell transportplanering: maktdynamik som formarplaneringens taktik: Slutrapport från projektet Klimatfrågans integrering i nationell transportplanering - en maktanalys. Stockholm, Swedish EPA. In Swedish. ISSN 0282-7298.

Larsson et al. (2022). Consumption based scenarios for Sweden - a basis for discussing new climate targets (sustainableconsumption.se)

Marmot, M. (2015). *Status Syndrome, How Your Place in the Social Gradient Directly Affects Your Health*. ISBN0747570493. http://www.bloomsbury.com/

Molander, P. (2015). Ojämlikhetens anatomi, In Swedish, ISBN9789175034157.

Molander, P. (2017). Condorcets misstag – Hoten mot staten och demokratin, In Swedish. ISBN 9789176811351.

MUCF. (2014). 10 reasons for dropping out. 10 reasons for dropping-out | MUCF.

Nilsson, I., & Wadeskog, A. (2009). En vägledning för att värdera effekterna av tidiga och samordnade insatser, SEEAB.SE, In Swedish. http://www.seeab.se-SkolSamv-skolsamvrkan_091101U.htm

Palm, V., Wood, R., Berglund, M., Dawkins, E., Finnveden, G., Schmidt, S., & Steinbach, N. (2019). Environmental pressures from Swedish consumption – A hybrid multi-regional input-output approach. *Journal of Cleaner Production*, 228, 634–664. https://doi.org/10.1016/j.jclepro.2019.04.181

SCB. (2020). Swedish report on vulnerable groups. Leaving no one behind: Statistical review of the implementation of the 2030 Agenda in Sweden. Leaving no one behind (scb.se).

SEI. (2021). Production Gap Report 2021. PGR2021_web_rev.pdf (productiongap.org).

Steffen, W., Rockström, J., Richardson, K., Lenton, T. M., Folke, C., Liverman, D., Summerhayes, C. P., Barnosky, A. D., Cornell, S. E., Crucifixi, M., Donges, J. F., Fetzer, I., Steven, J., Lade, S. J., Scheffer, M., Winkelmann, R., & Schellnhuber. H. J. (2018). Trajectories of the Earth System in the Anthropocene (pnas.org). *PNAS*, 115(33), 8259.

Svenfelt, Å., Alfredsson, E. C., Bradley, K., Fauré, E., Finnveden, G., Fuehrer, P., Gunnarsson-Östling, U., Isaksson, K., Malmaeus, M., Malmqvist, T., Skånberg, K., Stigson, P., Aretun, Å., Buhr, K., Hagbert, P., & Öhlund, E. (2019). Scenarios for sustainable futures beyond GDP growth 2050. *Futures*, 111, 1–14.

Swedish Government. (2021). In Swedish Förslag om ett nytt och förenklat reseavdrag - Regeringen.se.

UNSD. (2021). The sustainable development goals report 2021. The-Sustainable-Development-Goals-Report-2021.pdf (un.org).

Wilkinson, R. G., & Picket, K. E. (2019). *The Inner Level: How More Equal Societies Reduce Stress, Restore Sanity and Improve Everyone's Well-Being*. London: Penguin Press. ISBN 9780525561224.

5. Quantitative approaches to explore synergies and trade-offs among Sustainable Development Goals (SDGs)

Prajal Pradhan and Anne Warchold

5.1 INTRODUCTION

No country is currently on track to meet the 2030 Agenda for Sustainable Development (UN, 2022). The 2030 Agenda calls for transformative changes to shift the world onto a sustainable and resilient path by balancing the three sustainability dimensions – social, economic, and environmental. It comprises 17 Sustainable Development Goals (SDGs) and 169 targets to be achieved by 2030. So far, countries have selectively implemented SDGs without considering their complex interactions, resulting in a limited transformative political impact (Biermann et al., 2022). Depending on context- and location-specific mechanisms, SDGs interact positively (that is, synergies) or negatively (that is, trade-offs) (Pradhan et al., 2017). For example, achieving food security (SDG 2) through intensive agriculture can negatively impact water (SDG 6), land (SDG 15), biodiversity (SDGs 14 and 15), and climate (SDG 13). In contrast, sustainable land and water use can also ensure food security. Doing so will positively affect water quality, restore land, conserve biodiversity, and sequestrate soil carbon (Mirzabaev et al., 2021; Pradhan et al., 2021). Positive interactions where advancement in one SDG or target favours progress in another are called synergies. Negative interactions or trade-offs are outcomes of the current imbalance across the three sustainability dimensions, where the progress of one SDG or target hinders another's advancement. Actions balancing the three sustainability dimensions can resolve these trade-offs, generating win-win solutions and enabling transformative changes (Messerli et al., 2019).

Currently, the world is facing crises characterized by conflicts, climate catastrophes, pandemics, massive displacement, and other socioeconomic challenges. Due to these cascading and intersecting crises, SDGs are regressing. Underachieved SDGs will jeopardize lives and livelihoods and worsen socioeconomic and environmental situations (Pradhan, 2023). The UN SDG Report 2022 highlights the following impacts of the current crises (UN, 2022). Ninety-three million more people were pushed into extreme poverty in 2020. For the first time in a decade, immunization coverage dropped, resulting in increased deaths from tuberculosis and malaria. Twenty-four million students were at risk of not returning to school. In the meantime, one-quarter of the global population is now living in conflict-affected countries (UN, 2022). Due to global warming, climate extremes are becoming more frequent, co-occurring, and persistent, negatively impacting social, economic, and environmental systems (Pradhan et al., 2022). Therefore, voices to rescue SDGs have become more prominent in recent months. For example, United Nations Secretary-General Antonio Guterres called on the international community to make SDGs a top priority and get back on track to building a better world that "leaves no one behind".

SDGs are considered systems of interacting components instead of just a collection of goals, targets, and indicators (Pradhan, 2019). Due to this integrated and indivisible nature, untangling complex SDG interactions to leverage synergies and tackle trade-offs is a challenge. In particular, making progress on SDGs is the main hurdle for practitioners and policy makers, who tend to be organized in silos represented by sectors, ministries, and agencies. Understanding SDG interactions allows policy makers to prioritize SDGs where transformative actions can maximize synergies and resolve trade-offs, leading to progress across SDG systems. They will also recognize which sectors could be allies and where negotiations would be required. Such an understanding clarifies how the SDG puzzle fits together in a particular context. It promotes better governance by encouraging coalitions between ministries, agencies, businesses, and local communities to achieve synergies and facilitates negotiations for compromise among competing priorities. Consequently, identifying key synergies and trade-offs between the targets can help the efficient implementation of SDGs by improving the opportunities to focus policy attention and actions on the most relevant sustainability issues. However, the challenge is to provide empirical evidence based on quantitative and qualitative research on the context-specific analysis of SDG interactions.

SDG interaction research accommodates an increasing diversity of approaches to analysing and identifying the interlinkages. They range from literature reviews to modelling, requiring different data types and expertise (Allen et al., 2021). Analysing the growing field of SDG interaction studies, Bennich and colleagues mapped the diverse research landscape on SDG interactions (Bennich et al., 2020). They provided a guide to frame studies' research design. Accordingly, SDG interaction studies can be mapped based on four themes: (1) policy challenges addressed, (2) SDG interaction conceptualization, (3) data source, and (4) methods of analysis.

This chapter provides an overview of quantitative studies that holistically conceptualize SDG interactions at goal, target, and/or indicator levels. We mainly focus on studies using statistical analysis, network analysis, and quantitative modelling based on official SDG databases. The spatial focus of these studies varies from local to global scales, and the temporal focus from immediate impacts to long-term projections. Due to data limitations and the multidimensionality of SDGs, quantitative analyses need to be based on data from multiple sources. Therefore, this chapter also gives an overview of the diverse data landscape. We provide insights into selected studies on SDG interactions and the data used, methods applied, and findings obtained, which have steered further research. However, our overview does not aim for complete coverage of quantitative methods and studies. Instead, we intend to guide the further development of science-based quantifications for understanding SDG interactions to provide a solid foundation for policy implementation.

5.2   DATA ON SUSTAINABLE DEVELOPMENT GOALS

Access to timely, high-quality data is fundamental to tracking progress toward achieving the 2030 Agenda and, thus, scientific evidence for transformative changes, developing implementation strategies, and managing resource allocations. However, leveraging this data requires a solid SDG framework and set of indicators to monitor local, national, regional, and global progress.

5.2.1   Global SDG Databases

Global SDG databases provide access to the world and regional aggregates as well as country-level data. The United Nations (UN), the World Bank Group (WB), and the Bertelsmann Stiftung & Sustainable Development Solutions Network (BE-SDSN) currently provide global SDG frameworks and corresponding databases widely used by scientists, policy makers, and practitioners.

Together with national statistical offices, the Inter-agency and Expert Group on SDG Indicators (IAEG-SDGs) develops methodologies and compiles data for SDG indicators. National statistical offices provide data to the UN Statistics to generate the *Global SDG Indicators database* (United Nations Statistics Division, 2022). The frequently updated database covers various countries and areas worldwide and provides a comprehensive disaggregation of indicators (Table 5.1). Disaggregated data, considering demographic factors (for example, gender, age, or rural-urban) as well as non-demographic factors (for example, cities, sectors, or products), improves the understanding

Table 5.1   SDG data availability

Parameter/databases	UN	WB	BE-SDSN
Countries and areas	259	217	206
Goals	17	17	17
Targets	156	77	—
Disaggregation level	35	9	—
Disaggregated indicators	3303	388	99*

Note: The 17 goals and 169 targets are according to the UN global indicator framework; however, BE-SDSN indicators are not assigned to SDG targets. The disaggregation level refers to an indicator being disaggregated by demographic (for example, age, gender) and non-demographic factors (for example, type of industry). However, BE-SDSN indicators are not disaggregated

Source: Sustainable Development Goals (SDGs) data availability provided by the United Nations (UN) (United Nations Statistics Division, 2022), the World Bank Group (WB) (World Bank Group, 2022), and the Bertelsmann Stiftung & Sustainable Development Solutions Network (BE-SDSN) (Sachs et al., 2020) in June 2022 for a comparable period of 2000 to 2022

of marginalized groups within a population and enables more specific insights into aspects of our society. For example, SDG indicator 6.2.1, "Proportion of population using (a) safely managed sanitation services and (b) a hand-washing facility with soap and water", has three different sub-indicators. They are: (1) the proportion of the population with basic hand-washing facilities; (2) the proportion of the population using safely managed sanitation services; and (3) the proportion of the population practising open defecation (per cent). Each of these 6.2.1 sub-indicators is further disaggregated into either rural or urban living populations.

As one observer and a custodian agent in the IAEG-SDGs, the WB is directly responsible for several SDG indicators. It provides technical input and data for the *Global SDG Indicators database*. Additionally, the WB extracts relevant indicators from their premier data compilation – the World Development Indicators (WDI) – reorganizing them according to the goals and targets of the 2030 Agenda and creating their own global SDG database (Table 5.1) (World Bank Group, 2022).

Parallel to the work of the IAEG-SDGs, the BE-SDSN outlined how a comprehensive indicator framework and associated monitoring systems might be established to support the 2030 Agenda. The data itself comes from a mix of official and nonofficial data sources. BE-SDSN states that including nonofficial statistics, like model-based estimates, helps to fill data gaps and reduce time lags in official statistics (Sachs et al., 2020). This open-access SDG data, however, is only mapped to the 2030 Agenda at the goal level and is not yet disaggregated (Table 5.1).

Only two global SDG data providers consider the proposed official SDG indicator framework, at least at the target level. Therefore, there are significant contradictions in indicator consideration, data availability, and consistency between them (Table 5.1). Warchold and colleagues filled this gap by building a unified SDG database and highlighted that indicator selection can lead to substantially different evaluations of SDG interactions (Warchold et al., 2022). Thus, unifying SDG data via enhanced collaboration among various stakeholders and data sources is needed to offer a reliable and accurate representation of SDGs, targets, indicators, and their interactions. By compiling the three presented global SDG databases, UN, WB, and BE-SDSN, into one unified SDG database, Warchold and colleagues demonstrated this representation value (Warchold et al., 2022). Based on the lowest common denominator of the years 2000 to 2019 as a comparison period, they assigned all provided indicators to match the 17 SDGs and 169 targets of the officially adopted global SDG indicator framework. The assignment maximized the number of indicators per target, which also covered more aspects of their multidimensionality. For identical indicators or indicators with similar descriptions/units, the ones with the highest data availability over time and space were included. These steps result in a unique indicator list from multiple sources that form the unified SDG database, allowing for more consistent data over time, space, and targets and greater disaggregation. However, several SDG targets remain uncovered or insufficiently covered by data, especially concerning the environmental SDGs. Most disaggregations refer to non-demographic aspects, and marginalized groups of society are hardly represented. Therefore, there is a need to continuously improve the 2030 Agenda data but also to understand the limitations of the SDG data.

5.2.2   National SDG Databases

Despite significant efforts by international organizations to acquire SDG data, with the support of national statistical offices, comparable data and indicators for SDGs are still creating some tension between global and national perspectives. Although the goals of the 2030 Agenda are universal, not all targets and indicators apply to all countries. For example, SDG target 3.3 aims to prevent diseases such as AIDS, tuberculosis, malaria, neglected tropical diseases, hepatitis, and so on, which are not all relevant to every country. Therefore, national governments aim to identify data gaps for measuring SDG indicators that are relevant to and prioritized by their country. Thus, a definition of potential data providers within and outside the national statistical system (civil society organizations, foundations, universities, research institutes, and the private sector) is needed. It requires an assessment of when national and international data sources are appropriate. For example, considering SDG targets 16.5 and 16.6, about bribery, corruption and accountable institutions, and the sensitivity of those matters, external or unofficial data might make sense as official data may not exist or be trusted to provide an independent, impartial picture of such sensitive issues (MacFeely, 2018).

Consequently, various governments already provide national SDG data besides the official SDG indicator framework. Voluntary National Reviews (VNRs) also report national efforts and SDG progress. For strategic alignment of the country's plans and policies with the 2030 Agenda, the national alignment process encompasses the identification of SDGs, targets, and indicators that reflect its reality, needs, and interlinkages. For example, in light of the German Sustainable Development Strategy (DNS) and to monitor progress, Germany's statistical authority launched a national open online reporting platform.[1] It presents time series and related metadata in an edited, interactive, and downloadable way. The SDGs have also been well-integrated into Nepal's national development frameworks. Besides VNRs and roadmap reports, Nepal provides an SDG analysing platform[2] with SDG indicator projections until 2030 and accessible SDG data.

5.2.3   Sub-National and Local SDG Databases

SDG progress and interactions may vary within a country. SDG data at a sub-national scale is required to capture these variations, which may not be visible in the country-scale data. Thus, there are efforts to create sub-national SDG databases. For example, Zhang and colleagues reconstructed SDG indicator data for the Chinese provinces based on the official SDGs indicator framework and the relevant literature (Zhang et al., 2022b). They mapped 88 indicators to 71 SDG targets and 16 SDGs and compiled their data from different statistical departments since 1990. Due to a lack of coastal regions in more than half of China's provinces, they did not compile indicators for SDG 14 (Life below Water) related to marine ecosystems. Many landlocked countries, for example, Nepal, also do not include indicators for SDG 14 in their national SDG database.

Similarly, accelerating local SDG implementation depends on timely, reliable data on the hurdles and opportunities faced by governments and other stakeholders operating at the local level. More realistically, SDG data must be supplemented with local qualitative data to provide a complete picture of the progress needed. Local opinions and experiences must be considered rather than relying solely on remote, contextless databases to truly leave no one behind. For example, tracking SDG progress on a city level allows decentralized, local responses. This tailoring of data generation focuses on the city's needs and the communities within these cities. For example, BE-SDSN offers various municipal SDG indices, for example, Bolivian[3] and European.[4]

Already those few examples show the diversity of SDG indicators and data development and the adaption of the *global indicator framework* at various levels. Liverpool is the latest amongst a fleet of global cities and the second in the UK (after Bristol) to unveil its local Sustainable Development Goal (SDG) Platform.[5]

5.3   QUANTITATIVE APPROACHES AND THEIR APPLICATIONS

Researchers have investigated SDG interactions, including their networks, using a broad range of qualitative and quantitative approaches. Qualitative approaches mainly consist of literature reviews, expert elicitation, or stakeholder perspectives (Weitz et al., 2018; Pham-Truffert et al., 2020; Hernández-Orozco et al., 2021). Quantitative approaches analyze available data on SDG indicators using different statistical methods (Pradhan et al., 2017; Kroll et al., 2019; Lusseau & Mancini, 2019; Xu et al., 2020; Warchold et al., 2021). A few studies also mixed qualitative and quantitative approaches to investigate SDG interactions, for example, quantitatively analysing information obtained from qualitative methods (Zhou and Moinuddin, 2017; Mainali et al., 2018; Smith et al., 2021). This section mainly focuses on data-driven statistical analyses of SDG interactions, their application and complementary methodologies.

5.3.1   Statistical Analysis

Since the SDGs are carefully underpinned by data, a subsequent step in deciphering their interactions is analysing the data statistically. Correlation analysis is one of the statistical methods widely used to investigate SDG interactions, and it enables the identification of no, weak, or strong SDG interactions. Such a statistical classification of SDG interactions is a starting point for reducing the complexity of SDG systems. Here, we briefly introduce the different methods of correlation analysis and their applications and highlight a few landmark studies on SDG interactions based on correlation analysis.

5.3.1.1   Correlation analysis methods
The appropriate use of correlation coefficients depends on several aspects, which is why their uncareful application can lead to misinformation. Certain correlation measurements are often able to reveal specific types of relationships but are blind to others (Anscombe, 1973). Thus, the scientific community has diverse views on the question of what correlation coefficient should be used. Every type of correlation coefficient contains unique descriptions through its usage. Therefore, it also requires understanding the data and the problem to be solved. Characteristics include the strength and direction of the

association, the ratio of change (linear vs non-linear), the number of variables (bivariate vs multivariate), the scale type of variables (nominal, continuous, interval, ordinal, binary, and so on), the amount of data per variable/sample size, and/or the noisiness level of data.

In bivariate analysis, the most commonly applied correlation is that by Francis Galton and Karl Pearson. They designed the well-known Pearson correlation coefficient r to measure linear associations between variables (Galton, 1889a, 1889b; Pearson, 1920). The correlation coefficient r is easy to calculate and interpret for positive or negative correlations. The coefficient signs indicate the direction of the relationship. A "+ sign" means a positive relationship, and a "– sign" shows a negative relationship. However, it measures only linear dependence. Spearman's rank correlation coefficient (Spearman's *rho*) owes its name to Charles Spearman. It is often represented by the Greek letter ρ (*rho*) or as r_s in distinction to Pearson's correlation coefficient. In statistics, the Spearman correlation is a nonparametric measure that captures the strength of monotonic relations (Spearman, 1904).

Recently, newer correlation methods have come to the forefront in the measurements of monotone non-linear and non-monotone dependence due to the increasing realization that those are often as necessary and likely more common than linear ones (Wang et al., 2017; Deebani & Kachouie, 2018). The maximal information coefficient (MIC) has been described as a twenty-first-century correlation with roots in information theory (Speed, 2011). The MIC proposed belongs to the nonparametric methods (Reshef et al., 2011). The MIC score indicates the strength of the linear or non-linear association in a two-variable dataset. MIC is described as satisfying two heuristic properties: generality and equitability. Generality implies that with sufficient sample size, the statistic should observe functional and non-functional relationships without being limited to certain types. Equitability intends that similar scores will be seen in relationships with similar noise levels regardless of the kind of relationship.

5.3.1.2   Application of correlation analyses

The correlation analyses can be applied to understand relationships between indicators at a single point in time, over a period, or by combining both. Cross-sectional studies provide information about specific demographics at a given time, enabling the detection of similarities and differences among selective groups. The temporal bias is a particular problem inherent to cross-sectional studies limiting the ability to ascertain whether the exposure precedes the observed outcomes. Since no dimensions of time exist, no indication of the sequence of the event can be given. When the application of cross-sectional analysis is based on historical data, it provides information on the existing relations which could be used for predictions. However, suppose these relations, for example, trade-offs, need to be transformed to achieve SDGs. In this case, the method does not provide forward-looking information, an ex-ante evaluation of achieving the 2030 Agenda, or predictions of the effectiveness of future policy measures.

A longitudinal or temporal study is the opposite of a cross-sectional study in that it repeatedly observes the same participants over a period of time. It offers insights into processes and changes that might occur over time. It can better establish the events' sequence and allow insights into potential cause-and-effect relationships.

Both cross-sectional and longitudinal studies may prove helpful, so a combination of the two is incorporated into panel data analysis. Panel data analyses are repeated measures of one or more variables on one or more persons. Panel data contains more information, more variability, less collinearity, and more efficiency than pure time series data or cross-sectional data. Panel data often involves observing many variables simultaneously to maximize the size of the analysis. For example, panel data may comprise annual income information and individuals over nine years of age. However, the distortion due to measurement errors is also high, leading to data management errors and biased regression results.

5.3.1.3 Quantitative SDG interactions

Pradhan and colleagues conducted the first holistic, systematic quantification of synergies and trade-offs within and across SDGs (Pradhan et al., 2017). They applied a data-driven longitudinal correlation analysis, accounting for all countries worldwide. Based on UN SDG data, SDG interactions are categorized as synergies and trade-offs based on (anti-)correlations between pairs of SDG indicators, considering country and country-disaggregated data. The study highlights the existence of typically more synergies than trade-offs within and among the SDGs in most countries. The observed synergies show broad compatibility of SDGs where progress in one goal can leverage the fulfilment of the other goals. They highlighted that SDG 1 (No Poverty) and SDG 3 (Good Health and Well-Being) could positively influence most other SDGs. However, SDG 12 (Responsible Consumption and Production) has trade-offs with most other goals, making it a bottleneck in achieving the 2030 Agenda. It is mainly because improvements in human well-being and economic prosperity are currently coupled with increased environmental and material footprints. These trade-offs must be identified, governed, and tackled to successfully implement the 2030 Agenda. Since its publication in 2017, this approach has been applied in many other SDG interaction studies.

Kroll and colleagues built on the correlation approach by projecting SDG interactions until 2030, applying a cross-sectional analysis based on BE-SDSN data (Kroll et al., 2019). They studied the development of SDG synergies and trade-offs between 2010 and 2018 and also evaluated interactions in the projected SDG trends until 2030. They reported positive changes with notable synergies for SDGs related to poverty alleviation and strengthening the economy, innovation, and modern infrastructure as a basis for achieving other SDGs. However, tackling challenges in making our cities and communities more sustainable and implementing climate actions are crucial because of their current trade-offs with many goals. Their results highlight that strategies for achieving SDGs deemed feasible in developed nations may not be optimal in developing or least developed nations. Many countries could leverage poverty alleviation and economic growth synergies to achieve the 2030 Agenda. However, while doing so, special attention is also required to tackle the trade-offs of conventional economic development strategies.

Likewise, adapting the pair-wise correlation method and classification of SDG interactions, Warchold and colleagues conducted a cross-sectional correlational analysis for 2016 (Warchold et al., 2021). The cross-sectional study enabled them to understand SDG interactions under the entire development spectrum using UN data. The authors applied several correlation methods to identify synergies or trade-offs considering population, location, income, and regional groups. Their innovative approach characterizes synergies or trade-offs according to their monotony and linearity at different scales. Resulting in highly context-specific SDG interactions, the analysis also revealed the existence of non-linear SDG interactions. Identifying these non-linear interactions is crucial because development is generally not linear, which may also hold for SDGs. Their findings highlight that there are more synergies than trade-offs among SDGs, and these relations are more linear than non-linear. There are variations in SDG interactions according to a country's income and region, along with the gender, age, and location of its population. Thus, fulfilling the 2030 Agenda's pledge to "leave no one behind" further plays a crucial role in leveraging the achievements of SDGs, as gender, age, and location disparities are highly linked to poverty, health, and education (Figure 5.1). These findings shed light on how SDG implementation could be prioritized across different groups and whether rapid progress towards SDGs could follow non-linear paths.

Other statistical approaches use a multiple-factor analysis to quantify the spatial differences in the SDG interactions and their temporal variation. Zhang and colleagues applied a multiple-factor analysis to untangle SDG interactions in China at a sub-national scale (Zhang et al., 2022b). They highlighted that China needs to enhance SDG 12 (Responsible Production and Consumption) and SDG 7 (Affordable and Clean Energy) for a balanced development across its provinces (Zhang et al., 2022b). Lusseau and Mancini used the WB data to estimate the association between each indicator pair using linear mixed-effect models (Lusseau and Mancini, 2019). Another study assessed the

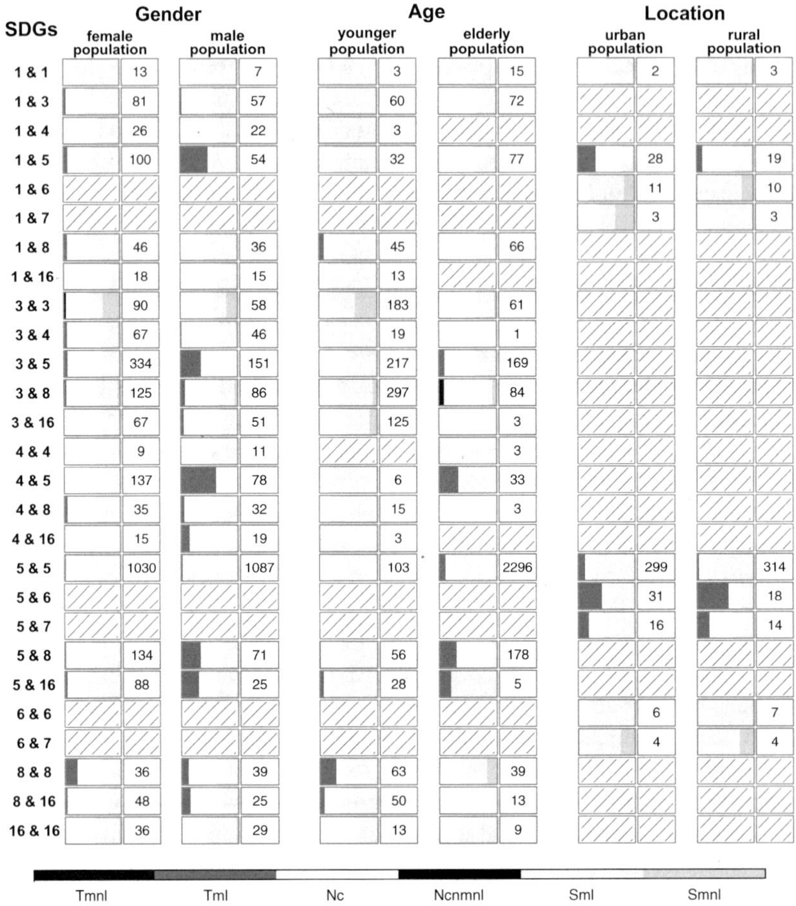

SDGs	Gender — female population	Gender — male population	Age — younger population	Age — elderly population	Location — urban population	Location — rural population
1 & 1	13	7	3	15	2	3
1 & 3	81	57	60	72	(dashed)	(dashed)
1 & 4	26	22	3	(dashed)	(dashed)	(dashed)
1 & 5	100	54	32	77	28	19
1 & 6	(dashed)	(dashed)	(dashed)	(dashed)	11	10
1 & 7	(dashed)	(dashed)	(dashed)	(dashed)	3	3
1 & 8	46	36	45	66	(dashed)	(dashed)
1 & 16	18	15	13	(dashed)	(dashed)	(dashed)
3 & 3	90	58	183	61	(dashed)	(dashed)
3 & 4	67	46	19	1	(dashed)	(dashed)
3 & 5	334	151	217	169	(dashed)	(dashed)
3 & 8	125	86	297	84	(dashed)	(dashed)
3 & 16	67	51	125	3	(dashed)	(dashed)
4 & 4	9	11	(dashed)	3	(dashed)	(dashed)
4 & 5	137	78	6	33	(dashed)	(dashed)
4 & 8	35	32	15	3	(dashed)	(dashed)
4 & 16	15	19	3	(dashed)	(dashed)	(dashed)
5 & 5	1030	1087	103	2296	299	314
5 & 6	(dashed)	(dashed)	(dashed)	(dashed)	31	18
5 & 7	(dashed)	(dashed)	(dashed)	(dashed)	16	14
5 & 8	134	71	56	178	(dashed)	(dashed)
5 & 16	88	25	28	5	(dashed)	(dashed)
6 & 6	(dashed)	(dashed)	(dashed)	(dashed)	6	7
6 & 7	(dashed)	(dashed)	(dashed)	(dashed)	4	4
8 & 8	36	39	63	39	(dashed)	(dashed)
8 & 16	48	25	50	13	(dashed)	(dashed)
16 & 16	36	29	13	9	(dashed)	(dashed)

Legend: Tmnl — Tml — Nc — Ncnmnl — Sml — Smnl

Note: Detected interactions within and across gender-, age-, and geographical-disaggregated sustainable development goals (SDGs) in 2016. The bar represents the shares of monotone non-linear synergies (Smnl), monotone linear synergies (Sml), not-classifieds (Nc), non-monotone non-linear not-classifieds (Ncnmnl), monotone linear trade-offs (Tml), and monotone non-linear trade-offs (Tmnl). The dashed bar depicts insufficient data for the analysis. The numbers in the boxes represent the number of data pairs used for the analysis, and the numbers on the left-hand side of the figures represent the SDG pairs

Source: Reprinted from Warchold et al., 2021

Figure 5.1　*Detected interactions within and across gender-, age- and geographical-disaggregated sustainable development goals (SDGs) in 2016*

two-way interactions among the Water-Energy-Food nexus using the Panel Vector Autoregressive model for provinces in China (Zhang et al., 2022a). Their results highlight that adequate actions can effectively transform SDG trade-offs into synergies. Another study identifies synergetic SDGs using the Boosted Regression Trees model, a machine learning and data mining technique (Asadikia et al., 2021).

5.3.2 Applications of Statistical Results

Statistical analysis is one of the first steps in examining SDG interactions. Its results can be used in further applications such as network analysis, quantitative modelling, or scenario analysis. The 17 SDGs were not conceptualized as siloed goals. The 2030 Agenda is already a framework in which SDG linkages have been established through targets and indicators referring to multiple sustainability dimensions. For example, biodiversity, gender equality, or disaster reduction are topics reoccurring as indicators in several SDGs. In this context, network analyses enable us to untangle the complex SDG interactions by better visualizing how multiple SDG dimensions interact. For example, sustainable and healthy diets provide climate change adaptation and mitigation synergies with many co-benefits (Rosenzweig et al., 2020). Adequate nutrition helps children to perform better in school. Therefore, health and nutrition policies also need to consider their implications for education. Better education creates awareness of healthy diets (Ospina-Forero et al., 2022). Thus, causality in SDG interactions needs to be considered to understand SDG networks better.

Most importantly, sustainable development is not unidimensional; instead, it is a coevolutionary process across multiple dimensions. Unravelling those development clusters could also be a potential investment focus because investing in one could bring various benefits. However, just as importantly, it could also tackle trade-offs. Due to the nature of SDGs, statistical applications such as networks and models require an integrated approach to benefit SDG planning, implementation, and governance.

5.3.2.1 Network analysis
The essential components of statistical networks are nodes and edges. Nodes represent the units in the network, for example, SDG indicators, targets, or goals, and the edges represent the interactions between the nodes, for example, based on correlation analysis or text analysis. A positive correlation means that improvements in one node, such as increased action or investment in an SDG, are likely to benefit neighbouring nodes in the network and vice versa. A negative correlation implies a negative impact on adjacent nodes in the network. For example, Putra and colleagues highlighted the networks of

water, energy, and food security nexus, building on the statistical analysis (Putra et al., 2020).

In most cases, correlation-based network analyses are bivariate and undirected or one-directional. Other network analysis techniques are required to support relevant knowledge. Those networks can include weighted edges and nodes according to their role in the system, provide the directionality of the interaction, and consider feedback loops. Detecting network clusters is a complex network's most crucial topological property. However, an SDG network that meets all of the desirable properties identified by Ospina-Forero and colleagues, such as scalability, replicability, specificity, directionality, and validity, has yet to be explored (Ospina-Forero et al., 2022). The network accuracy depends on the estimation of the data used in the network. Therefore, data remains another challenge as networks identify the most positively and negatively connected SDG goals and targets which might be data-biased.

Warchold and colleagues showed how the structure of the SDG networks changes at goal and target levels with SDG data selection (Warchold et al., 2022). Generally, there are more positive than negative connections within the networks. Nevertheless, these networks also represent several negative connections at the goal and target levels. The different levels of aggregation can tell different stories – SDG goal versus target level (Figure 5.2). Therefore, it is necessary to vary the levels of aggregation to confirm tendencies and understand at which point the results diverge or reverse. Lastly, the research shows the high interconnectedness of targets. Targets with significant links to other targets tend to be relatively consistent regarding the degree of centrality within the network. The network in Figure 5.2 shows that each target has dozens of positive and negative connections. Consequently, it can be argued that there is not one central element in the SDG system but many connections that cause feedback loops. These need to be uncovered utilizing directionality embedded in SDG system models.

5.3.2.2 SDG systems model
Anderson and colleagues built a more holistic SDG systems model considering the influence of all SDGs and their targets based on a statistical analysis of SDG interactions (Anderson et al., 2022). Most SDG interaction studies focus on first-order effects, that is, direct interactions between two SDGs or targets. In contrast, Anderson and colleagues also accounted for second-order effects or beyond (indirect interactions that include more than two SDGs or targets) to build an SDG systems model. In other words, their model considered direct and indirect interactions among SDGs, including their directionality. They applied this model to identify levers and hurdles for achieving the 2030 Agenda at a target scale. They considered SDGs and targets with overall synergies and trade-offs based on direct and indirect interactions as

levers and hurdles, respectively. The model highlighted that many SDGs and targets act as levers rather than hurdles in achieving other goals and targets (Figure 5.3). In particular, efforts at achieving SDGs 5 (Gender Equality) and 17 (Partnerships for the Goals) may accelerate progress across many other SDGs. At the same time, conventional efforts to achieve SDGs 10 (Reduced Inequalities) and 16 (Peace, Justice, and Strong Institutions) need to be transformed. Anderson and colleagues identified these SDGs as potential hurdles.

5.3.3 Beyond Statistical Analysis

Besides statistical analysis, many other approaches are used to quantify SDG interactions. One such approach is scenario analysis based on integrated assessment models. In the case of scenario analysis, Sörgel and colleagues analyzed sustainable development pathways using the coupled energy–economy–land–climate modelling framework REMIND–MAgPIE (Soergel et al., 2021). They highlighted the extent to which interventions significantly increase SDG progress while facilitating the achievement of ambitious climate targets. Most integrated assessment models currently analyze energy, economy, climate, and land interactions but insignificantly cover social aspects. Recently, researchers also proposed the concept of "target space", comprising 36 indicators and associated thresholds for quantitative scenario analysis of sustainable development pathways (van Vuuren et al., 2022).

Although quantitative analysis provides an understanding of SDG interactions, mechanisms underlying these interactions are highly dependent on local context and other local characteristics, as highlighted by many studies (Kroll et al., 2019; Warchold et al., 2021). In such a case, the quantitative analysis at a global, regional, or national level would be the first step. It must be advanced to context-specific, holistic, evidence-based SDG interactions that can easily be translated into policy recommendations at various levels. Data availability could be another limitation in conducting a quantitative analysis. Therefore, further qualitative studies are required to understand the underlying mechanisms and to erase biases from data limitations.

Transformative actions to achieve SDGs and ensure sustainability must be based on the best available scientific evidence by applying a combination of different analytical methods to improve the overall quality of the formulated policy advice. These methods might include meta-analyses of the literature, expert elicitations, qualitative literature analysis, and/or stakeholder involvement. For example, systematic literature analysis can synthesize evidence on SDG interactions' mechanisms and the effects of (under)achieving SDGs, including new insights on the most pressing global challenges. However, there might be two limitations: statistical noise due to studies' context- and location-specific dependencies and limited literature on specific topics related to

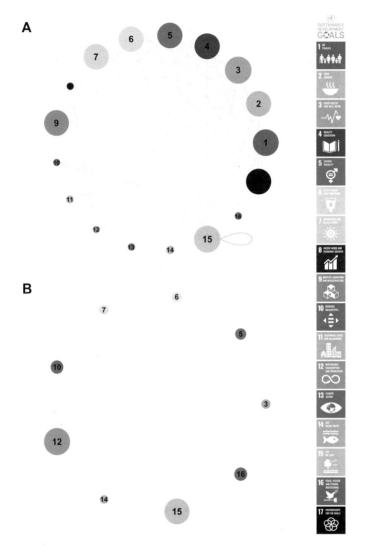

Note: Sustainable Development Goal (SDG) (left) and target (right) network for (A) synergies and (B) trade-offs based on the UN SDG database. Each node indicates an SDG target, coloured according to the respective SDG. The node size reflects the SDG target's eigenvector centrality, emphasizing the structural significance of nodes in the network. Edges indicate synergistic (solid line) or impeding (dashed line) interactions between targets. The edge's thickness and colour reflect the share (s) of synergies and trade-offs (light grey with 30% < s ≤ 60%, grey with 60% < s ≤ 90%, and dark grey with s > 90%), emphasizing structurally significant interactions in the network
Source: Reprinted from Warchold et al., 2022

*Figure 5.2   Sustainable Development Goal and target network for syner-
gies and trade-offs*

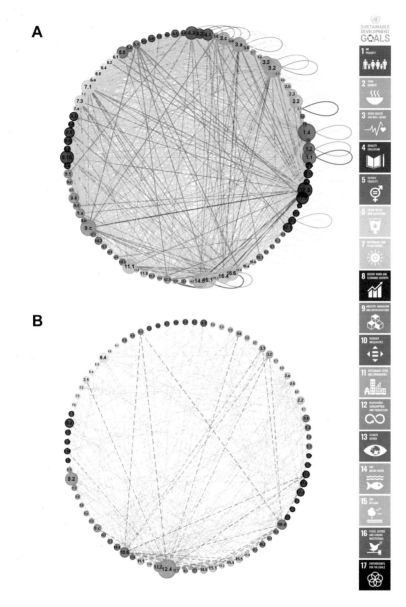

Figure 5.2   (Continued)

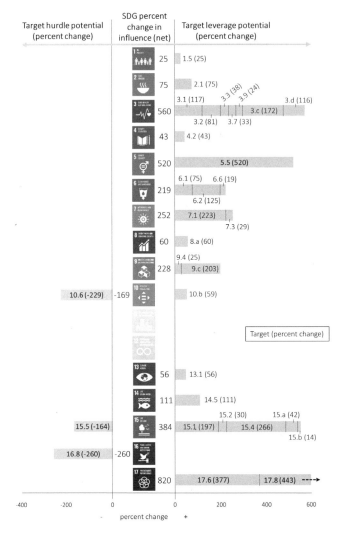

Figure 5.3   *Sustainable Development Goal and target influences in the causal SDG systems model*

SDGs and sustainability. Expert elicitations can address these limitations by filtering the noise and filling the gaps in the literature. Additionally, quantitative methods can be applied to investigate further generated qualitative data, leading to a mixed-method approach either way.

Various studies have conducted literature analysis-based studies to understand SDG interactions or interlinkages between SDGs and specific strategies. For example, Ladha and colleagues highlighted that optimum nitrogen fertilizer management positively impacts most SDGs (Ladha et al., 2020). Meeting the 2030 Agenda could also provide enabling conditions for optimum fertilizer management. In contrast, agricultural systems with low fertilizer application result in a vicious cycle of poverty, malnutrition, and a poor economy due to low crop productivity. Excess fertilizer application leads to environmental hazards, land degradation, and economic loss (Ladha et al., 2020). Similarly, sustainable food system transformation can convert the current negative linkages of food systems with SDGs into positive ones. Mainly, the current food systems fail to provide healthy diets for all and exhibit substantial socioeconomic and ecological impacts, creating obstacles to achieving numerous SDGs (Pradhan et al., 2021).

Additionally, we highlight an example of an expert elicitation-based study on the impacts of the COVID-19 pandemic on SDGs. It has affected humankind worldwide, slowing down and even reversing the progress in achieving SDGs. Pradhan and colleagues applied a mixed-method approach to understanding the impacts of the COVID-19 pandemic on SDGs in Nepal (Pradhan et al., 2021). They followed a five-step knowledge co-creation process with experts from various professional backgrounds. These steps included an online survey, virtual workshop, expert opinion assessment, review and validation, and revision and synthesis. Their study highlighted that the pandemic negatively impacts most SDGs' progress. However, it has also opened a short-lived window of opportunity for sustainable transformation. Many adverse effects may subside in the medium and long term.

5.4   DISCUSSION

This chapter briefly summarized the five-year evolution from simple correlation methods for analysing SDG interactions to developing an SDG systems model to unentangle the SDG systems' complexity. Since these statistical approaches are based on SDG data, we have indicated official global, national, regional, and local data and identified existing data discrepancies. If the 2030 Agenda and SDGs are viewed as a plan for a near-perfect world in which the needs of societies and the planet are carefully balanced, rapid transformative changes are required. Currently, however, countries are not on track but instead are failing to achieve the 2030 Agenda. So far, SDGs have had discursive impacts, only affecting understanding and communication on sustainable development (Biermann et al., 2022).

Thus, there is an urgent need to rescue the 2030 Agenda within a limited time by prioritizing SDGs at the target level. Such prioritization requires identifying SDG targets where transformative actions can maximize synergies and resolve trade-offs, leading to progress across SDG systems. For this, science should provide more evidence that is easily manageable for the government and practitioners within their limited resources and can easily be translated into decision-making. Thus, methodological advances require more transparent and reliable assessment of SDG interactions.

The strength of quantitative studies is that they provide descriptive data, offer objectiveness and replicability, and give a snapshot of reality, but we encounter difficulties in interpreting them. For example, while significance tests may tell us whether an interlinkage exists, it does not tell us about the importance of the interlinkage. In this respect, one suggestion has been to report measures of effect sizes, which refer to the magnitude of an interlinkage. The larger the effect size, the stronger the relationship between the two variables. In principle, statistical significance indicates whether the results are actual, while effect size indicates how important they are. In addition, increasing the sample size can enhance the statistical power of the results, as in the case of MIC, and the generalization of the results is more reliable.

Nonetheless, the correlation coefficient cannot provide information about the cause-and-effect relation, meaning which indicator represents the dependent variable (the cause) and which is the independent variable (the effect). However, various statistical methods are available to evaluate causal interlinkages, for example, transfer entropy and non-linear Granger causality (Edinburgh et al., 2021). These methods can be applied to assess causal SDG interactions, enabling the building of directional SDG networks and causal SDG systems models. However, these statistical analyses cannot provide information about the underlying mechanisms of interactions. Based on existing literature and stakeholder knowledge, a conceptual interpretation of SDG interactions, that is, qualitative analysis, is required. Thus, a way forward is to combine quantitative and qualitative methods to understand the mechanisms underlying SDG interactions. This understanding is crucial to derive adequate actions to resolve the current trade-offs among SDGs, resulting in win-win solutions.

Additionally, limitations of the current SDG interaction research need to be overcome. First, SDG data gaps still exist. The SDG data must consider all possible disaggregation levels to focus on leaving no one behind (Pradhan et al., 2022). Further, data must be generated from multiple sources. These sources could more strongly interact with one another by sharing data, knowledge, and capacities to improve activities along the data value chain. Members of these data communities can be stakeholders from official statistical agencies, ministries, banks, civil society organizations, academia, and the private sector (Cázarez-grageda & Zougbede, 2019). It is also vital to ensure this SDG data is open source and accessible to multi-stakeholder audiences rather than just academia or the public sector. Second, improvements in the analytical approaches are needed. Identifying suitable methods to detect causal SDG interactions beyond their statistical associations is still challenging (Pradhan et al., 2022). In addition, there is still only a handful of SDG systems models. Third, various areas of SDG interactions have not yet been adequately researched. For example, whether achieving the SDGs is synonymous with staying within planetary boundaries needs to be explored. Similarly, there is a need to identify the required extra efforts besides meeting SDGs to ensure sustainability beyond 2030. Ensuring sustainability requires building social prosperity and foundations within planetary boundaries, that is, a safe and just corridor for people and the planet (Rockström et al., 2021).

Concerning the four themes of SDG interaction studies, Bennich and colleagues highlighted that policy implications are addressed only to a limited extent (Bennich et al., 2020). Most studies presented in this chapter also devote little attention to policy challenges and innovation to facilitate actual transformative change. One way to enable a more policy-oriented analysis is by estimating SDG networks and then using them as inputs for an agent-based model of the policy making process (Ospina-Forero et al., 2022). Combining different analytical methods improves the overall quality of policy advice to inform and guide SDG implementation (Toth et al., 2022). This chapter, therefore, elaborates on an understanding of current methodological approaches to show the choice of the best multi-method application for approaching specific cases and their related policy challenges in SDG implementation. Future SDG interaction research should incorporate multiple conceptualizations by combining analytical approaches, considering policy implications, and understanding underlying mechanisms (Pradhan, 2023).

ACKNOWLEDGEMENTS

We acknowledge funding from the German Federal Ministry of Education and Research (BMBF) for the BIOCLIMAPATHS project (grant agreement No. 01LS1906A) under the JPI Climate AXIS ERA-NET and from the German Academic Exchange Service (DAAD) for the ForHimSDG project with financial support from the Federal Ministry for Economic Cooperation and Development of Germany (BMZ).

NOTES

1. https://sdg-indikatoren.de/en/
2. https://nepalindata.com/sdg/
3. https://sdsnbolivia.org/atlas/
4. https://euro-cities.sdgindex.org/
5. https://liverpool-sdg-data.github.io/

REFERENCES

Allen, C., Metternicht, G., & Wiedmann, T. (2021). Priorities for science to support national implementation of the sustainable development goals: A review of progress and gaps. *Sustainable Development*, 29(4), 635–652. https://doi.org/10.1002/sd.2164

Anderson, C. C. et al. (2022). A systems model of SDG target influence on the 2030 agenda for sustainable development. *Sustainability Science*, 17(4), 1459–1472. https://doi.org/10.1007/s11625-021-01040-8

Anscombe, F. J. (1973). Graphs in statistical analysis. *The American Statistician*, 27(1), 17. https://doi.org/10.2307/2682899

Asadikia, A., Rajabifard, A., & Kalantari, M. (2021). Systematic prioritisation of SDGs: Machine learning approach. *World Development*, 140, 105269. https://doi.org/10.1016/j.worlddev.2020.105269

Bennich, T., Weitz, N., & Carlsen, H. (2020). Deciphering the scientific literature on SDG interactions: A review and reading guide. *Science of the Total Environment*, 728, 138405. https://doi.org/10.1016/j.scitotenv.2020.138405

Biermann, F. et al. (2022). Scientific evidence on the political impact of the sustainable development goals. *Nature Sustainability*. https://doi.org/10.1038/s41893-022-00909-5

Cázarez-grageda, K., & Zougbede, K. (2019). *National SDG Review : Data challenges and Opportunities*. Bonn and Eschborn. http://files/95/Paris 21 Partners for review – National-SDG_Review2019_rz.pdf

Deebani, W., & Kachouie, N. N. (2018). *Ensemble Correlation Coefficient*. ISAIM. https://www.semanticscholar.org/paper/Ensemble-Correlation-Coefficient-Deebani-Kachouie/34c65e8d55f776e5bf88f82c2c105784c70dca0c

Edinburgh, T., Eglen, S. J., & Ercole, A. (2021). Causality indices for bivariate time series data: A comparative review of performance. *Chaos: An Interdisciplinary Journal of Nonlinear Science*, 31(8), p. 083111. https://doi.org/10.1063/5.0053519

Galton, F. (1889a). I. Co-relations and their measurement, chiefly from anthropometric data. *Proceedings of the Royal Society of London*, 45(273–279), 135–145. https://doi.org/10.1098/rspl.1888.0082

Galton, F. (1889b). *Natural Inheritance*. London: Macmillan & Co. https://galton.org/books/natural-inheritance/pdf/galton-nat-inh-1up-clean.pdf

Hernández-Orozco, E. et al. (2021). The application of soft systems thinking in SDG interaction studies: A comparison between SDG interactions at national and subnational levels in Colombia. *Environment, Development and Sustainability*. https://doi.org/10.1007/s10668-021-01808-z

Kroll, C., Warchold, A., & Pradhan, P. (2019). Sustainable Development Goals (SDGs): Are we successful in turning trade-offs into synergies? *Palgrave Communications*, 5(1), 140. https://doi.org/10.1057/s41599-019-0335-5

Ladha, J. K. et al. (2020). Achieving the sustainable development goals in agriculture : The crucial role of nitrogen in cereal-based systems. In D. Sparks (Ed., 1st edn), *Advances in Agronomy*. Elsevier Inc. https://doi.org/10.1016/bs.agron.2020.05.006

Lusseau, D., & Mancini, F. (2019). Income-based variation in sustainable development goal interaction networks. *Nature Sustainability*, 2(3), 242–247. https://doi.org/10.1038/s41893-019-0231-4

MacFeely, S. (2018). *The 2030 Agenda: An Unprecedented Statistical Challenge*. New York. http://library.fes.de/pdf-files/iez/14796.pdf

Mainali, B. et al. (2018). Evaluating synergies and trade-offs among Sustainable Development Goals (SDGs): Explorative analyses of development paths in South Asia and Sub-Saharan Africa. *Sustainability*, 10(3), 815. https://doi.org/10.3390/su10030815

Messerli, P. et al. (2019). *Global Sustainable Development Report 2019: The Future is Now – Science for Achieving Sustainable Development, United Nations*. New York.

Mirzabaev, A. et al. (2021). *Climate Change and Food Systems: Food Systems Summit Brief Prepared by Research Partners of the Scientific Group for the Food Systems Summit, May 2021*. https://doi.org/10.1146/annurev-environ-020411-130608

Ospina-Forero, L., Castañeda, G., & Guerrero, O. A. (2022). Estimating networks of sustainable development goals. *Information and Management*, 59(5). https://doi.org/10.1016/j.im.2020.103342

Pearson, K. (1920). Notes on the history of correlation. *Biometrika*, 13(1), 25–45. https://doi.org/10.1093/biomet/13.1.25

Pham-Truffert, M. et al. (2020). Interactions among sustainable development goals : Knowledge for identifying multipliers and virtuous cycles. *Sustainable Development*, 28(5), 1236–1250. https://doi.org/10.1002/sd.2073

Pradhan, P. et al. (2017). A Systematic Study of Sustainable Development Goal (SDG) interactions. *Earth's Future*, 5(11), 1169–1179. https://doi.org/10.1002/2017EF000632

Pradhan, P. (2019). Antagonists to meeting the 2030 agenda. *Nature Sustainability*, 2(3), 171–172. https://doi.org/10.1038/s41893-019-0248-8

Pradhan, P. (2023). A threefold approach to rescue the 2030 Agenda from failing. *National Science Review*, nwad015, https://doi.org/10.1093/nsr/nwad015

Pradhan, P. et al. (2021). The COVID-19 pandemic not only poses challenges, but also opens opportunities for sustainable transformation. *Earth's Future*, 9(7), e2021EF001996. https://doi.org/10.1029/2021EF001996

Pradhan, P., Seydewitz, T. et al. (2022). Climate extremes are becoming more frequent, co-occurring, and persistent in Europe. *Anthropocene Science*, 1(2), 264–277. https://doi.org/10.1007/s44177-022-00022-4

Pradhan, P., van Vuuren, D. et al. (2022). Methods for analysing steering effects of global goals. In F. Biermann, T. Hickmann, & C.-A. Senit (Eds.), *The Political Impact of the Sustainable Development Goals* (pp. 172–203). Cambridge: Cambridge University Press. https://doi.org/10.1017/9781009082945.008

Pradhan, P., Sapkota, T. B., & Kropp, J. P. (2021). Why food systems transformation is crucial for achieving the SDGs. *Rural*, 21, 10–12.

Putra, M. P. I. F., Pradhan, P., & Kropp, J. P. (2020). A systematic analysis of water-energy-food security nexus: A South Asian case study. *Science of The Total Environment*, 728, 138451. https://doi.org/10.1016/j.scitotenv.2020.138451

Reshef, D. N. et al. (2011). Detecting novel associations in large data sets. *Science*, 334(6062), 1518–1524. https://doi.org/10.1126/science.1205438

Rockström, J. et al. (2021). Identifying a safe and just corridor for people and the planet. *Earth's Future*, 9, 1–7. https://doi.org/10.1029/2020EF001866

Rosenzweig, C. et al. (2020). Climate change responses benefit from a global food system approach. *Nature Food*, 1(February), 1–4. https://doi.org/10.1038/s43016 -020-0031-z

Sachs, J. et al. (2020). *The Sustainable Development Goals and COVID-19. Sustainable Development Report 2020*. Cambridge: Cambridge University Press.

Smith, T. B. et al. (2021). Natural language processing and network analysis provide novel insights on policy and scientific discourse around sustainable development goals. *Scientific Reports*, 11, 22427. https://doi.org/10.1038/s41598-021-01801-6

Soergel, B. et al. (2021). A sustainable development pathway for climate action within the UN 2030 Agenda. *Nature Climate Change*, 11(8), 656–664. https://doi.org/10 .1038/s41558-021-01098-3

Spearman, C. (1904). The proof and measurement of association between two things. *The American Journal of Psychology*, 15(1), 72. https://doi.org/10.2307/1412159

Speed, T. (2011). A correlation for the 21st century. *Science*, 334(6062), 1502–1503. https://doi.org/10.1126/science.1215894

Toth, W. et al. (2022). Deepening our understanding of which policy advice to expect from prioritizing SDG targets: introducing the analytic network process in a multi-method setting. *Sustainability Science*, 17(4), 1473–1488. https://doi.org/10.1007/ s11625-021-01009-7

UN. (2022). *The Sustainable Development Goals Report 2022, United Nations*.

United Nations Statistics Division. (2022). *SDG Indicators: United Nations Global SDG Database*. https://unstats.un.org/sdgs/indicators/database/ (Accessed: 30 June 2022)

van Vuuren, D. P. et al. (2022). Defining a sustainable development target space for 2030 and 2050. *One Earth*, 5(2), 142–156. https://doi.org/10.1016/j.oneear.2022.01 .003

Wang, Y. et al. (2017). Bagging nearest-neighbor prediction independence test: An efficient method for non-linear dependence of two continuous variables. *Scientific Reports*, 7(1), 12736. https://doi.org/10.1038/s41598-017-12783-9

Warchold, A. et al. (2022). Building a unified sustainable development goal database: Why does sustainable development goal data selection matter? *Sustainable Development*, 30(5), 1278–1293. https://doi.org/10.1002/sd.2316

Warchold, A., Pradhan, P., & Kropp, J. P. (2021). Variations in sustainable development goal interactions: Population, regional, and income disaggregation. *Sustainable Development*, 29(2), 285–299. https://doi.org/10.1002/sd.2145

Weitz, N. et al. (2018). Towards systemic and contextual priority setting for implementing the 2030 agenda. *Sustainability Science*, 13, 531–548. https://doi.org /10.1007/s11625-017-0470-0

World Bank Group. (2022). *DataBank: Sustainable Development Goals (SDGs)*. https://databank.worldbank.org/reports.aspx?source=sustainable-development -goals-(sdgs) (Accessed: 30 June 2022)

Xu, Z. et al. (2020). Assessing progress towards sustainable development over space and time. *Nature*, 577, 74–78. https://doi.org/10.1038/s41586-019-1846-3

Zhang, J. et al. (2022a). Mapping the complexity of the food-energy-water nexus from the lens of Sustainable Development Goals in China. *Resources, Conservation and Recycling*, 183(2016), 106357. https://doi.org/10.1016/j.resconrec.2022.106357

Zhang, J. et al. (2022b). Untangling the interactions among the sustainable development goals in China. *Science Bulletin*, 67(9), 977–984. https://doi.org/10.1016/j.scib.2022 .01.006

Zhou, X., & Moinuddin, M. (2017). *Sustainable Development Goals Interlinkages and Network Analysis: A practical tool for SDG integration and policy coherence, IGES Research Report.*

6. Network analysis of SDG interlinkages

Jonathan H. P. Dawes

6.1 INTRODUCTION

This chapter aims to introduce and explain a number of general methods and ideas from network science, illustrating their use on two specific interlinkage matrices for the Sustainable Development Goals (SDGs). Formally a network comprises (i) a set of nodes (or vertices) and (ii) a set of edges between them. For the SDGs, the set of nodes could be chosen to be either the 17 goals, or the 169 separate targets, or subsets of these, as is commonly done when discussing a 'nexus' such as water–energy–food (Weitz et al., 2014; Yillia, 2016; Fader et al., 2018; van Noordwijk et al., 2018; Putra et al., 2020). Edges describe interactions at the relevant level and carry varying kinds of information. Generally speaking, networks have (at least) three independent properties associated with each edge: (i) edges have direction: there is a direction of influence along each edge in the network; (ii) edges have weights: different interactions have different strengths; and (iii) edges have signs: edges can be negatively weighted (corresponding to trade-offs) or positively weighted (corresponding to co-benefits).

Depending on the data source and construction methodology, an SDG network may not exhibit all three features. Most obviously, networks based on correlations between data sources alone result in undirected networks since correlation does not in itself confer a direction of influence or causation. The fact that the construction and interpretation of a network may indeed rule out one of these properties is entirely natural; for example in disease transmission networks if the edges are associated with probabilities of transmission, these will all be non-negative quantities and so such edges do not have property (iii) above – they do not have signs.

From the text of the original resolution adopted by the UN General Assembly onwards, the SDGs have been framed as one 'integrated and indivisible' agenda; see paragraphs 18 and 55 in particular of the resolution text

(UN General Assembly, 2015). Yet the SDG agenda comprises 169 separate, and highly diverse, targets combined into 17 overarching goals. This tension between the unity of the whole and the diversity of the component parts has, from the launch of the SDGs onwards, made a description in terms of a network particularly appealing as a mode of thinking about Agenda 2030 (Le Blanc, 2015). A particular benefit is that it allows the application of quantitative methods of analysis of the SDGs, with the conceptual clarity that quantitative analysis offers.

With its focus on network science, this chapter naturally avoids discussing a number of important societal and political aspects of the SDGs. Two of these, for example, are (i) which sets of policy actors (government, business, third sector organisations, individual citizens) are enabled to carry out, or are responsible for, SDG implementation, and (ii) the relation between SDG interlinkages and policy coherence for sustainable development. The debate on the extent to which policy actions can be measured to have additional positive or negative additional influences (often referred to as 'co-benefits' and 'trade-offs', respectively, in the SDG literature) is clearly extremely important in understanding SDG interactions but is omitted here.

6.1.1   Networks

Network-type problems arise in many fields of social and natural science and engineering, for example bioinformatics, behavioural ecology, national infrastructure, and telecommunications (Newman, 2018). Methods appropriate to each of these have been particularly well-studied over the last two decades; of course in many cases, notably in social sciences, the roots of these methodologies lie much deeper (Bonacich, 1972; Wasserman & Faust, 1994). More recent developments in network science, which we do not comment on further here but which clearly offer exciting directions for future research, include the analysis of multiplex (or multilayer) networks (Bianconi, 2018), in which the same collection of nodes may be connected by edges of different kinds (for example one layer corresponding to social interactions and a second layer corresponding to travel times between locations), and the analysis of networks in which interactions involve not just pairs of nodes, but 'higher-order' effects such as being reinforced in interactions between triples of nodes (Arrigo et al., 2020).

The richness and variety of network science tools mean that there are challenges in selecting appropriate tools, with transparent methodologies, so that the results can be interpreted in light of the specific field. With this caveat, it is notable that systems thinking in general provides a flexible bridge between quantitative and qualitative insights into complex phenomena. Moreover, complex systems ideas of emergence and of phenomena that reach across scales indicate that it is necessary to apply this kind of thinking in order to show how system-level outcomes result from smaller-scale interactions.

Figure 6.1 shows an illustrative example of a network defined by a collection of nodes (here, a subset of nine SDGs), together with directed edges (arrows) indicating directions of influence between pairs of nodes. Arrowheads indicate positive influences, while round dots indicate negative influences. Each edge has a positive or negative weight associated with it; different edges have different weights. For convenience we assume that (by rescaling) the weights will all lie between +1 and −1. Several points of interest can be clearly seen from Figure 6.1, such as the mutually reinforcing interlinkages between SDGs 6, 7, and 13 on the left-hand side of the figure, the negative influences of SDGs 2 and 11 on SDG 14, and more subtly, the fact that while SDGs 5 and 16 reinforce each other, neither receives any additional positive influence from the remainder of the network. But the overall net effect of the interlinkages is harder to quantify from Figure 6.1; our need to understand the overall system-level response motivates the tools that we discuss in this chapter.

As a first step we encode the weighted directed influences into an *adjacency matrix A* which is simply a square array of the edge weights, with the array entry A_{ij} being the weight of the edge from node j to node i. Although this might seem to be slightly 'backwards' as a definition, it helps later on to ease the mathematical notation. The entry A_{ij} corresponds to the ith

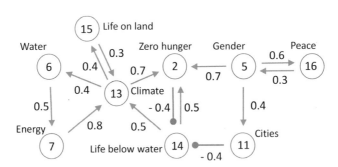

Notes: Interlinkages are indicated by the arrows. An arrow $j \rightarrow i$ indicates the positive influence of (progress on) SDG j on SDG i. A line with a round end indicates a negative influence of SDG j on SDG i
Source: Adapted under CC-BY-4.0 from figure 2 in Dawes (2020)

Figure 6.1   An example network for a subset of nine of the SDGs

row and the jth column. Hence the adjacency matrix A corresponding to Figure 6.1 is

$$
\begin{array}{c}
2 \\ 5 \\ 6 \\ 7 \\ 11 \\ 13 \\ 14 \\ 15 \\ 16
\end{array}
\left(
\begin{array}{ccccccccc}
0 & 0.7 & 0 & 0 & 0 & 0.7 & 0.5 & 0 & 0 \\
0 & 0 & 0 & 0 & 0 & 0 & 0 & 0 & 0.3 \\
0 & 0 & 0 & 0 & 0 & 0.4 & 0 & 0 & 0 \\
0 & 0 & 0.5 & 0 & 0 & 0 & 0 & 0 & 0 \\
0 & 0.4 & 0 & 0 & 0 & 0 & 0 & 0 & 0 \\
0 & 0 & 0 & 0.8 & 0 & 0 & 0.5 & 0.3 & 0 \\
-0.4 & 0 & 0 & 0 & -0.4 & 0 & 0 & 0 & 0 \\
0 & 0 & 0 & 0 & 0 & 0.4 & 0 & 0 & 0 \\
0 & 0.6 & 0 & 0 & 0 & 0 & 0 & 0 & 0
\end{array}
\right)
\qquad (6.1)
$$
$$
\begin{array}{ccccccccc}
2 & 5 & 6 & 7 & 11 & 13 & 14 & 15 & 16
\end{array}
$$

where we have included row and column labels to indicate precisely how the network nodes (that is, the subset of the SDGs) correspond to the rows and columns of the matrix. Note, for example, the two negatively weighted edges in the seventh row, corresponding to SDG 14, due to the negative influences on SDG 14 from SDGs 2 and 11. The adjacency matrix corresponds exactly to the 'node and edge' pictorial version of the network, and one can be reconstructed immediately from the other. For larger networks with more edges we will not write out the numerical values but present a grey-scale 'heatmap' of the adjacency matrix, as in Figure 6.2. This is an easier way to present a greater amount of information when the network diagrams become more complicated and the adjacency matrix has more non-zero entries. When we turn to consideration of adjacency matrices for 16 or all 17 SDGs, the adjacency matrix expands in size to become 16×16 or 17×17 respectively, but this is the only change in its interpretation.

6.1.2   Network Data and Quantitative Approaches

Although not the main focus of this chapter, a note on the possible underlying sources of information for the construction of networks is appropriate here. SDG interlinkage networks are typically constructed from one of (broadly speaking) five possible sources of data: expert analysis; linguistic approaches (for example, the identification of shared keywords across the literature); literature reviews and meta-analysis; statistical analyses, such as the analysis of correlations in time series for SDG indicators (see for example Pradhan et al., 2017); and the output of computational models, most obviously integrated

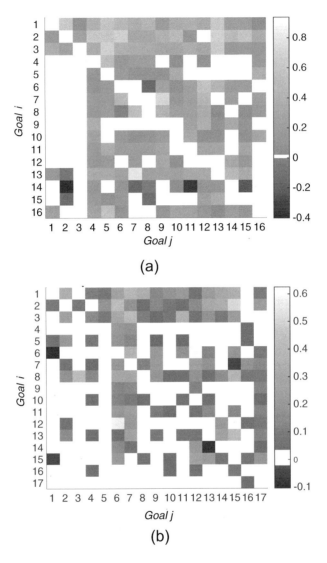

(a)

(b)

Notes: (a) The 16 × 16 ICSU matrix (SDG 17 was omitted from their analysis). (b) The 17 × 17 GSDR 2019 interlinkage matrix. Each cell corresponds to an interlinkage: the SDG labelling the column (*j*) influences the SDG labelling the row (*i*). Whitespace indicates that the interlinkage is close to zero; colour bars to the right give the scaled strength of interlinkages in each case
Source: Adapted under CC-BY-4.0 from figure 1 in Dawes (2022)

Figure 6.2   *Heatmaps showing the distribution of positive and negative interlinkages in the SDG interaction matrices used as examples here*

assessment models (van Soest et al. (2019) or bespoke models such as the iSDG framework (Pedercini et al., 2019). This five-fold classification and the need to integrate systemic features such as a gender perspective into this variety of analytical approaches are discussed further by Pollitzer (2022a, 2022b). A slightly more detailed but essentially similar typology of data sources is given by Bennich et al. (2020) who propose 7 types of data source and 9 groups of analytical approaches, based on a sample of 70 papers from the academic literature. It is also of interest to note that some SDG interlinkage studies combine aspects of multiple approaches, for example the interlinkage matrices constructed by IGES (Zhou & Moinuddin, 2017, 2019; Dawes et al., 2022) that combine expert analysis which determines which interlinkages exist *a priori*, with data-driven correlation analysis at a country-specific level which then determines the strength of those interlinkages. A similar combination of data and expert opinion was used by Anderson et al. (2022). Such interlinkage matrices can capture asymmetric interactions (via the expert opinion) while using correlation measures that are in themselves symmetric.

While data-driven approaches might appear to be the most preferable, given the concerns that will always exist around information gleaned through more sociological sources such as expert analysis, it needs to be borne in mind that data-driven methods have their own limitations and that these are often serious. The level of complexity that the suite of over 200 indicator time series bring, in their attempt to capture progress target-by-target, is compounded by at least three significant effects. First, the SDG indicator measure may only be a proxy for progress on a particular target, because the data required to monitor direct progress is not sufficiently widely available or sufficiently reliable. Second, the SDG target in question is often not framed sufficiently precisely that the relevant statistical indicator can be unambiguously defined and so may vary in its interpretation by different national statistical agencies. Third, the data required may simply not be available and so the indicator time series cannot be constructed for the time frame or national coverage required. This is a particularly important issue in respect of SDG 5 where gender-disaggregated statistics are in embarrassingly short supply worldwide.

In addition to these three effects, there is a more subtle issue, which perhaps is a specific instance of the more general observation that all data sources have their limitations: data-driven approaches tend to be historical and describe how progress arose in the past, but with shifts in policy or politics, these may well not be any guide to the future. In such a case, expert analysis for example may provide a more appropriate framework and describe one of a range of possible futures but help to decide priorities and actions that enable it. The interpretation of SDG interlinkage matrices naturally will depend on the data used in their construction.

Our focus here on quantitative, mathematical, methods demands that the connections between nodes must be numerically quantified. How one moves from qualitative to quantitative is often open to criticism and so must always be explicitly defined. Ideally the sensitivity of the results to changes in that part of the process should also be fully explored. One explicit relation between qualitative and quantitative views of SDG interlinkages that has gained popularity is the seven-point scale proposed by Nilsson et al. (2016) and presented in Table 6.1. As discussed above, behind this scale sits, implicitly or explicitly, a sense of the scope of likely, or perhaps merely possible, policy actions and the effects that a policy action aimed at one SDG might have on others, either for better (a 'co-benefit') or worse (a 'trade-off').

It is of interest to note that this scale, while numerical, may not actually be amenable to numerical manipulation: for example if there are two separate effects that would lead to a linkage being scored as either +2 or −1, a net score of 0.5 (the arithmetic mean) or perhaps +1 as a compromise might not be appropriate if the two underlying effects operated over different timescales or had different probabilities of arising.

6.1.3   Complete SDG Interlinkage Networks

Having used the relatively simple example network presented in Figure 6.1 as an initial example, we illustrate the concepts developed in this chapter with two complete goal-level interlinkage matrices for the SDGs. The first of these was generated in Dawes (2020) from an expert analysis (ICSU-ISSC, 2015) and is the network from which the example presented in Figure 6.1 was abstracted; in what follows we therefore use the complete version rather than this simplified

Table 6.1   The seven-point scale for scoring the influence of one specific SDG or target on another

Score	Name	Explanation
+3	Indivisible	Inextricably linked to the achievement of another goal
+2	Reinforcing	Aids the achievement of another goal
+1	Enabling	Creates conditions that further another goal
0	Consistent	No significant positive or negative interactions
−1	Constraining	Limits options on another goal
−2	Counteracting	Clashes with another goal
−3	Cancelling	Makes it impossible to reach another goal

Source: Nilsson, Griggs and Visbeck (2016)

version of the network. The expert analysis was conducted by the International Science Council in 2015 when it was known as the International Council for Science (ICSU), in partnership with the International Social Science Council (ISSC); we therefore refer to this as the ICSU Report. Although based on a qualitative analysis of policy interlinkages rather than historic data, this is one of the few reports to treat all the SDGs identically (but not quite – it omits SDG 17). Dawes (2020) describes in detail the methodology through which the expert opinions were turned into a quantitative cross-impact matrix. Essentially this involved interpretation of the direction of interlinkages from the report's text, combined with an indication of the strength of an interlinkage given by the number of targets in the SDG that was being influenced that were mentioned as being impacted by progress on the influencing SDG. The initial example presented in Figure 6.1 is in fact the subset of the ICSU network consisting of high-weight edges that form closed loops in the network; this can be seen by comparing the non-zero entries in the adjacency matrix (Equation 6.1) with the very light grey and very dark grey cells in Figure 6.2a.

The second interlinkage matrix we use is based on the Global Sustainable Development Report (GSDR, 2019; Pham-Truffert et al., 2019, 2020). This report carried out a literature survey of 177 global scientific assessments, UN flagship report, and scientific articles on SDG interlinkages, wherever possible looking at the level of targets; here we consider their results aggregated to goal-level. A hand-coding of statements in these articles resulted in a set of 4,976 separate positive and 782 negative interactions. Although there is considerable value in preserving the distinction between the positive and negative interactions separately, as discussed in more detail elsewhere (Dawes, 2022), for reasons of brevity we will discuss in this chapter only the 'net interlinkage' matrix obtained by summing positive and negative interlinkages.

Figure 6.2 shows the interlinkage matrices derived from the ICSU and GSDR reports. Interlinkages were scaled to lie in the range [–1, 1] and those close to zero are replaced by white space to improve the readability of the figures. Diagonal entries were removed from the GSDR matrix to make this more directly comparable with the ICSU matrix; removing these entries turns out to have only a very minor effect on the overall results (Dawes, 2022). In both cases we observe that almost every SDG influences SDGs 1–3, as shown by the densely populated top three rows of each plot. But there are fewer influences from SDGs 1 to 3 on the remaining goals, as is shown by the relatively sparsely coloured first three columns on the left-hand side of each plot. This highlights what appears to be a fundamental asymmetry in Agenda 2030: the first three SDGs are those on which most attention is focused, with SDGs 4 to 17 in some sense playing a subordinate role, supporting the fundamental development agenda, and continuation from the Millennium Development Goals, that SDGs 1–3 represent.

The interlinkage matrices in Figure 6.2 clearly differ from each other, and this highlights the obvious fact that interlinkage matrices constructed from different data sources vary and often vary considerably. The point is not to find a single interlinkage matrix that is somehow the most appropriate, or optimal, one, but to be able to link aspects of the detailed construction of any one interlinkage matrix with the system-level implications of those goal-by-goal or indeed target-by-target influences. Indeed, even being forced to address issues such as the directionality of interlinkages often helps to clarify what a particular interlinkage matrix is attempting to capture.

6.1.4   Chapter Organisation

The remainder of this chapter is organised as follows. In Section 6.2 we explain and apply the key idea of *centrality*, that is, the relative importance of different nodes in a network. Of the many different ideas of centrality we focus on the idea known as 'eigencentrality' (Bonacich, 1972; 2007; Newman, 2018; Bali Swain & Ranganathan, 2021) which in a strict sense does not apply to complex networks with both positive and negative interlinkages but has an alternative and extremely useful interpretation making it an important and applicable system-level statistic (Dawes, 2020).

Already above we have noted that the robustness of any network-based measures is an important aspect of these quantitative approaches. In Section 6.3 we discuss two possible measures of the sensitivity of the eigen-centrality measure to perturbations to the network (that is, the addition or removal of new interlinkages). This also leads naturally to methods to answer the question of where best to introduce new interlinkages in order to improve the self-reinforcements already present in a network.

Section 6.4 discusses the third idea: the notion of hierarchy among an interlinkage network for the SDGs. Measures of overall hierarchy and directionality in complex networks have their roots in the computation and analysis of ecosystems, for example food webs, but lend themselves also to the systemic analysis and quantification of prioritisation between the SDGs. Prioritisation of SDGs that lie further 'upstream' of others should enable those goals to be met while at the same time allowing benefits to flow through the network and so allow the whole system to benefit. In contrast, prioritisation of SDGs that lie far 'downstream', and hence have much lower levels of influence on other goals, would not allow all SDGs to be met. We develop and discuss measures of hierarchy that help to identify points of leverage and maximum 'downstream benefit' to other SDGs in the network. We conclude in Section 6.5 and offer perspectives and directions for further research.

6.2 CENTRALITY MEASURES

A common observation in network science is that some nodes appear to be more important or more 'central' to the network than others. The most fundamental notion of centrality is simply to count the edge weights of the edges by which other nodes are connected to the node under consideration. This gives rise to the centrality measures

$$k_i^{\text{in}} = \sum_{j=1}^{n} A_{ij} \quad \text{and} \quad k_i^{\text{out}} = \sum_{j=1}^{n} A_{ji} \qquad (6.2)$$

which are the (weighted) in-degree k_i^{in} and out-degree k_i^{out} of node i, respectively. We note that in situations where edges weights may be negative as well as positive, it might be more appropriate to take the absolute value of the edge weights A_{ij} in order to avoid cancellation between positive and negative contributions. Compact expressions for the vectors of in-degrees and out-degrees can be written making use of the vector 1 which denotes the vector $(1,1,\ldots,1)$ in which every element is one. Then $k^{\text{in}} := A1$ and $k^{\text{out}} := A^T 1$ where A^T denotes the transpose of the matrix A, that is, the matrix in which the $(i, j)^{\text{th}}$ element is the entry A_{ji}.

Pham-Truffert et al. (2020) refer to nodes that have a large in-degree as 'buffers' since in some sense they serve to combine the effects of many different nodes together, and they refer to nodes that have a large out-degree as 'multipliers' as they may propagate the influence of a node to many other parts of the network. The total degree $k_i = k_i^{\text{in}} + k_i^{\text{out}}$ of node i is a natural measure of the relative importance of node i in the network; this is commonly referred to as the *degree centrality* of the node.

Other popular and long-studied measures of centrality, which we will not consider further here, include 'betweenness centrality' (Freeman, 1977) and 'closeness centrality' (Bavelas, 1950). To compute betweenness centrality we first compute the set of shortest paths between every pair of nodes in the network. The betweenness centrality of a node is then proportional to the number of shortest paths that pass through that node. Closeness centrality is the average length of the shortest path between the given node and all other nodes in the network. Both definitions are most straightforward to apply to unweighted, undirected, and connected networks; various generalisations and improvements account for cases in which the network is either weighted, directed, or disconnected (a network is disconnected if its set of nodes divides into two subsets for which there are no edges linking any pair of nodes chosen so that one node lies in each subset).

6.2.1   Eigencentrality

While simple, the concept of degree centrality has an inherent drawback – it is a purely local calculation. By 'local' we mean that degree centrality counts the numbers of direct neighbours of a node but does not make any allowance for how connected those nodes themselves might be. A node with a large number of 'unimportant' neighbours is perhaps less important itself than a node with a smaller number of 'very important' neighbours. A more robust measure of importance could therefore be obtained differently, through a slightly self-referential definition: the importance of a node is given by the weighted sum of the importance of the nodes to which it is connected. Mathematically we can define the importance v_i of node i to be given by the weighted sum

$$v_i = \frac{1}{\lambda} \sum_{j=1}^{n} A_{ij} v_j \qquad (6.3)$$

where λ is a 'normalisation' or rescaling parameter. This definition appears to be unfortunately circular since it demands knowing the importances v_j of the nodes j to which node i is connected. One can imagine some kind of iterative scheme, starting with estimated values for the v_i and then re-calculating them according to Equation 6.3 until they converge. Such an approach indeed works (for almost all initial choices of the v_i) although it involves estimating the value of λ as well. In more mathematical language, λ is the largest or 'leading' eigenvalue of the matrix A and $\mathbf{v} = (v_1,\ldots,v_n)$ is the leading eigenvector. The calculation of λ and $\mathbf{v}$ is numerically straightforward in many software packages. Further mathematical remarks are given in Box 1.

BOX 6.1   EIGENVALUES AND EIGENVECTORS

In the generic case, an $n \times n$ matrix A has n distinct eigenvalues $\lambda_1,\ldots,\lambda_n$ each with a corresponding eigenvector $\mathbf{v}^{(1)},\ldots,\mathbf{v}^{(n)}$. Each eigenvector is a column vector with n elements. We order the eigenvalues so that $Re(\lambda_1) \geq Re(\lambda_2) \geq \cdots \geq Re(\lambda_n)$ where Re denotes the real part of the eigenvalue λ_i which is possibly a complex number even when the matrix A is real.

The eigenvalues and eigenvectors are defined by the equation $A\mathbf{v}^{(i)} = \lambda_i \mathbf{v}^{(i)}$. In practice we usually find eigenvalues first, by solving the equation $P(\lambda) := \det(A - \lambda I) = 0$, where $\det$ denotes the determinant of the matrix, and I denotes the $n \times n$ identity matrix. $P(\lambda)$ is a polynomial of degree n in λ and so (generically) has n distinct roots which are the eigenvalues $\lambda_1,...,\lambda_n$. For each eigenvalue one can then find the column vector $\mathbf{v}$ that satisfies $(A - \lambda_i I)\mathbf{v}^{(i)} = \mathbf{0}$. Eigenvectors are typically scaled ('normalised') so that the sum of the squares of their entries is one; if this is carried out then each entry lies in the range from −1 to +1.

For a typical matrix A that has no negative entries the Perron–Frobenius Theorem (Meyer, 2000, Chapter 8) guarantees that the largest eigenvalue λ_1 is real and positive and it has a corresponding eigenvector $\mathbf{v}^{(1)}$ that has no negative entries. In this case, for typical positive initial guesses, iterations of Equation 6.3 when $\lambda = \lambda_1$ converge to $\mathbf{v}^{(1)}$.

The elements of the leading eigenvector $\mathbf{v}^{(1)}$ define a centrality measure describing the relative importance of each of the nodes; this is known as eigenvector centrality, abbreviated sometimes to *eigencentrality*. Eigencentrality is a remarkably old concept, dating back at least as far as the article by Landau (1895) on scoring in chess tournaments; further historic references include Leontief (1941) and Seeley (1949). If the matrix A has no negative entries then the eigencentrality scores for each node lie in the range zero to one, assuming the normalisation described in Box 1 is carried out.

6.2.2 Interpretation

Eigencentrality as an importance measure is related to the in-degrees of the nodes rather than their out-degrees in the sense that, for a directed network (as we consider in this chapter), a large eigencentrality score relates to a high accumulation of co-benefits provided by other nodes. Therefore, in the context of SDG interlinkage networks, eigencentrality according to Equation 6.3 measures the extent to which a node receives co-benefits (or trade-offs) from other nodes, rather than the extent to which it generates these co-benefits and confers them onto other nodes. Therefore, the elements of $\mathbf{v}^{(1)}$ provide a measure of the extent to which nodes are 'sinks', rather than 'sources'.

While the Perron–Frobenius Theorem referred to in the last paragraph within Box 1 is mathematically well-defined only for non-negative matrices, it is often the case that a network with only a relatively small number of negative links will also have a leading eigenvector that has all entries non-negative; in such a case it is tempting to continue to interpret the leading eigenvector as a centrality measure. But there is an additional context for interpreting the leading eigenvector – it is the dominant 'response' of the network when we consider the interlinkage network as dynamically generating reinforcements, or trade-offs between progress on different nodes over time. For example, taking the simplest possible case, consider the evolution equation

$$\frac{dx_i}{dt} = \sum_{j=1}^{n} A_{ij} x_j,$$ (6.4)

which states that the rate of change in time t of a state variable x_i related to node i depends linearly on each of the state variables x_j at the nodes j that have influence on, and feed into, node i, mediated in each case by the strength and sign of the interaction between the two nodes as captured by the interlinkage A_{ij}. The solution $\mathbf{x}(t)$ to the differential equation (Equation 6.4) is dominated, apart from perhaps over a short initial transient phase, by the form of the leading eigenvector because the leading eigenvector describes the mode of maximum growth rate – the eigenvalues $\lambda_1,\ldots,\lambda_n$ are the growth rates of these different modes of response, but $\mathbf{v}^{(1)}$ dominates since (by definition) λ_1 is larger than all the others. For completeness, we note that in special cases there might be other eigenvalues equal to λ_1 but this is not a generic behaviour and so in the interests of simplicity, and because it does not arise in practical examples of SDG interlinkage networks, we gloss over this point in our exposition here. Indeed, in the examples below we will see that the leading eigenvalue is substantially larger than the remaining $n-1$ eigenvalues and so provides a good guide to the overall system dynamics.

To summarise, the leading eigenvector can be interpreted as the intrinsic mode of self-reinforcing growth of the state variables $\mathbf{x}(t) = (x_1(t),\ldots,x_n(t))$ caused solely by their interactions. In the context of this work, and conscious of many caveats around the simplistic nature of Equation 6.4 and the coarse-grained representation this implies, we can view $x_1(t),\ldots,x_n(t)$ as the relative levels of progress made on each of the SDGs, interpreting the interlinkages as reinforcing or constraining effects due to policy actions.

6.2.3   A Measure of Influence

We now briefly contrast the interpretation of eigencentrality above (that reveals which nodes benefit the most from positive interlinkages in the network) with a closely related but distinct question: which nodes have the greatest influence on others, across the network? That is, instead of asking which nodes receive the greatest number of co-benefits (as 'sinks'), we ask which nodes provide the most co-benefits, as 'sources'. Let y_i denote the influence across the network of node i. As in the earlier discussion, we can frame an answer to deducing the relative levels of influence through a similar but subtly different self-referential definition: the influence of node i is given by the weighted sum of the influences of the nodes that node i is itself able to influence. Mathematically we can define the influence y_i of node i to be given by

$$y_i = \frac{1}{\lambda} \sum_{j=1}^{n} y_j A_{ji}. \tag{6.5}$$

The key difference between Equations 6.5 and 6.3 is the directionality of the interlinkages: note the term A_{ji} in Equation 6.5 rather than A_{ij}. A node i that has no outgoing edges (that is, where $k_i^{\text{out}} = 0$) will have zero influence on the network: this agrees with Equation 6.5 since $k_i^{\text{out}} = 0 \Rightarrow y_i = 0$. However, a node with no outgoing edges may still have a positive in-degree $k_i^{\text{in}} > 0$ and hence $v_i > 0$. The distinction between the levels of 'influence' and 'benefits received' for each node is crucial for directed networks of the kind that we consider here.

Mathematically, Equation 6.5 implies that $\mathbf{y}$ satisfies the equation $\mathbf{y}^T A = \lambda \mathbf{y}^T$. The row vector $\mathbf{y}^T$ is the left eigenvector corresponding to the eigenvalue λ, in contrast to $\mathbf{v}$ which is the (usual) right eigenvector. Equivalently, $\mathbf{y}^T$ is the right eigenvector of the transpose matrix A^T defined by swapping the elements of A so that $(A^T)_{ij}$ is the element A_{ji}.

6.2.4 Katz Centrality

Finally, we briefly mention a centrality measure that 'interpolates' between eigencentrality and degree centrality (Katz, 1953). Consider the importance x_i of node i to be given by the weighted sum of the importances of its neighbours as in Equation 6.3, with a weighting parameter α, but also including a constant term so that every node has importance at least one:

$$x_i = \frac{1}{\alpha} \sum_{j=1}^{n} A_{ij} x_j + 1. \tag{6.6}$$

Written in matrix-vector terms this is equivalent to writing $\mathbf{x} = \alpha A \mathbf{x} + 1$ where 1 is the column vector having a one in every element. Re-arranging we obtain

$$x = (I - \alpha A)^{-1} 1 = (I + \alpha A + \alpha^2 A^2 + \alpha^3 A^3 + \cdots) 1, \tag{6.7}$$

where I denotes the $n \times n$ identity matrix having ones on the main diagonal and zeros in all other entries, and the power series expansion indicated by the ellipsis is valid for $0 \le \alpha < 1/\lambda_1$. The parameter α measures the 'discount rate' at which the contribution to the importance of node i from ever more distant nodes drops off as the distance through the network increases. For very small α only the immediate neighbours of node i really count, and so the centrality measure $x_i \approx 1 + \alpha k_i^{\text{in}}$ and we recover (apart from the constant 1 and the scaling by α which do not affect the relative values of the centralities) the in-degree centrality. In the opposite limit, as $\alpha \rightarrow 1/\lambda_1$ we recover the eigen-centrality measure v_i.

Similarly, if we replace A by its transpose in Equations 6.6 and 6.7 we obtain measures of the influence u_i of node i, with successive terms in the sum on the right-hand side of Equation 6.7 corresponding to contributions from nodes at successive distances from node i. This is precisely what the analysis by Weitz et al. (2020) aimed to capture in the analysis of a cross-impact matrix for a set of 34 SDG targets in a country-level analysis for the case of Sweden. Their overarching aim was to understand how to answer the question (as they posed it) 'If progress is made on target x, how does this influence progress on target y?'. Weitz et al. proposed the idea that the total influence of a node should be a combination of the direct ('first order' in their terminology) and indirect ('second order') influences. This combination of direct and indirect influences led Weitz et al. to propose the measure of total influence $\mathcal{I}_i^{\text{total}}$ of a node i as a weighted sum of its out-degree k_i^{out} and the out-degrees of its neighbours, multiplied by the interlinkage strength A_{ij} (noting that they used the convention that A_{ij} is the strength of the edge $i \rightarrow j$ and so their A is our A^T):

$$\mathcal{I}_i^{\text{total}} = k_i^{\text{out}} + \frac{1}{2}\sum_{j=1}^{n} A_{ij} k_j^{\text{out}}. \tag{6.8}$$

In light of the discussion above we can see this as a truncation of the series expansion in Equation 6.7, ignoring the $\alpha^2 A^3$ and higher-order terms, and with A replaced by A^T in order to compute influences rather than importances. In our notation, letting $\mathcal{I}_i^{\text{total}} = (u_i - 1)/\alpha$, and setting $\alpha = 1/2$, their definition in Equation 6.8 above becomes

$$(u-1)/\alpha = A^T 1 + \frac{1}{2}\left(A^T\right)^2 1 = [A^T + \alpha(A^T)^2]1,$$
$$\Rightarrow u = (I + \alpha A^T + \alpha^2 (A^T)^2)1,$$

(using the fact that $I1 = 1$) which is precisely the truncation of Equation 6.7 ignoring the A^3 term and all higher powers. Again, in the limit as $\alpha \rightarrow 1/\lambda_1$ (and including the higher-order terms in α) the influence measure $\boldsymbol{u}$ converges to the eigenvector-based influence measure $\boldsymbol{y}$ discussed previously.

6.2.5 Illustrations of Centrality

It is numerically straightforward to compute the eigenvalues and eigenvectors for the interlinkage matrices shown in Figure 6.2; the results are given in Figure 6.3. Figure 6.3a plots the eigenvalues. In both cases there is a leading eigenvalue that appears far to the right of the remaining ones, leaving a significant gap between the leading eigenvalue and the next-largest, for both the ICSU eigenvalues (squares) and GSDR eigenvalues (round dots). This indicates that the behaviour of the networks is dominated by the form of their leading eigenvectors and that this fact is robust to perturbations of individual interlinkages. The form of the leading eigenvectors themselves is shown in Figure 6.3b, again with the GSDR eigenvector in black and the ICSU one in red. The lines joining the dots are added just as a guide to the eye; the data points show the components of the eigenvectors for each of the SDGs. The ICSU eigenvector has only 16 components since the ICSU analysis omitted SDG 17.

The asymmetry noticed above is reflected in the high values of the eigenvector components for SDGs 1–3: these three SDGs are positively supported by many of the others which therefore act to promote greater progress on goals 1–3, in the dynamical sense, and for them to be identified as among the most important in a centrality sense. The GSDR matrix has a particularly high component also for SDG 8 (decent work and economic growth) which is perhaps expected due to the relatively full row of interactions supporting SDG 8 in the interaction matrix in Figure 6.2b. The corresponding row for the ICSU matrix in Figure 6.2a also strongly supports SDG 8, but in this case the support is stronger for other SDGs and so SDG 8 does not emerge as relatively better off. Most concerning is the negative component of the leading eigenvector for SDG 14 (life below water) for the ICSU matrix. This suggests that the internal dynamics of the ICSU network would result in negative progress on SDG 14 when positive progress is made elsewhere. In terms of the interlinkage matrix there are two strongly negative links, from SDG 2, and from SDG 11, to SDG 14 – these are coloured dark blue in Figure 6.2a and point to significant trade-offs between the goals on zero hunger and sustainable cities, and progress on life below water.

Figure 6.4 reveals that the most influential sources of co-benefits are SDGs 12, 9, 5, and 4 (in that order) for the ICSU interlinkage network (and these in effect generate the co-benefits that result in greatest progress on SDGs 1–3 as revealed by Figure 6.3b). For the GSDR network SDGs 12, 6 and 7 are the most influential in generating co-benefits for other SDGs (and from Figure 6.3b we see that these benefits accrue most to SDGs 1–3 and 8 for the GSDR network). We see also that for the ICSU matrix SDGs 2 and 3 are a source of trade-offs within the network, while SDG 1 is the only SDG that is a source of (net) trade-offs for the GSDR interlinkage matrix.

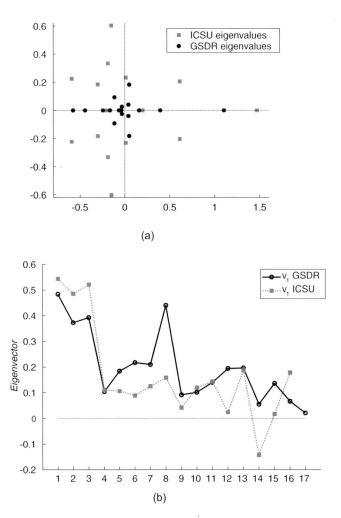

(a)

(b)

Notes: (a) Eigenvalues of the adjacency matrices *A* in the two cases, shown in the complex plane (that is, the horizontal axis corresponds to the real part of the eigenvalue and the vertical axis to the imaginary part). The leading eigenvalues are real and are located at approximately $\lambda_1 = 1.47$ for the ICSU matrix and $\lambda_1 = 1.10$ for the GSDR matrix (both to 2 decimal places). In both cases there are significant horizontal gaps between this leading eigenvalue and those that are next-largest. (b) The leading eigenvectors $\mathbf{v}^{(1)}$ for the ICSU and GSDR adjacency matrices, with the components for each SDG plotted against the SDG number on the horizontal axis. The vertical scale is arbitrary since eigenvectors are defined only up to a scale factor and are normalised here as described in Box 1 (so that the sums of the squares of the components add up to one)
Source: Adapted under CC-BY-4.0 from figure 2 in Dawes (2022)

Figure 6.3   *Eigenvalues and (right) eigenvectors for the ICSU and GSDR interlinkage matrices*

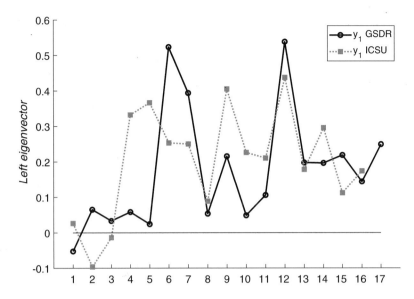

Notes: Components corresponding to each SDG are plotted against the SDG number on the horizontal axis. The vertical scale is arbitrary since eigenvectors are defined only up to a scale factor. Here, as is customary and convenient, we normalise so that the sum of the squares of the components adds up to one

Figure 6.4 *The components of the left eigenvectors $\boldsymbol{y}^{(1)}$ corresponding to the leading eigenvalue λ_1 for the ICSU and GSDR adjacency matrices*

6.3   SENSITIVITY TO INDIVIDUAL LINKAGES

Given the importance of eigenvalues and eigenvectors in summarising the overall dynamics of an interlinkage network, it is important and useful to be able to relate them directly to variations in the microscopic individual links in the network. This enables us to explore, for example, whether and how we might be able to influence the overall dynamics through changes to one or a small number of linkages. This discussion of the sensitivity of centrality results to the addition of new network linkages is linked to long-standing and well-known perturbation results in applied mathematics and yields useful analytical results. It also yields readily to interpretations, building on the results of the previous section and the concepts of right and left eigenvectors introduced there. The discussion in this section is based on Dawes (2022).

First, we distinguish between two possible senses in which we might want to improve the co-benefits that the interlinkage matrix results in. Our first measure, which we term 'growth rate sensitivity', describes the change in the leading eigenvalue which is the overall rate at which interlinkages generate overall changes (which we hope are largely positive) in progress on the SDGs. The second measure, which we term 'equality sensitivity', describes the extent to which a change in a particular interlinkage affects the distribution across the SDGs of these self-reinforcing benefits so that progress becomes more equal across the whole set of SDGs.

6.3.1   Growth Rate Sensitivity

A suitable mathematical measure of the sensitivity of the growth rate to perturbations is to consider the rate of change of the leading eigenvalue λ_1 of the interlinkage matrix to perturbations in one element A_{ij} of the adjacency matrix. We therefore define the 'multiplier effect' sensitivity matrix S^m to be the $n \times n$ matrix whose (i, j) entry is $S_{ij}^m := (1/\lambda_1)\partial\lambda_1 / \partial A_{ij}$. The factor of $1/\lambda_1$ is included so that S^m computes relative changes in λ_1 rather than absolute changes. In the cases of interest here, S_{ij}^m turns out to have a simple expression in terms of the left and right eigenvectors ($\mathbf{y}^{(1)T}$ and $\mathbf{v}^{(1)}$, respectively) for the leading eigenvalue λ_1. A straightforward calculation, presented in Appendix B of Dawes (2022) and also summarised in Box 2, leads to the formula

$$S_{ij}^m = \frac{1}{\lambda_1} \frac{y_i^{(1)} v_j^{(1)}}{\mathbf{y}^{(1)T}\mathbf{v}^{(1)}} \tag{6.9}$$

Thus S_{ij}^m is a measure of the sensitivity of the leading eigenvalue of the adjacency matrix to an increase in the interlinkage A_{ij}.

The growth rate sensitivity formula (Equation 6.9) has an intuitive explanation that builds on the interpretations of $\mathbf{y}^{(1)}$ as the sources of co-benefits (or trade-offs) in the network, and $\mathbf{v}^{(1)}$ as the resulting 'sinks' of co-benefits or trade-offs. Consider the two cases in Figure 6.5 where we show, as a thought-experiment, two nodes labelled i and j and part of their interlinkage network.

For simplicity, suppose that initially the nodes are not linked, and consider the effect on the network overall of introducing a new edge from j to i. In case (a), corresponding to Figure 6.5a, suppose that node i has only incoming edges and no outgoing ones: $k_i^{out} = 0$. (We make no assumptions about the nodes that j is connected to; suppose j has both incoming and outgoing edges.) Then node i is unable to propagate co-benefits or trade-offs further through the network; column i in the interlinkage matrix must consist entirely of zeros: $A_{pi} = 0$ for all $p = 1,\ldots,n$. Then from Equation 6.5 we conclude that we must have $y_i = 0$ for any left eigenvector $\mathbf{y}$. So in particular this is true for the leading left eigenvector $\mathbf{y}^{(1)}$ and hence $S_{ij}^m = 0$ from Equation 6.9, and so the addition of the new link $j \to i$ does not change the growth rate λ_1. Intuitively, if i only

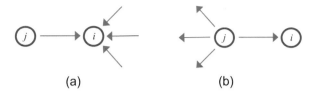

(a)   (b)

Notes: Illustrations of the two cases in which we would expect the growth rate sensitivity to the addition of an edge from node *j* to node *i* to be zero. (a) Suppose that *j* has a mixture of incoming and outgoing edges (not shown), but that *i* has only incoming edges, and that we add a new edge $j \rightarrow i$. (b) Suppose in this case that *i* has a mixture of incoming and outgoing edges (not shown), but that *j* has only outgoing edges, and that we add a new edge $j \rightarrow i$

Figure 6.5   Insensitivity of the growth rate to the addition of an edge

receives benefits from other nodes and is not a source itself, then adding a new edge pointing towards node *i* does not change that situation, and so the network as a whole does not gain or lose.

In case (b), corresponding to Figure 6.5b, consider adding the new edge $j \rightarrow i$ when *j* has no incoming edges, only outgoing ones (and we suppose that *i* might have both incoming and outgoing edges). Then node *j* is unable to receive the results of co-benefits or trade-offs from other nodes: row *j* of the adjacency matrix contains only zeros: $A_{jq} = 0$ for all $q = 1,\ldots,n$. Hence, from Equation 6.3 we see that v_j must be zero, that is, the jth entry of any (right) eigenvector **v** must be zero. Then from Equation 6.9 we see that $S_{ij}^{m} = 0$ and so the addition of the new edge $j \rightarrow i$ does not change the growth rate for the network at all.

To summarise, Equation 6.9 can be justified intuitively as stating that, for a new edge $j \rightarrow i$ to affect the network dynamics, it is necessary that node *i* already propagates co-benefits or trade-offs through to other nodes in the network (that is, $k_i^{\text{out}} > 0$), and that node *j* already receives co-benefits or trade-offs from other nodes (that is, $k_j^{\text{in}} > 0$). The sensitivity of the network to the addition of the new edge $j \rightarrow i$ is proportional to the product of the level of co-benefits currently offered by node *i* and received by node *j*.

BOX 6.2   DERIVATION OF THE SENSITIVITY MATRIX S^{m}

Following Greenbaum et al. (2020) here we summarise the derivation of Equation 6.9 that describes the effect on the growth rate λ_1 of a perturbation to the interlinkage from *j* to *i*, that is, the entry A_{ij}. Let the matrix A have distinct eigenvalues $\lambda_1,\ldots,\lambda_n$, with corresponding right and left eigenvectors $\mathbf{v}^{(1)},...,\mathbf{v}^{(n)}$ and $y^{(1)},...,y^{(n)}$ normalised so that $\|\mathbf{v}^{(i)}\| = \|\mathbf{y}^{(i)}\| = 1$ for all $i = 1,...,n$.

Now consider the adjacency matrix A to be a function of a parameter ε that changes the interlinkage from j to i (this will be made explicit in a moment), writing $A(\varepsilon)$ where $A \equiv A(0)$. Suppose that $A(\varepsilon)$ has an eigenvalue $\lambda_1(\varepsilon)$ and a right eigenvector $\mathbf{v}^{(1)}(\varepsilon)$ that vary smoothly with ε, so that $A(\varepsilon)\mathbf{v}^{(1)}(\varepsilon) = \lambda_1(\varepsilon)\mathbf{v}^{(1)}(\varepsilon)$. Differentiating with respect to ε and setting $\varepsilon = 0$ we obtain

$$A'(0)\mathbf{v}^{(1)}(0) + A(0)\mathbf{v}^{(1)\prime}(0) = \lambda_1'(0)\mathbf{v}^{(1)}(0) + \lambda_1(0)\mathbf{v}^{(1)\prime}(0),$$

where $'$ denotes a derivative with respect to ε. Now multiply on the left by the left eigenvector $\mathbf{y}^{(1)T}(0)$ and observe that the second term on the left-hand side will cancel with the second term on the right hand side since they are both $\lambda_1(0)\mathbf{y}^{(1)T}(0)\mathbf{v}^{(1)\prime}(0)$. Hence we obtain

$$\lambda_1'(0) = \frac{\mathbf{y}^{(1)T}(0)A'(0)\mathbf{v}^{(1)}(0)}{\mathbf{y}^{(1)T}(0)\mathbf{v}^{(1)}(0)}. \tag{6.10}$$

This expression holds for any perturbation to the interlinkage matrix A; we now specialise to the case that the perturbation is to a single network edge $j \rightarrow i$, for which the derivative matrix $A'(0)$ is just the outer product $A'(0) = \mathbf{e}_i \mathbf{e}_j^T$ where $\mathbf{e}_i$ is the column vector whose i^{th} entry is 1 and all other entries are 0. For this case, omitting the parameter dependence in the notation, Equation 6.10 becomes

$$\lambda_1' = \frac{y_i^{(1)} v_j^{(1)}}{\mathbf{y}^{(1)T}\mathbf{v}^{(1)}}$$

which describes the rate of change of the eigenvalue λ_1 with respect to the value of the network edge from $j \rightarrow i$. This result is well-known (Jacobi, 1846) and was re-derived more recently in the ecological literature (see Equation (23) in Neubert & Caswell, 1997) in the context of ecosystem resilience.

Finally, the matrix S^m introduced in Equation 6.9 is precisely the $n \times n$ matrix of rates of change with respect to perturbations in each element of A in turn, scaled by a factor of λ_1. We may define:

$$S_{ij}^{\text{m}} := \frac{1}{\lambda_1}\frac{\partial \lambda_1}{\partial A_{ij}} = \frac{1}{\lambda_1}\frac{y_i^{(1)} v_j^{(1)}}{\mathbf{y}^{(1)T}\mathbf{v}^{(1)}}. \tag{6.11}$$

The factor of $1/\lambda_1$ is included in our definition so that S^m computes relative changes in the magnitude of the leading eigenvalue: this allows better comparison of the values of S^m computed from different matrices with different absolute values of λ_1.

6.3.2 Equality Sensitivity

The second sensitivity measure is also easy to define in terms of eigenvectors, although some of the mathematical details are a little more complicated and are omitted here. We define the equality sensitivity S_{ij}^{eq} of the leading eigenvector $\mathbf{v}^{(1)}$ to be

$$S_{ij}^{\text{eq}} := \hat{\mathbf{n}} \cdot \frac{\partial \mathbf{v}^{(1)}}{\partial A_{ij}}, \qquad (6.12)$$

that is, a 'scalar product' (sometimes referred to just as the 'dot product') between two vectors, one being the vector $\hat{\mathbf{n}} := 1/\sqrt{n}$ that describes complete equality of progress on all $n = 17$ SDGs, and the other being the rate of change in the leading eigenvector $\mathbf{v}^{(1)}$ when the $(i, j)^{\text{th}}$ element of A changes. The scalar product measures the extent to which the two vectors are pointing in the same direction, or not: if the vectors are at right angles to each other then the scalar product is zero. The entries of the matrix S^{eq} therefore measure the extent to which a perturbation to A_{ij} increases the alignment of the leading eigenvector $\mathbf{v}^{(1)}$ with the vector $\hat{\mathbf{n}}$ which corresponds to complete equality of progress across all the SDGs. Mathematical details concerning Equation 6.12 are given in Appendix 2 of Dawes (2022). The details are a little more complicated than for the growth rate sensitivity S_{ij}^m for unfortunately technical and purely mathematical reasons: because eigenvectors are defined only up to a normalisation, which we take to be the standard one that $| \mathbf{v}^{(1)} | = 1$, this normalisation has to be accounted for in the calculation of S_{ij}^{eq} so that an increase in one eigenvector component is compensated for by decreases elsewhere. For that reason we omit mathematical details here and refer the interested reader to Appendix B of Dawes (2022).

6.3.3 Illustrations of Sensitivity Analysis

Figures 6.6 and 6.7 illustrate the theory of the previous sections with calculations of the growth rate sensitivity S^m from Equation 6.9 and the equality

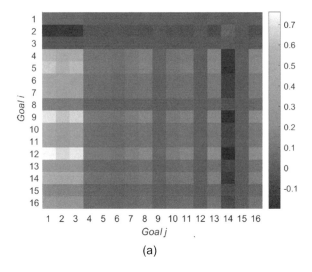

(a)

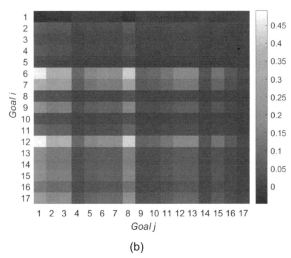

(b)

Notes: Growth rate sensitivities S^m for the leading eigenvalues λ_1 of (a) the ICSU network illustrated in Figure 6.2a; and (b) the averaged GSDR interaction network, illustrated in Figure 6.2b. Each square in the grid is coloured according to the relative increase in the growth rate (that is, S^m that would result from a small increase in that specific interlinkage, keeping the remainder of the network the same). Lighter grey entries in the matrix indicate where increases in those interlinkages would increase S^m (and hence increase the leading eigenvalue λ_1); darker grey entries indicate where increases in an interlinkage would decrease S^m (and hence decrease the leading eigenvalue λ_1)
Source: Adapted under CC-BY-4.0 from figure 5 in Dawes (2022)

Figure 6.6   Growth rate sensitivities for the leading eigenvalues

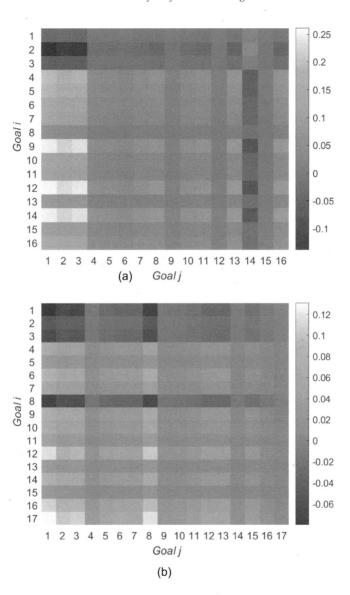

Notes: Light grey colours indicate that increasing those interlinkages serves to make the components of the leading eigenvector $\mathbf{v}^{(1)}$ more equal. Dark grey colours indicate that increasing an interlinkage will make the leading eigenvector more unbalanced. The relative differences between matrix entries are significant; the absolute differences between the colour scales in (a) and (b) are not significant

Source: Adapted under CC-BY-4.0 from figure 6 in Dawes (2022)

Figure 6.7   *Equality sensitivities S^{eq} for (a) the ICSU matrix and (b) the GSDR matrix*

sensitivity S^{eq} from Equation 6.12 for the ICSU and GSDR interlinkage matrices shown in Figure 6.2.

As we would anticipate from Figures 6.3b and Figure 6.4, the growth rate sensitivities are largest when both $\mathbf{y}^{(1)}$ and $\mathbf{v}^{(1)}$ take their most positive values, corresponding to changes in edges from nodes that are currently benefitting the most from the network structure (for example nodes 1–3 for the ICSU interlinkage matrix), to nodes that have the highest influences on other nodes (for example, nodes 12, 9, 5, and 4 for the ICSU matrix). Hence increasing the value of edges $\{1,2,3\} \rightarrow \{4,5,9,12\}$ increase the overall growth rate of system-wide co-benefits the most, for the ICSU network. Similarly, for the GSDR network we would expect edges from $\{1,2,3,8\} \rightarrow \{6,7,12\}$ to affect the overall growth rate the most, and this is confirmed by Figure 6.6b.

Figure 6.7 is a little harder to interpret, as the sensitivities plotted here reveal the extent to which the distribution of the co-benefits to different SDGs becomes more uniform as the weight of a specific edge is increased. But the general message is similar: increasing the interlinkages from SDGs 1-3 tends to re-balance the expected distribution of co-benefits across the SDGs, and this effect is particularly apparent when, for the ICSU network, the interlinkages are from $\{1,2,3\} \rightarrow \{4,5,9,12,14\}$. For the GSDR network, the edges that are most useful in this respect are those from $\{1,2,3,8\}$ to $\{12,17\}$.

6.4   HIERARCHY

Building interlinkage matrices with *directed* edges between nodes, rather than *undirected* ones (which could be interpreted only as either mutually beneficial or mutually antagonistic relationships), immediately provokes questions at the system level as to whether the network taken as a whole has a sense of directionality to it. To a certain extent this has been present in the background to the discussions in Section 6.2 since we have looked to identify nodes that are greater recipients of co-benefits, in some sense lying further 'downstream' of other nodes, and nodes that have the greatest influence and are providers of those benefits, in some sense lying further 'upstream' of other nodes. Thus there is implicitly a sense of directed order across the network. In this section we tackle this question of hierarchy directly.

It is clear that some directed networks do not have an overarching sense of hierarchy; for example consider the case of a network consisting of a cyclic ring of directed edges of equal edge weights. In such a network all nodes must lie at the same 'level' by symmetry. Contrastingly, a chain of positive directed edges all pointing in the same direction confers a clear hierarchy since, in our SDG context, progress on SDGs corresponding to nodes earlier in the chain results in co-benefits shared with SDGs further along the chain, but the reverse is not true. In the context of the SDGs it feels likely that there is at least some sense of hierarchy; for example it is clear that while progress on goals related to societal change such as SDG 5 (gender equality) and SDG 10 (reduced inequalities) are highly likely to lead to progress on 'human development' goals such as SDG 1 (no poverty) and SDG 3 (good health and well-being), it is not so clear that all policy actions taken to reduce poverty or to improve healthcare would necessarily have co-benefits that included progress on SDG 5 or SDG 10; progress (at least to some extent) on SDG 1 or SDG 3 could be made through policy choices that fail to address persistent inequalities in gender or other population characteristics. Indeed, the persistent failure of sufficient data collection to monitor SDG 5 means that it may be difficult to quantify this effect although it surely exists (Pollitzer, 2022b).

In this section we look at a quantitative approach to deciding whether a given interlinkage network implies the existence of a hierarchy, and if it does, to computing the relative 'level' for different SDGs in the network.

6.4.1   Trophic Confusion

Following Mackay et al. (2020) we assign a level h_i to each node i (that is, each SDG in our goal-level analyses), and the challenge is to find a choice for the levels that minimises a function F which measures the overall lack of directionality in the network (that is, we aim to choose levels in order to maximise the amount of directionality that exists). Mackay et al. (2020) refer to F as the amount of 'trophic confusion' in the network, motivated by food webs where the structure of the trophic network is a key quantity of interest in order to understand an ecosystem. A generalisation of their initial idea is to include a collection of pre-specified quantities g_{ij}, not necessarily related to the adjacency matrix A, that provide a set of target spacings between the levels h_i. The values of the levels h_i that minimise F can then be determined by minimising, for example, the function

$$F(\mathbf{h}) := \frac{\sum_{ij} |A_{ij}| (h_i - h_j - g_{ij})^2}{\sum_{ij} |A_{ij}|}. \tag{6.13}$$

The form of $F(\mathbf{h})$ in Equation 6.13 guarantees that it takes positive values or is zero. F clearly has a minimum value zero that is achieved when the spacings between levels satisfy exactly the requirements given by the g_{ij}, if this is possible. If it is not, then minimising F attempts to get as close to satisfying this situation as possible. The denominator provides a normalisation of the values of F, enabling comparisons between different networks if the distributions of edge weights are the same; otherwise it does not affect the values of the levels h_i that minimise F. Mathematically, by considering how F depends on the value chosen for a level h_i, it can be shown that the set of levels h_i that minimise F are equivalently given by solving the equation

$$\Lambda \mathbf{h} = \text{vecdiag}(AG^T - A^T G), \tag{6.14}$$

where the matrix $\Lambda := \text{diag}(\mathbf{k}) - A^T - A$, G is the matrix whose entries are given by the elements g_{ij}, and vecdiag(M) means the operation that extracts just the elements of the main diagonal of the matrix M and forms these elements into a column vector. Note also that $\mathbf{k}$ is the vector of total degrees $\mathbf{k} := \mathbf{k}^{\text{in}} + \mathbf{k}^{\text{out}}$ defined towards the start of Section 6.2, G is the matrix whose entries are the target spacings g_{ij}, and the notation diag($\mathbf{v}$) means the square matrix with the elements of the vector $\mathbf{v}$ as the main diagonal of the matrix, with zeros elsewhere. In the case $g_{ij} = 1$ for all i and j, the right-hand side vecdiag($AG^T - A^T G$) reduces to the difference between the (weighted) in-degree and out-degree.

Despite this rather detailed set of definitions, minimising the 'trophic confusion' quantity F is straightforward to implement computationally and provides a representation of a network that as far as possible provides an overall sense of directionality. This enables a visualisation of which nodes are furthest 'upstream' in the network and so influence most others, and which are furthest downstream and hence benefit most from co-benefits due to other SDGs.

6.4.2   Illustrations of Hierarchy

In Figure 6.8 we show the results of minimising the trophic confusion measure F defined in Equation 6.13 for the ICSU and GSDR networks. In both parts of the figure, the relative levels of the SDGs are determined so that as many of the directed edges point upwards as possible. The relative horizontal positions of different SDGs have no meaning in terms of interlinkages; they are purely to make the figures as easy to interpret as possible. The influences between pairs of SDGs therefore generally run from the bottom of each figure to the top. We see that consistently SDGs 1–3 appear close to the top of the figures, and SDG 12 appears low down. SDG 17 does not appear in Figure 6.8a since it was not included in the ICSU analysis. One surprise in Figure 6.8b is the relatively high position of SDG 5 (gender equality). This illustrates that the construction of these hierarchies depends on the robustness of the underlying data; as noted above, SDG 5 is rather sparsely represented in the literature on which the GSDR review was built. One useful direction for future research

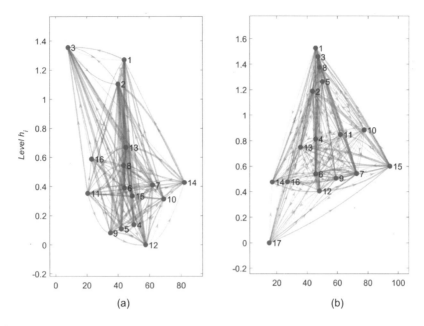

Figure 6.8   *Hierarchies of nodes in the two networks*

would clearly be to develop measures of the robustness or sensitivity of these hierarchy calculations to missing or suspected biases in the underlying data.

6.5   SUMMARY AND DISCUSSION

The aim of this chapter has been to introduce a number of concepts in network science and illustrate how they are able to contribute to the understanding of the study of SDG interlinkages. In particular they illuminate the challenge of drawing system-level inferences from a set of individual pairwise interactions between the 17 SDGs. Such system-level inferences would similarly be possible if we had started with data at the level of the 169 individual targets, or, indeed, at the even more granular level of indicator time series; the figures would have been more complicated to interpret but the methodology would apply unchanged. The extent to which SDG interlinkages reinforce each other, generating co-benefits, illustrates exactly the concept of policy coherence, with, naturally, some care required in the interpretation of these results depending on whether the interlinkage data are historic, related to current policy actions, or hypothesised as potentially existing if future policy actions are carried out.

In the public policy literature a central distinction is made between policy instruments (or tools, or techniques) and policy goals (outcomes). In terms of SDG interlinkages, the policy goals are made much more explicit than the policy instruments that might influence them; the mechanisms or inputs required to achieve the SDGs are often, as noted above, only described implicitly. The discussion of the relation between policy instruments and policy goals stretches back at least to the work of Jan Tinbergen who suggested that in typical situations, if n independent policy goals were to be achieved, then a set of at least n policy instruments would in general be required (Tinbergen, 1952; Schaeffer, 2019). But of course, any degree of alignment or coherence between policy goals might enable a reduction in the number of policy instruments required. A set of 17 separate policy instruments to achieve the SDGs would seem both awkward and at variance with the call for policy coherence, yet perhaps policy coherence is in many cases the atypical situation and needs to be 'designed in' to policy rather than being frequently and easily available.

The scope of the SDG agenda is so wide that the pursuit of some minimal number of policy 'tasks' that might generate policy coherence, or at least provide focal points for policy formulation, appears to be advocated by a number of recent proposals such as the Six Transformations proposed by the Sustainable Development Solutions Network (SDSN) (Sachs et al., 2019, 2020) or the six 'entry points' listed by the Global Sustainable Development Report 2019 (GSDR, 2019).

Three topics were discussed in this chapter: centrality in Section 6.2, sensitivity in Section 6.3, and hierarchy in Section 6.4. Each topic was illustrated with results for two example networks; one based on expert review (the ICSU network, elaborated from the ICSU–ISSC report published in 2015) and the other on a substantial literature survey (GSDR, 2019). These were presented mainly in order to illustrate the mathematical tools, but it is of interest to note the many similarities in the structure of the two networks built from these different data sources. It should be noted that the data sources are largely, but not quite fully, independent: one of the 177 assessments used by GSDR (2019) was ICSU-ISSC (2015). The results illustrated the kinds of overall conclusion that could be drawn about the structure of the interlinkage networks that was less obvious, and certainly less quantifiable, without carrying out the mathematical analysis set out above.

In Section 6.2 the discussion focussed on 'eigencentrality'; in the context of directed networks, this corresponds to the idea that the most important nodes are those that receive the largest co-benefits from other nodes. As long as an interlinkage network does not contain too many negative entries (trade-offs), the interpretation of the eigenvector corresponding to the largest eigenvalue as a centrality score makes sense. It certainly continues to make sense as a measure of how much progress will be made on each SDG if the internal network dynamics and co-benefits or trade-offs within the network are left to dominate the dynamics of the system over time. Eigencentrality in the usual sense corresponds to the right eigenvector of the interlinkage matrix A. The left eigenvector of A has the dual interpretation: it shows which SDGs contribute the most to the co-benefits that are received by the SDGs that score highly in terms of eigencentrality (that is, those for which the corresponding entry in the right eigenvector is largest). For our illustrative examples, Figures 6.2b and 6.3 reveal that SDGs 1–3 (and for the GSDR network, SDG 8 also) have high eigencentrality scores, and SDG 12 (and SDGs 6 and 7 for the GSDR network) have high influence scores.

Section 6.3 considered the robustness of the leading eigenvalue λ_1 of an interlinkage matrix (that is, the overall rate at which network effects influence progress) to perturbations in the interlinkage network. Two possible measures of this sensitivity were presented in Equations 6.9 and 6.12 which describe either the sensitivity S^m of the growth rate λ_1 itself, or the sensitivity S^{eq} of the extent to which the network would result in equal progress across all SDGs, under perturbation. It turns out that S^m can be written elegantly as a product of the left and right eigenvectors of λ_1, but that S^{eq} is a little more complicated but yields similar results. These results show that adding interlinkages which allow goals that receive very high co-benefits to feed these back in and influence goals that received much lower levels of co-benefits are the ones that improve the overall rate of progress the most. While this is in line with our intuition, we have set out in this chapter a mathematical formulation that quantifies and justifies this statement. For our pair of example networks, we observe in Figures 6.6 and 6.7 that the largest improvements in growth rates arise when progress on SDGs 1–3 (and SDG 8 for the GSDR network) is allowed to influence progress on specific other SDGs (including for both networks SDG 12).

The eigencentrality idea is particularly powerful due to its dynamical interpretation via Equation 6.4; for an interlinkage matrix where there is a large gap between the leading eigenvalue and the remaining ones, eigencentrality reveals which SDGs will receive increasing shares of the overall co-benefits that are available. In cases where this gap is much smaller, more careful analysis may be required. There are of course many important additional caveats such as the need to consider interlinkages whose strength might vary over time and the level of direct investment in support of specific SDGs. These issues are discussed further in Dawes (2022). The discussion in the present chapter is intended to highlight how one might begin to analyse a complex network of interactions and to move securely between consideration of individual interactions and the overall system-level consequences.

Finally, in Section 6.4 we summarised another approach to this question of downstream response and upstream influence in the network, introducing a measure of hierarchy within the network, and computing the relative levels of different SDGs within the network (that is, how far upstream or downstream of other SDGs they are). Despite the differences in methodology, the results of the hierarchy calculations, shown in Figure 6.8, appear in many examples to be well-correlated with the difference, for each SDG, between their scores $\mathbf{v}^{(1)}$ for receipt of co-benefits and $\mathbf{y}^{(1)}$ for generation of influence. This can be mathematically justified through careful consideration of Equation 6.14; the solution for the levels $\boldsymbol{h}$ can be well-approximated by the formula

$$h_i \approx \frac{k_i^{\text{in}} - k_i^{\text{out}}}{k_i^{\text{in}} + k_i^{\text{out}}} \approx \frac{v_i^{(1)}(\mathbf{v}^{(1)} \cdot \mathbb{1}) - y_i^{(1)}(\mathbf{y}^{(1)} \cdot \mathbb{1})}{v_i^{(1)}(\mathbf{v}^{(1)} \cdot \mathbb{1}) + y_i^{(1)}(\mathbf{y}^{(1)} \cdot \mathbb{1})},$$

where the last expression on the right hand side is a further approximation in the limit in which the leading eigenvalue λ_1 is much larger than the remaining eigenvalues $\lambda_2, \ldots, \lambda_n$ in which case the 'network response' given by the eigencentrality measures $\mathbf{v}^{(1)}$ and $\mathbf{y}^{(1)}$ effectively captures the whole network response. Note that the coefficients in parentheses, for example $(\mathbf{v}^{(1)} \cdot \mathbb{1})$, represent scalar ('dot') products of two vectors and are a convenient way to denote the sum of the entries in (in this example) the vector $\mathbf{v}^{(1)}$. The form of these coefficients is not particularly relevant for this discussion – of more interest is that this expression for h_i essentially looks like the difference $v_i^{(1)} - y_i^{(1)}$. In other words, the 'trophic levels' $\boldsymbol{h}$ are closely related to the (relative) differences between the influences received and the influences exerted, for each node in the network.

Of the many directions for future research we will touch on a couple of the most obvious and pressing. First, the degree to which the results are sensitive to biases, missing input data, and the details of the construction of any interlinkage network are obviously extremely important if the results are to be robust and valuable. In part, detailed knowledge of the limitations or indeed the rationale behind any one interlinkage network should be known and understood at the time of construction or data collection. The results for that network must then be interpreted in that light; without that context and background understanding interpretation of the results is likely always to be misleading. That is one reason to include the second topic, on sensitivity analysis, here.

It is likely that similar approaches can be developed in order to understand the robustness of the hierarchy calculations presented in Section 6.4 as well. The hierarchy calculations can also be formulated in many different ways, for example making different choices for the target spacings g_{ij} in Equation 6.13. There are indeed a number of different 'natural' choices for g_{ij}, and more generally g_{ij} allows the formulation of some kind of 'prior structure' that one might wish to impose on the answer, for example pairs of SDGs whose levels should be more or less closely aligned than other pairs of SDGs due to some structural influence or geographical restriction. These issues deserve to be the subject of future investigation. One concrete example of a set of targets that thematically cut across the SDGs are the 'access-related' targets listed by Pollitzer (2022b), see pages 18–19 and 38–39 therein. More prosaically, one could use the g_{ij} terms to link together targets within each goal, to explore how hierarchy results are affected by the potential for unanticipated spill-overs and co-benefits to exist between targets that lie within the same SDG.

Other centrality measures, building on eigencentrality, might also be useful in order to explore more fully the connected nature of the network; this motivated the inclusion of the short discussion of Katz centrality in Section 6.2.4 and the discussion of the related work by Weitz et al. (2018) that followed. There is related recent literature that allows the inclusion of three-way interactions between nodes in a directed network (Arrigo et al., 2020, and references therein); this may be another helpful direction for SDG interlinkage networks in particular due to the prevalence of 'nexus' thinking between, for example, water, energy, and food (Weitz et al., 2014; Yillia, 2016; Fader et al., 2018; van Noordwijk et al., 2018; Putra et al., 2020).

To conclude, while the construction of interlinkage networks is in itself a demanding and complex task, it appears to be gaining momentum as a way to visualise structure within the set of SDGs; it follows that appropriate network tools should be used to extract the system-level metrics and conclusions that follow from the interlinkage network. This second step, while of course inheriting biases present in the network data, is crucial in understanding in policy terms the emergent features that the interlinkage network represents and how best they should be addressed. Moreover, network science tools directly offer insights that should challenge and provoke policy coherence and so lead to better policy development.

REFERENCES

Anderson, C. C., Denich, M., Warchold, A., Kropp, J. P., & Pradhan, P. (2022). A systems model of SDG target influence on the 2030 agenda for sustainable development. *Sustainability Science*, 17, 1459–1472.

Arrigo, F., Higham, D. J., & Tudisco, F. (2020). A framework for second-order eigenvector centralities and clustering coefficients. *Proceedings of the Royal Society A*, 476, 20190724.

Bali Swain, R., & Ranganathan, S. (2021). Modeling interlinkages between sustainable development goals using network analysis. *World Development*, 138, 105136.

Bavelas, A. (1950). Communication patterns in task-oriented groups. *Journal of the Acoustical Society of America*, 22, 725–730.

Bennich, T., Weitz, N., & Carlsen, H. (2020). Deciphering the scientific literature on SDG interactions: A review and reading guide. *Science of the Total Environment*, 728, 138405.

Bianconi, G. (2018). *Multilayer Networks: Structure and Function.* Oxford: Oxford University Press.

Bonacich, P. (1972). Factoring and weighting approaches to clique identification. *Journal of Mathematical Sociology*, 2, 113–120.

Bonacich, P. (2007). Some unique properties of eigenvector centrality. *Social Networks*, 29, 555–564.

Dawes, J. H. P. (2020). Are the sustainable development goals self-consistent and mutually achievable? *Sustainable Development*, 28, 101–117.

Dawes, J. H. P. (2022). SDG interlinkage networks: Analysis, robustness, sensitivities, and hierarchies. *World Development*, 149, 105693.

Dawes, J. H. P., Zhou, X., & Moinuddin, M. (2022). System-level consequences of synergies and trade-offs between SDGs: Quantitative analysis of interlinkage networks at country level. *Sustainability Science*, 17, 1435–1457.

Fader, M., Cranmer, C., Lawford, R., & Engel–Cox, J. (2018). Toward an understanding of synergies and trade-offs between water, energy, and food SDG targets. *Frontiers in Environmental Science*, 6, 112.

Freeman, L. C. (1977). A set of measures of centrality based on betweenness. *Sociometry*, 40(1), 35–41.

Greenbaum, A., Li, R.-C., & Overton, M. L. (2020). First-order perturbation theory for eigenvalues and eigenvectors. *SIAM Review*, 62(2), 463–482.

Independent Group of Scientists appointed by the Secretary-General. (2019). *Global Sustainable Development Report 2019: The Future is Now – Science for Achieving Sustainable Development*. United Nations: New York, USA.

International Council for Science (ICSU); International Social Sciences Council (ISSC). (2015). *Review of the Sustainable Development Goals: The Science Perspective*. International Council for Science: Paris, France.

Jacobi, C. J. G. (1846). Über ein leichtes Verfahren die in der Theorie der Säcularstörungen vorkommenden Gleichungen numerisch aufzulösen. *Journal für die reine und angewandte Mathematik*, 30, 51–95.

Katz, L. (1953). A new status index derived from sociometric analysis. *Psychometrika*, 18, 39–43.

Landau, E. (1895). Zur relativen Wertbemessung der Turnierresultate. *Deutsches Wochenschach*, 11, 366–369.

Le Blanc, D. (2015). Towards integration at last? The sustainable development goals as a network of targets. UN Department of Economic & Social Affairs, DESA Working Paper No. 141.

Leontief, W. W. (1941). *The Structure of American Economy 1919–1929*. New Haven, CT: Harvard University Press.

MacKay, R. S., Johnson, S., & Sansom, B. (2020). How directed is a directed network? *Royal Society Open Science*, 7, 201138.

Meyer, C. D. (2000). *Matrix Analysis and Applied Linear Algebra*. Philadelphia, PA, USA: Society for Industrial and Applied Mathematics.

Neubert, M. G., & Caswell, H. (1997). Alternatives to resilience for measuring the responses of ecological systems to perturbations. *Ecology*, 78(3), 653–665.

Newman, M. (2018). *Networks: An Introduction* (2nd edn). Oxford: Oxford University Press.

Nilsson, M., Griggs, D., & Visbeck, M. (2016). Policy: Map the interactions between sustainable development goals. *Nature*, 534, 320–322.

Pedercini, M., Arquitt, S., Collste, D., & Herren, H. (2019). Harvesting synergy from sustainable development goal interactions. *Proceedings of the National Academy of Sciences*, 116(46), 23021–23028.

Pham-Truffert, M., Metz, F., Fischer, M., Rueff, H., & Messerli, P. (2020). Interactions among sustainable development goals: Knowledge for identifying multipliers and virtuous cycles. *Sustainable Development*, 1–15. https://doi.org/10.1002/sd.2073

Pham-Truffert, M., Rueff, H., & Messerli, P. (2019). *Knowledge for Sustainable Development: Interactive Repository of SDG Interactions*. CDEdatablog, Bern, Switzerland: CDE. https://datablog.cde.unibe.ch/index.php/2019/08/29/sdg-interactions/ (Accessed: 7 September 2020)

Pollitzer, E. (2022a). *Integrating a Gender Perspective into Implementation of Agenda 2030*. Guidance Note. Nairobi, Kenya: UN Women.

Pollitzer, E. (2022b). *Gender Analysis Toolkit for Prioritising SDG Goals and Targets: How to Improve the Knowledge Base for SDGs, Remove Gender Gaps in Evidence, and Integrate Gender Perspectives into Analyses of SDGs*. Nairobi, Kenya: UN Women.

Pradhan, P., Costa, L., Rybski, D., Lucht, W., & Kropp, J. P. (2017). A systematic study of Sustainable Development Goal (SDG) interactions. *Earth's Future*, 5, 1169–1179.

Putra, M. P. I. F., Pradhan, P., & Kropp, J. P. (2020). A systematic analysis of water-energy-food security nexus: A South Asian case study. *Science of the Total Environment*, 728, 138451.

Sachs, J., Schmidt–Traub, G., Kroll, C., Lafortune, G., & Fuller, G. (2019). *Sustainable Development Report 2019: G20 and Large Countries Edition*. New York: Bertelsmann Stiftung and Sustainable Development Solutions Network (SDSN).

Sachs, J., Schmidt–Traub, G., Kroll, C., Lafortune, G., Fuller, G., & Woelm, F. (2020). *The Sustainable Development Goals and COVID-19. Sustainable Development Report 2020*. Cambridge: Cambridge University Press.

Schaeffer, P. V., & Willardsen, K. (2019). *A Note on the Tinbergen Rule*. Working paper. https://www.petervschaeffer.com/publications.html (Accessed July 2021)

Seeley, J. R. (1949). The net of reciprocal influence: A problem in treating sociometric data. *The Canadian Journal of Psychology*, 3(4), 234–240.

Tinbergen, J. (1952). *On the Theory of Economic Policy*. New York: North-Holland.

United Nations. (2015). *Transforming Our World: The 2030 Agenda for Sustainable Development*. A/RES/70/1, New York: United Nations General Assembly.

van Noordwijk, M., Duguma, L. A., Dewi, S., Leimona, B., Catacutan, D. C., Lusiana, B., Öborn, I., Hairiah, K., & Minang, P. A. (2018). SDG synergy between agriculture and forestry in the food, energy, water and income nexus: Reinventing agroforestry? *Current Opinion in Environmental Sustainability*, 34, 33–42.

van Soest, H. L., van Vuuren, D. P., Hilaire, J., Minx, J. C., Harmsen, M. J. H. M., Krey, V., Popp, A., Riahi, K., & Luderer, G. (2019). Analysing interactions among sustainable development goals with integrated assessment models. *Global Transitions*, 1, 210–225.

Wasserman, S., & Faust, K. (1994). *Social Network Analysis: Methods and Applications*. Cambridge: Cambridge University Press.

Weitz, N., Carlsen, H., Nilsson, M., & Skånberg, K. (2018). Towards systemic and contextual priority setting for implementing the 2030 agenda. *Sustainability Science*, 13, 531–548.

Weitz, N., Nilsson, M., & Davis, M. (2014). A nexus approach to the post-2015 agenda: Formulating integrated water, energy, and food SDGs. *SAIS Review of International Affairs*, 34(2), 37–50.

Yillia, P. T. (2016).Water-energy-food nexus: Framing the opportunities, challenges and synergies for implementing the SDGs. *Österreichischer Wasser- und Abfallwirtschaftsverband*, 68, 86–98.

Zhou, X., & Moinuddin, M. (2017). Sustainable Development Goals interlinkages and network analysis: A practical tool for SDG integration and policy coherence. Research Report. IGES.

Zhou, X., Moinuddin, M., & Li, Y. (2019). SDG interlinkages analysis & visualisation tool (V3.0) https://sdginterlinkages.iges.jp/index.html

7. An integrated approach to the Sustainable Development Goals from an interlinkage perspective: methodology, decision support tool and applications

Xin Zhou and Mustafa Moinuddin

7.1 INTRODUCTION: AN INTEGRATED APPROACH TO THE SUSTAINABLE DEVELOPMENT GOALS

The thematic coverage of the 2030 Agenda for Sustainable Development is very broad. The 17 Sustainable Development Goals (SDGs) and their associated 169 targets encompass virtually all the aspects of social, economic and environmental issues, ranging from addressing poverty to creating jobs and mitigating climate risks. Unlike past development policy processes, the 2030 Agenda calls for implementing the SDGs in an 'integrated and indivisible manner', thus bringing in a unique feature with both opportunities and challenges. Each of the individual SDGs addresses a specific thematic area, but these thematic areas are inherently interlinked and hence their implementation needs to reflect this as well. These interlinkages can be either mutually reinforcing (synergistic) or conflicting (involving trade-offs). For instance, policies to enhance food security (Goal 2) and employment (Goal 8) are likely to increase agricultural productivity and reduce poverty (Goal 1) but could put stress on water resources and thus affect people's access to drinking water (Goal 6).

While the concept of sustainable development is not new, earlier approaches failed to take account of the aspect of cross-sectoral integration, causing incoherence in policy development (Le Blanc, 2015). Policies often mention sustainable development as a main objective, but eventually they tend to prioritise traditional economic growth, leading to trade-offs in other aspects of development, including social inequalities and environmental deterioration. Through a holistic, integrated approach, the SDGs intend to overcome this drawback and enhance policy coherence. The significance of an integrated approach and policy coherence has been highlighted in many reports and scholarly studies, including a handbook for Voluntary National Reviews (VNRs) by the United Nations Department of Economic and Social Affairs calling for an integrated approach in SDG planning (UNDESA, 2018) and the United Nations Development Group report stressing horizontal policy coherence (UNDG, 2015). Zusman and Amanuma (2018) further pointed out the need for vertical integration across various decision-making levels.

Adopting an integrated approach, however, is anything but trivial. It entails shifting away from the existing silo-based institutions and daily practices that policy makers are used to. An integrated approach is something new that has not yet been explored much, nor does the 2030 Agenda elaborate about how the SDGs are interconnected. Without proper information and guidance, policy makers will not know how or why to coordinate with other agencies. Put simply, they do not have the means to identify the reinforcing or conflicting measures and hence cannot reflect this in policy (Nilsson et al., 2016). Recognising the need for developing scientific knowledge in this area, several institutions and scholars have taken initiatives to better understand SDG integration and provide methodologies and tools to analyse the interlinkages among the SDGs. The approaches, scope and levels of analysis as well as coverage in these studies are diverse. Table 7.1 presents a brief summary of some of the most relevant literature in this area.

While these initiatives indicate a good start to analysing SDG integration, there are still huge gaps remaining, particularly in terms of the comprehensiveness (covering all the goals and targets), detailed knowledge on how the SDGs are interlinked, quantification of the SDG interlinkages and the applications to practical case studies at the national and sub-national levels. The SDG Interlinkages Analysis and Visualisation Tool (Zhou & Moinuddin, 2017; Zhou et al., 2017, 2018, 2019, 2021b), which is developed by the Institute for Global Environmental Strategies (IGES), has attempted to address some of the above-mentioned gaps. The IGES methodology and the associate tool help identify, quantify and visualise the SDG interlinkages at the target level for 27 countries in Asia and Africa. Subsequent developments in the methodology have also expanded its use in sub-national analysis (Zhou, Moinuddin, et al., 2022) and on specific thematic issues such as COVID-19 impacts and implications (Zhou & Moinuddin, 2021).

This chapter introduces the IGES methodology of SDG interlinkages analysis and the online visualisation tool. Section 7.2 of the chapter explains the methodology for building an SDG interlinkage model. Section 7.3 presents the SDG Interlinkages Analysis and Visualisation Tool, its functions and applications. Section 7.4 provides two case studies in Bangladesh and Indonesia to demonstrate how the tool can be used to support integrated SDG planning

Table 7.1   *Summary of selected literature on SDG interlinkages*

Literature	Scope	SDG coverage	Level of interlinkages analysis	Nature of interlinkages analysis
Zhou and Moinuddin (2017); Zhou et al. (2017, 2018, 2019 and 2021b)	National; 27 countries in Asia (22) and Africa (5)	All	Target level	Qualitative analysis, quantitative analysis, network analysis, synergies and trade-offs dashboards, an online visualisation tool
European Commission (2019)	General cumulative; policy mapping focuses in EU 27 region	All	Goal level and target level	Qualitative analysis, policy mapping, network analysis
Miola et al. (2019)	Regional (EU 27 region) National (Austria case study)	All	Target level	Qualitative analysis, quantitative analysis, network analysis
Allen et al. (2019)	Regional (22 countries in the Arab region)	All	Target level	Multicriteria analysis, network analysis
Millennium Institute (2018)	General; customisable to any country	All	Goal level and target level	Integrated simulation, quantitative analysis
Weitz et al. (2018)	General; case study in Sweden	All	Target level	Systems analysis, network analysis
ICSU (2017)	Global; national (country-specific illustrative examples)	Goals 2, 3, 7, 14	Goal level and target level	Qualitative analysis
UNESCAP (2017)	Sectoral; national (pilot application in Fiji and Tajikistan; issue-based examples in Japan, Nepal and Singapore)	Goal 6	Target level	Qualitative analysis
Nilsson et al. (2016)	General; conceptual	—	Target level	Analytical framework
Elder et al. (2016)	General; conceptual	All	Goal level	Systemic and functional way to classify the SDGs
Niestroy (2016)	General; regional perspectives (EU, OECD)	All	Goal level	Conceptual framework for clustering the SDGs
Le Blanc (2015)	General	All	Goal level and target level	Qualitative analysis, network analysis

Source: Authors' compilation

and implementation. Section 7.5 concludes the chapter by highlighting the potential of the tool, the limitations of the current version and the plans for further development.

7.2   METHODOLOGY

7.2.1   A Four-Step Methodology for Building an SDG Interlinkage Model

To study the interlinkages among the SDGs, IGES developed a methodology to identify, quantify and visualise the SDG interlinkages at the target level. A free online tool, SDG Interlinkages Analysis and Visualisation Tool (https://sdginterlinkages.iges.jp/visualisationtool.html), covering 27 countries in Asia and Africa, was developed to support integrated SDG planning and prioritisation by informing about the synergies and trade-offs among the SDGs (Zhou & Moinuddin, 2017; Zhou et al., 2021b). The methodology includes four steps (see Figure 7.1).

7.2.1.1   Step I: Identification of the SDG causal relationships and building a qualitative SDG interlinkage model

Not every target interacts with all other targets. Our assumption is that one target may have causal relationships with some targets but not necessarily all of them. For example, maintaining genetic diversity of seeds, cultivated plants and farmed and domesticated animals (Target 2.5) will enhance agricultural productivity (Target 2.3), indicating an intrinsic causal relationship between the two targets. However, there is no direct causal relationship between Target 2.5 and the access of small-scale industrial enterprises to financial services (Target 9.3). Identifying the causal links between SDGs is important to understand the drivers and potential impacts in the system of SDGs and find viable solutions from a systemic perspective.

We define a link with direction from Target *a* to Target *b* as a causal link, indicating the influence of achieving *a* on achieving *b* (or achieving *b* driven by achieving *a*). The identification of the causal links between SDG targets is conducted through a reference approach by reviewing the linkages identified in relevant literature (Zhou & Moinuddin, 2017). For example, for Goal 6, UNESCAP (2017) is used as a major reference for building the links between the targets of Goal 6 and other SDGs. Based on the literature review, more than 8000 directional links between 169 targets were identified and presented in a binary matrix (see Figure 7.2). The matrix model of the SDG interlinkages is a qualitative model indicating whether two targets in a pair have a causal relationship (defined as 1) or not (defined as 0).

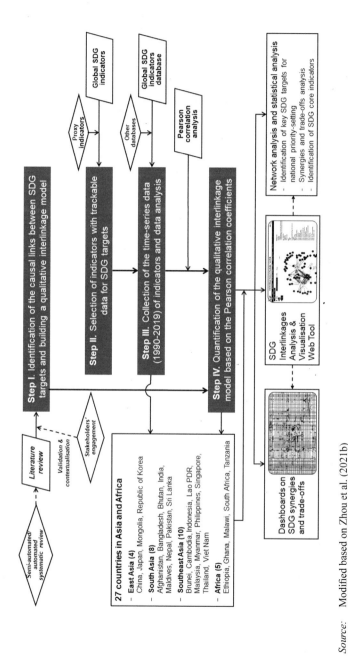

Source: Modified based on Zhou et al. (2021b)

Figure 7.1   A four-step methodology for the identification and quantification of SDG interlinkages

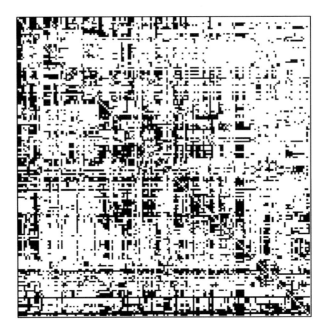

Note: Shaded entries indicate that paired targets have a causal relationship, and blank entries indicate that paired targets have no causality. Rows are read as causes, and columns are read as effects
Source: Compiled based on Zhou et al. (2021b)

Figure 7.2   IGES qualitative matrix model of SDG interlinkages

A literature review based on a limited number of references may not cover all SDG targets nor the full scope of the linkages. A large amount of literature related to the SDGs can be found in bibliographic databases such as Scopus. For example, there are more than 2 million references in Scopus by querying keywords related to Goal 2, such as 'hunger, food, nutrition or agriculture', in the titles, abstracts or keywords. Due to the comprehensiveness of the SDGs and the complexity of their linkages, it is important to include a wide range of literature that is relevant to the topic. Zhou, Moinuddin, et al. (2022) applied a systematic review following the preferred reporting items for systematic reviews and meta-analyses (PRISMA) (Moher et al., 2009) to select literature and review the interlinkages between selected SDGs (Goals 6, 7, 11, 13 and 15) at the river basin scale.

Through a systematic review, it is possible to extract the key issues studied in the literature, the major factors involved in these key issues and the relationships between major factors. The key issues, major factors and the relationships between major factors constitute a system of SDG interactions under study. By mapping the key issues and major factors with SDG targets, a qualitative system model of SDG interlinkages can be built at the target level.

The review of a large amount of literature based on a manual process is laborious and largely involves the subjective judgement of experts. To systematically extract the information from selected literature, text mining and content analysis supported by relevant software (for example, KH Coder and Nvivo) are used (Zhou, Moinuddin, et al., 2022). Software-based text data processing, such as extracting terms (n-grams) from strings, sorting terms by their frequency and identifying connections between terms based on word associations and co-occurrences, can reduce subjective judgement and improve data processing in a systematic way.

To further automate the process of a systematic review, artificial intelligence-based natural language processing (NLP) techniques are applied to extract information and discover corresponding relationships. Zhou, Jain, et al. (2022) demonstrate an automated process that applies NLP techniques to systematically extract the key interlinkages of SDG 13 (climate action) from selected climate change literature.

The SDG interlinkage model built through a literature review is generic. Due to different national and local circumstances, it is often necessary to tailor the generic model to a particular country or region. In a couple of case studies conducted by IGES at the national and sub-national levels (see Section 7.4.1), the SDG interlinkages identified through literature reviews were validated and contextualised through engagement with national and local stakeholders (Baffoe et al., 2021; Moinuddin et al., 2021; Zhou, Moinuddin, et al., 2022).

7.2.1.2 Step II: Selection of indicators for SDG targets

The qualitative model of the SDG interlinkages is quantified through a Pearson correlation analysis, which uses SDG indicators and their time series data (United Nations Statistics Division, 2019). As of March 2019,[1] among 231 global SDG indicators, 114 indicators (classified as Tier 1) have established methodologies and data collected regularly by at least 50 per cent of countries (IAEG-SDGs, 2019). The remaining indicators, classified as Tier 2 or Tier 3, lack data or methodologies. Even for Tier 1 indicators, data availability varies across countries. Particularly, the gaps in the indicators of some environment-related SDGs (Goals 11, 12, 13 and 14) are larger than other SDGs. To fill in the gaps in indicators and data, proxy indicators are selected from various sources, such as the World Development Indicators (World Bank, 2019). A total of 145 indicators are selected, covering 113 SDG targets, with some targets corresponding to multiple indicators (Zhou et al., 2021b). As of 30 November 2022, an updated tier classification contains 148 Tier 1 indicators, 77 Tier 2 indicators and 6 indicators that have multiple tiers.

Rapid improvement in SDG indicators also helps close the data gap. These new developments were not reflected in the current version of the quantified SDG interlinkages model.

7.2.1.3   Step III: Data collection and processing

The time-series data (1990–2019) of selected indicators is collected for 27 countries in Asia and Africa (Zhou et al., 2021b). Only data with at least two data points in the time series is included. Data availability varies across targets and countries. The average data availability at the indicator level for all countries is 56 per cent (measured by dividing the number of indicators with data by the total number of indicators). At the goal level, data availability is higher for Goals 3, 7, 8, 9, 15 and 17 (more than 65 per cent) but lower for Goals 4, 5, 6, 11 and 12 (less than 50 per cent).

In many cases, a full time-series covering 30 data points (1990–2019) is not available. The average data availability at the time point level for all indicators and all countries (measured by dividing the number of time points with data by the number of time points in the full time-series) is 35 per cent. Complete time-series data is required for conducting a Pearson correlation analysis. Missing data is imputed using the least square method based on the available data.

7.2.1.4   Step IV: Quantification of the SDG interlinkage model

The qualitative SDG interlinkage model built from Step I is quantified to indicate how strong the links are and whether the links are positive or negative. Each causal link defined in the qualitative model (represented as 1 in the binary matrix) is quantified by using the Pearson correlation coefficient calculated from two corresponding time-series. The Pearson correlation coefficient measures a linear relationship between two datasets. Quantification using Pearson correlation coefficients represents linear causality between the targets.

Quantitative models were built for 27 countries based on the qualitative model and the time-series data of individual countries. Because of the specific circumstances and development levels of individual countries, the interlinkages among SDGs may vary from one country to another. Using national data for quantification of the SDG interlinkages enables country-specific assessment. Figure 7.3 shows the SDG interlinkage model for Bangladesh and Indonesia, respectively. The Pearson correlation coefficients, ranging between [−1, 1], indicate a positive relationship if the correlation coefficient is greater than 0 or a negative relationship if the correlation coefficient is less than 0. A correlation coefficient between [0.7, 1] indicates a strong positive relationship, and a correlation coefficient between [−1, −0.7] indicates a strong negative relationship.

Bangladesh:

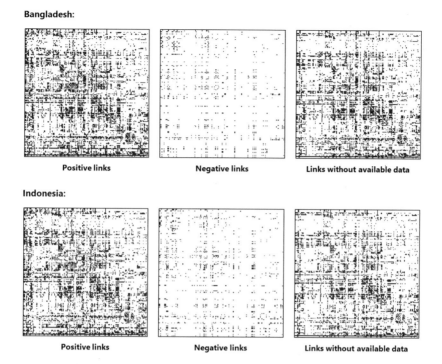

Source: Compiled based on Zhou et al. (2021b)

Figure 7.3   *Quantitative SDG interlinkage models for two countries*

7.2.2   Scope and Types of SDG Linkage

In terms of the scope of SDG linkage, it can be defined as a link between two goals, between a goal and a target or between two targets. In addition, links can be defined by a direct relationship between two targets or an indirect relationship via a third or more intermediate targets. Furthermore, a link can be defined by causation or other relationships (for example, social relationships). In our research, we define a linkage between two targets as a direct causal relationship with direction from cause to effect.

The causal relationship between two paired targets can reflect different situations. Suppose that two targets, *T1* and *T2*, have a causal relationship where *T1* is the cause and *T2* is the effect. Based on the development trend of *T1* and *T2*, there can be four different linkage types (see Table 7.2). When both targets are progressive, *T1* and *T2* develop synergistically in a progressive trend (Type A). When both targets are regressive, *T1* and *T2* are coupled in a

Table 7.2   Four types of SDG linkage

Development trend of paired targets	*T2*: Progressive	*T2*: Regressive
T1: Progressive	A Synergy	B Trade-off
T1: Regressive	C Development drag	D Coupled regression

Source: Modified based on Zhou and Moinuddin (2021)

regression trend (Type D). When *T1* is progressive but *T2* is regressive, *T2* is a trade-off of improving *T1* (Type B). When *T1* is regressive but *T2* is progressive, *T1* is a drag affecting *T2*'s development (Type C).

7.2.3   Network Analysis of the SDG Interlinkages

The SDG interlinkage matrix model can be transformed into a network model in which the 169 targets and their causal links can be presented as nodes and edges. Since the causal links defined in the SDG interlinkage model are directional and quantified links, the corresponding network of SDG interlinkages is a weighted and directed network.

In a network, the number of nodes and how a node connects with other nodes determine the structure of the network. Understanding the structure of the SDG interlinkage network and the importance of nodes can help improve the ability of the network to perform its functions and achieve the goals. Dawes et al. (2022) used hierarchical analysis to understand the characteristics of the network structure.

A network analysis based on various metrics, such as centrality, can help assess the importance of nodes and identify key nodes that play strategic roles in the network. In practical policy making, identifying important nodes in the network of SDG interlinkages can help identify key issues and find systems solutions by addressing the mechanisms among drivers, impacts and responses. This is particularly important for achieving multiple goals given limited financial resources and social capacity. Table 7.3 is an example of the top 20 important nodes in the network of SDG interlinkages in Ethiopia by ranking various centrality metrics, namely degree centrality, weighted degree centrality, closeness centrality, betweenness centrality and eigenvector centrality. For a detailed description of the centrality metrics and the methodology, please refer to a previous study (Zhou & Moinuddin, 2017). In Ethiopia, Targets 13.1 (climate adaptation), 8.1 (economic growth), 2.3 (agricultural productivity improvement), 11.2 (development of transport systems) and 17.9 (capacity building on SDG planning and implementation), among others, are identified as important targets in the network. These important targets can be set as national priorities for SDG planning.

Table 7.3   *Top 20 important nodes (SDG targets) in the network of SDG interlinkages in Ethiopia*

Top targets	Degree	Weighted degree	Closeness	Betweenness	Eigen	Average
13.1	3	3	4	10	9	5.8
8.1	4	15	5	6	5	7.0
2.3	5	2	15	12	3	7.4
11.2	6	7	6	13	14	9.2
17.9	1	1	1	4	44	10.2
12.2	9	6	12	22	7	11.2
8.4	10	10	13	21	13	13.4
8.2	11	16	25	14	11	15.4
15.5	15	9	16	27	17	16.8
1.1	7	5	52	19	1	16.8
1.2	8	4	51	20	2	17.0
15.2	14	8	18	29	18	17.4
8.5	13	18	45	18	4	19.6
1.5	16	13	17	31	23	20.0
11.1	12	11	31	28	20	20.4
11.5	17	14	19	32	25	21.4
9.a	2	82	3	9	16	22.4
15.1	19	12	24	39	21	23.0
15.4	22	64	11	1	32	26.0
3.b	27	22	42	16	24	26.2

Note: Values in columns 2–6 are the ranking results of 81 targets which have indicators and data. The average is calculated by summing the values in columns 2–6 and dividing by 5
Source: Calculated based on the data of Ethiopia (Zhou et al., 2021b)

Graphical visualisation of all or part of the SDG interlinkage network helps track upstream and downstream impacts, both direct and indirect, through chains of influence. This can help in pinpointing the drivers of a problem, understanding the mechanisms of the impacts and finding solutions and planning their implementation (see Section 7.4.2 for the practical case of Bangladesh).

7.2.4   Extension to Sub-National Scales

The methodology developed to identify and quantify SDG interlinkages at the national level has been extended to the sub-national levels through several case studies. One of the case studies assesses the synergies and trade-offs in achieving the SDGs across regions of a large river basin. The aim is to address spatial inequalities resulting from the implementation of relevant national policies, such as forest conservation for water source protection in the upstream and its impacts. A qualitative SDG interlinkage model at the basin scale was developed and used for an empirical study in China's Luanhe River Basin (Zhou, Moinuddin, et al., 2022). The qualitative model on the SDG interlinkages for river basins was built based on the causal framework of drivers-pressures-state-impacts-responses (DPSIR) through a systematic review of relevant literature found by searching ScienceDirect. The systematic review was supported by a machine-based text analysis. The results from the literature review were further validated through an expert survey and tailored to the Luanhe River Basin through a field campaign and stakeholders' consultation meetings. Figure 7.4 shows a qualitative SDG interlinkage model for river basins in a network graph. The model was further quantified for 27 counties located in the Luanhe River Basin using county-level statistical data collected for relevant indicators. A free online tool, the Interactive SDG Tool for River Basins (Zhou et al., 2021a), was developed to visualise the SDG interlinkages of 27 counties in the Luanhe River Basin. The qualitative generic model and the quantitative methodology are replicable for other large-scale river basins.

7.3   SDG INTERLINKAGES ANALYSIS AND VISUALISATION TOOL

To help explore the issues related to specific SDGs, their drivers and impacts through the interlinkages among the SDGs, as well as to communicate about possible solutions, IGES developed a free online tool, the SDG Interlinkages Analysis and Visualisation Tool (Zhou et al., 2017, 2018, 2019 and 2021b). The tool provides the following functions (see Figure 7.6):

  i) Select a country to analyse;
 ii) Select SDGs and targets and visualise their linkages;
iii) Save selections for repeated use;
iv) Select different ways to visualise the linkages, including:
   • Out-degree (downstream) and in-degree (upstream) links;
   • Positive and negative links;
   • Strength of the links and so on;
 v) Edit links, including:
   • Add new links;
   • Modify the strength of links;
   • Add new targets; and
   • Create new datasets based on the changes;
vi) Export visualisation graphs and relevant datasets.

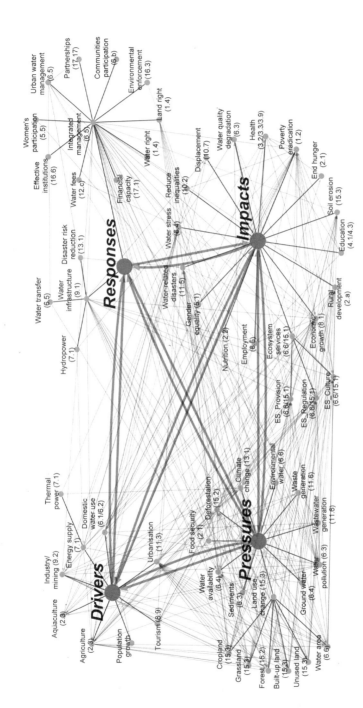

Source: Zhou, Moinuddin, et al. (2022)

Figure 7.4   SDG interlinkage model at the river basin scale

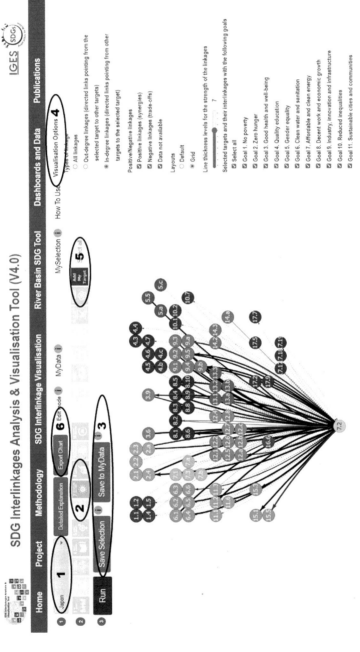

Source: Zhou et al. (2021b)

Figure 7.5 The SDG Interlinkages Analysis and Visualisation Tool (4.0) and functions

The tool was used to support practical policy development in a couple of countries in Asia. The national model for Indonesia was used to support the development of a chapter on the interlinkages of 17 goals in the Roadmap of SDGs Indonesia (Ministry of National Development Planning of Republic of Indonesia, 2019a). The tool was also used in the VNR of Indonesia to elaborate on the integration of the social, economic and environmental dimensions represented by six focused SDGs, namely Goal 4 (quality education) under the social pillar, Goals 8 (decent work and economic growth), 10 (reduced equalities) and 17 (partnerships) under the economic pillar, Goal 13 (climate action) under the environmental pillar and Goal 16 (peace, justice and strong institutions) under the law and governance pillar (Ministry of National Development Planning of Republic of Indonesia, 2019b).

The national model for Viet Nam was used to support the formulation of the National Action Plan on Sustainable Consumption and Production (Ministry of Industry and Trade, 2020). In the policy development process, the tool was used to assess the synergies and trade-offs of the preliminary measures of the action plan proposed by the Ministry of Industry and Trade. The assessment results, particularly on the trade-offs, were used by the Ministry of Industry and Trade in consultation with other ministries to make a final decision on the measures (King et al., 2020).

7.4   CASE STUDIES FOR THE APPLICATIONS OF THE SDG INTERLINKAGES TOOL

The IGES SDG Interlinkages Tool and its methodology have been applied in a couple of case studies. This section will introduce two case studies in Indonesia and Bangladesh. The first case study provides an example of our work on SDG interlinkages at the sub-national level in Indonesia's West Java Province. It focuses on the relevance of local context and the importance of engaging local stakeholders in the policy process of integrating climate actions and the SDGs. The challenges and priorities vary not only across countries but also among regions and cities within a country. This is an important aspect that needs to be taken into consideration in SDG interlinkage studies. The second case study reports the application of the IGES SDG interlinkages methodology to provide technical advice on integrated SDG planning and institutional arrangements at the national level in Bangladesh. This study was developed by taking into consideration the relevant national development plans and policies, and it explains how the methodology was used to recommend key SDG targets and which institutions should be involved in the implementation of these targets. Based on this, the study makes recommendations on how to prioritise SDGs and develop inter-agency collaboration from an interlinkage perspective.

7.4.1   Case Study in West Java, Indonesia: Integration of Climate Actions and SDGs through Stakeholder Consultation[2]

Climate actions and sustainable development are closely linked processes requiring committed efforts in the areas of the economy, society and the environment. Related instruments, namely the Paris Agreement and the SDGs, are global commitments, but they need to be implemented at the local level, since many of the policy-related competencies for land use, housing, infrastructure or climate change fall within the scope of local authorities such as cities and regions. Implementing actions at the local level necessitates proper understanding of local contexts – including not only local challenges, but also the priorities and opportunities at hand. Furthermore, these local-level actions need to be aligned with local and national development plans and take the climate action–SDG linkages into consideration. Involvement of local stakeholders in the planning and implementation processes, therefore, is indispensable. It is important to know how policy makers, local communities and other stakeholders view the potential synergies and trade-offs between climate action (Goal 13) and SDGs in West Java. In addition, stocktaking of the existing institutions and policies and identifying the barriers for taking an integrated approach is needed. Climate-SDG integration is a relatively new area and the issue has not yet been explored enough, particularly using surveys and consultations reflecting the views and opinions of the stakeholders. From this perspective, IGES partnered with the Center for Sustainable Development Goals Studies (SDGs Center) at Universitas Padjadjaran, to develop and conduct a study by involving local stakeholders in West Java on the issue of integrating climate actions and the SDGs at the provincial level (Moinuddin et al., 2021).

The stakeholder engagement process consisted of two parts: an online questionnaire survey of around 100 stakeholders, which was then followed by a focus group discussion among more than 20 members. The steps in the consultation process are shown in Figure 7.6. The exercise aimed at identifying the key challenges, synergies and trade-offs between climate actions and the SDGs and governance gaps, which can provide the basis for tailoring the generic SDG interlinkage model to West Java.

The study identified key issues facing West Java in four dimensions, that is, economy, community, environment and governance, and their linkages with Goal 13. Figure 7.7 shows the interlinkages of the identified issues under each dimension with Goal 13. Under the economic dimension, the respondents found linkages of all four key issues – especially infrastructure and economic growth and stability – with SDG 13 on climate action (Figure 7.8a). Goals 1, 2, 3 and 8 are the SDGs that the survey found to be highly linked with the four issues. The social issues in West Java are also found to be linked with

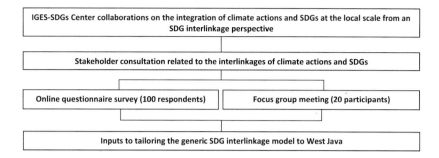

Figure 7.6   *Overview of the steps in the stakeholder's consultation in West Java*

climate actions to some extent, with almost 30 per cent of respondents highlighting access to energy as a major area that needs attention (Figure 7.8b). The respondents found West Java's environmental issues to be highly linked with climate actions as well as with other SDGs (Figure 7.8c). Climate action itself was found to be most linked with health (Goal 3) and water (Goal 6) and also linked with poverty and hunger (Goals 1 and 2), energy (Goal 7), water and land biodiversity (Goals 14 and 15). On the governance side (Figure 7.8 (d)), the rule of law and relations with the central government are found to be highly relevant for West Java's climate actions. The second issue, that is, aligning local actions with national ones, is especially important because policies and regulations related to climate change and the environment are mainly developed by the central government.

The results of the stakeholder's consultation as well as the details of the underlying methodology were compiled in a discussion paper (see Moinuddin et al. 2021). It is worth briefly noting some of the major issues, challenges and priorities that were emphasised by the stakeholders in this study.

- The engagement with stakeholders helped us identify the issues, challenges and priorities that should be reflected in West Java's local climate change and SDG policies. For instance, the region's widespread poverty, high dependence on the informal sector, infrastructure inadequacy and prolonged environmental degradation are directly linked with sustainable development and climate change. Addressing these issues will require, among others, integrating policies aimed at reducing poverty, increasing the resilience of the poor and supporting small and informal businesses.
- Feedback from the stakeholders indicated that the challenges and issues facing West Java are not in any particular sector; rather these are spread across the three dimensions of sustainable development: economic

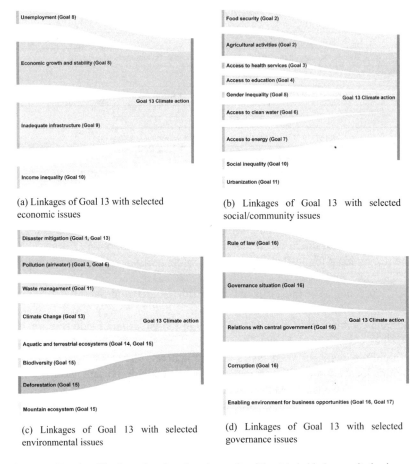

(a) Linkages of Goal 13 with selected economic issues

(b) Linkages of Goal 13 with selected social/community issues

(c) Linkages of Goal 13 with selected environmental issues

(d) Linkages of Goal 13 with selected governance issues

Source: Developed by the authors based on the results of the stakeholder's consultation in West Java

Figure 7.7   Linkages of selected key issues related to the economy, community, environment and governance with Goal 13 on climate action

(growing income inequality, inadequate jobs and income generating opportunities, and high dependence on the informal sector), social (widespread poverty, unequal access to public services such as education and gender inequality) and environmental (high level of environmental pollution, excessive industrial wastes, overexploitation of natural resources, lack of clean water and continued land-use change from agriculture to

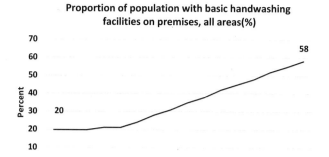

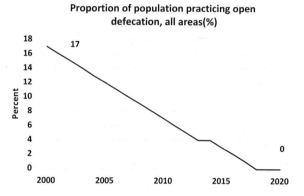

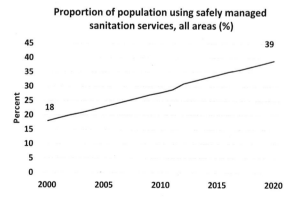

Source: Based on the data from UNSD (n.d.)

Figure 7.8   *Bangladesh's performance in sanitation and hygiene in recent years, selected indicators for Target 6.2*

built-up land for industrial and residential development). All these issues can adversely affect local climate actions and the SDGs in West Java.

• Addressing the above-mentioned issues is urgent. Along with the already existing climate- and environment-related measures in the province, public awareness building initiatives are needed. Access to education in West Java has been relatively limited, which has aggravated human resources scarcity, unemployment and socio-economic inequality and kept public environmental awareness at a low level. This has led people to overexploit natural resources to secure their livelihood, which results in aggravated environmental degradation. Environmental pollution and degradation, depleting natural resources and other environmental disasters increase West Java's vulnerability to climate risks.

• The stakeholders highlighted poor governance and institutional infrastructure as some of the major issues in West Java that require urgent attention and action. An enabling governance mechanism is needed for policies, plans and actions to be carried out efficiently and smoothly. Policy coherence among governmental agencies, for instance, is one such issue. The usual siloed working style of these agencies does not consider the connections between the social, the economic and the environmental sectors. An integrated approach with appropriate institutional arrangements and coherent delegation of responsibilities is needed to implement climate actions and the SDGs. Aligning and harmonising all localisation processes with national processes are also necessary.

The findings from the stakeholders' consultation indicate that due to the overlaps between climate actions and sustainable development, it is important that policy makers make an effort to integrate and co-develop the implementation plans by considering not only the local context and priorities but also the interlinked aspects of these two policy processes. Developing adequate knowledge and understanding of these interlinkages at the local level therefore is a prerequisite for enabling SDGs and climate actions to be aligned with and integrated into development plans. The results of this stakeholder consultation exercise can help develop the design of this integrated approach. Doing so will also require consideration of the socio-economic and environmental characteristics, issues and priorities of West Java within the broader national and local development plans. An integrated approach can help develop local policies consistently with national-level policies by bridging the gap between these policy processes. Strengthened governance and institutional setup and clarified budget lines are needed in order to create the enabling conditions for localising and integrating climate actions and the SDGs. Finally, an empowered civil society is expected to enhance accountability and transparency for spending and policy decisions on climate actions and the SDGs.

The insights and knowledge acquired through this stakeholder engagement exercise will also be essential for bottom-up science-based studies, such as in-depth SDG interlinkage analyses at the sub-national levels. In particular, the local stakeholders can provide inputs into the specific context and validate the generic SDG interlinkage model. This can provide important insights and practical support to local policy processes including, but not limited to, the development of Voluntary Local Reviews on SDG progress. The experience from this stakeholder consultation activity is expected to provide a basis for similar activities in other localities or cities within and outside Indonesia.

7.4.2   Case Study in Bangladesh: Application of the SDG Interlinkage Model to Inform Integrated SDG Planning[3]

Soon after the development of the IGES SDG Interlinkages Tool, it was applied to develop a case study on integrated priority setting and institutional arrangements for SDGs planning and implementation in Bangladesh. Bangladesh is an early starter in SDGs. The country made impressive progress in the implementation of the Millennium Development Goals (MDGs) and intends to carry the momentum to the SDGs as well. SDGs receive strong support from the highest level of political office, with SDG coordination led by the Principal Coordinator for SDG Affairs at the Prime Minister's Office. An inter-ministerial SDG monitoring and implementation committee has been established, and the General Economics Division of the Planning Commission serves as the secretariat. SDGs were aligned with the country's 7th Five Year Plan (FYP) for 2016–2020 (GED, 2015, 2016b). The government has also developed Bangladesh's SDG financing strategy (GED, 2017c), identified the interactions among policies directed to achieve the SDGs (GED, 2016b), mapped SDGs at goal and target levels with implementation activities including the lead/associate governmental agencies/ministries (GED, 2016a), conducted a data gap analysis (GED, 2017a) and developed an online SDGs Tracker as a data repository (GED, 2017b; PMO-Bangladesh, 2017). Bangladesh has submitted its VNR reports twice, in 2017 and 2020. The VNR documents provide details of the governmental plans and progress in implementing the SDGs, including national indicators and data, priority areas and localisation efforts.

In 2018, as part of the governmental effort to strengthen SDG implementation, the Governance Innovation Unit of the Prime Minister's Office of Bangladesh (GIU-PMO) developed an initial list (GIU-PMO draft list) of 38 priority targets across all 17 SDGs (GIU, 2018). This list reflected the primacy of the three core themes (growth acceleration, inclusiveness and environmental sustainability) of the 7th FYP in the country's SDG planning. The 38 country-specific targets were mapped with 33 official SDG targets across all of the 17 goals.[4]

During an informal consultation meeting between the GIU-PMO and IGES in Dhaka in May 2018, it was suggested that IGES would conduct an SDG interlinkages analysis to identify key targets for Bangladesh and compare them with this draft priority list, and review one specific target (Target 6.2 on sanitation and hygiene) in more detail including suggestions for institutional arrangements for its implementation. As the list received was not part of any formal report (as of the time of drafting of this chapter), the authors treat the list as a document in progress. An official SDG priority indicators list was adopted by the Government of Bangladesh later,[5] but the IGES analysis was based on the draft priority list received from the GIU-PMO.

7.4.2.1   SDG interlinkages analysis

Using the SDG Interlinkages Tool (V2.0) for Bangladesh, a network of interlinkages including more than 4000 direct causal connections between 169 targets could be obtained and visualised. For this massive and complicated network of interlinkages, IGES further used network analysis techniques to identify a set of 30 key SDG targets which play strategic roles in connecting other targets in the network. The key SDG targets were identified based on the ranking of various centrality metrics, namely degree centrality, betweenness centrality, closeness centrality and eigenvector centrality,[6] which measure the importance of individual targets in the network of connections (Zhou & Moinuddin, 2017). The derived list of the key targets is referred to as 'IGES recommended key targets'. Table 7.4 presents the results by combining the priority targets provided from the GIU-PMO draft SDG targets list and those proposed by IGES. The upper part lists the common targets in both lists, while the lower part shows other priority targets in each list. An important feature apparent in both lists is that the priority/key targets are not concentrated within a few goals; rather they are spread across the SDGs.

The government list reflects the priority areas of the 7th FYP from the near-term social-economic development perspective, the country's long-term vision (the Perspective Plan (GED, 2012)) and urgent issues to be addressed. The IGES list of key targets, on the other hand, emphasises the importance of interlinkages and key areas for joint planning and joint implementation. A combination of the two lists can be expected to support effective and efficient policy making for SDG planning and implementation. On one hand, it addresses the national social-economic development priorities and existing urgent issues to be solved. On the other hand, it pinpoints the areas which can be expected to leverage the generation of multiple benefits and remove major trade-offs to release the system's capacity to achieve more (the efficiency and cost-effectiveness aspects). Both perspectives are indispensable for Bangladesh, a thriving developing country with impressive socio-economic development experience in recent decades but facing the challenges relating to the limited availability of financial, economic and human resources.

Table 7.4   Priority/key targets for Bangladesh

Priority targets that are identified by both GIU-PMO and IGES

1.1 End extreme poverty	7.1 Universal access to energy
1.2 Halve national poverty	8.5 Decent work for all
2.2 End malnutrition	8.6 Improve youth employment
2.4 Build sustainable food production systems	10.1 Income growth of bottom 40 per cent of population
5.5 Enhance women's participation in decision-making	10.7 Improve equality of migrants
6.1 Universal access to safe drinking water	11.2 Universal access to sustainable transport system
6.2 Universal access to sanitation and hygiene	15.1 Sustainable use of terrestrial and inland freshwater

GIU-PMO draft priority targets

3.2 End preventable young children deaths	12.5 Reduce waste generation
3.6 Halve traffic deaths	13.1 Strengthen resilience to climate change
4.1 All for free primary and secondary education	14.5 Conserve 10 per cent of coastal areas
4.4 Increase skilled workers for decent jobs	15.3 Combat desertification and soil degradation
4.a Improve education facilities	16.9 Provide legal identity to all
5.3 Eliminate forced marriage	16.a Capacity building for preventing violence and terrorism
7.2 Increase renewable energy	17.1 Capacity building for tax collection in developing countries
8.1 Sustain inclusive economic growth	17.8 Enhance ICT in LDCs
9.1 Develop resilient infrastructure	
9.2 Promote inclusive and sustainable industrialisation	
9.c Universal and affordable access to ICT	

IGES recommended key targets

1.5 Build resilience of the poor to climate and other disasters	9.a Enhance international aid to build sustainable infrastructure
2.1 End hunger	11.5 Reduce losses from disasters
2.3 Double agriculture productivity	11.a Strengthen development planning for sustainable cities
3.4 Reduce pre-mature mortality from non-communicable diseases	12.8 Enhance awareness of sustainable lifestyles
4.5 Estimate gender disparities in all levels of education	13.2 Integrate climate change measures into national policies
4.7 Acquire knowledge needed for sustainable development	14.2 Sustainable management of marine ecosystems
5.c Strengthen policies for gender equality	15.2 Sustainable management of forests
6.4 Increase water use efficiency	16.6 Develop accountable institutions
9.4 Resource-efficient and clean technology-based industrial retrofit	

Source: Authors' analysis based on GIU (2018) and Zhou and Moinuddin (2017)

7.4.2.2 Analysis of Target 6.2 on sanitation and hygiene for Bangladesh

According to a UN Water Analytical Brief, Goal 6 on clean water and sanitation tends to have a bidirectional interdependence with all the other goals, and hence it plays a central role in SDG integration (UN Water, 2016). This appears to be one of the most important goals for Bangladesh as well. In recent years, the country has made commendable progress in water, sanitation and hygiene (Fan & Azad, n.d.). As of 2015, roughly 88 per cent of the country's total population had access to safely managed drinking water services (GIU, 2018).

Progress can also be seen in sanitation and hygiene (Figure 7.8). The open defecation level in Bangladesh declined from over 18 per cent in 2000 to nearly zero in 2015. The use of sanitation services has also increased over the years, but the overall condition remains below par, particularly among poor and marginal communities. In addition, rural and urban areas are likely to face a looming sanitation crisis due to the inability to properly dispose of the massive volume of untreated sludge (Sacosan-VII, 2018; WaterAid Bangladesh, n.d.).

Target 6.2 appears in the GIU-PMO draft priority targets list and the IGES list from the interlinkage perspective (see Table 7.3 and Figure 7.9). Figure 7.10 provides a visualised network image of how Target 6.2 is interconnected (influencing other targets and also being influenced by other targets) with targets under other goals in the case of Bangladesh. The network chart shows that sanitation and hygiene are connected to as many as 87 targets under all of the 17 goals.[7] Many links are observed with targets under Goal 1 (no poverty), Goal 3 (good health and well-being), Goal 4 (quality education), Goal 5 (gender inequality), Goal 6 (clean water and sanitation), Goal 9 (industry,

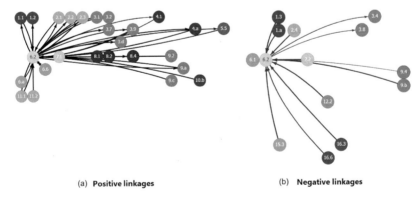

(a) **Positive linkages**   (b) **Negative linkages**

Source: Generated using the IGES SDG Interlinkages Analysis and Visualisation Tool (V4.0)

Figure 7.9   *Positive and negative linkages of Target 6.2*

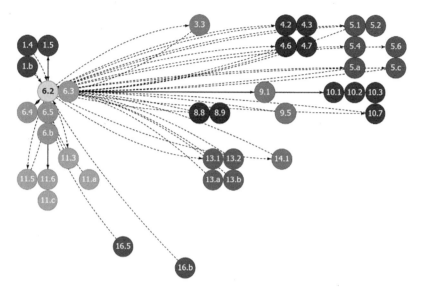

Source: Generated using the IGES SDG Interlinkages Analysis and Visualisation Tool (V4.0)

Figure 7.10   Linkages of Target 6.2 without available data

innovation and infrastructure), Goal 10 (reduced inequalities), Goal 11 (sustainable cities and communities) and Goal 17 (partnership for the goals). The results conform to an intuitive understanding of these issues. For example, sanitation and hygiene are expected to be linked with health and well-being and are reflected in the network chart with Target 6.2 having connections with 8 out of 13 targets under Goal 3. Notice, however, that not all links are positive; the presence of red lines between Target 6.2 and any other given target (for instance Target 3.8 on universal health coverage) indicates that these two target-pairs are mutually conflicting, meaning that progress towards achieving one target will create trade-offs for the other. It may appear counter-intuitive that a health target is negatively linked with sanitation and hygiene, but there could be many reasons behind such a tendency, and it is related to the country's context, particularly the allocation of resources and the state of progress in the concerned targets. For instance, depending on the availability of resources, efforts towards achieving Target 6.2 might require the reallocation of resources from Target 3.8 on universal health coverage, thereby causing the trade-off. The synergies and trade-offs as presented in the network chart may provide important insights for formulating policies and plans to leverage co-benefits from reinforcing targets and to take precautionary measures and minimise the trade-offs among the conflicting targets.

Focusing on how sanitation and hygiene can influence other areas, a shows that the progress made in Target 6.2 will have a positive effect on 17 out of the 87 linked SDG targets. Target 6.2's reinforcing effects will be felt across several SDGs: Goals 1, 2, 3, 4, 5, 6, 8, 9 and 11. On the other hand, this progress may negatively affect two targets under Goal 3 (Figure 7.9b). Target 6.2 also affects 26 other targets, but due to data unavailability, the nature (synergistic or conflicting) of the effect could not be identified (Figure 7.10). The missing data issue, which can cause bias, needs to be addressed to better understand the nature of Target 6.2's interlinkages and for monitoring progress in the related targets.

Some observations on the nature of the interlinkages of Target 6.2 and its impact on other goals and targets are discussed below.

- Target 6.2 on sanitation and hygiene has a strong influence on the targets under Goal 3 on good health and well-being. The analysis found that Target 6.2 influences 8 out of the 13 targets under the health goal.
- Improved sanitation and hygiene policies also reinforce poverty reduction and the fight against hunger and improving nutrition in Bangladesh. For instance, several targets under Goal 1 (no poverty) and Goal 2 (zero hunger) are positively impacted by progress in Target 6.2.
- The gender dimension of sanitation and hygiene is quite strong. All seven of the nine targets under Goal 5 (gender inequality) are positively or negatively affected by the progress made in Target 6.2 in Bangladesh.
- Sanitation and hygiene are closely linked with social inclusiveness and the development of sustainable cities and communities: several targets under Goal 10 (reduced inequalities) and Goal 11 (sustainable cities and communities) are affected by Target 6.2.

Formulating policies will not be effective unless well-coordinated institutional arrangements for SDG implementation are made. The Government of Bangladesh underscores that achieving the SDGs needs 'a strong and effective collaboration involving all stakeholders including public representatives, government bureaucracy, private sector, civil society, knowledge community, media, and development partners' (PMO-Bangladesh, 2017). The GED of the Bangladesh Planning Commission has conducted a mapping study to assign the lead, co-lead and associate ministries, agencies and divisions for each of the 169 SDG targets. Based on IGES SDG interlinkages analysis, some additional recommendations are made to enhance synergies and mitigate conflicts in the implementation of Target 6.2 (Table 7.5). The table first presents those institutions that are identified by both the GED and IGES, and then the rest are presented as GED mapping results and IGES recommendations. Institutions

Table 7.5   *Initial recommendations for institutional arrangements for SDG Target 6.2 in Bangladesh (sanitation and hygiene)*

Lead/co-lead	Associates	
Lead: Local government division	***Ministries and divisions that are identified by both GED and the authors***	
	Ministries: Education/Primary and Mass Education; Environment; Food; Health; Women and Children Other organisations: Statistics and information division	
	Additional recommendations provided by GED	***Additional recommendations by the authors***
	Ministries: Information Other organisations: Prime Minister's Office	Ministries: Agriculture; Commerce; Fisheries; Foreign Affairs; Health; Housing and Public Works; Industries; Labour; Land; Railways; Science and Technology; Social Welfare; Textile; Water Resources Divisions: Cabinet; Economic Relations; Finance, General Economics; ICT; Posts; Road Transport; Law and Justice; Legislative and Parliamentary Affairs; Programming

Source: Authors' analysis based on GIU (2018) and Zhou and Moinuddin (2017)

that have strong links with SDG Target 6.2, and those that have relatively weak links, are also duly categorised. Based on the results of the interlink-ages analysis, it is recommended to expand the list of institutions that need to be involved in the institutional framework for implementing Target 6.2 in Bangladesh. GED mapping is certainly commendable and timely, but to ensure an integrated approach, it may be necessary to consider other institutions that may be affected by the implementation of Target 6.2. For this, the ministries and divisions under the 'strong links' category will be of particular relevance, since their work will be significantly affected. For instance, the previous section of the chapter noted that Target 6.2 has a synergistic effect on reducing poverty (Goal 1) and combatting hunger (Goal 2). The lead minis-tries/divisions identified by GED for implementing the relevant targets under Goals 1 and 2 are the Cabinet Division and the Ministry of Agriculture. It is recommended to involve these two entities within the overall institutional framework as associates so that Target 6.2 can be implemented in a more coordinated, integrated manner. Such institutional coordination, together with an understanding of the interlinkages, will be critical in leveraging synergies and minimising trade-offs in implementing the SDGs.

Key insights from the Bangladesh case study include:

- The effective implementation of the SDGs with optimal resource use calls for prioritising the goals and targets and progressive stage-based planning. This prioritisation should be based on scientific evidence and with due consideration of the country situation, keeping in mind that the priorities should change over time to eventually consider the whole set of SDGs and the associated targets.
- In this context, the draft priority targets identified by the Governance Innovation Unit of the Prime Minister's Office of Bangladesh and the key targets recommended by IGES provide a basis for further fine-tuning the priority list in the first instance. Further analysis using the IGES SDG Interlinkages Tool in consultation with the concerned government authorities will help to fully link the two sets and develop a refined list of priority targets.
- Adopting an integrated approach in implementing the SDGs requires a solid understanding of the trade-offs and synergies associated with the goals/targets. Innovative instruments such as the IGES SDG Interlinkages Tool can help identify these interlinkages among the goals and targets.
- Inter-agency collaboration is needed for policy coherence and the integrated implementation of the SDGs. Bangladesh's mapping of relevant agencies could be further enhanced by taking into consideration the interlinkages of the goals and targets. This will help minimise conflicting policies across the targets and improve the overall integrated implementation by fostering synergies, synchronising the activities of various ministries and avoiding repetitive works by various agencies.
- The SDGs are indivisible and call for leaving no one behind and leaving no goals behind. The initial prioritisation, phased implementation and then regular review of progress should lead Bangladesh to reorient its SDG priorities periodically leading up to 2030. It is only through such phasing of priorities that Bangladesh can effectively adopt the crucial integrated approach, ensuring that no one is left behind.

7.5   CONCLUSION

The IGES SDG interlinkages analysis methodology follows four steps for the identification and quantification of the causal links between SDG targets. The qualitative analysis of the SDG interlinkages based on a literature review has recently been improved by using a systematic review supported by artificial intelligence-based natural language processing techniques. Expert survey and stakeholder consultation were applied to validate and localise the results in a couple of case studies at the sub-national levels. The IGES SDG Interlinkages Tool, by visualising quantified interlinkages in graphs, works as a policy support instrument to help explore potential synergies and trade-offs among the SDGs. This can help policy makers make informed plans and policies and set priorities based on key SDG targets that play strategic roles in the network of SDG interlinkages. The results of the interlinkages analysis and SDG prioritisation can be used to develop a coherent institutional arrangement for implementing the SDGs. Based on the causal relationships among the SDGs, the tool can help identify the drivers and impacts and explore systems solutions to maximise the synergies and mitigate the trade-offs.

The IGES Tool was selected as one of ten successful practices for exhibition at the 2020 High Level Political Forum (UNDESA, 2020) and was featured in UNESCAP's SDG Help Desk Toolboxes (UNESCAP, 2018). The tool was also applied to inform relevant policy making in several countries such as Indonesia (BAPPENAS, 2019), Bangladesh (Section 4.2) and Viet Nam (King et al., 2020). The use of the IGES SDG interlinkages analysis methodology at the national and local levels in these countries revealed several important points. There is great interest and merit in better understanding the SDG interlinkages. The 2030 Agenda is intended to be implemented in a holistic manner, but scientific knowledge about these interlinkages, including the nature and strength of such relations, is limited, making it difficult for policy makers to develop coherent, integrated policies. The IGES methodology can provide important insights and analysis in this regard. For example, the IGES Tool and the methodology were extensively consulted when Indonesia developed its National SDGs Roadmap (Ministry of National Development Planning of Republic of Indonesia, 2019a) and the 2021 VNR report (Ministry of National Development Planning of Republic of Indonesia, 2019b, 2021). The experience in Bangladesh and Viet Nam shows that the tool can be used as an instrument to provide evidence of and communicate knowledge on SDG interlinkages among various governmental agencies and ministries, which are otherwise more accustomed to working in silos. The case study at the sub-national level, that is, in the West Java province of Indonesia, highlights the importance of local context, challenges and priorities – which are often very different from the national level – in SDG implementation and the urgency of involving local stakeholders in policy processes.

With further improvement in the methodology for the identification and quantification of SDG interlinkages, together with strengthened stakeholder engagement, the SDG Interlinkages Tool has great potential to support practical policy making at national and sub-national levels. To promote further applications of the tool, the following suggestions for improvement can be used as a focus of future research:

- Improve the qualitative analysis of all targets based on a systematic review through an automated, transparent and replicable process supported by advanced natural language processing techniques.
- Fill the data gaps by using statistical data imputation methods.
- Enhance stakeholder engagement through improving the selection of stakeholders, questionnaire design and the facilitation of focused group discussions, and so on.
- Develop a user manual on tailoring the generic SDG interlinkages model and methodology to specific sectors or locations.
- Promote applications of the tool through collaborations with international organisations and governmental organisations at the national and sub-national levels.

NOTES

1. It is the time when indicator selection and data collection were conducted for the SDG interlinkage analysis.
2. This part is based on Moinuddin et al. (2021).
3. This part is based on Moinuddin and Zhou (2019).
4. Note that the mapping of the 38 targets GIU-PMO draft priority targets list with 33 official SDG targets was conducted by the authors.
5. Note that the Government of Bangladesh adopted a final list of 40 priority SDG indicators in December 2018. The official list includes 40 (39+1) priority indicators: 39 indicators from the 17 SDGs and 1 additional indicator addressing the specific needs of different districts/sub-districts (that is, it is different for different districts) (Government of the People's Republic of Bangladesh, 2020).
6. These different types of centrality metrics capture different aspects of the role of a given 'node' (a target in the case of SDG interlinkages) in a given interconnected network. Degree centrality, for example, reflects not only the number of connections that a target has, but also whether the target influences other targets or is influenced by others. Betweenness centrality, closeness centrality and eigenvector centrality take into consideration the extent of the position of a target in the path of other targets, the distance of one target from others and the significance of the neighbouring targets of a given target. For further information on these centrality measures, see chapter 5 in Zhou and Moinuddin (2017).
7. To learn more about the indicators and data used in the analysis, please visit the IGES SDG Interlinkages Tool.

REFERENCES

Allen, C., Metternicht, G., & Wiedmann, T. (2019). Prioritising SDG targets: Assessing baselines, gaps and interlinkages. *Sustainability Science*, 14(2), 421–438. https://doi.org/10.1007/s11625-018-0596-8

Baffoe, G., Zhou, X., Moinuddin, M., Somanje, A. N., Kuriyama, A., Mohan, G., Saito, O., & Takeuchi, K. (2021). Urban–rural linkages: Effective solutions for achieving sustainable development in Ghana from an SDG interlinkage perspective. *Sustainability Science 2021*, 16(4), 1341–1362. https://doi.org/10.1007/S11625-021-00929-8

BAPPENAS. (2019). *Voluntary National Reviews (VNR) 2019, Republic of Indonesia*. https://sdgs.un.org/sites/default/files/documents/23423INDONESIA_E_File_Final_VNR_2019_Indonesia.pdf

Dawes, J. H. P., Zhou, X., & Moinuddin, M. (2022). System-level consequences of synergies and trade-offs between SDGs: Quantitative analysis of interlinkage networks at country level. *Sustainability Science*, 1, 1–23. https://doi.org/10.1007/s11625-022-01109-y

Elder, M., Bengtsson, M., & Akenji, L. (2016). An optimistic analysis of the means of implementation for sustainable development goals: Thinking about goals as means. *Sustainability*, 8(9), 962. https://doi.org/10.3390/su8090962

European Commission. (2019). *KnowSDGs Platform – European Commission*.

Fan, Q., & Azad, M. A. K. (n.d.). *Towards a Cleaner Bangladesh: Safe Water, Sanitation, and Hygiene for all | End Poverty in South Asia*.

GED. (2012). *Perspective Plan of Bangladesh 2010–2021: Making Vision 2021 a Reality* (Issue April).

GED. (2015). 7th Five Year Plan FY2016 – FY2020: Accelerating Growth, Empowering Citizens. In *7th Five Year Plan FY2016 – FY2020 Accelerating Growth, Empowering Citizens; Part 2: Sector Development Strategies, Sector 5: Power and Energy*. Bangladesh Planning Commission.

GED. (2016a). *A Handbook Mapping of Ministries by Targets in the Implementation of SDGs Aligning with 7th Five Year Plan (2016–2020)* (Issue September).

GED. (2016b). *Integration of Sustainable Development Goals into the 7th Five Year Plan* (Issue February).

GED. (2017a). *Data Gap Analysis of Sustainable Development Goals (SDGs): Bangladesh Perspective*.

GED. (2017b). *SDG Tracker: Bangladesh's Development Mirror*.

GED. (2017c). *SDGs Financing Strategy: Bangladesh Perspective*.

GIU. (2018). *Shuchoker bhittitey Bangladesher SDG ogradhikar talika (SDG Priorities for Bangladesh by Indicators (in Bengali)*.

Government of the People's Republic of Bangladesh. (2020). *Bangladesh Voluntary National Reviews (VNRs) 2020: Accelerated Action and Transformative Pathways: Realizing the Decade of Action and Delivery for Sustainable Development* (Issue June).

IAEG-SDGs. (2019). *Tier Classification for Global SDG Indicators*. https://unstats.un.org/sdgs/iaeg-sdgs/tier-classification/

ICSU. (2017). *A Guide to SDG Interactions: From Science to Implementation*. International Council for Science. https://doi.org/10.24948/2017.01

King, P., Mao, C., Pham, N. B., Nguyen, L., Nguyen, A. T., Zhou, X., & Moinuddin, M. (2020). *Development of the National Action Plan on Sustainable Consumption and Production (2021–2030) in Vietnam: An Assessment of the Progress in 2016–2020 and Recommendations for 2021–2030*. https://www.switch-asia.eu/site/assets/files/2689/vietnam_scp_assessment_report_en.pdf

Le Blanc, D. (2015). Towards integration at last? The sustainable development goals as a network of targets. *Sustainable Development*, 23(3), 176–187. https://doi.org/10.1002/sd.1582

Millennium Institute. (2018). *iSDG Integrated Simulation Tool: Policy Coherence and Integration to Achieve the Sustainable Development Goals.*

Ministry of Industry and Trade. (2020). *National Action Plan on Sustainable Consumption and Production for the Period of 2021–2030 in Vietnam.* Ministry of Industry and Trade, The Socialist Republic of Vietnam. https://www.switch-asia.eu /site/assets/files/2533/national_action_plan_on_scp_vietnam_pdf_pdf.pdf

Ministry of National Development Planning of Republic of Indonesia. (2019a). *Roadmap of SDGS Indonesia: A Highlight.* https://www.unicef.org/indonesia/ reports/roadmap-sdgs-indonesia

Ministry of National Development Planning of Republic of Indonesia. (2019b). *Voluntary National Reviews (VNR): Empowering People and Ensuring Inclusiveness and Equality.* https://sustainabledevelopment.un.org/content/ documents/2380320190708_Final_VNR_2019_Indonesia_Rev3.pdf

Ministry of National Development Planning of Republic of Indonesia. (2021). *Indonesia's Voluntary National Review (VNR) 2021: Sustainable and Resilient Recovery from the COVID-19 Pandemic for the Achievement of the 2030 Agenda.* https://sustainabledevelopment.un.org/content/documents/2380320190708_Final _VNR_2019_Indonesia_Rev3.pdf

Miola, A., Borchardt, S., & Neher, F. (2019). *Interlinkages and Policy Coherence for the Sustainable Development Goals Implementation (JRC Technical Reports).* European Commission/ Joint Research Centre. https://doi.org/10.2760/472928

Moher, D., Liberati, A., Tetzlaff, J., & Altman, D. G. (2009). Preferred reporting items for systematic reviews and meta-analyses: The PRISMA statement. *BMJ (Online),* 339(7716), 332–336. https://doi.org/10.1136/bmj.b2535

Moinuddin, M., & Zhou, X. (2019). Integrated priority setting for SDGs planning and implementation: A practical case study on Bangladesh. In X. Zhou and M. Moinuddin (Eds.), *An Integrated Approach to Sustainable Development Through SDG Interlinkages.* Presentation made at the Thematic Trace Session on 'Practical Guidance for SDG Integration through Interlinkages Analysis and Visualisation' at the International Forum for Sustainable Asia and the Pacific, 19 July 2018, Pacifico Yokohama Conference Centre, Yokohama. Institute for Global Environmental Strategies (IGES). https://isap.iges.or.jp/2018/pdf/tt7/TT7_Mustafa_Moinuddin.pdf

Moinuddin, M., Zhou, X., Anna, Z., & Satriatna, B. (2021). *Integration of Climate Actions and SDGs at the Sub-National Scale: Results from Stakeholder Consultation in West Java.* https://www.iges.or.jp/en/publication_documents/pub/ discussionpaper/en/11837/West-Java_Integrating-climate-and-SDGs_Nov2021.pdf

Niestroy, I. (2016). *How Are We Getting Ready? The 2030 Agenda for Sustainable Development in the EU and its Member States: Analysis and Action So Far.* Discussion Paper 9/2016. Bonn: German Development Institute / Deutsches Institut für Entwicklungspolitik (DIE). https://www.idos-research.de/uploads/media/DP_9 .2016.pdf

Nilsson, M., Griggs, D., & Visback, M. (2016). Map the interactions between sustainable development Goa. *Nature.* https://doi.org/10.1038/534320a

PMO-Bangladesh. (2017). *SDG Tracker: Bangladesh's Development Mirror.* Bangladesh: Prime Minister's Office.

Sacosan-VII. (2018). *Bangladesh Country Paper Presented at the Seventh South Asian Conference on Sanitation* (Issue April).

UN Water. (2016). *Water and Sanitation Interlinkages Across the 2030 Agenda for Sustainable Development.* 48.

UNDESA. (2018). *Handbook for the Preparation of Voluntary National Reviews: The 2019 Edition* (Vol. 66).

UNDESA. (2020). *2020 High Level Political Forum Exhibitions.* https://sustainable development.un.org/hlpf/2020#exhibit

UNDG. (2015). *Mainstreaming the 2030 Agenda for Sustainable Development: Reference Guide to UN Country Teams* (Issue October).

UNESCAP. (2017). *Integrated Approaches for Sustainable Development Goals Planning: The Case of Goal 6 on Water and Sanitation.*

UNESCAP. (2018). *Toolboxes | SDG Help Desk.* https://sdghelpdesk.unescap.org/toolboxes?field_sdgs_target_id=All&title=&page=8

United Nations Statistics Division. (2019). *Global SDG Indicators Database.* https://unstats.un.org/sdgs/dataportal

UNSD. (n.d.). *Global SDG Indicators Data Platform.* https://unstats.un.org/sdgs/dataportal

WaterAid Bangladesh. (n.d.). *WaterAid Bangladesh and SDG 6.*

Weitz, N., Carlsen, H., Nilsson, M., & Skånberg, K. (2018). Towards systemic and contextual priority setting for implementing the 2030 agenda. *Sustainability Science*, 13(2), 531–548. https://doi.org/10.1007/s11625-017-0470-0

World Bank. (2019). *World Development Indicators.* https://datatopics.worldbank.org/world-development-indicators/

Zhou, X., Jain, K., Moinuddin, M., & McSharry, P. (2022). Using natural language processing for Automating the identification of climate action interlinkages within the sustainable development goals. *Proceedings of the AAAI 2022 FALL SYMPOSIA FS-22-07 The Role of AI in Responding to Climate Challenges*, 4.

Zhou, X., & Moinuddin, M. (2017). *Sustainable Development Goals Interlinkages and Network Analysis: A Practical Tool for SDG Integration and Policy Coherence.* Institute for Global Environmental Strategies (IGES). https://pub.iges.or.jp/pub/sustainable-development-goals-interlinkages

Zhou, X., & Moinuddin, M. (2021). Impacts and implications of the COVID-19 crisis and its recovery for achieving Sustainable Development Goals in Asia: A review from an SDG interlinkage perspective. In A. L. Ramanathan, C. Sabarathinam, M. P. Jonathan, M. V. Prasanna, P. Kumar, and F. Arriola (Eds.), *Environmental Resilience and Transformation in Times of COVID-19: Climate Change Effects on Environmental Functionality* (1st ed., pp. 273–288). Elsevier. https://www.elsevier.com/books/environmental-resilience-and-transformation-in-times-of-covid-19/ramanathan/978-0-323-85512-9

Zhou, X., & Moinuddin, M. , & Li, Y. (2017). *SDG Interlinkages and Data Visualisation Web Tool (V1.0).* Institute for Global Environmental Strategies (IGES). https://www.iges.or.jp/en/pub/sdg-interlinkages-and-data-visualisation-web/en

Zhou, X., Moinuddin, M., & Li, Y. (2018). *SDG Interlinkages Analysis & Visualisation Tool (V2.0).* Institute for Global Environmental Strategies (IGES). https://www.iges.or.jp/en/pub/sdg-interlinkages-analysis-visualisation-tool/en

Zhou, X., Moinuddin, M., & Li, Y. (2019). *SDG Interlinkages Analysis & Visualisation Tool (V3.0).* Institute for Global Environmental Strategies (IGES). https://www.iges.or.jp/en/pub/sdg-interlinkages-web-tool-v3/en

Zhou, X., Moinuddin, M., & Li, Y. (2021a). *Interactive SDG Tool for River Basins.* Institute for Global Environmental Strategies (IGES). https://sdginterlinkages.iges.jp/luanhe/SDGInterlinkagesAnalysis.html

Zhou, X., Moinuddin, M., & Li, Y. (2021b). *SDG Interlinkages Analysis & Visualisation Tool (V4.0).* Institute for Global Environmental Strategies (IGES). https://sdginterlinkages.iges.jp/visualisationtool.html

Zhou, X., Moinuddin, M., Renaud, F., Barrett, B., Xu, J., Liang, Q., Zhao, J., Xia, X., Bosher, L., Huang, S., & Hoey, T. (2022). Development of an SDG interlinkages analysis model at the river basin scale: A case study in the Luanhe River Basin, China. *Sustainability Science*, 1, 1–29. https://doi.org/https://doi.org/10.1007/s11625-021-01065-z

Zusman, E., & Amanuma, N. (Eds.). (2018). *Governance for Integrated Solutions to Sustainable Development and Climate Change: From Linking Issues to Aligning Interests*. Hayama: Institute for Global Environmental Strategies (IGES). https://www.iges.or.jp/en/pub/governance-integrated-solutions-sustainable/en

8. Measuring global interlinkages between SDGs applying linear dimensionality reduction tools

Jean-Pierre Cling and Clément Delecourt

8.1 INTRODUCTION

The Sustainable Development Goals are designed to be universally applicable to all countries. They provide guidelines for policy making and embody a blueprint for sustainable development adaptable enough to encompass all the major issues faced in the world (Long, 2015). The 2030 Agenda covers the three economic, social and environmental dimensions of sustainable development, to which a fourth dimension is added (governance and the rule of law). The width of this Agenda, combined with the strong heterogeneity of countries regarding their distances from the SDGs, raises the question of global interlinkages between SDGs: the fact that, when progressing towards one SDG, a country's progress towards others can be either positively or negatively influenced. Indeed, it is widely accepted that general progress towards the 2030 Agenda requires these interlinkage conditions be taken into account.

The objective of this chapter is to measure these global interlinkages between countries through an analysis of correlations between the SDGs and their associated indicators, complemented by country clustering, which allows us to check the consistency of our analysis. Given the highly political and empirical nature of the SDG process, this approach is suitable for measuring interlinkages between them, by putting them on an equal footing (Zhang et al., 2022). Indeed, correlation analysis has the advantage, in this context, of not requiring the introduction of prior hypotheses on the relationships between the SDGs and not estimating causalities between them, contrary to an econometric model that would univocally estimate the impact of one or several SDGs on the performance of another (Bali Swain & Wallentin, 2020).

In addition, and in line with this approach, we use non-parametric methods because they do not require the assumption of probability distributions on the data and unearth results on interlinkages at the global level derived from point clouds (distributions of countries over SDG indicators). To assess these inter-linkages, in this chapter we apply linear dimensionality reduction methods on cross-sectional data from the United Nations Global SDG Database, the official source which gathers data for the 231 indicators selected by the UN for monitoring SDGs across the 193 UN member countries. This is the first study at the global level conducted on this database.

The *first section* of this chapter lays out the two-step approach adopted by the authors to build a working dataset drawn from the UN Global SDG Database, which required using robust missing data imputation techniques after making an in-depth analysis of this database. The *second section* gives an overview of the main principles of the two dimensionality reduction tools employed, multiple factor analysis (MFA) and hierarchical cluster analysis (HCA), and of the methodological choices made to implement them. The *third section* presents the results of the MFA in terms of analysis of the variance of the dataset and interlinkages between SDGs (in particular the RV coefficients for each pair of SDGs). The *fourth section* describes the three consistent country clusters derived from the HCA.

8.2   A MAJOR STAKE: BUILDING A DATASET AT THE GLOBAL LEVEL FROM THE UN GLOBAL SDG DATABASE

As of 2020, the United Nations has endorsed a comprehensive list of 231 indicators (247 when counting duplicates) for monitoring the progress of countries towards the goals. One of the advantages derived from these indicators is that they allow for the quantitative analysis of correlations between them and they can be expanded in order to build and understand interlinkages between the 17 goals. To achieve this raises the question of data availability for the SDG numerous indicators.

The UN Global SDG Database, which is an official database of the United Nations, has been considered for the purpose of this study to represent the best source among the several international databases that exist on SDGs. In this regard, our work follows Bali Swain and Ranganathan (2021), the first to rely on this database for measuring interlinkages. This database is the broadest available and the official source used for the production of the annual SDG report of the United Nations (UN, 2022), as well as other SDG reports of UN Regional Commissions. Moreover, using the UN Global SDG Database has many advantages, bringing together data from multiple sources (official statistics produced by national statistical offices, by custodian agencies, computed from international models or surveys and so on) in a harmonised format that is theoretically ready-to-use, accompanied by detailed metadata that describe a supposedly common methodology (for an extensive evaluation of this database, see Dang & Serajuddin, 2020). After proceeding to an in-depth assessment of the profusion of data available in the UN Global SDG Database, a precise set of rules is defined for building a dataset that is then analysed.[1]

8.2.1   First Step: Keeping Widely Available Indicators Which Are Comparable between Countries

The strategy chosen for data selection in order to establish this dataset can be summed up by the following rules, stemming from a thorough examination of the UN Global SDG Database:

- Indicators which are not widely available (that is, classified in Tier II) are removed from the outset and only the 130 widely available indicators are kept (Tier I);[2]
- Only indicators that determinedly allow comparability between countries are selected (to that end, all indicators of SDG 14 "Life below water" are removed, as this SDG does not apply to landlocked countries). To adopt a standard Euclidean metric[3] when analysing the point cloud, qualitative and ordinal data series are also excluded. Twenty-seven additional indicators are therefore removed from the dataset;
- For the 103 remaining indicators, there are often not only many sub-indicators available in the database, but also sometimes they have several disaggregations (for indicator 4.1.1, 18 data series are available for instance). In order not to over-represent certain indicators over others, only one data series is selected per indicator, favouring ratios over absolute quantities and indicators as aggregated as possible and as filled as possible;
- Too few countries have comparable data over a common set of years, so this study is cross-sectional. Considering data from 2010 to 2020, for each data point, the most recent observation was kept. Observations for which the most recent data available dates from before 2010[4] are considered too old to be used and marked as missing.

Over the 19 879 resulting data points (for 103 indicators and 193 countries), 18 per cent are missing (3600). SDG 4 "Quality education" is the SDG for which indicators are the least well filled, missing on average for 72 countries. SDG 7 "Affordable and clean energy" is the best filled: only three countries lack data for two indicators, six for one indicator and all the others filling perfectly the four indicators of this SDG. Delving deeper, a link between this ranking of countries (fulfilment of SDGs' indicators) and development can be hypothesised.

Somewhat unexpectedly, there is an absence of correlation between the missing data rates[5] and the level of development as measured by GNI per capita (0 per cent). In fact, many countries with the highest missing data rates are middle-income micro-states. Countries with low missing data rates are much more diverse in terms of income levels (Ghana, which is a middle-income country, exhibits the most data, with all but three indicators filled). The way the UN Global SDG Database is built partly explains this absence of correlation: some indicators like malaria incidence measure phenomena that do not exist in developed countries and that are therefore not measured (because their value would be zero or almost zero), and those are marked as missing data for those countries. This illustrates the fact that fulfilling indicators for SDGs monitoring is not an issue only for least developed countries. This reinforces as well the fact that SDGs can and do apply to all countries. As a matter of fact, if these missing data percentages are taken as a proxy for indicator 17.18.1 of the SDGs (statistical capacity indicator for SDG monitoring, which is currently a Tier II indicator), then no country meets this target yet.

Applying the aforementioned rules set does not lead to an equally distributed selection of indicators throughout the SDGs. The various SDGs are covered very unequally in the dataset:

- First of all, there are gaps in the size of SDGs as measured by their number of indicators (for example, SDG 7 "Affordable and clean energy" is only monitored through 6 indicators, while 28 indicators are listed for monitoring SDG 3 "Good health and well-being");
- Second, SDGs present considerable discrepancies in terms of data coverage. For instance, while Tier II indicators represent 75 per cent of the indicators for SDG 13 "Climate action", SDG 7 has no Tier II but only Tier I indicators. While 75 per cent indicators of SDG 3 can be kept in the dataset, only one indicator is kept for SDG 13 (see Figure 8.1).

This explains why, despite the broad perspective of this study, not all aspects of SDGs can be appropriately included, and why the analysis is restricted to SDGs and related indicators, excluding the targets associated with SDGs.[6] The specificities of this monitoring dashboard must be acknowledged when applying dimensionality reduction techniques: otherwise, results would be artificially affected by SDGs that are profusely measured. To counter these imbalances, multiple factor analysis is a technique that accounts for the fact that indicators are not to be pitted against each other straightforwardly, but to be assigned each to one SDG, making up a collection of indicators, as defined by the statisticians of the UN Inter-Agency Expert Group (see Section 8.3).

8.2.2   Second Step: Selecting Countries and Indicators with Missing Data below a Fixed Threshold

Taking stock of this situation, overarching missing data (missing data deemed too prominent to be kept) is dealt with by eliminating altogether countries

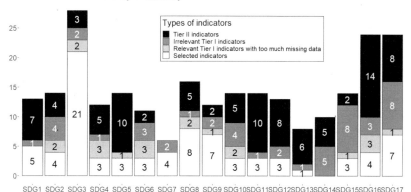

Number of indicators by availability

Source: United Nations SDG Indicators Global Database; authors' calculations

Figure 8.1   An unequal distribution of the SDG Indicators

whose missing data rate exceeds a threshold of 25 per cent, effectively removing 33 countries (out of 193).[7] This threshold is found empirically to optimise the trade-off between the number of countries and the range of missing data. Then, setting a threshold of 20 per cent for selecting indicators to keep amounts to the removal of 24 indicators; hence 79 indicators are kept (more than three-quarters of the 103 statistically relevant Tier I indicators). This more demanding threshold on indicators is yielded by the fact that indicators are removed after countries. After applying these two thresholds in turn, the maximum missing data rates in our dataset are pretty similar: they amount to 21.5 per cent for countries (Fiji) and to 22.5 per cent for indicators (number of researchers in the population).[8]

Apart from introducing new information on countries' SDGs monitoring capacity, this work on the availability of SDG indicators shows that there are few consequences as to whether missing data is handled starting from the countries' or from the indicators' perspective. By way of consequence, removing a handful of key countries and indicators is enough to significantly and coherently reduce the overall missing data rate (the percentage of empty cells in the dataset) to only 6 per cent. Once this processing is done, a correlation of –31 per cent is measured between the missing data rate of countries and their GNI per capita. This negative correlation evidences that high-income countries comply better with the requirements for monitoring SDGs than low-income ones, once outliers have been removed (that is, the 33 countries with the highest missing rate, most of which are small middle- or high-income countries with low statistical capacities because of their size): overall, national statistical systems perform better in rich than in poor countries, Africa, which includes mostly low-income countries, lagging behind in this respect (Bedecarrats et al., 2016).

The final step in building the dataset consists of imputing missing data. Indeed, the methods pertaining to multidimensional data analysis that are applied only work on files that are completely filled in. A one-size-fits-all mean substitution method is chosen to correct the remaining missing data. Mean substitution is favoured over hot-deck because it has the advantage of reducing the variance of indicators proportionally to their amount of missing data.[9] Incomplete indicators are artificially brought towards the centre of the point cloud and then have a limited risk of appearing as fake outliers when conducting multiple factor analysis. Such a guarantee, deemed necessary when applying variance analysis techniques, is not provided when applying hot deck. More precisely, to limit the impact of imputation on the reduction of variance of the point cloud, imputation was carried within the four classes of countries calculated by the World Bank from GNI per capita.[10] Indeed, within those classes, the missing data is more random than globally (see the correlation between missing data rate and GNI per capita mentioned above, after removing countries with the most missing data), which improves the imputation.

8.3   FACTOR AND CLUSTER ANALYSIS: HIGH-PERFORMANCE TOOLS FOR MEASURING GLOBAL INTERLINKAGES

This study is carried out by conducting nonparametric multidimensional analysis. This approach, using multiple factor analysis and hierarchical cluster analysis, is based on the idea that SDGs are comparable to collections of indicators: the dataset can be seen as 17 joined datasets.

Multiple factor and hierarchical cluster analyses are powerful tools for understanding relations between numerous variables without making assumptions beforehand on their relations. In this respect, they are highly appropriate for analysing interlinkages, in the framework of this chapter where interlinkages are considered to be akin to macro-correlations (as in correlations between datasets), expanded from the correlations between the variables that compose them. One of the principal advantages of these methods is that they require no assumptions on the data (like assuming normality for instance, as is the case in Gaussian mixture models) and little data processing. In fact, in practice, they only require the standardisation of the dataset, to allow the comparison of indicators regardless of their scale. In the context of SDGs, where available data is far from always being usable, as described above, limiting the tweaking of the data is undoubtedly desirable. These methods produce results solely from observing the data rather than from a priori models and are therefore convenient when tackling new and unknown relationships, such as interlinkages between SDGs.

Moreover, it is also useful to know if the results presented in our study depend on how the dataset has been constructed. In this context, cluster analysis can help confirm or infirm the robustness of the dataset, by comparing the clusters obtained on different datasets, for which missing data has been rectified in different ways. In addition, cluster analysis helps in finding similar countries in the world and measuring the discrepancies at play between interlinkages when considering homogeneous subsets of countries versus when considering all countries at once.

8.3.1 Multiple Factor Analysis and the Correlations between SDGs

Multiple factor analysis is a multivariate data analysis method that aims at reducing the dimensions of the whole dataset taking into account the expected relations within each group of indicators (that theoretically measure the same broad phenomena). It works by constructing ordered principal components, each including as much as possible of the initial variance of indicators, in decreasing order (Abdi et al., 2013; Escofier & Pagès, 1990). From this set of principal components, a sub-space is then designed onto which countries and indicators are symmetrically projected, to highlight key relations within the dataset (on both countries and indicators).

Among dimensionality reduction techniques, MFA has the advantage of accounting for indicators that are expected to measure the same broad phenomena and that are classified a priori. Thus, here, it weights indicators according to how they are correlated with other indicators of the SDGs they are attached to, so that results are not influenced by the very unequal number of indicators related to each SDG (that is, the contribution of one SDG to a factor is not overestimated and conversely the contribution of others is not underestimated for opposite reasons). For instance, SDG 3 is consequently underweighted as compared to the others. This is a prerequisite considering the high number of indicators selected in our dataset for this SDG (knowing that this SDG has the highest number of indicators of all SDGs) and also the way many of these indicators are calculated: they are not derived from national official statistics (which are mostly inexistent on this subject) but are the outputs of econometric modelling conducted by UN agencies at the global level. This increases the risk of spurious correlations between the indicators of SDG 3 and therefore overestimates its internal consistency (incidentally, SDG 3 has the highest Cronbach's alpha of all SDGs, at 0.93).[11]

Another specificity of MFA is that it enables the calculation of RV coefficients, which can be likened to generalised correlations between datasets (that is, between sets of indicators). By definition, RV coefficients vary between

0 and 1 (maximum correlation). They provide a measure of interlinkages between SDGs, going beyond relations between indicators. Those RV coefficients make for quantitative measures of interlinkages between SDGs (Zhang et al., op. cit.). In addition, MFA allows for a measurement of proximities between countries and of countries' scores on the factors uncovered.

A user's decision is required to select the number of factors kept for interpretation as a result of multiple factor analysis. Here, the Kaiser criterion (Kaiser, 1960) identifies 23 relevant factors (factors that carry more of the point cloud inertia than the average of 1 of the 79 indicators), and 12 factors are necessary to account for 70 per cent of the point cloud inertia. Those automatic strategies to find the accurate number of factors undoubtedly over-extract (the twelfth factor only accounts for a supplementary 2 per cent of the initial inertia). In reality, it seems clear there is a lot of noise in the dataset: many indicators measure similar phenomena for which countries behave in similar patterns, as evidenced by the fact that from the fourth factor onwards, the variance decreases by less than 1 per cent from one factor to the next one.

This hints that there are definitely interwoven indicators of which the variance is contributed by the first factors. In the meantime, the results of the criteria mentioned above highlight that other indicators interconnect deeply, even at smaller scales. This shows how paramount interlinkages are within the SDG model, even though a clear, defined subset of them especially prevails. Three factors are selected, accounting for 42 per cent of the initial inertia. This selection of the first three factors for the remainder of the study derives from the correlations of factors with GNI per capita, the traditional proxy for measuring development used in lieu of a better synthetic index in this study. Only the first three Pearson correlations[12] (respectively equalling +72 per cent, +24 per cent and –34 per cent) are statistically significant at the level of 1 per cent, according to Student's t-test.

8.3.2 Homogeneous Country Clusters Derived from Hierarchical Cluster Analysis

From this set of proximities, hierarchical cluster analysis then allows the building of homogeneous country clusters. The high value of the Hopkins statistics[13] for the dataset (0.77) proves that countries tend to form statistical clusters when it comes to sustainable development (Hopkins & Skellam, 1954) and that it is indeed advisable to look for clusters in the data.

Countries are projected onto the first three factors of the MFA and then clustered. There exist several clustering strategies: hierarchical clustering is chosen because, in line with the empirical approach of this study, it automatically decides the number of appropriate clusters, by maximising the relative loss of inertia, rather than leaving it to the user. Using HCA, four algorithms are computed: average linkage, single linkage, complete linkage and Ward linkage. All algorithms find three to be the optimal number of clusters into which to partition the countries, except for average linkage which breaks down the dataset into five clusters.[14] To strengthen the classifications found, algorithms are run 30 times to limit the risk of falling into local optima: this situation is likely not encountered, as all 30 classifications are exactly the same. The best classification is then chosen between the four algorithms, by maximising the between sum of squares (a measurement of the inertia between the classes).

Classifications are consolidated: as expected, they are found in all cases to be more robust when consolidated (consolidation is the computation of a k-means algorithm on an existing classification, to draw more decisively the frontiers of each group of the classification). Interestingly, single linkage, complete linkage and Ward linkage all systematically yield the same clustering scheme after consolidation (and even no matter whether the Forgy/ Lloyd, MacQueen or Hartigan-Wong methods (Morissette & Chartier, 2013) are applied for k-means). Therefore, there seems to be an almost natural way in which countries are grouped. The only peculiarity is the case of the average linkage algorithm.

This protocol for partitioning countries is carried out on two datasets: a dataset where indicators are imputed through their average within the four classes of countries defined by the World Bank, and a dataset imputed through a direct average substitution, computed from what is observed on all countries for which there is data. Results are fully consistent from one dataset to another (all algorithms find three clusters save for average linkage, consolidation systematically increases the results and so on), the only difference lying in the values of the criteria for selecting the best classifications. In this regard, the criterion is found to be always higher (admittedly, by 0.02) when correcting missing data through imputation within classes rather than directly, further underlining the appropriateness of the missing data imputation technique selected and the advantage of limiting the reduction of variance when imputing. Simultaneously, classifications never stray far from each other: the Adjusted Rand Index[15] (Rand, 1971) on the best classifications from these two sets is equal to 0.92, indicating that most countries are classified in the same manner anyway. This also shows the reassuring imperviousness of the dataset to different decisions (in selecting data, in handling missing data and so on): overall, within the framework of dimensionality reduction, no matter how bountiful, the UN Global SDG Database is very stable as regards the results extracted from it. This reinforces the significance of the following results, because it means they cannot be attributed to how data is processed and as a consequence are rather evidence of real trends.

Consequently, multidimensional methods for data analysis are definitely methodologically appropriate for analysing SDGs at the global level and more precisely their interlinkages. Those methods can evaluate the shortcomings in the coverage of the UN Global SDG Database as well as the influence of corrections on the consistency of the results. Their empirical nature is recommendable because there is no leeway for data processing to influence the results. Subsequently, the results are relevant and lay bare a lot about statistically existing interlinkages.

8.4   STRONG INTERLINKAGES BETWEEN SDGS AT THE GLOBAL LEVEL

Multiple factor analysis shows the three main factors contributing to the variance of the dataset (and the corresponding SDGs and indicators), as well as the correlations and proximities between SDGs (especially by measuring RV coefficients). Without aiming at clustering SDGs into completely separate categories (for a description of such attempts, see for instance Tremblay et al. (2017)), this approach aims to understand the characteristics of the data, at the level of indicators, and their implications for relations between SDGs, seen as collections of indicators.

8.4.1   Human Development Is the Dimension Contributing the Most to the Variance of the Dataset

The first four SDGs are among the main contributors to the *first factor axis of the MFA*. These SDGs have in common that they relate to the three main dimensions that the United Nations Development Programme (UNDP) recognises as part of human development (UNDP, 1994): healthy life (SDG 2 "Zero hunger"[16] and SDG 3 "Good health and well-being"), knowledge (SDG 4 "Quality education") and a decent standard of living (indicators of SDG 1 "No poverty" can be considered as measuring that). This factor, which explains 30 per cent of the variance, is also strongly correlated with GNI per capita as mentioned in Section 8.2. According to Dawes et al. (2022), these SDGs (and especially the first three) are the most likely to be achieved. SDG 3 especially plays a determinant role in building this factor (in spite of the fact that the MFA technique actively underweights its contribution). This confirms that health is an essential component of human development, in agreement with the works of Deaton (2013).

Two other SDGs contribute to a lesser extent to this factor: SDG 8 "Decent work and economic growth" and SDG 17 "Partnerships for the goals". These two SDGs are the most correlated with the GNI per capita, both at +78 per cent, while SDGs on average are correlated at +55 per cent with GNI per capita. This high correlation for SDG 8 is due to the fact that four of its eight indicators kept in the dataset have correlations above 50 per cent in total with GNI per capita: "proportion of youth not in education, employment or training", "proportion of children engaged in economic activity", "number of ATMs per 100,000 adults" and "proportion of adults with an account at a bank or financial institution or with a mobile-money-service provider". In the case of SDG 17, its contribution is mostly due to indicators related to access to science and information (the indicator "fixed Internet broadband subscriptions per 100 inhabitants" standing out for instance), which is closely related to the economic development of a country.

Four different SDGs, all related to the environment, are among the main contributors to the *second factor axis*, which explains 7 per cent of the total variance. These are SDG 7 "Affordable and clean energy", SDG 9 "Industry, innovation and infrastructure", SDG 11 "Sustainable cities and communities" and SDG 15 "Life on land". Among these, SDG 15 is the best contributor to this factor, reflecting the central position of biodiversity protection within the environmental issues tackled by the 2030 Agenda. SDG 5 "Gender equality" and SDG 10 "Reduced inequalities" also contribute to this second factor. A parabolic pattern appears when projecting countries on the plane made of the first two factors (Figure 8.2). Indeed, the poorest and richest countries of the dataset have good performances for these SDGs, especially as regards their energy schemes: for example, as they are not oil producers and do not have heavy industries, they do not emit much CO_2 per unit of GDP, and they also have a high renewable energy share in their total final energy consumption. At the other end of the development spectrum, high-income countries have a high demand for environmental quality, while in-between, developing countries with intermediate levels of income pollute the most, especially those that are oil producers. Apart from SDG 7 and SDG 15, the second factor appears to be made up of key indicators which have an outstanding weight within their respective SDGs: especially "CO_2 emissions per unit of GDP" for SDG 9 and "Annual mean levels of fine particulates" for SDG 11. Those indicators show that within the monitoring dashboard of SDGs, environmental information is not concentrated within dedicated SDGs as is the case for human development (as seen on the first factor) but is rather scattered across broad SDGs.

The distribution of countries on the plane made up of the first two factors is reminiscent of the environmental Kuznets curve (Grossman & Krueger, 1993).[17] Indeed, the environmental Kuznets curve theorises that countries that have rather low or high development do not greatly degrade their environment, while countries with middle levels of development degrade it more. Nevertheless, there are two caveats to keep in mind about the interpretation of the U-shaped curve observed. First, a high observed share of renewable energy in final energy consumption can be ambiguous in the case of poorer countries, as it comes from their mostly using wood for cooking and heating, which causes deforestation and causes countries to move away from

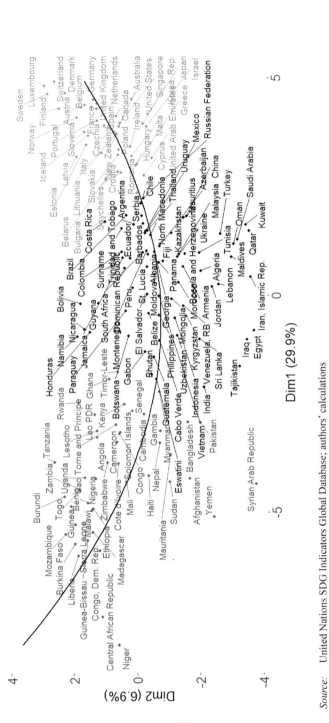

Source: United Nations SDG Indicators Global Database; authors' calculations

Figure 8.2   Countries' representation on the first plane of the MFA

biodiversity targets. Second, the curve does not mean there is a mandatory trade-off for poor countries between increasing national income and protecting the environment. Observing the situation as of today for countries is not equal to measuring the extent of perennial interlinkages towards realising the 2030 Agenda (Cling & Delecourt, 2022).

SDG 5 "Gender equality", SDG 15 "Life on land" and SDG 16 "Peace, justice and strong institutions" contribute the most to the *third factor axis*, which explains 5 per cent of the total variance. SDG 16 is a composite goal that includes in the notion of sustainable development the topics of the rule of law, of institutions and more broadly of governance and especially represents the added fourth dimension of governance in sustainable development. These three SDGs have in common that they are all related in one way or another to the quality of government policies and, to summarise, to the quality of their governance. The inclusion of this dimension makes sense, as data indicates that it indeed makes up a third group of SDGs distinct from those found in the first two factors. Looking at indicators belonging to those SDGs at a detailed level, significant correlations (but not causality!) are found: countries with strong gender inequalities are also violent countries with high homicide rates. Conversely, countries with low gender inequalities have generally very low homicide rates.

8.4.2 Strong Synergies and No Trade-Offs between SDGs

When looking at the RV coefficients, a clearly defined set of SDGs registers strong correlations between themselves, never sharing RV coefficients lower than 0.5 (Figure 8.2). These are exactly the six SDGs that stand out on the first factor of the MFA: SDG 1 "No poverty", SDG 2 "Zero hunger", SDG 3 "Good health and well-being" and SDG 4 "Quality education", as well as SDG 8 "Decent work and economic growth" and SDG 17 "Partnerships for the goals", plus rather unexpectedly an additional one – SDG 7 "Affordable and clean energy". Kroll et al. (2019) find similar synergies between these SDGs (except for SDG 7). Their correlations with the first factor range from +84% to +95 per cent. Together, this group of SDGs has the particularity of being the best measured SDGs (they are all in the top 10 SDGs with the most indicators included in the analysis, amounting to 49 indicators, that is, two-thirds of the total), and their strong intertwining with human development calls for structural policies for human development, as supported by Pritchett (2020). Finally, the particular case of SDG 7 shows that energy matters for human development, the question of access to electricity and its indicator ("proportion of population with access to electricity") being at the heart of these interlinkages. There is also a strong RV coefficient (0.5) between SDG 5 "Gender equality" and SDG 16 "Peace, justice and strong institutions", which especially reflects a correlation at the global level between gender inequalities and the incidence of crime.

Strikingly enough, SDGs related to the environment (such as SDG 15 "Life on land") are not correlated with each other or with other SDGs (even SDG 7 already mentioned). They do represent a different set of SDGs, notably distinct from the ones related to human development contributing the most to axis 1. The relationships within the environmental dimension that appear on the second factor are not mirrored in the RV coefficients. For SDG 6, SDGs 9 to 12 and SDG 15, only low correlations are identified through the RV coefficients,[18] as though each of these SDGs is uncorrelated to others and policies to achieve them have limited influence on other SDGs. This is mainly a matter of internal consistency. These SDGs are evidently more transversal, and each of them measures completely different phenomena, including the environment (as stated above, environmental measures are peppered throughout the SDGs and remarkably are not as concentrated as is the case for the measures of the components of human development, within the SDGs).

The fact that these SDGs are less coherent than the SDGs related to human development is for instance illustrated with SDG 6 "Clean water and sanitation": its indicator on "Water Use Efficiency" is the fourth most contributing to the third factor (highlighting water management as a definite component of governance), while its indicator on "Open defecation" is the third most contributing to the first factor (this practice being widely acknowledged as one of the main obstacles to human development). The case of SDG 10 "Reduced inequalities" is also worth noting for different reasons: unlike SDG 6, it does not seem to be at the crossroads of the different dimensions of sustainable development, but rather intrinsically oddly built. Indeed, SDG 10 incorporates the same SDG issues pertaining to inequalities both within a country and among countries. Those two kinds of inequalities appear to be very different and almost irreconcilable, in that no common patterns are found on those two sub-dimensions of inequalities among countries. The low value of Cronbach's alpha for this SDG (0.10, the lowest of all SDGs) confirms that it stands out from other SDGs in this respect.

As RV coefficients are by definition always positive, they do not give any information on synergies or trade-offs between SDGs. To measure these, we project SDGs on the first two factors of the MFA (Figure 8.4). All SDGs are located on the top right quadrant.[19] Rather than being antagonistic, this confirms that SDGs within one of the three categories identified really co-benefit from each other. All in all, these findings suggest that SDGs either reinforce each other (within a category) or do not influence one another (between categories) but do not compete. Looking at indicators instead of at SDGs, and projecting them on the correlation circle of the MFA, Cling and Delecourt (op. cit.) draw the same conclusions on the prevalence of synergies. In the case of the environment, there is an apparent contradiction: on the one hand,

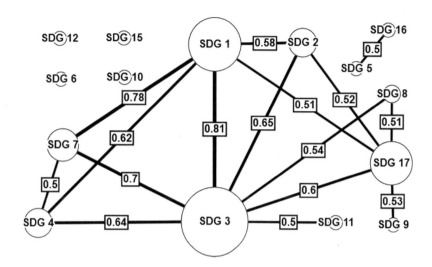

Note: The more interlinkages an SDG has, the bigger its representation is
Source: United Nations SDG Indicators Global Database; authors' calculations

Figure 8.3   *RV coefficients above 0.50*

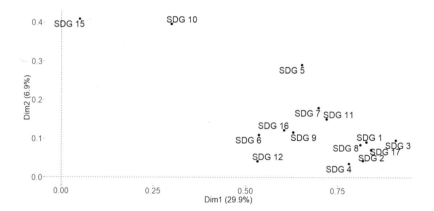

Note: The further from the origin an SDG is projected on this plane, the stronger its contribution to this axis. The closer two SDGs are, the likelier they measure the same phenomenon

Source: United Nations SDG Indicators Global Database; authors' calculations

Figure 8.4   *Projection of SDGs on the first two axes*

SDGs covering this dimension are not correlated with each other as mentioned before; on the other hand, several of these SDGs contribute to factor axis 2 which is a sort of "environmental" factor (and simultaneously to factor axis 1). This contradiction derives mostly from the fact that indicators monitoring the environment are spread along several SDGs which do not exclusively cover this dimension.

8.5   PARTITIONING COUNTRIES INTO THREE CLUSTERS: DIFFERENT LEVELS OF DEVELOPMENT, SAME INTERLINKAGES AT PLAY

Partitioning the countries highlights distinctive groups, within which countries are relatively homogeneous (that is, they share a similar level of sustainable development). Remarkably, the three country clusters deriving from the hierarchical cluster analysis – that are called "poor", "intermediate" and "rich" countries in this section – correspond roughly to the World Bank classification of low-income, middle-income and high-income countries (the Rand Index between this partition and the classification of the World Bank equals 0.76). This validates that the GNI per capita-induced classification of the World Bank is actually a classification of sustainable development.

8.5.1   Three Clusters of Countries Depending Mainly on Their Level of Economic Development

Calculating the v-test values within each country cluster[20] allows for a more in-depth analysis of the consistency of these three clusters. As this clustering is based on the first three factors of the MFA, it is expected that the three clusters will have distinctive performances along the different dimensions of sustainable development of the MFA. Indeed, poor countries stand out especially because of their low score on human development. Intermediate countries have a higher level of human development but have in common low scores for environment and mid-rankings on governance. The remainder, that is, rich countries, significantly fare well on all three factors. More specifically, this means that sustainable development cannot be reduced exclusively to its economic and social component, and the two other components (environment and governance) play distinctive roles as well. In this spirit, Guerini et al. (2022) study the limitations of GNI per capita in capturing well-being in all its components, in a dimensionality reduction framework.

To illustrate the specificities of these three clusters as regards these three dimensions, a selection of indicators, which differentiate the three clusters especially well according to their v-tests, is presented in Table 8.1.

Table 8.1 *Simple averages of outstanding indicators for differentiating the three clusters*

SDGs	Indicators	"Poor" countries	"Intermediate" countries	"Rich" countries	World
SDG 1: No poverty	Proportion of the population living below the international poverty line (%)	37.6	3.6	0.5	12.6
	Proportion of population above statutory pensionable age receiving pensions (%)	19.7	66.2	94.1	60.1
SDG 2: Zero hunger	Prevalence of children moderately or severely stunted (%)	32.2	13.7	1.2	15.7
SDG 3: Good health and well-being	Under-5 mortality rate (per 1000 live births)	61.9	17.1	4.1	26.6
	Proportion of women of reproductive age who have their need for family planning satisfied with modern methods (%)	49.6	64.9	97.4	69
	Universal Health Coverage Index	45.1	69.4	79.9	65.2
SDG 4: Quality education	Completion rate at the end of lower secondary (%)	37.8	81	97.6	72.9
SDG 5: Gender equality	Proportion of women aged 20–24 years who were married or in a union before 18 (%)	33	15.5	0.5	16.6
	Proportion of women in managerial positions (%)	26.8	32.3	32.9	30.1
SDG 6: Clean water and sanitation	Water use efficiency (USD per cubic meter)	15.6	18.7	124.5	45.6

(Continued)

179

Table 8.1 (Continued)

SDGs	Indicators	"Poor" countries	"Intermediate" countries	"Rich" countries	World
SDG 7: Affordable and clean energy	Proportion of population with access to electricity (%)	50.8	96.6	100	84.4
	Proportion of population with primary reliance on clean fuels and technology (%)	16.8	82.3	98.7	67.8
	Renewable energy share in the total final energy consumption (%)	62	21.9	20.1	32.9
SDG 8: Decent work and economic growth	Proportion of adults with an account at a bank or financial institution or with a mobile-money-service provider (%)	34.3	57.1	92.1	59.7
SDG 9: Industry, innovation and infrastructure	CO_2 emissions per unit of GDP (kg per PPP USD of GDP)	0.2	0.3	0.2	0.2
	Researchers (in full-time equivalent) (per million inhabitants)	145.1	760.2	4182.6	1482
SDG 10: Reduced inequalities	Labour share of GDP (%)	44.4	45.6	54.3	47.5
SDG 11: Sustainable cities and communities	Proportion of urban population living in slums (%)	54.1	23.4	2.3	26.7
SDG 12: Responsible consumption and production	Annual mean levels of fine particulate matter (µg per cubic meter)	35.1	26.6	13.2	25.5

SDG 15: Life on land	Average proportion of Terrestrial Key Biodiversity Areas covered by protected areas (%)	43.7	32.6	68.2	45.1
SDG 16: Peace, justice and strong institutions	Homicide rate (per 100 000 individuals)	6.4	9.7	1.6	6.6
SDG 17: Partnerships for the goals	Total government revenue as a proportion of GDP (%)	19.9	27.4	40.4	28.7
	Fixed Internet broadband subscriptions (per 100 inhabitants)	0.7	10.9	33.8	14
GNI per capita (USD)		1247	8170	39 264	14 342

Source: United Nations SDG Indicators Global Database, World Bank national accounts data; authors' calculations

8.5.2   Interlinkages within SDGs Bring to Light Three Types of Countries

An in-depth examination of these three clusters highlights their specificities concerning interlinkages between SDGs.

The *first cluster*, of 46 countries, is made up of all of the countries classified as low-income countries by the World Bank (except for Tajikistan), as well as a handful of lower-middle-income countries (mainly from South-East Asia and sub-Saharan Africa). These countries have in common the characteristics of low-income countries: high poverty rates (more than 50 per cent in many of them), child stunting and child mortality, very low school completion rates at the end of lower secondary (lower than 10 per cent in some African countries), low access to electricity and the internet, a majority of urban people living in slums and so on. These countries illustrate the cumulative aspect of development: indicators measuring economic and social development are all well correlated. Remarkably, these indicators, that explain for the most part the situation of these "poor" countries within the reduced space of the factor analysis, all belong to components of human development as defined by the UNDP and are all well inter-correlated.

As regards the two other components of sustainable development, results are more nuanced. As far as the environment is concerned, "poor" countries fare better than "intermediate" countries on the whole, but their relative performance depends on the indicators. On the one hand, these countries appear to rely heavily on renewable energies (62 per cent of their total final energy consumption being due to renewable energies), to emit low amounts of CO_2 emissions per unit of GDP and to have a high proportion of protected areas. On the other hand, their level of annual mean levels of fine particulate matter is much higher than anywhere else in the world and they rely little on clean fuels (17 per cent of their population rely primarily on them), which is the counterpart of their reliance on wood for cooking (a source of deforestation as mentioned before). As regards social inequalities, no distinctive pattern is discernible which is not the case for gender inequalities: child marriage is rife in this first cluster (33 per cent), and other gender inequalities (such as the proportion of women in managerial positions) are higher on average, highlighting the existence of a gender–environment nexus (OECD, 2021).

The *second cluster*, the widest one (72 countries), brings together all but two upper-middle-income countries (Belarus and Bulgaria) and all remaining lower-middle-income countries; it also includes one low-income country (Tajikistan) and a small number of high-income countries (mostly small islands and Gulf countries). In short, practically, it merges more or less the two lower- and upper-middle-income groups identified by the World Bank. These countries have a higher level of human development on average but with a high heterogeneity within the group. These countries inspire many discussions on the trade-off between growth and environment for developing countries (see ODI, 2017, which imagines a fictional developing country). Many of the indicators contributing greatly to factor 1 are for these countries close to the global average: the number of fixed Internet broadband subscriptions per 100 inhabitants for instance. These countries for these reasons are "intermediate" between the "poor" and the "rich", hence the name of the cluster they belong to. Depending on the two other dimensions measured, these countries can sway closer to or farther from one of the other two clusters. For instance, when it comes to gender inequalities as measured by the proportion of women in managerial positions, these countries are very close to the rich countries. When it comes to the homicide rate however, these countries are closer to the "poor" countries. Their homicide rate (especially in Latin America and South Africa) is much higher than the world average. As for the environment dimension, the countries of this category, especially oil producers, register among the worst performers of the word: some of the Arab emirates report 0 per cent reliance on renewable energies.

The *third cluster* consists of 42 mostly high-income countries (except for those in the second cluster) plus Belarus and Bulgaria. Overall, these countries perform very well on all SDGs and their three main dimensions as shown by our analysis: they are the most advanced in terms of human development and environment protection; they are also democracies with relatively low inequalities on the whole. Human development is on track as attested by the share of adults with a bank account (close to 100 per cent). Extreme poverty virtually does not exist; access to birth control is universal (97 per cent on average against 69 per cent in the whole world), child stunting is hardly an issue (1 per cent against 16 per cent), as well as social protection (31 countries of this cluster report a 100 per cent share of the population above statutory pensionable age receiving a pension). Policies are pursued to safeguard the environment, resulting in a high degree of protection of the Terrestrial Key Biodiversity Areas and moderately low CO_2 emissions (0.20 kg per unit of GDP on average, close to the level of "poor" countries and much lower than "intermediate" countries). Indicators related to governance are also much better than in the two other clusters. The government domestic capacity, as measured by the total government revenue in GDP, makes up a high percentage of GDP. Water use efficiency, which measures the value added of a cubic meter of water, is significantly higher than in the other two categories and the number of researchers (in full-time equivalent) per million inhabitants is very high as well. All of these facts evidence the soundness of those countries' governance and highlight the cumulative aspect of all three factors for most developed countries.

To sum it up, the qualitative analysis conducted in this section underlines that similar patterns are observed overall concerning the interlinkages between SDGs in each of the clusters resulting from the HCA. The sub-components of human development in its broad sense especially appear to reinforce each other, with mediocre performances in "poor" countries for most indicators, excellent performances in "rich" countries and in-between for the "intermediate" countries. The same applies concerning the environment, although interlinkages appear to be more tenuous. For governance issues, relations seem to be more country-specific. Cling and Delecourt (op. cit.) also draw this general conclusion when applying MFA to each homogeneous cluster of countries. Indeed, they observe that each MFA as well as that carried out on all countries have similar first components, with approximately the same SDGs and indicators contributing to them in each case.

8.6   CONCLUSION

The multiple factor analysis conducted in this chapter identifies three key dimensions in the data as regards sustainable development: human development, the environment and governance. We also observe the existence of an environmental Kuznets curve linking the first two of these dimensions. Human development is found to be the main driver in explaining the countries' variance and to be highly correlated with GNI per capita. This strong contribution of human development is partly due to the fact that this dimension of sustainable development is better covered than others in the SDGs (conversely, only SDG 16 "Peace, justice and strong institutions" tackles governance strictly speaking, despite it being one of the three empirical dimensions of sustainable development uncovered in this study). Three homogeneous country clusters are derived from the hierarchical cluster analysis, with a strong gradient in terms of GNI per capita. The aim of the SDGs was to take a holistic approach to development beyond the measurement of GDP, which is often misused as a summary indicator of development and well-being (Stiglitz et al., 2009). These results suggest, however, that the differences between countries on the SDG indicators stem largely from their level of development, as measured by their income per capita.

Policies attached to certain SDGs are surely not expected to affect other SDGs in the same way in all countries in which they are pursued. For instance, Miola et al. (2019) demonstrate how the rippling effects of development policies across SDGs depend on the political context. However, although the countries' performance is very different along the three dimensions of sustainable development highlighted above, the multiple factor analysis finds broadly the same types of interlinkages both globally and within each country cluster. This study confirms that there exist strong positive interlinkages at play between SDGs, when looking at the global level or within each country cluster, without any negative interlinkages. The RV coefficients derived from the multiple factor analysis especially show strong correlations between SDGs related to human development, as well as with the last SDG, which measures the capacity and efforts of countries to get closer to the goals. SDGs related to the environment are of a different nature: they are not correlated to each other or to other SDGs. This illustrates their transversality, as each of these SDGs measures different phenomena and consequently seems unlinked to the others.

The possibilities with this family of extremely powerful tools have not been exhausted with this study. In particular, potential prolongations could focus on confirmatory factor analysis (following Spaiser et al., 2016), to assess the reliability and unidimensionality of SDGs: how indicators within an SDG measure a common phenomenon and how this phenomenon is accurately measured by its indicators. The results would undoubtedly open up avenues for improvement in the measure of sustainable development. In stating this, the issue of the availability of data comes up again in full force: there is no use for sophisticated models without good data.

This study has demonstrated the usefulness of the UN Global SDG Database for improving our understanding of the consistency of SDGs and their interactions. However, data is still lacking on many dimensions of sustainable development, especially on SDGs covering new domains such as the environment and governance. Because of these shortcomings, there is actually a trade-off between conducting cross-section analysis and time series analysis on indicators of the database. This study has chosen the former option, but fully comprehending interlinkages must take into account variations over time. Knowing that, it would be very useful in the future to repeat the cross-section analysis conducted in this chapter. Data is unfortunately insufficient for now to reconcile both options. One can hope that some progress will be made before the deadline of Agenda 2030 and that increased data availability will help to keep improving knowledge on interlinkages at the global level.

NOTES

1. In this chapter, the dataset designed by Cling and Delecourt (2022) is used, following the approach described in this section.
2. SDGs indicators are distributed into two categories, Tier I and Tier II. According to the United Nations, data for Tier I indicators needs to be regularly produced by countries for at least 50 per cent of countries and of the population in every region where the indicator is relevant.
3. The Euclidean distance was favoured because it gives the same importance to all dimensions, a preferable property in this case of interest.

4. The threshold of 2010 represents an empirical break, as most available data is for recent years in the database: the missing data rate steadily diminishes when the window is expanded until 2010. Opening it further does not significantly raise the missing data rate any more.

5. The percentage of SDG indicators for which countries did not report data since 2010 can be taken as a rough measure of the statistical capacity of each country for SDG monitoring.

6. Analysing all 169 targets raises many issues. For instance, some targets do not have monitoring indicators at all (as of 2022, there is no Tier I indicator for the target of SDG 2 that aims at doubling the agricultural productivity of small-scale food producers by 2030), while some others have not enough recent data (the most filled indicator for the target of SDG 4 related to upgrading education facilities, which measures the proportion of schools with access to electricity, is filled only for 40 per cent of countries over the period considered).

7. Countries with very low data availability for monitoring SDGs are the four European microstates (Andorra, Liechtenstein, Monaco and San Marino), 17 of the 38 small island developing states (Antigua and Barbuda, Bahamas, Comoros, Dominica, Grenada, Kiribati, Marshall Islands, Micronesia, Nauru, Palau, Papua New Guinea, Saint Kitts and Nevis, Saint Vincent and the Grenadines, Samoa, Tonga, Tuvalu and Vanuatu) and 11 countries whose statistical systems are fragile for various reasons, war for example (Bahrain, Brunei, Chad, Cuba, Djibouti, Equatorial Guinea, Eritrea, Libya, North Korea, Somalia, South Sudan and Turkmenistan).

8. The missing data rate for indicators rises to 22.5 per cent because cells in the dataset for which the most recent value available dates prior to 2010 are erased. This is to ensure results correspond to a definite and consistent time window, that is, the 2010s.

9. Stochastic regression is not considered because of its inherent risk of introducing implausible values (a ratio over one for instance). No auxiliary information is considered satisfactory for all 49 indicators with missing data, so to avoid building so many models (which enhances the risk of mistakes and may introduce spurious relations in the dataset), deterministic regression and nearest-neighbour methods are not considered either.

10. The World Bank breaks down the world into four classes of countries as follows (as of July 1, 2020): high income (GNI per capita > 12 536 USD), upper-middle income (4 046 US < GNI per capita < 12 535 USD), lower-middle income (1 036 USD < GNI per capita < 4 045 USD) and low income (GNI per capita < 1 035 USD). GNI per capita is measured in current dollars according to the Atlas method.

11. The issue of internal consistency can be measured with Cronbach's alpha (Cronbach, 1951): ranging from 0 to 1, the higher its value the better the internal consistency.

12. Attention is paid to linear measures of correlations for consistency purposes, factors being themselves linear combinations of the initial variables of the dataset.

13. The Hopkins statistic, ranging from 0 to 1, measures the tendency to form clusters of a dataset: the closer to 1 it is, the more likely it is to form clusters. Close to 0, it indicates data is distributed according to a uniform process. A random dataset typically scores around 0.5 for this statistic.

14. In the case of the average linkage algorithm, clusters uncovered are found to be more homogeneous: with average linkage, countries are more centred around

their centroid. In spite of that, these results are rejected because this algorithm is deemed to have less reliable theoretical grounds, as well as because a partition into three clusters as opposed to five clusters is considered to allow for easier interpretation (see Section 8.3).

15. The Adjusted Rand Index, ranging from 0 to 1 (identical classifications), measures how similar two classifications are. It works even when they have a different number of clusters.

16. In this respect, it is interesting to note the duality of SDG 2, which deals with both agriculture and health, its health components taking precedence over its agriculture components here.

17. Relationships between indicators of human development and of inequalities (social and gender-based) are too thin to compare this curve to a strict Kuznets curve, in the sense of its inventor (Kuznets, 1955).

18. That is, the RV coefficient is significantly inferior to the middle threshold of 0.5, set in Figure 8.3.

19. It is also the case when looking at the relations between the third and the two first factors.

20. The v-test is a generalised measure of how far from the mean of the point cloud the countries of one cluster are, identifying what determines why clusters form in the way they do.

REFERENCES

Abdi, H., Williams, L. J., & Valentin, D. (2013). Multiple factor analysis: Principal component analysis for multitable and multiblock data sets. *Wiley Interdisciplinary Reviews: Computational Statistics*, 5(2), 149–179.

Bali Swain, R., & Ranganathan, S. (2021). Modelling interlinkages between sustainable development goals using network analysis. *World Development*, 138, Article 105136.

Bali Swain, R., & Wallentin, F. Y. (2020). Achieving sustainable development goals: Predicaments and strategies. *International Journal of Sustainable Development & World Ecology*, 27(2), 96–106.

Bedecarrats, F., Cling, J.-P., & Roubaud, F. (2016). The data revolution and statistical challenges in Africa: Introduction to the special report. *Afrique contemporaine*, 258(2), 297–334.

Cling, J.-P., & Delecourt, C. (2022). Interlinkages between the sustainable development goals. *World Development Perspectives*, 25, Article 100398.

Cronbach, L. J. (1951). Coefficient alpha and the internal structure of tests. *Psychometrika*, 16, 297–334.

Dang, H.-A., & Serajuddin, U. (2020). Tracking the sustainable development goals: Emerging measurement challenges and further reflections. *World Development*, 127, Article 104570.

Dawes, J. H. P., Zhou, X., & Moinuddin, M. (2022). System-level consequences of synergies and trade-offs between SDGs: Quantitative analysis of interlinkage networks at country level. *Sustainability Science*, 17(4), 1435–1457.

Deaton, A. (2013). *The Great Escape: Health, Wealth and the Origins of Inequality*. Princeton: Princeton University Press.

Escofier, B., & Pagès, J. (1990). Multiple factor analysis. *Computational Statistics & Data Analysis*, 18(1), 121–140.

Grossman, G. M., & Krueger, A. B. (1993). Environmental impacts of a North American free trade agreement. In P. M. Garber (Ed.), *The Mexico-U.S. Free Trade Agreement.* Cambridge, MA: The MIT Press, pp. 1–10.

Guerini, M., Vanni, F., & Napoletano, M. (2022). *E pluribus, quaedam.* Gross domestic product out of a dashboard of indicators. FEEM Working Paper.

Hopkins, B., & Skellam, J. G. (1954). A new method for determining the type of distribution of plant individuals. *Annals of Botany*, 18(70), 213–227.

Kaiser, H. F. (1960). The application of electronic computers to factor analysis. *Educational and Psychological Measurement*, 20(1), 141–151.

Kroll, C., Warchold, A., & Pradhan, P. (2019). Sustainable Development Goals (SDGs): Are we successful in turning trade-offs into synergies? *Palgrave Communications*, 5, Article 140.

Kuznets, S. (1955). Economic growth and income inequality. *American Economic Review*, 45(1), 1–28.

Long, G. (2015). The idea of universality in the sustainable development goals. *Ethics & International Affairs*, 29(2), 203–222.

Miola, A., Borchardt, S., Neher, F., & Buscaglia, D. (2019). *Interlinkages and Policy Coherence for the Sustainable Development Goals Implementation: An Operational Method to Identify Trade-Offs and Co-Benefits in a Systemic Way.* Luxembourg: Publications Office of the European Union.

Morissette, L., & Chartier, S. (2013). The *k*-means clustering technique: General considerations and implementation in Mathematica. *Tutorials in Quantitative Methods for Psychology*, 9(1), 15–24.

Organisation for Economic Co-operation and Development. (2021). *Gender and the Environment; Building Evidence and Policies to Achieve the SDGs.* Paris: OECD.

Overseas Development Institute. (2017). *The Sustainable Development Goals and Their Trade-Offs.* London: ODI.

Pritchett, L. (2020). Randomizing development; Method or madness? In F. Bedecarrats, I. Guerin, and F. Roubaud (Eds.), *Randomized Control Trials in the Field of Development: A Critical Perspective.* Oxford: Oxford University Press.

Rand, W. M. (1971). Objective criteria for the evaluation of clustering methods. *Journal of the American Statistical Association*, 66(336), 846–850.

Spaiser, V., Ranganathan, S., Bali Swain, R., & Sumpter, D. J. T. (2016). The Sustainable Development oxymoron: Quantifying and modelling the incompatibility of Sustainable Development Goals. *International Journal of Sustainable Development & World Ecology*, 24(6), 457–470.

Stiglitz, J. E., Sen, A., & Fitoussi, J.-P. (2009). *Report by the Commission on the Measurement of Economic Performance and Social Progress.* Paris: CMEPSP.

Tremblay, D., Fortier, F., Boucher, J.-F., Riffon, O., & Villeneuve, C. (2017). Sustainable Development Goals interactions: An analysis based on the five pillars of the 2030 Agenda. *Sustainable Development*, 28(6), 1584–1596.

United Nations. (2022). *The Sustainable Development Goals Report.* New York: United Nations.

United Nations Development Programme. (1994). *Human Development Index: Methodology and Measurement.* New York: UNDP.

Zhang, J., Wang, S., Pradhan, P., Zhao, W., & Fu, B. (2022). Untangling the interactions among the Sustainable Development Goals in China. *Science Bulletin*, 67(9), 977–984.

9. Improving data availability in Colombia to find interlinkages across the 2030 Agenda

Karen Chavez Quintero and
Natalia Alonso Ospina

9.1   INTRODUCTION

Along with the foundation of the 2030 Agenda and the Sustainable Development Goals (SDG), there was an agreement to tackle and monitor the advances made towards the targets' achievement using quantitative measures. The Inter-agency and Expert Group on SDG Indicators (IAEG-SDGs) was tasked with establishing and implementing a global set of indicators which were methodologically sound, consistent, and comparable across countries. The IAEG-SDGs developed the indicator framework that was adopted by the United Nations General Assembly and has almost finished the approval processes for the metadata for all of the 248 (231 unique) indicators that are currently part of the global framework. While metadata is a necessary and useful tool for information producers, the implementation of the framework also requires data to be available to compute measures.

Countries have been overcoming challenges to strengthen their statistical capacities and reduce data gaps with strategies (i) to improve the knowledge of SDG indicator methodologies agreed at the global level and (ii) to widen information sources to reduce data gaps with the required level of disaggregation leaving no one behind. Beyond statistical strengthening to better monitor progress, increasing data availability enhances the identification of interlinkages between indicators/targets/goals by quantifying the direction, significance, and magnitude of statistical relationships. These are relevant aspects considering the large number of indicators, targets, and goals to tackle in each country and the absence of theories to define the interlinkages across all of them. Thus, quantifying interlinkages across the elements of the 2030 Agenda is a key input when defining public policy priorities to identify catalyst indicators/targets.

These catalyst indicators/targets are those producing either higher impact for the overall achievement of the goals or higher impact when allocating additional resources to improve performance. The latter involve data modeling exercises, for which available SDG indicator measures are required inputs. This also shows that the availability of SDG indicators fosters the use of data when establishing policy measures to maximize the overall advance towards the goals and beyond individual follow-ups on data series. Given that we are less than a decade away from the end of the 2030 Agenda and the completion of SDG data hasn't been achieved, strategies to accelerate statistical strengthening are still in demand.

Looking at the current state of SDG indicator production at the global level and using the defined TIER classification of IAEG-SDGs,[1] we found evidence of a general increase in the data availability of SDG indicators in the period 2016–2022; however, no country/region in the world has achieved data availability for all SDG indicators to date, and furthermore, the data gaps to be filled are still greater than the observed increases. Table 9.1 shows that, by July 2022, 144 out of 248 SDGs are classified as TIER I, meaning that 144 SDGs indicators have data availability of at least 50 percent at the global level. This represents a growth from 98 indicators in 2016; nonetheless, the

Table 9.1   SDGs TIER classification by number of indicators (2016–2022)

TIER classification	2016	2022
TIER I	98	144
TIER I (a)/TIER II (b)		1
TIER I (a)/TIER II (b, c)		1
TIER I/II depending on index		1
TIER I/II depending on resource		1
TIER II	48	99
Unclassified	30	1
TIER I/II	2	
TIER I/II/III	1	
TIER I/III	1	
TIER II/III	1	
TIER III	67	
Total	**248**	**248**

Source: Own elaboration based on the results of the IAEG-SDGs TIER Classification of July 9, 2022

positive variation of 46 indicators contrasts with the 104 additional indicators that remain outside the TIER I level.

Following the lack of data at the global level for SDGs, this chapter examines the statistical capacity (data availability, strategies to strengthen statistical capacity, and challenges) to implement the SDG indicator framework in Latin American and Caribbean countries, in the first section. Afterwards, in the second section, it describes the actions developed around statistical capacity strengthening in Colombia, ending with a conclusion on good practices that could help to boost the progress made so far by these countries.

9.2   SDG STATISTICAL CAPACITY IN LATIN AMERICAN AND CARIBBEAN COUNTRIES

9.2.1   Data Availability, Strategies to Strengthen Statistical Capacity, and Challenges

In the Latin American and Caribbean region, the Statistics Division of the Economic Commission for Latin America and the Caribbean (ECLAC) designed the "National Statistical Capabilities Questionnaire for the Production of SDG Indicators" which aimed to (i) map the capacities of the region's countries to measure SDG indicators, (ii) collect information on the production processes of each country, and (iii) identify those countries that require support and those that could provide support, as a way to start building collaborative networks among ECLAC countries.

The first consultation process for the capabilities questionnaire was submitted in 2016 by the National Statistical Offices, and it was an exercise with the participation of other national entities of the National Statistical System producing information for SDG indicators. Subsequently, in 2017 and 2018, additional consultation processes were conducted, and results showed that— on average—31 percent of the global framework indicators were produced by ECLAC countries, and this percentage could increase to 46 percent when considering indicators for which the information exists but calculations have not been made.

Likewise, the results showed great heterogeneity among the countries in the percentages of indicators that can be produced from the available information. For example, while in Haiti and St. Vincent and the Grenadines the production percentages were 25 percent and 26 percent, respectively, in Argentina the production percentage was 71 percent. However, examining the actual SDG production, only Costa Rica, Uruguay, and Panama reported global indicator production of more than 50 percent (ECLAC, n.d.).

Based on the above, the Latin American and Caribbean countries have established strategies to improve statistical capacities. According to ECLAC,

Chile and the Dominican Republic developed national classifications that allowed them to gather data according to their national priorities (ECLAC, n.d.). Other countries in the region such as Colombia and Uruguay have begun to take advantage of data available from non-traditional sources. Uruguay's National Institute of Statistics used gender statistics from a civil society organization to report information about SDG 3 "Health and Well-being" (Cázarez-Grageda & Zougbede, 2019).

Some of the challenges evidenced for the fulfillment of the 2030 Agenda are in the public policy approach in formulating actions to counteract the effects of climate change and support the most vulnerable populations, as well as in the data approach to ensure the availability of measures, noting that "what is not measured usually goes unnoticed" (ACNUDH, 2012). In this regard, ECLAC formulated some recommendations described below (CEPAL, 2017):

1. Taking advantage of the data revolution, the use of new data sources should be fostered to generate capacities for the use of these recent developments. It is necessary to enhance alliances between different actors (private sector, civil organizations, and academia) in the development of innovations within the new data ecosystems.
2. Improve the quality, timeliness, disaggregation, transparency, and access to statistics for better data that reflects the reality and needs of public policy, either through traditional sources or alternative sources of information.
3. Under the leadership of National Statistical Offices and with the support of national cooperation agencies, the national, regional, and global monitoring mechanisms should be strengthened to collect, analyze, and exchange information on SDG indicators.
4. Financing and budget identification concerning SDGs require articulation between planning and budgeting that allows planning, the allocation of resources, and the effective materialization of results.
5. Greater investment is required to take advantage of new sources of information that are sustainable over time.

9.3   STATISTICAL CAPACITY STRENGTHENING IN COLOMBIA TO IMPROVE DATA AVAILABILITY FOR SDGS

Considering the data challenges posed by the 2030 Agenda for many countries, this section aims to describe the work developed in Colombia, formulated and led by the *SDG Indicators Unit of DANE* (acronym in Spanish for National Statistics Institute), shedding light on how other countries can also improve data availability and highlighting the lessons learned and the challenges that persist. For this purpose, this section is divided into the following subsections: the Colombian context, the production of global indicators, the dissemination of information, challenges, and lessons learned.

9.3.1   Colombian Context

Colombia is one of the 193 countries that adopted the post-2015 development agenda and made a commitment to the framework of the United Nations General Assembly of 2015. The country decided to implement a plan for the achievement of the SDGs, and three key strategies have been developed by the Colombian government:

- In February 2015, the country established the *National High-Level Interinstitutional Commission for the Preparation and Effective Implementation of the Post-2015 Development Agenda and its Sustainable Development Goals* (hereinafter the SDG High-Level Commission) through Decree 280 of 2015. This SDG High-Level Commission is a formal space for monitoring and decision-making on the implementation of the 2030 Agenda, through public policies, plans, actions, and programs that ensure an integrated and participatory vision of the dimensions of sustainable development (DNP, 2015). It is composed of three ministries and four administrative departments, including the National Planning Department (DNP), which acts as chair, the Technical Secretariat of SDGs in Colombia, and the National Administrative Department of Statistics (DANE).
- One of the main achievements of the SDG High-Level Commission was the development of the public policy document "Strategy for the Implementation of the Sustainable Development Goals in Colombia",[2] and it was approved by the *CONPES* (acronym in Spanish for National Council on Social and Economic Policy) in March 2018. This policy document sets out the national SDG targets and strategies and is based on four main objectives: (i) to define a national indicators framework for *monitoring and reporting progress*, with each indicator having a quantitative baseline and intermediate and/or final quantitative targets, (ii) to define a plan to *strengthen the statistical capacities* in the production and management of data, (iii) to establish *strategic lines* for the national government *to accompany local governments*, and (iv) to develop guidelines for *dialogue with non-governmental actors*, materializing the multi-stakeholder approach of the 2030 Agenda (DNP, 2018).
- Also, the National Development Plans (PND, acronym in Spanish) have been aligned with SDG. First, *PND 2014–2018: All for a New Country* linked SDGs based on an ex-post analysis. Then, *PND 2018–2022: Pact*

for Colombia, Pact for Equity linked the SDGs from its formulation in such a way that policy lines, goals, and strategies contained in the document are a mechanism for SDG implementation; as a result, 98.2 percent of the indicators for monitoring PND *2018–2022* are associated with one or more SDG targets (DNP, 2021).

Furthermore, the indicators for monitoring the progress towards SDG were jointly defined identifying national entities with responsibilities as providers of sources of information and responsibilities for the computation of indicators, in addition to the definition of entities responsible for the targets from a public policy perspective and according to their mission. In addition, DANE has the task of managing the SDG national indicators database, as well as the coordination of the production of global SDG indicators to fill information gaps through coordinated work with other entities within the National Statistical System, highlighting the joint work with custodian agencies, specifically the ones that are part of the *Colombian UN Interagency SDG Indicators Working Group* (see description below).

9.3.1.1 Colombian UN Inter-Agency Working Group on Sustainable Development Goals

In 2017, DANE and the United Nations System (UN System) in Colombia created the *Colombian UN Inter-Agency Working Group on Sustainable Development Goals*, which seeks to close information gaps, adopt global methodologies at the national level, and build the right conditions for the generation of information that did not exist and were considered necessary to measure SDG indicators. The activities of this group were included in Guideline 2 "Statistical Strengthening Plan" of the public policy document CONPES 3918 and in product 3.1.1 of the Colombian United Nations Sustainable Development Cooperation Framework (UNSDCF) 2020–2023.

This group is made up of the following UN Colombian bodies:

- Resident Coordinator's Office in Colombia
- United Nations Population Fund (UNFPA) in Colombia as the technical secretariat
- Food and Agriculture Organization (FAO) in Colombia
- International Labor Organization (ILO) in Colombia
- Office of the High Commissioner for Human Rights (OHCHR) in Colombia
- Pan-American Health Organization (PAHO)
- UN Environment Programme (UNEP) in the ECLAC region
- UN Refugee Agency (UNHCR) in Colombia
- UN Women in Colombia
- UN-Habitat in Colombia

- United Nations Children's Fund (UNICEF) in Colombia
- United Nations Development Programme (UNDP) in Colombia
- United Nations Industrial Development Organization (UNIDO) in Colombia
- United Nations Office on Drugs and Crime (UNODC) in Colombia

9.3.2 Global Indicators Production in the Colombian Context

The objective of this section is to describe the strategies used by the Colombian Inter-Agency Group to enlarge the availability of data on SDG measures, highlighting the main advances and achievements during the work period. The *Colombian UN Inter-Agency Working Group on SDG* has developed different innovative strategies to fulfill the purposes for which it was created; among these strategies, we pinpoint the release of the *Guide to Measuring and Reporting on the Global Indicators*,[3] the Barometer for monitoring indicator production advances, experimental statistics, and the promotion of disaggregations.

9.3.2.1 Guide to measuring and reporting on the global indicators in the United Nations Sustainable Development Cooperation Framework

Based on Colombia's experience in the measurement of SDG indicators, in 2021, DANE, the UNFPA, and the FAO launched the *Guide to Measuring and Reporting on the Global Indicators in the United Nations Sustainable Development Cooperation Framework*, which establishes seven steps as a sequence of actions to calculate and report global SDG indicators in the country, including coordination strategies across the National Statistics System in the joint work between the National Statistical Office, the entities that are sources of information, and the custodian agencies (DANE, 2021). The steps set out in the guide are:

Step 1: Indicator prioritization
    To define the indicators that will be worked on throughout the year, DANE, the UN System, and national entities participate in a prioritization exercise. This process considers public policy needs, the interests of the custodian agencies, and the work carried out in previous years.
Step 2: Information availability analysis
    For each indicator, an analysis of the available information and possible sources of information to measure the indicator is performed. This exercise makes it possible to determine the information requirements and to draw up a work plan aimed at satisfying information requirements.

Step 3: Working plans development

In line with the previous point and again for each indicator, relevant stakeholders for the SDG are defined, considering the possible sources of information and custodian agencies. Stakeholders involved define the work plan for the development of activities.

Step 4: Communication pathway

To ensure that the activities proposed in the work plan are carried out, a communication route is ensured in which the responsible actors are determined and, for each stakeholder, the focal points of contact are established.

Step 5: Boost the work

The custodian agencies can keep providing support to DANE and can establish agreements to continue the articulated work to collect all the information on the agreed work plans and to document, monitor, and implement the work plans.

Step 6: Document the process

A good statistical practice is the documentation of the cooperation process with the custodian agency(ies) and other stakeholders, since it allows traceability to be maintained and proposals to be improved as appropriate. This documentation process is built up through the work plans, and the mechanism used to save the information is called a logbook. A logbook is a document containing a record of the criteria that have already been met in the production process of the indicator and contains evidence for every met criterion (DANE, 2021).

Step 7: Progress and challenges

Every six months, a follow-up report is prepared and the main advances in the measurement of the indicators are presented, as well as a section on the main challenges identified to establish joint actions within the framework of the Colombian Working Group, to allow progress in the measurement *of the indicators.*

9.3.2.2   The Barometer and the logbook

The *Barometer* tool was developed by DANE to establish homogeneous criteria when characterizing the status of an indicator's measurement and to streamline the work with the Colombian UN System and thus achieve effective communication between the partners involved in the indicator's measurement and reporting. It was designed based on the first version of the "Survey of National Statistical Capacity for the Production of SDG Indicators", developed by the Statistical Conference of ECLAC. In this sense, the Barometer has four categories (A, B, C, and D) for a quantitative characterization of the status of the production process of the indicator; the categories are:

- Category A (green): the indicator is produced.
- Category B (light green): the indicator is not produced, but it can be produced with the existing information sources.
- Category C (yellow): some information is available, but it needs to be improved or supplemented to produce the indicator.
- Category D (red): there is no information available to produce the indicator.

Additionally, the following general aspects were defined for the *Barometer*:

1. Each category was equally weighted to make up 100 percent; that is, each category has a weighting of 25 percent.
2. Criteria were associated with each category. Overall, 17 criteria were identified as key aspects to be considered in the measurement processes. For each criterion, whether the indicator fulfills it or not is examined.
3. The weighting of each criterion was calculated by dividing the 25 percent of each category by the number of criteria in the category. For example, category A is composed of six criteria, and each criterion has a weighting of 4.16 percent (25%/6) in the *Barometer* (DANE, 2021).

9.3.2.3   Progress in measuring SDG indicators

Following the above, with the approval of the UNSDCF 2020–2023 in the country, it was established that the Colombian UN Inter-Agency Working Group on SDGs would focus its efforts on an initial set of 106 indicators, which could be increased depending on the requirements of the custodian agencies, new measurement projects through alternative sources, or new public policy needs (DANE, 2021). Given this, currently, there is a set of 132 indicators that have been, are being, or are expected to be worked on. It is important to note that, following the first step of the *Guide*, a subset of this list of indicators is prioritized annually to be included as part of the work in filling SDG data gaps throughout the year.

For a baseline that allows a follow-up on the progress made, in 2020, the Barometer was calculated for all SDG indicators of the global framework, for the first time. Subsequently, the Barometer has been updated at least four times a year for the prioritized indicators, which has made it possible to know whether the work plans developed have accelerated the production of the indicators or if there have been difficulties slowing down the production. Additionally, the results of the Barometer for the prioritized indicators are used to elaborate reports, showing both the progress and the challenges, and these documents are published in the SDG portal of DANE's website.[4] After the release of the Guide and to date, two reports have been published, one that summarizes the results of 2021[5] and another that describes the results from the first half of 2022.[6]

Table 9.2 Barometer: a tool for characterizing the measurement status of an indicator

%	Categories		Criterion		Response		Percentage per criterion (%)
					Yes	No	
0%–25%	D. No information is available to produce the indicator	1.	Contact was made with the custodian agency				8.33
		2.	The possible sources have been identified				8.33
		3.	Information sources	Own			8.33
				Mixed (ANNEX 1)			
25%–50%	C. Some information is available, but it needs to be improved or supplemented to produce the indicator	4.	The sources/information are complete	Yes			6.3
				No (ANNEX 2)			
		5.	Inter-institutional coordination took place: Referring to working groups and methodological transfer (if necessary)				6.3
		6.	A work plan for data extraction exists				6.3
		7.	Agreement exists regarding the conceptual and methodological definition to be used				6.3

50%–75%	**B. The indicator is not produced, but it can be produced with the existing information sources**	8.	The data required to calculate the indicator is produced	6.3
		9.	The required data to calculate the indicator has sufficient statistical quality	6.3
		10.	The custodian agency validated the produced measure	6.3
		11.	DANE validated the produced measure Yes No (ANNEX 3)	6.3
75%–100%	**A. The indicator is produced**	12.	Clarity exists regarding the statistical operation	4.16
		13.	The collection of input data has a defined and guaranteed frequency for producing the indicator	4.16
		14.	A record is kept of the time period for which the information required to produce the indicator is available	4.16
		15.	The required regularity for the dissemination of the indicator is ensured	4.16
		16.	The indicator is reported globally and has been validated by the country	4.16
		17.	The indicator produced is reported globally and is part of the national monitoring framework	4.16
			RESULT	100

Note: In the original version the colors represent a traffic light, where category A is green, B is light green, C is yellow, and D is red

Source: National Administrative Department of Statistics (DANE) and Colombian UN System

199

For example, in 2022, 66 indicators were prioritized, and the progress made in the statistical production processes of these SDG indicators is shown in Figure 9.1. In the period July 2021 to July 2022, there was an increase in the total number of indicators belonging to *Category A*, from 22 to 30 indicators, as well as an increase in the number of indicators in *Category B*, from 17 to 20 indicators. These increases coincide with decreases in the number of indicators in Category C (from 19 to 11 indicators) and Category D (from 8 to 2 indicators). The results evidence how the articulation processes for statistical strengthening have boosted the production of SDG data, and this is also an example of how the *Barometer* is a tool for checking progress in filling data gaps.

On the other hand, recognizing that DANE does not have a monopoly on the production of official statistics in Colombia and there is coordinated work with the National Statistical System's entities, 31 out of the 66 SDG indicators prioritized in 2022 were worked on with additional public entities; among these, the two entities working on the highest number of

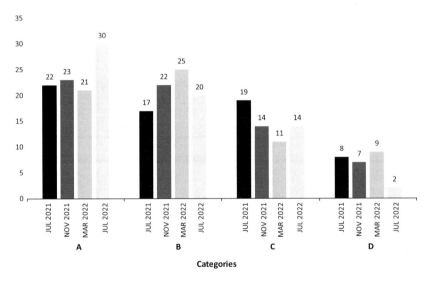

Note:　**Category A.** The indicator is produced. **Category B.** The indicator is not produced, but it can be produced with the existing information sources. **Category C.** Some information is available, but it needs to be improved or supplemented to produce the indicator. **Category D.** No information is available to produce the indicator

Source:　Elaborated by the National Administrative Department of Statistics (DANE)

Figure 9.1　　*Measurement Barometer diagnosis: 66 SDG indicators prioritized and worked on in 2022*

indicators—excluding DANE—in 2022 were the Ministry of Environment and Sustainable Development (11 indicators prioritized) and the Institute of Hydrology, Meteorology and Environmental Studies (8 indicators). Table 9.3 lists all public entities and the number of indicators each worked on in 2022; it should be noted that work may be carried out on an indicator by more than one national entity, depending on the subject and the source of information.

In addition, Table 9.4 shows the number of indicators worked on by the agencies of the United Nations System in Colombia.

Due to these advances, 46 additional SDG indicators belonging to the global monitoring framework have been produced in the past two years (Table 9.5). These indicators have their data series and technical sheets (which follow the structure of the global metadata, as well as national guidelines) and have been validated either by the custodian agencies when the indicator is produced at the national level or by the country when the indicator is produced by the agency at the global level. On the production of these global indicators, DANE has requested for the National SDG Technical Secretariat to incorporate them into the national monitoring framework, which will increase the number of indicators in the national framework from 180 to 226 indicators.

In addition to the production of SDG indicators, some specific achievements deserve to be highlighted. On one hand, by 2019 the country did not have enough information for the indicators of Goal 5 "Gender Equality", and from the statistical strengthening developed, the number of indicators produced has increased from two indicators in 2019 to nine in 2022. Another example in the progress made is in the measurement of SDG 16 indicators; out of the 24 total indicators for this goal, at the beginning of 2019 in Colombia, there was only 1 global indicator within the national monitoring framework, and currently, there are 8 new indicators measured.

9.3.2.4 Experimental statistics

Given that one of the main challenges in the process of measuring SDG indicators is the availability of data with which compute the indicators, Colombia has implemented strategies for the use of non-traditional sources in the line of experimental statistics as an alternative for the measurement of SDG indicators. Experimental statistics are those derived from new sources of information and/or new methods used and/or by a new subject not previously measured. Likewise, these statistics are considered experimental because they have not yet reached sufficient maturity in terms of reliability, stability, or data quality to be included in the list of standard statistical operations (DANE, n.d.-a).

In this context, 6 of the 46 new indicators were produced using non-traditional sources such as satellite images and citizen-generated data. Here it is

Table 9.3　Entities of the National Statistical System with which indicators are worked on and the number of indicators worked on in 2022 with each entity

National Statistical System entities	Number of indicators
National Administrative Department of Statistics (DANE, acronym in Spanish)	33
Ministry of Environment and Sustainable Development (MADS, acronym in Spanish)	11
Institute of Hydrology, Meteorology and Environmental Studies (IDEAM, acronym in Spanish)	8
Ministry of Health and Social Protection (MSPS, acronym in Spanish)	7
Ministry of National Education (MEN, acronym in Spanish)	4
National Planning Department (DNP, acronym in Spanish)	3
Colombian Institute of Family Welfare (ICBF, acronym in Spanish)	3
National Unit for Disaster Risk Management (UNGRD, acronym in Spanish)	3
National Aquaculture and Fishing Authority (AUNAP, acronym in Spanish)	2
Presidential Council for Human Rights	2
Instituto de Investigaciones Marinas y Costeras José Benito Vives de Andrés (INVEMAR)	2
Ministry of Agriculture and Rural Development (MADR, acronym in Spanish)	2
Rural Development Agency (ADR, acronym in Spanish)	2
National Institute of Legal Medicine and Forensic Sciences (INMLCF, acronym in Spanish)	2
Ministry of Labor	2
Mining and Energy Planning Unit (UPME, acronym in Spanish)	2
Inter-sectoral Commission for Comprehensive Early Childhood Care (CIPI, acronym in Spanish)	1
Administrative Department of Public Service (DAFP, acronym in Spanish)	1
Office of the Human Rights Ombudsman of Colombia	1
Department of Social Prosperity (DPS, acronym in Spanish)	1

(*Continued*)

Table 9.3   (Continued)

National Statistical System entities	Number of indicators
National Public Procurement Agency – Colombia Efficient Purchase	1
Humboldt Institute	1
Ministry of Culture	1
Ministry of Defense	1
Office of the Attorney General of the Republic of Colombia	1
Ministry of the Interior	1
Colombia's Presidential Cooperation Agency (APC Colombia, acronym in Spanish)	1
Ministry of Mines and Energy	1
Ministry of Finance and Public Credit (MHCP, acronym in Spanish)	1
Superintendency of Residential Public Services	1
Unit for the Attention and Integral Reparation to Victims (UARIV acronym ins Spanish)	1
Unit of Rural Agro-economic Planning (UPRA, acronym ins Spanish)	1

Source: Elaborated by the National Administrative Department of Statistics (DANE)

also important to note that new data sources are not used in isolation but are combined with other sources of information (traditional and non-traditional). An example of this is SDG indicator 11.7.1, which was calculated in partnership with the German Cooperation Agency (GIZ Data Lab), using satellite imagery, Open Street Map, and census data.

Regarding this point of the use of non-traditional sources, it is also emphasized that economies of scale are being generated where, although the learning exercises are developed specifically for an indicator, this knowledge is applied to the measurement of other indicators beyond SDGs. This is because the sources and methods are considered "agnostic" to the topics, meaning that if, for example, satellite imagery is processed and computed for a particular SDG, the same images and procedures could be applied when measuring other SDGs or other measures.

On the other hand, it is relevant to mention the work carried out under the *Data for Now* strategy, which aims to identify data needs for the identification of resources to increase the availability of information for the measurement of SDG indicators. Currently, the strategy is composed of four thematic areas: poverty (SDG 1), education (SDG 4), justice and institutions (SDG 16), and

Table 9.4   Agencies of the United Nations System with which the prior-
itized indicators are worked on in 2022, by number of indica-
tors worked on with each agency

Custodian agencies	Number of indicators
Food and Agriculture Organization	12
International Labor Organization	7
UN Environment Programme (UNEP) in ECLAC region	7
United Nations Educational, Scientific and Cultural Organization (UNESCO)	6
United Nations Population Fund (UNFPA)	5
United Nations Children's Fund (UNICEF) in Colombia	4
Office of the High Commissioner for Human Rights (OHCHR) in Colombia	4
UN-Habitat in Colombia	3
Pan-American Health Organization (PAHO/WHO)	3
United Nations Office for Disaster Risk Reduction (UNISDR)	3
United Nations Office on Drugs and Crime (UNODC) in Colombia	2
United Nations Statistics Division	2
International Energy Agency (IEA)	2
World Bank	1
Data for Now	1
Joint United Nations Programme on HIV/AIDS (UNAIDS)	1
Organization for Economic Co-operation and Development (OECD)	1

Source: Elaborated by the National Administrative Department of Statistics (DANE)

price monitoring, in addition to two cross-cutting areas (technological architecture and geospatial information).

This strategy prioritizes exercises that integrate different sources of information, as well as promoting the use of alternative sources (such as satellite
images, administrative records, and big data sources/techniques, among others). Among the achievements are:

- The estimation of the census Multidimensional Poverty Index using
  machine learning and satellite imagery, disaggregated for municipalities
  and at per block level (for municipal capitals).

Table 9.5   *List of indicators produced as part of the Colombian UN Inter-Agency Working Group on Sustainable Development Goals work since 2020*

ID	SDG indicators	Entity source
1.5.1G 11.5.1G 13.1.1G	Number of deaths, missing persons, and directly affected persons attributed to disasters per 100 000 population	UNGRD
1.5.3G 11.b.1G 13.1.2G	1.5.3 Number of countries that adopt and implement national disaster risk reduction strategies in line with the Sendai Framework for Disaster Risk Reduction 2015–2030	UNGRD
1.5.4G 11.b.2G 13.1.3G	Proportion of local governments that adopt and implement local disaster risk reduction strategies in line with national disaster risk reduction strategies	UNGRD
2.a.1G	The agriculture orientation index for government expenditures	DANE FAO
2.c.1G	Indicator of food price anomalies	DANE FAO
3.3.1G	Number of new HIV infections per 1000 uninfected population, by sex, age, and key populations	MSPS
3.7.1G	Proportion of women of reproductive age (aged 15–49 years) who have their need for family planning satisfied with modern methods	MSPS
3.7.2G	Adolescent birth rate (aged 10–14 years; aged 15–19 years) per 1000 women in that age group	DANE
3.c.1G	Health worker density and distribution	MSP
4.2.2G	Participation rate in organized learning (one year before the official primary entry age), by sex	DANE (UNESCO UIS)
4.c.1G	Proportion of teachers with the minimum required qualifications, by education level	MEN (UNESCO UIS – Questionary)
5.1.1G	Whether or not legal frameworks are in place to promote, enforce, and monitor equality and non-discrimination on the basis of sex	DANE Questionary Agencies
5.2.1G	Proportion of ever-partnered women and girls aged 15 years and older subjected to physical, sexual, or psychological violence by a current or former intimate partner in the previous 12 months, by form of violence and by age	MSPS

(Continued)

Table 9.5   (Continued)

ID	SDG indicators	Entity source
5.4.1G	Proportion of time spent on unpaid domestic and care work, by sex, age, and location	DANE
5.5.1b. G	Proportion of seats held by women in (a) national parliaments and (b) local governments	National Civil Registry Office
5.5.2G	Proportion of women in managerial positions	DANE
5.6.2G	Number of countries with laws and regulations that guarantee full and equal access to women and men aged 15 years and older to sexual and reproductive health care, information, and education	DANE UNFPA
5.a.2G	Proportion of countries where the legal framework (including customary law) guarantees women's equal rights to land ownership and/or control	DANE FAO
5.c.1G	Proportion of countries with systems to track and make public allocations for gender equality and women's empowerment	DANE (Questionnaire agencies)
8.3.1G	Proportion of informal employment in total employment, by sector and sex	DANE ILO
8.8.2G	Level of national compliance with labor rights (freedom of association and collective bargaining) based on International Labour Organization (ILO) textual sources and national legislation, by sex and migrant status	DANE ILO
8.9.1G	Tourism direct GDP as a proportion of total GDP and in growth rate	DANE
9.1.1G	Proportion of the rural population who live within 2 km of an all-season road	DANE
9.4.1G	CO_2 emission per unit of value added	UPME
9.b.1G	Proportion of medium- and high-tech industry value added in total value added	DANE
11.1.1G	Proportion of urban population living in slums, informal settlements, or inadequate housing	DANE
11.2.1G	Proportion of population that has convenient access to public transport, by sex, age, and persons with disabilities	DANE
11.3.1G	Ratio of land consumption rate to population growth rate	DANE

(Continued)

Table 9.5   *(Continued)*

ID	SDG indicators	Entity source
11.4.1G	Total per capita expenditure on the preservation, protection, and conservation of all cultural and natural heritage, by source of funding (public, private), type of heritage (cultural, natural), and level of government (national, regional, and local/municipal)	DANE
11.7.1G	Average share of the built-up area of cities that is open space for public use for all, by sex, age, and persons with disabilities	DANE
11.b.1G	Number of countries that adopt and implement national disaster risk reduction strategies in line with the Sendai Framework for Disaster Risk Reduction 2015–2030	UNGRD
11.b.2G	Proportion of local governments that adopt and implement local disaster risk reduction strategies in line with national disaster risk reduction strategies	UNGRD
12.7.1G	Number of countries implementing sustainable public procurement policies and action plans	DANE UNEP information system at the global level
12.b.1G	Implementation of standard accounting tools to monitor the economic and environmental aspects of tourism sustainability	DANE
16.1.4G	Proportion of population that feel safe walking alone around the area they live after dark	DANE
16.2.2G	Number of victims of human trafficking per 100 000 population, by sex, age, and form of exploitation	Ministry of the Interior
16.3.1G	Proportion of victims of violence in the previous 12 months who reported their victimization to competent authorities or other officially recognized conflict resolution mechanisms	DANE
16.3.3G	Proportion of the population who have experienced a dispute in the past two years and who accessed a formal or informal dispute resolution mechanism, by type of mechanism	DANE

(Continued)

Table 9.5   (Continued)

ID	SDG indicators	Entity source
16.5.1G	Proportion of persons who had at least one contact with a public official and who paid a bribe to a public official, or were asked for a bribe by those public officials, during the previous 12 months	DANE
16.7.2G	Proportion of population who believe decision-making is inclusive and responsive, by sex, age, disability, and population group	DANE
16.b.1G	Proportion of population reporting having personally felt discriminated against or harassed in the previous 12 months on the basis of a ground of discrimination prohibited under international human rights law	DANE
17.14.1G	Number of countries with mechanisms in place to enhance policy coherence of sustainable development	DNP

Note: The coding of the global SDG indicators responds to the codes established at the national level for the SDG indicators. In this sense, the letter G represents indicators belonging to the global framework and the letter P to proxy indicators. Although not presented here, there is a third category C, which represents complementary indicators, that is, indicators that are 100 percent related to the country's needs
Source: Elaborated by the National Administrative Department of Statistics (DANE)

- The estimation of complementary information for indicator 16.b.1, "Proportion of the population that reports having felt personally discriminated against or harassed in the last 12 months on a ground of discrimination prohibited by international human rights law", and indicator 16.7.2, "Proportion of the population that considers decision-making to be inclusive and responsive, by gender, age, disability and population group" (United Nations, 2018), using information from social networks and natural language processing techniques, to identify whether people make comments associated with some of the forms of discrimination determined by indicator 16.b.1 and whether these comments can identify some of the aspects associated with citizens' political representativeness, as part of indicator 16.7.2.
- The development of a data lake as the IT base of the statistical information system for education, associated with "Quality education", that seeks the integration and interoperability of different sources of information for computing measures associated with educational public policy designs.
- The calculation and analysis of the distances of students to schools and the correlation with dropout rates. These results were published as a *Statistical Brief*, "Analysis of Accessibility to Educational Centers" (DANE, 2022).[7]

9.3.2.5 Disaggregation approach

Under the premise of "leaving no one behind", the production of disaggregated SDG data has been included in strategies for strengthening subnational statistical capacities and the Differential and Intersectional Approach in DANE, as described below.

- **Territorial Statistical Capacity Index (ICET, acronym in Spanish)**, developed by DANE to measure the statistical capacity at subnational levels, allows the identification of aspects (knowledge, skills, resources, and institutional environment) that require intervention by national and territorial entities that contribute to improvements in the production, availability, quality, and use of statistical information at the subnational level (DANE, n.d.-b).
- **Territorial Strategy in PDET Municipalities** was a pilot project carried out in 2020 by the DNP, the Territorial Renewal Agency, DANE, and UNFPA, in 18 Development Programs with a Territorial Approach (PDET, acronym in Spanish) municipalities, to develop a territorialization strategy and promote alliances to accelerate the 2030 Agenda, including statistical capacity.
- **Guide on the availability of territorial information for the SDGs and Dashboard for SDG indicators in the Territory**[8] is a document that diagnoses the availability of SDG indicators in municipalities and departments.
- On the differential and intersectional approach, DANE's SDG working group works with the Differential and Intersectional Approach Group, and this joint work follows the parameters established in the Guide on the differential and intersectional approach to production of the National Statistical System.

9.3.3   Dissemination of Information Related to the 2030 Agenda

DANE has established a strategy for disseminating SDG information based on quantitative descriptions. This strategy is developed under two lines of action:

1. Infographic publications on Twitter:
    On the United Nations International Days, and subject to data availability, some publications are issued on the SDG indicator(s) related to the celebrated topic. For this purpose, a relationship is established between the international days and the goals, and then relevant information is identified. Some of these publications are developed with the support of the UN System in Colombia and/or public entities that have some policy responsibility for the topic.

2. Statistical Brief Series:

The objective of DANE's *Statistical Briefs*[9] is to encourage analysis and decision-making based on available data on topics of public interest, for which they gather information from different statistical sources to characterize the country's situation on a single topic. DANE's Statistical Briefs include measurements that belong to the regular statistical production, as well as measurements that belong to the area of *experimental statistics*. In this context, the *Statistical Briefs* series emphasizes the differential and intersectional approach in the production of data to "leave no one behind" in line with the 2030 Agenda for Sustainable Development, thus promoting analyses that contribute to making visible the life situations, particular gaps, and inequalities between different population groups (DANE, n.d.-c).

Since 2021, about 27 Statistical Briefs have been published of which, according to Table 9.6, 21 are directly related to 1 or more SDGs and 6 are indirectly related to 1 or more SDGs. Likewise, it should be noted that, since 2021, multi-stakeholder participation in the publication of these documents has been strengthened, with the participation not only of the UN System but also of national government entities and civil society organizations.

9.3.4   Challenges

Although progress in the measurement of SDG indicators is recognized, it is also important to note that there are still challenges to overcome. As mentioned

Table 9.6   List of indicators produced as part of experimental statistics

ID	SDG indicators	Source
1.2.2	Proportion of men, women, and children of all ages living in poverty in all its dimensions according to national definitions	DANE
9.1.1.	Proportion of the rural population who live within 2 km of an all-season road	DANE
11.1.1.	Proportion of urban population living in slums, informal settlements, or inadequate housing	DANE
11.2.1.	Proportion of population that has convenient access to public transport, by sex, age, and persons with disabilities	DANE
11.3.1	Ratio of land consumption rate to population growth rate	DANE
11.7.1	Average share of the built-up area of cities that is open space for public use for all, by sex, age, and persons with disabilities	DANE

Source: Elaborated by the National Administrative Department of Statistics (DANE)

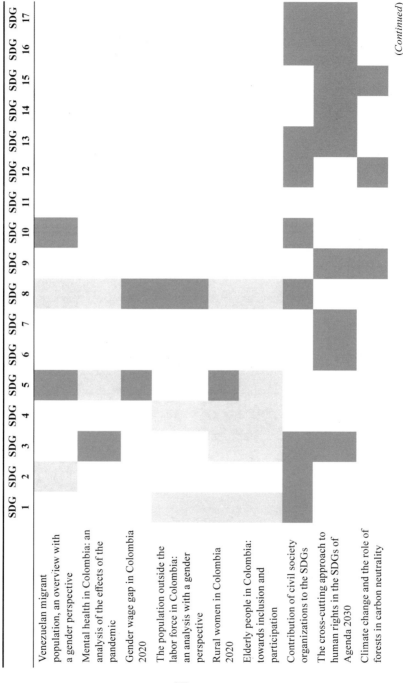

Table 9.7   Relation between DANE's published Statistical Brief and the SDGs

	SDG 1	SDG 2	SDG 3	SDG 4	SDG 5	SDG 6	SDG 7	SDG 8	SDG 9	SDG 10	SDG 11	SDG 12	SDG 13	SDG 14	SDG 15	SDG 16	SDG 17
Venezuelan migrant population, an overview with a gender perspective		■			■			■		■							
Mental health in Colombia: an analysis of the effects of the pandemic			■		■			■									
Gender wage gap in Colombia 2020					■			■									
The population outside the labor force in Colombia: an analysis with a gender perspective		■		■	■			■									
Rural women in Colombia 2020		■		■	■												
Elderly people in Colombia: towards inclusion and participation								■									
Contribution of civil society organizations to the SDGs			■					■		■	■		■			■	■
The cross-cutting approach to human rights in the SDGs of Agenda 2030						■	■		■			■		■	■	■	
Climate change and the role of forests in carbon neutrality												■	■		■		

(Continued)

Table 9.7 (Continued)

	SDG 1	SDG 2	SDG 3	SDG 4	SDG 5	SDG 6	SDG 7	SDG 8	SDG 9	SDG 10	SDG 11	SDG 12	SDG 13	SDG 14	SDG 15	SDG 16	SDG 17
Demographic, educational, and labor profile of the Venezuelan migrant population in Colombia 2014–2021										X							
Youth in Colombia																	
Poverty in Colombia, an analysis with a gender perspective	X				X												
Births to girls and adolescents in Colombia			X		X												
Economic census: national count of economic units (CNUE 2021)								X									
Decision-making and bargaining power within the household					X			X									
The situation of children and adolescents in Colombia—COVID-19	X		X	X													
Analysis of accessibility to educational centers				X													
Current status of disability measurement in Colombia	X		X					X									

212

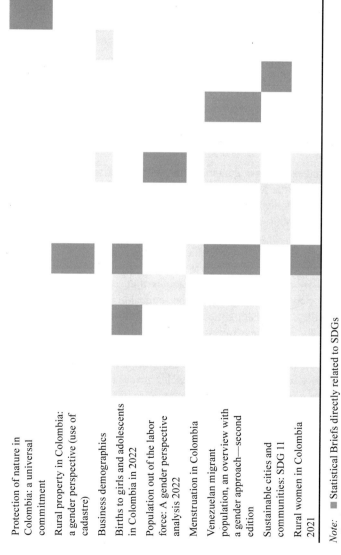

Protection of nature in Colombia: a universal commitment

Rural property in Colombia: a gender perspective (use of cadastre)

Business demographics

Births to girls and adolescents in Colombia in 2022

Population out of the labor force: A gender perspective analysis 2022

Menstruation in Colombia

Venezuelan migrant population, an overview with a gender approach—second edition

Sustainable cities and communities: SDG 11

Rural women in Colombia 2021

Note: ■ Statistical Briefs directly related to SDGs
  Statistical Briefs indirectly related to SDGs
Source: Elaborated by the National Administrative Department of Statistics (DANE)

above, these challenges are linked to the availability of information for both total and disaggregated data, based on the disaggregation suggested in the metadata and moreover with the aim of leaving no one behind and characterizing vulnerable populations. Overcoming this challenge demands greater efforts to make visible diverse groups of the population located in different geographical areas.

It is also necessary to strengthen cooperation and communication mechanisms among stakeholders to accelerate the production of indicators in *Categories C* and *D* of the Barometer. In addition, the timeliness of information from statistical operations that are not regularly conducted, which provide information for many SDG indicators, should be strengthened.

It should also be possible to estimate the costs to finance the production process of the prioritized indicators up to 2030 and in this way to look for alternatives to finance data at a larger scale. Finally, coordination and organization with other entities, agencies, and other actors must be strengthened, as well as high-level technical and political support in the management of resources and responses to requests for the acceleration of the production of SDG indicators.

Finally, additional exercises of data modeling with the existing data to make an overall evaluation of the progress made in Colombia towards the SDGs are still a pending issue, despite the fact that the relevance of these exercises has been recognized and discussed.

9.4   CONCLUSIONS: LESSONS LEARNED

This chapter ends by emphasizing the strategies that, based on Colombian experience in filling SDG data gaps, could be replicable in other countries to boost data availability: establishing mechanisms to follow up advances in the statistical process for each measure; articulating and coordinating the work across the entities of the National Statistical System, identifying relevant stakeholders for each SDG based on responsibilities in terms of data and also from the policy perspective with the custodian agencies always involved; and including the SDGs in the core of crosscutting data policies like subnational capacities strengthening, differential data approaches, and experimental statistics.

The described also represents ways to strengthen overall statistical capacity by enhancing innovations in technical aspects and also in the establishment of partnerships across the National Statistical System.

ACKNOWLEDGMENTS

The activities described in this chapter included the work of people who were part of the SDG Indicators Taskteam of DANE's General Direction under the lead of Juan Daniel Oviedo as Chief Statistician. At the same time, the authors acknowledge the work done by former and current members of the group: Alexandra Barreto, Katizza Carvajal, Ivon Diaz, Juan Sebastian Muñoz, Luisa Natalia Monroy, María Alejandra Cepeda, Paola Fernanda Medina, Patricia Contreras, Raul Chimbi, and Victor Arevalo.

NOTES

1. For further information visit: https://unstats.un.org/sdgs/iaeg-sdgs/tier-classifi cation/
2. For further information visit: https://assets.ctfassets.net/27p7ivvbl4bs/c15L6fP oswiGYUy64Uy4k/d2d1c2b218757846743c6eb335d5b380/CONPES_3918_ Anexos.pdf
3. For further information visit: https://www.dane.gov.co/files/indicadores-ods/ Guide-to-measuring-and-reporting-on-the-global-SDG-indicators.pdf
4. The DANE's SDGs website is https://www.dane.gov.co/index.php/servicios-al- ciudadano/servicios-informacion/objetivos-de-desarrollo-sostenible-ods
5. The 2021 progress report is published at https://www.dane.gov.co/files/indica- dores-ods/Reporte-avance-Indicadores-ODS-prio.pdf
6. The progress report for the first half of 2022 is published at https://www.dane.gov. co/files/indicadores-ods/Reporte-avance-Indicadores-ODS-prio.pdf
7. For further information visit: https://www.dane.gov.co/files/investigaciones/notas- estadisticas/ago_Nota-estadistica-accesibilidad-ingles-20220805.pdf
8. For further information visit: https://www.dane.gov.co/files/indicadores-ods/Guia- sobre-disponibilidad-%20informacion-territorial-ODS.pdf
9. For further information visit: https://www.dane.gov.co/index.php/servicios-al-ciu- dadano/servicios-informacion/serie-notas-estadisticas

REFERENCES

ACNUDH. (2012). *Indicadores de Derechos Humanos. Guía para la medición y la aplicación.*

Cázarez-Grageda, K., & Zougbede, K. (2019). *National SDG Review: Data Challenges and Opportunities.* Deutsche Gesellschaft für Internationale Zusammenarbeit (GIZ) GmbH. Retrieved November 30 https://paris21.org/sites/default/files/ inline-files/National-SDG_Review2019_rz.pdf

CEPAL. (2017). *Informe anual sobre el progreso y los desafíos regionales de la Agenda 2030 para el Desarrollo Sostenible en América Latina y el Caribe.*

DANE. (n.d.-a). *Estadísticas experimentales.* Retrieved September 29, 2022, from https://www.dane.gov.co/index.php/estadisticas-por-tema/estadisticas -experimentales

DANE. (n.d.-b). *Índice de Capacidad Estadística Territorial (ICET).* Retrieved October 18, 2022, from https://www.dane.gov.co/index.php/estadisticas-por-tema /informacion-regional/indice-de-capacidad-estadistica-territorial-icet

DANE. (n.d.-c). *Statistical Brief.* Retrieved November 30, 2022, from https://www .dane.gov.co/index.php/servicios-al-ciudadano/servicios-informacion/serie-notas -estadisticas

DANE. (2022). *Statistical Brief: Analysis of Accessibility to Educational Centers.* https://www.dane.gov.co/files/investigaciones/notas-estadisticas/ago_Nota -estadistica-accesibilidad-ingles-20220805.pdf

DANE, FAO, OCR, OHCHR, OIM, OIT, OMS/OPS, ONU Mujeres, PNUMA, PNUD, UNFPA, UNIDO, UNESCO, UN-Habitat, & UNODC. (2022). *Reporte de avance de Indicadores-ODS priorizados: Primer semestre de 2022.* https://www.dane.gov .co/files/indicadores-ods/Reporte-avance-Indicadores-ODS-prio.pdf

DANE, FAO, & UNFPA. (2021). *Guide to Measuring and Reporting on the Global Indicators in the United Nations Sustainable Development Cooperation Framework.* https://www.dane.gov.co/files/indicadores-ods/Guide-to-measuring -and-reporting-on-the-global-SDG-indicators.pdf

DNP. (2015). *Decreto 280 de 2015 – Gestor Normativo – Función Pública.* https:// www.funcionpublica.gov.co/eva/gestornormativo/norma.php?i=66611

DNP. (2018). *Estrategia para la implementación de los Objetivos de Desarrollo Sostenible (ODS) en Colombia.* https://assets.ctfassets.net/27p7ivvbl4bs/c15L6f PoswiGYUy64Uy4k/d2d1c2b218757846743c6eb335d5b380/CONPES_3918_ Anexos.pdf

DNP. (2021). *Acelerar la implementación para una recuperación sostenible. Reporte Nacional Voluntario 2021.* https://downloads.ctfassets.net/27p7ivvbl4bs/5QH MJWk16oeBIbmAuhlkaO/346d94400d11453bc9523ee63be7cacd/VNR_2021 _Colombia.pdf

ECLAC. (n.d.). *National Statistical Capabilities of the Countries of Latin America and the Caribbean to Produce the Global SDG Indicators.* Retrieved November 14, 2022, from https://agenda2030lac.org/estadisticas/national-statistical-capacities- produce-sdg-indicators.html

United Nations. (2018). *Global Indicator Framework for the Sustainable Development Goals and Targets of the 2030 Agenda for Sustainable Development.*

10. Mainstreaming gender in environment goals across the SDG monitoring framework

Sara Duerto Valero and Sharita Serrao[1]

10.1 INTRODUCTION

An increasing body of evidence is now available to demonstrate the connections between environmental sustainability and gender equality and women's empowerment (OECD, 2021) (UNEP, 2019) (SPC, UN Women, 2022). These connections, often referred to as the gender–environment nexus, are present in the context of natural resource management; environmental conservation; vulnerability, exposure to, and capacity to cope with and adapt to climate change and disasters; and even gender differentiated contributions to environmental degradation.

The Sustainable Development Goals, set out for the achievement of Agenda 2030, along with their monitoring framework, place a strong emphasis on environmental sustainability through several goals such as goals 6–7 and goals 11–15. They also recognize the importance of gender equality through goal 5 and select gender indicators integrated across several of the other goals and targets. However, the gender–environment nexus is not sufficiently recognized across the SDG framework.

The wider literature indicates that women and men have different levels of agency and their access to natural resources differs as well. For instance, although women's livelihoods are disproportionately reliant on natural resources, their limited ownership of productive assets renders them vulnerable in coping with disasters and environmental degradation. Furthermore, they do not always make decisions pertaining to water, forest management, or fishery utilization. As such, their contribution to environmental conservation is often limited by these access barriers.

The changing climate and its effects have a differing impact on women and men. For instance, job segregation may affect their levels of exposure to various hazards. Pre-existing gender inequalities in poverty, given that globally women are more likely to live in extreme poverty than men during reproductive years (UN Women, 2021); women's exposure to violence; and their disproportionate likelihood of being engaged in informal jobs (ILO, 2008), for instance, make them more vulnerable to environmental crises. At the same time, women's dependence on natural resources and the barriers they face in owning productive assets also limit their capacity to cope with job and income loss, food insecurity, displacement, and the many other consequences of climate change.

As women typically make decisions about household purchases (ASEAN, UN Women, 2021), they also have a role to play in environmental use and degradation, which differs from that of men, who disproportionately make these decisions at work. For instance, men are more likely to engage in polluting industries such as logging, fishing, chemical production, mining, and extraction. Although women engage substantially in other environmentally damaging industries such as garment production, social norms often hamper their engagement in decision-making at various levels, including in the context of environmentally friendly or damaging practices. Women face barriers to getting involved in environmental decision-making in politics, with only an estimated 15 percent of top jobs in environment-related ministries held by women globally (IUCN, 2020). Yet, in many countries, women, particularly rural and indigenous, are holders of traditional agricultural and environmental knowledge, some of which may hold the key to resolving or mitigating many of the environmental problems we face today.

10.2 THE GENDER–ENVIRONMENT NEXUS IN THE SDG MONITORING FRAMEWORK

As stated above, the 2030 Agenda is ambitious in recognizing the importance of both environmental sustainability and gender equality and women's empowerment as necessary conditions for the achievement of sustainable development. Although the United Nation's General Assembly's Resolution on Transforming our World: The 2030 Agenda for Sustainable Development (A/RES/70/1) recognizes the relevance of identifying interlinkages across all of the goals, the SDG monitoring framework does not include indicators that enable countries to measure the gender–environment connections adequately. This contributes substantially to a global lack of evidence on the nexus, which may delay the achievement of sustainable development as a whole.

For instance, according to whether or not each of the goals includes one or more gender-related indicators, the SDG goals can be classified into three groups: gender-specific, if they include more than one gender-relevant indicator; gender-sparse if they only include one gender-related indicator; or gender blind if they include no gender-relevant indicators (UN Women, 2018). While in goals on the elimination of poverty or the achievement of universal health and education, for instance, gender considerations are well mainstreamed, in most of the environment-related goals, gender indicators are largely absent (Figure 10.1). Goal 5 on gender equality and women's empowerment also lacks indicators pertaining directly to the environment, with the exception of 5.a.1 on land ownership and secure tenure.

SDG 13 on climate action and 15 on life on land, for instance, are among the gender-blind goals, as they do not include any gender-related indicators. However, indicators such as 13.1.1 (number of deaths, missing persons, and directly affected persons attributed to disasters per 100 000 population) and 15.7.1/ 15.c.1 (proportion of traded wildlife that was poached or illicitly trafficked) could both be of relevance from a gender perspective if data were disaggregated. However, no specific call for disaggregation is included in these indicators.

Even if sex-disaggregation were to be included, the indicators currently in the SDG framework are insufficient to measure the multiple interrelated gender dimensions pertaining to the environment. For instance, we now know that increases in temperatures and their impact on agricultural yield, biodiversity, and ecosystem loss could potentially increase economic stress on families and communities, and this in turn can increase child marriage practices

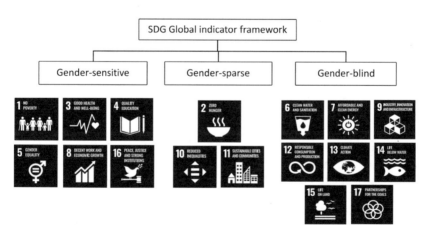

Note: Classification updated based on the available list of SDG indicators as of 30 August 2022 (A/RES/71/313)

Source: Based on the available list of SDG indicators as of 30 August 2022

Figure 10.1   *Uneven distribution of gender indicators across the SDG global monitoring framework*

and subsequently adolescent births, particularly in regions where these practices are already prevalent (see Chapter 11).

Also, changes in rainfall patterns can affect gender outcomes (see Chapter 11). For instance, increased aridity, which is often accompanied with land degradation, affects the availability of clean water and fuels, both of which have a significant effect on women's wellbeing, given that women and girls are in charge of water collection in 80 percent of the world's households for which water collection is necessary (UN Women, 2019), and they are also typically in charge of fuel collection and cooking. Although issues such as the availability of water, clean fuels, child marriage, and adolescent births are all reflected in various parts of the SDG framework, the connections between these and climate change are not adequately elucidated.

Similarly, issues around the differentiated gender roles pertaining to the management and use of land, for instance, are absent in Goal 15. Labor statistics show that, across Asia and Africa, women in employment are more likely to engage in agriculture than employed men (Paneque-Gálvez et al., 2018). They are also more likely to use land for subsistence farming and engage disproportionately in selling agricultural produce in markets. However, when it comes to decision-making in agricultural practices, such as pesticide and fertilizer use that may contribute to environmental degradation, these decisions often fall outside of the hands of women, as it is landowners who decide.

Indigenous and rural women, who are often key holders of traditional environmental knowledge, could make substantial contributions to environmental conservation if they were allowed to be involved in related decision-making. In Pacific Island countries, for instance, women hold key knowledge on practices such as angling roots to drain salt, which could help cope with the effects of salinization (Elizabeth Mcleod et al., 2018). Women also have knowledge on fallowing land, which contributes to the replenishment of nutrients in the soil and higher longer-term yields. Indigenous women in the Amazon are also known holders of knowledge on swidden cultivation-fallow management systems of agroforestry (Shiva, 1992). Recognizing these issues, including through targeted indicators, is important to generate necessary evidence that could inform national policies and action on land and biodiversity conservation.

No SDG indicators recognize the important gender aspects attached to accessing clean water, sanitation, and fuels, infrastructure, sustainable consumption and production, and life below water, whether oceans or freshwater. And yet, these are some of the most important gender–environment considerations for human wellbeing and biodiversity conservation. For instance, having access to an improved water source in or near the household is essential for human health. In most Asian and African countries, for instance, women are typically responsible for collecting water regularly, and their health is often adversely affected by walking long distances and carrying heavy weights while fetching water. This also potentially exposes them to violence and impinges on their time available for paid work or self-care and leisure activities.

While goal 7 of the SDG framework addresses the need for affordable and clean energy, this goal does not as such address women's limited access to clean cooking fuels and its adverse effects on women's health, as solid fuels and kerosene affect indoor air quality, and it is usually women who spend more time cooking and at home. Lack of access to electricity, in addition, may worsen women's domestic burdens, as it limits the possibility of using appliances and labor-saving devices for household chores.

Women's participation in, and contribution to, decision-making, as we know, is limited across most fields and at all levels, including in the designing and building of infrastructure related to clean water and energy (Morgan, 2020). For instance, data from 18 Pacific power utility firms indicates that only in one territory (American Samoa) was there an equal number of women and men managers, with most countries showing the proportion of women in managerial positions in these industries falling far below 50 percent. In the Federated States of Micronesia (FSM), Tahiti, Tuvalu, and Vanuatu, no women held managerial positions in power utilities. Furthermore, in FSM, the Marshall Islands, Palau, and Samoa no women held technical positions (UN Women, 2022). Promoting women's engagement in STEM and TVET education could greatly contribute to their engagement in these industries and thus open the door for their contribution to more sustainable consumption and production practices.

Women also play a key role in fisheries and life underwater. Although men are more likely to engage in fishing, women are often involved in aquaculture and are more likely to participate in post-processing operations, such as fish cleaning, packaging, drying, and selling. These contributions of women are not reflected in the SDG framework, including in goal 14. In the context of climate change, measuring women's participation in these sectors is important to put in place just transition policies that respond to women's needs as well.

In many regions, fish stocks have declined dramatically. Globally, only 66 percent of them are within biologically sustainable levels (United Nations Economic and Social Council, 2022). This has direct consequences not only on the livelihoods of fishermen, but also on those of people working on related secondary operations. Also, biodiversity loss poses a key challenge for all those residing in coastal areas. These hold 90 percent of all marine species, and losing key species such as sharks and rays is expected to trigger dramatic losses across overall marine environments, with consequences for both men and women. Oceanic sharks and rays have declined by 71 percent since 1970, the loss of which leads to a decline in coral reefs and seagrass beds and the loss of commercial fisheries (Pacoureau, 2021). These ecosystem changes affect marine vegetation and coral reefs. Women, who often remain in coastal areas while their male family members go out at sea, can play a key role in their conservation, for instance, through the management of mangrove forests and oversight of coastal practices regarding pollution or the discarding of nets and other fishing gear. Building their capacity and eliminating barriers to their contribution to ocean conservation is key. Oceans currently capture 25 percent of global carbon emissions, so the stakes are high in marine conservation for human and ecosystem wellbeing (UN, n.d.).

10.3   WHERE SDG INDICATORS EXIST, GENDER–ENVIRONMENT DATA ARE INCREASINGLY PRODUCED, AND THEY CAN SHOWCASE IMPORTANT CONNECTIONS

The gender–environment nexus is complex, and some cross-country data illustrating this nexus are now slowly emerging. Available data reinforce the strong interconnections indicated in the wider literature and that gender equality and women's empowerment are necessary conditions for the achievement of overall environmental sustainability and sustainable development as a whole.

One of the few SDG indicators that pertains to the gender–environment nexus and has some data availability is indicator 2.3.2 (average income of small-scale food producers, PPP (constant 2011 international $)). Analysis of data since 2015 reveals that, in most countries, women small-scale food producers earn less than men (Figure 10.2).

Women are also more likely than men to engage in small-scale operations. In these operations, gender gaps in income are large in many countries. Among small-scale food producers, the income of men-headed production units is systematically larger than the income of those headed by women. In half of the countries with available data in 2022, women-headed small-scale food production units earned between 50 and 70 percent of the income of those headed by men (United Nations Economic and Social Council, 2022).

The availability of sex-disaggregated data on land ownership and secure tenure continues to progressively increase, thanks to efforts by FAO and UN Women in supporting data reprocessing and collection across countries.[2] Data on SDG indicator 5.a.1 on the percentage of agricultural population with ownership or secure rights over agricultural land are largely unavailable, but efforts are ongoing to fill data gaps. Where available, preliminary data show that, in most countries, women are either at a disadvantage or on par with men. In some sub-regions, such as South Asia, large gender gaps exist. For instance, in India and Nepal, men are more than 15 percentage points more

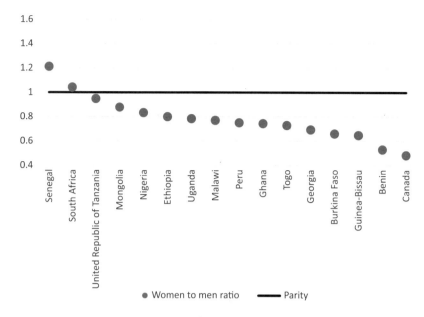

Source: Global SDG Database, available from https://unstats.un.org/sdgs/dataportal/database

Figure 10.2   *Women to men ratio for average income of small-scale food producers, PPP (constant 2011 international $), latest available datapoint since 2015*

likely than women to own land. Few countries showed gaps with women at an advantage; one instance was Cambodia, with a gap larger than 7 percentage points.[3]

The availability of these data is essential to help inform corrective policies. For instance, acknowledging women's and men's job segregation into small- and large-scale food production can help set up measures that support women's advancement into larger-scale operations, including by eliminating barriers to accessing loans, machinery, or other productive assets. Similarly, measuring the gender gaps in income among small-scale producers is important to identify their causes and put in place measures to tackle these inequalities.

Looking at other environmental SDGs from a gender angle is also of key importance, regardless of whether or not these goals and their indicators were initially designed to reflect gender issues. For instance, the WHO-UNICEF Joint Monitoring Programme is working to integrate new questions in multiple indicator cluster surveys, able to generate water and sanitation SDG indicators from a gender angle.[4] Similarly, UN Women supports countries with the implementation of surveys on gender and the environment, which are increasingly generating data on numerous gender–environment indicators (see next section).[5] Although countries producing these data may initially encounter barriers to reporting sex-disaggregated estimates to the international statistical system, as no sex-disaggregated indicators on water and fuel are currently part of the SDG monitoring framework, the availability of these estimates can inform national policies to address gender inequalities in the context of water and fuel management, environmental conservation and degradation, and unpaid work, among many other areas.

10.4   THE GENDER–ENVIRONMENT NEXUS: ISSUES BEYOND THE SDGS

Key issues of relevance for the gender–environment nexus that are currently absent from the SDG framework could be reflected through additional indicators for the existing SDGs and targets, while others may require the addition of new goals or targets. In 2019, consultations were conducted in the Asia-Pacific region to collate a set of indicators capturing the gender–environment issues relevant to the Asia-Pacific region (SPC, UN Women, 2022) (ESCAP, 2020). The intention was to provide a resource to countries in the region, which could be adapted and used based on country needs and interests to measure this nexus. Gender–environment policy issues relevant to the Asia-Pacific region were identified and classified into six key thematic areas: (A) land and biodiversity; (B) natural resources, including food, energy, and water; (C) climate change and disasters; (D) sustainable consumption, production, and waste; (E) health, wellbeing, and sanitation; and (F) environmental decision-making. The SDGs were first examined as a starting point to see if they had indicators to meet the data needs for these thematic areas. Through a series of expert consultations, key gap areas in the SDG framework were identified by experts. While some of these could be complemented with indicators from the Sendai Monitoring Framework, the International Standard Classification of Occupations, and other frameworks, environmental experts noted some gap areas that required additional measures not existing in international frameworks at the time. These included:

(a) Exposure to disasters
(b) Environment-related conflict, migration, and displacement
(c) Gender-based violence in the context of environment
(d) Harnessing women's traditional ecological knowledge
(e) Women in environmental conservation roles
(f) Rural women's leadership on environmental issues

(g) Small-scale industries, environment-related employment, and livelihoods
(h) Sustainable production and consumption, including sustainable agricultural practices, organic farming, and waste management

Numerous statistical developments are underway to fill these information gaps. For instance, through the Evidence and Data for Gender Equality (EDGE) project, FAO, UNSD, and UN Women developed guidelines to measure asset ownership and women's entrepreneurship (Department of Economic and Social Affairs Statistics Division, 2017), which are key indicators for measuring resilience to disasters. ILO currently measures women's participation in managerial positions through labor force surveys and collates key information about the management of firms through establishment surveys and other tools, although internationally comparable measures on women CEOs by type of industry remain currently unavailable across all regions and countries (ILO, n.d.). These statistics are important to assess women's contribution to natural resource management and environmental decision-making. FAO, through agricultural surveys and censuses, supports countries in measuring uses of land, fisheries, and forestry, among other issues, and thus produces important estimates that can help shed light on these topics. A key challenge, however, is that these instruments often focus on agricultural households, with plots and other environmental assets as the unit of measurement, rather than the individual (FAO, Food and Agriculture Statistics, 2022) (FAO, World Programme for the Census of Agriculture, 2020). As a result, capturing gender inequalities may be challenging, and any uses of land beyond agricultural practices remain unaccounted for. Furthermore, the use of proxy respondents for data collection is the usual practice in some of these instruments, which is known to return inaccurate data for sex-disaggregation on many issues.

To fill data gaps at the individual level, in 2021, UN Women, in consultation with ESCAP, FAO, ILO, IUCN, SPC, UNDRR, and UNEP, developed a model questionnaire on gender and the environment (UN Women, 2022), along with enumerators and sampling manuals for gender and environment surveys and related materials for implementation using CAPI. UN Women is currently supporting National Statistics Offices with related data collection. At the time of writing, gender and environment surveys had been conducted in Bangladesh, Mongolia, and Tonga and were underway in Samoa, with multiple other countries having expressed interest in receiving this support. These national surveys, conducted by interviewing two adult members of the opposite sex in each household, are useful to fill data gaps on a wide range of environmental issues, many of which are not captured in other standardized surveys, such as women's resilience to disasters, the gender-differentiated effects of climate change, women's participation in environmental decision-making, gender differences in engagement and roles in environment-related livelihoods, and women's roles in sharing traditional environmental knowledge.

Preliminary findings from the countries that have implemented the surveys show that gender roles are markedly different when it comes to the environment. For instance, in the context of preparing for environmental hazards, including disasters, women are more likely to deal with food processing and collecting and saving water, while men are typically in charge of reinforcing household walls and building barriers, for instance. In the aftermath of these events, women appear more likely to lose their income or livelihoods, including due to their disproportionate engagement in informal work and their reliance on environmental assets. Importantly, preliminary findings also show women are more likely than men to note the time spent on childcare, adult care, and unpaid domestic work activities increased as a result of the effects of climate change.

Gender and environment surveys can generate more than 100 gender–environment indicators and are thus useful tools for national planning and reporting toward national and international commitments. For instance, the surveys can generate data for several SDG indicators for goals 6, 7, 13, 14, and 15. Similarly, they are also useful to generate Sendai indicator data and data for the Global Set of Climate Change indicators. As data collection efforts increase across countries, comparable estimates for gender–environment indicators are expected to become increasingly available.

Despite these efforts, gaps remain, and methodology and tools are still underdeveloped to measure areas such as climate change-induced migration and displacement, gender-based violence in the context of the environment, and gender differences in involvement in illicit wildlife trade, to name a few. Further developments will be needed to measure the many dimensions of the gender–environment nexus. These will require leveraging different data sources beyond just surveys. For instance, analyzing existing data from administrative sources could provide key insights on issues such as women's participation and decision-making power in natural resource-focused industries. When this analysis was conducted in Pacific power utility firms, it showed very few women engaged in technical and senior management roles (SPC, UN Women, 2022). Integrating data from various sources could also provide additional insights. When UN Women analyzed geospatial data integrated with demographic and health survey data, it found relevant correlations between climate-related variables and gender equality outcomes (see Chapter 11). Finally, leveraging big data and other forms of non-conventional data sources, such as citizen-generated data, can provide additional insights to help fill gender–environment data gaps.

Many actors are currently working towards generating data to gain a better understanding of the gender–environment nexus. To coordinate efforts and ensure the new estimates are widely used, a Gender-Environment Data Alliance (GEDA) was established in 2022 during the Generation Equality Forum. The alliance looks to bring together data producers and users, to promote the uptake of gender–environment data to inform policies, advocacy, and accountability. GEDA focuses on compiling existing data and communicating them in a user-friendly way for policy makers. The alliance works closely with grassroots organizations and numerous data producers of official and non-official statistics. Links beyond the work of the GEDA and that of international statistical mechanisms could be strengthened to further promote the use of available gender–environment statistics by decision-makers.

10.5   CONCLUSION

Despite the increasingly available body of evidence demonstrating clear connections between the environment and gender equality and women's empowerment, sufficient data to measure all the complex relations that characterize this nexus remains unavailable, with several thematic areas showcasing large data gaps. International commitments and their monitoring frameworks, such as the Sustainable Development Goals or the Sendai Monitoring Framework, lack sufficient appropriate measures on the gender–environment nexus. Even when these exist, data are rarely available across countries and are seldom sufficient for trend analysis and the calculation of regional aggregates.

International recognition of the importance of measuring this nexus is however on the rise. In its 53rd session, decision 51/115, the UN Statistical Commission "emphasized the need for statistical offices' commitment at all levels and stages in the process of mainstreaming a gender perspective into the work of the Commission." In response, the United Nations Statistics Division and UN Women are working towards mainstreaming gender in the Global Set of Climate Change indicators. This endeavor may include adjusting some indicators, adding new indicators to the set, and developing further methodological guidelines. Ultimately, this is expected to promote the availability of gender–environment data and ideally its use to inform inclusive environmental policies. This work may, in addition, contribute to promoting gender data availability for some environment-related SDG indicators.

This is critical for achieving the SDGs, including meeting the 2030 Agenda's promise of leaving no one behind. Given that, in most households that lack water and fuel infrastructure, women are typically the ones collecting water and fuels, the achievement of SDGs 6 and 7 would be incomplete without measuring these gender differences. Similarly, recognizing women's important roles in agriculture, including small-scale operations, and fisheries, including the marketing of seafood, is important to ensure SDGs 14 and 15 are achieved for all. Recognizing the differentiated roles men and women play in natural resource management, both at home and at work, is key to achieving SDG 12, while looking at the different barriers they face in owning assets and accessing credit is essential for understanding their levels of resilience to disasters and other effects of climate change.

These are just a few examples that illustrate the importance of continuing the development of methodology and supporting interested governments in measuring the gender–environment nexus. Ultimately, the availability of these data is the only avenue for the evidence-based design of inclusive environmental policies.

NOTES

1. The authors would like to acknowledge the research assistance provided by Tsz Yu Chang.
2. https://data.unwomen.org/news/un-women-help-fill-data-gaps-womens-owner-ship-agricultural-land-asia-pacific
3. The datapoints mentioned in this paragraph are preliminary and thus should be interpreted with caution. No official estimates for this indicator are published in the official SDG database at the time of publication. Thus, these estimates may be revised or change substantially. The Food and Agriculture Organization of the United Nations continues working on producing these data points and may recommend further adjustments.
4. https://washdata.org/monitoring/inequalities/gender
5. https://data.unwomen.org/sites/default/files/documents/Publications/Model-Questionnaire-Gender-Environment.pdf

REFERENCES

ASEAN, UN Women. (2021). ASEAN gender outlook.

Department of Economic and Social Affairs Statistics Division. (2017). Evidence and Data for Gender Equality (EDGE). Retrieved from https://unstats.un.org/edge#:~:text=The%20Evidence%20and%20Data%20for,better%2C%20evidence%2Dbased%20policies

ESCAP. (2019). ESCAP Working Paper Series (SD/WP/10/October 2019): Mainstreaming gender in environment statistics for the SDGs and beyond: Identifying priorities in Asia and the Pacific.

ESCAP. (2020). Work of the secretariat and partners on mainstreaming (ESCAP/CST/2020/INF/10).

FAO. (2020). World programme for the census of agriculture. Retrieved from https://www.fao.org/world-census-agriculture/wcarounds/wca2020/en/

FAO. (2022). Food and agriculture statistics. Retrieved from https://www.fao.org/food-agriculture-statistics/capacity-development/agrisurvey/en/

ILO. (2008). *Women, Gender and the Informal Economy*. Geneva: ILO.

ILO. (n.d.). ILOSTAT. Labour statistics on women. Retrieved from https://ilostat.ilo.org/topics/women/

IUCN. (2020). Environment and gender information. Retrieved from https://gen derandenvironment.org/egi/#:~:text=IUCN's%20new%20data%20reveals%20inc remental,compared%20to%2012%25%20in%202015.&text=environmental%2 0decision%20making-,IUCN's%20new%20data%20reveals%20incremental%2 0change%3A%20in%202020%2C%20women%20held,comp

Mcleod, E., et al. (2018). Raising the voices of Pacific Island women to inform climate adaptation policies. *Marine Policy*, 93, 178–185.

Morgan, G. B. A.-H. (2020). *Infrastructure for Gender Equality and the Empowerment of Women*. Copenhagen, Denmark: UNOPS.

OECD. (2021). Gender and the environment: Building evidence and policies to achieve the SDGs.

Pacoureau, N. R. (2021). Half a century of global decline in oceanic sharks and rays. *Nature*, 567–571.

Paneque-Gálvez, J., Pérez-Llorente, I., Luz, A. C. et al. (2018). High overlap between traditional ecological knowledge and forest conservation found in the Bolivian Amazon. *Ambio*, 908–923.

Shiva, V. (1992). Women's indigenous knowledge and biodiversity conservation. *India International Center Quarterly*, 19(1/2), 205–214.

SPC, UN Women. (2022). Gender equality and sustainable energy: Lessons from Pacific Island countries and territories. Retrieved from https://data.unwomen.org /publications/gender-equality-sustainable-energy-pacific

UN. (n.d.). Climate action. The ocean – The world's greatest ally against climate change. Retrieved from https://www.un.org/en/climatechange/science/climate -issues/ocean#:~:text=The%20ocean%20generates%2050%20percent,the %20impacts%20of%20climate%20change

UN Women. (2018). Turning promises into action: Gender equality in the 2030 agenda for sustainable development.

UN Women. (2019). Turning promises into action: Gender equality in the 2030 agenda for sustainable development. Retrieved from https://www.unwomen.org/en/digital -library/sdg-report

UN Women. (2021). From insights to action: Gender equality in the wake of COVID-19.

UN Women. (2022a). Gender equality and sustainable energy: Lessons from Pacific Island countries and territories.

UN Women. (2022b). Model questionnaire: Measuring the nexus between gender and Environment.

UNEP. (2019). Gender and environment statistics: Unlocking information for action and measuring the SDGs.

United Nations Economic and Social Council. (2022). Progress towards the sustainable development goals: Report of the Secretary-General, Supplementary Information.

11. The gendered impacts of climate change: evidence from Asia

Sara Duerto Valero and Sneha Kaul[1]

11.1 INTRODUCTION

According to the Intergovernmental Panel on Climate Change (IPCC), 'climate change refers to a change in the state of the climate that can be identified by changes in the mean climate and/or the variability of its properties, and that persists for an extended period, typically decades or longer' (IPCC, 2007). While its impacts are far reaching, not everyone is affected equally, with differences across regions, generations, age groups, income groups, occupations, and genders (IPCC, 2001). As women often own fewer assets than men (United Nations, 2019), are overrepresented among the poor during their reproductive years (UN Women, 2020), are more likely to engage in informal employment when they work (ILO, 2018), and face discriminatory social norms (UN Women, 2015), their capacity to cope with the effects of climate change may be hindered.

The 2030 Agenda calls on member states to take action to combat climate change and achieve a sustainable future for all (UN General Assembly, 2015). Implementing each of the Sustainable Development Goals (SDGs) from a gender perspective is essential to meet the promise of leaving no one behind. However, the SDG monitoring framework does not include sufficient indicators that reflect the gender–environment nexus and even less that address the connections between climate change and gender outcomes. For instance, although there is a goal on gender equality (SDG 5) and eight goals related to the environment (SDGs 6, 7, 9, 11, 12, 13, 14, and 15) gender-related indicators are largely missing from the environment goals, and only two environment-related indicators are included under SDG 5. This is likely both a cause and effect of the lack of gender-environment data (Valero et al., 2022). This chapter contributes to filling these data gaps, by exploring empirically the links between climate change and gender outcomes. It achieves this by utilizing household survey and geospatial data from Bangladesh, Cambodia, Nepal,

Philippines, and Timor-Leste. Random forest machine learning and binary logistic regression models were applied to undertake the analysis.

The most important contribution of this study is that it illustrates empirically multiple connections between climate change and gender outcomes across a variety of countries. Such cross-country multi-dimensional evidence was largely missing in the literature to date. These findings demonstrate the potential negative consequences that climate change may have on gender equality and women's empowerment. They are a warning sign that the two issues cannot be addressed in isolation and shed light on the importance of working towards filling gender–environment data gaps, including for SDG monitoring.

11.2   BACKGROUND

The negative impacts of climate change have become increasingly evident today, including long-term changes in average temperature and rainfall, changes in the intensity, timing, and geographical variation of rainfall, increases in the frequency of extreme weather events such as drought episodes and floods, and sea level rises (IPCC, 2007). Numerous factors may make women more vulnerable to these effects, including poverty-driven inadequate means of adaptation (O'Brien et al., 2008), reduced coping capacities dictated by limited ownership of assets (Goh, 2012), and social norms preventing women from participating in environmental decision-making (Siles et al., 2019), relegating them to some environmentally vulnerable jobs and limiting their agency and freedom to cope with hazards (in Bangladesh, for example, women were unable to evacuate flooded areas due to travel restrictions in the absence of a male chaperone) (Crate & Nuttall, 2009). Although existing research is useful in demonstrating some linkages between climate change and gender outcomes, the focus is largely on single-country studies and qualitative methods. This chapter approaches this issue empirically, multi-dimensionally, and across countries. Using data from Bangladesh, Cambodia, Nepal, Philippines, and Timor-Leste, it tests the association between drought, relative aridity, day land surface temperature, rainfall, flood risk, and proximity to water bodies (freshwater lakes, and sea), with five development indicators that affect women especially: (1) the prevalence of child marriage, (2) adolescent birth rates, (3) the prevalence of intimate partner violence in the past 12 months, (4) access to basic water sources, and (5) the use of clean cooking fuels. A brief literature review for evidence on the connections between climate change and these five outcomes is provided below.

11.2.1   Child Marriage

Child marriage affects personal agency and is known to result in poor educational (Nguyen & Wodon, 2014) attainment and heightened risk of adolescent births (Lee-Rife et al., 2012). Driven by socio-cultural norms, socio-economic status, faith, education, and many other factors (Malhotra et al., 2011), it affects girls disproportionately (UNICEF, 2014). Natural hazards, which aggravate poverty and may promote the use of child marriage as a coping strategy (Asadullah et al., 2021), are known risk factors. In Bangladesh, for instance, economic challenges exacerbated by climate change were found to be key drivers of child and forced marriages (Alston et al., 2014). In India, child marriage rates were found to increase after rainfall shocks (Corno et al., 2017), while in another study in Bangladesh, a higher number of dry months was significantly found to increase these rates (Tsaneva, 2020).

11.2.2   Adolescent Birth

Childbearing during adolescence has health consequences for mother and child (Singh, 1998) and may carry economic impacts, as young mothers are more likely to achieve lower pay later in life (WHO, Adolescent pregnancy, 2020). Young age at first marriage, lower educational attainment (WHO, 2014), poor knowledge of family planning, and lack of access to information and services (Kennedy et al., 2011) all worsen adolescent birth rates. A study from Lesotho suggests that women in drought-affected regions experienced barriers to accessing family planning services and saw increased unwanted pregnancies (UNFPA, 2020). However, whether women disproportionately affected by climate change are more likely to become adolescent mothers has remained empirically unexplored in existing literature.

11.2.3   Intimate Partner Violence

The frequency and intensity of intimate partner violence (IPV) are affected by factors such as educational attainment, age, social norms, legal protection, and levels of general violence in society (Muluneh et al., 2021). It is well acknowledged that IPV occurs in the aftermath of crises (Peterman et al., 2020). However, evidence is also emerging on the effects of slow-onset climate events on IPV (Gevers et al., 2019). In sub-Saharan Africa, evidence shows that women experiencing severe drought were more likely to report physical, sexual, or psychological violence (Epstein et al., 2020). Empirical cross-country evidence on this topic in Asia, however, was largely missing and inconclusive in existing literature.

11.2.4   Access to Basic Drinking Water Sources

Having safe drinking water at home is important for women's empowerment because women and girls shoulder the burden of fetching water in 80 percent of the world's households that lack it (UN Women, 2018). As changes in temperature and precipitation affect water availability and quality (Delpla et al., 2009), water fetching times may increase. Studies conducted in India and across South Asia confirm the heightened stress on rural women as some regions experience severe water scarcity (Yadav & Lal, 2018). Studies from Nigeria, similarly, confirm increased water collection times under climate-change-induced water stress (Chinwendu et al., 2017) (Oluwatayo, 2011). No such empirical literature was found for South-East Asia at the time of review.

11.2.5   Use of Clean Cooking Fuels

Evidence shows that exposure to fuel-related indoor air pollution and the burden of fuel collection disproportionately affect women, who spend more time at home and are often in charge of cooking and fuel collection chores (IEA, IRENA, UNSD, Bank, & WHO, 2020). As environmental degradation results in biodiversity loss and reduced forest cover (Hamdy & Aly, 2014), and as climate change reduces purchasing power (Kuhla et al., 2021) and thus the affordability of cleaner fuels, households are turning to inferior fuels and altering cooking and collection patterns (Das et al., 2017) (Oxfam, 2002). In Senegal, a case study found women using plastic and bedding as cooking fuels, as a result of wood depletion and deforestation (ELIAMEP, 2008). Little evidence, however, exists to empirically demonstrate how climate change affects women's fuel use and related health and time burdens across Asian countries.

11.3   METHODOLOGY

This study examines the association between climate change and gender outcomes across multiple South Asian countries. Specifically, it aims to test the hypothesis that changes in climate-related variables are associated with changes in gender outcomes in South Asian countries, as measured by five development indicators that affect women, especially child marriage rates, adolescent births rates, the prevalence of intimate partner violence, access to basic drinking water sources, and access to clean cooking fuels.

11.3.1   Data Sources

The study integrated survey data from demographic and health surveys (DHS) with data from the DHS Geospatial Covariates dataset (DHS, n.d.), UNDRR's

Global Disaster Risk Dataset (UNDRR, 2017), and the Global Self-Consistent Hierarchical, High-Resolution Geography Database (Wessel & Smith, 2017). In particular, DHS's women's recodes were utilized to calculate five indicators (one for each of the five gender outcomes considered). Thus, variables containing information on age at first marriage, age at first birth, exposure to intimate partner violence in the 12 months preceding the survey, type of water source used for drinking, time to water source, and type of cooking fuel used in the household for cooking were used for this analysis. Data was integrated using household cluster as the unique identifier.

11.3.2   Scope

The analysis was carried out in Bangladesh, Cambodia, Nepal, the Philippines, and Timor-Leste. The country selection process considered three criteria: (1) countries are highly climate-prone, in terms of frequency, fatalities, economic losses, or a combination thereof (Germanwatch, 2021), (2) both DHS microdata and geospatial information data are available and publicly accessible, and (3) the countries are sufficiently different from each other (from an environmental point of view) to add variability to the analysis, while keeping geographical representation across sub-regions in Asia.

11.3.3   Variables

Variables were selected based on the relevance (assessed from literature reviews) and availability of comparable data across the five countries. Table 11.1 presents a complete list of variables included.

11.3.4   Models

Random forest (RF) and multivariate logistic regression models were used to estimate the associations between climate change and gender outcomes. First, RF was used to identify which independent variables were important for classifying outcomes accurately (for example, the climate-related variables likely to explain the risk of occurrence of gender outcomes). Once importance was established, the multivariate binary logistic regression model was used to estimate the direction and strength of associations between the dependent variables (gender-related outcomes) and independent variables (climate variables). While a multivariate logistic regression analysis is a commonly used estimation technique in the climate change literature, random forest is a relatively new modeling technique in this field. Both have their strengths, and details on the application of these techniques are discussed below.

Table 11.1   *Description of variables for logistic regression analysis*

Type of variable	Name of variable	Description of variable
Dependent variables	Child marriage	Age at first marriage or cohabitation lower than 18
	Adolescent births	Age at first live delivery lower than 18
	Intimate partner violence	Experience of severe or less severe physical or sexual violence from an intimate partner in the 12 months preceding the survey[2],[3]
	Lack of access to basic water sources	Women living in households that lack piped water (into their dwelling or yard) or other improved sources such as public standpipes, tube wells, boreholes, protected wells, rainwater, or bottled water, within a 30-minute round trip
	Unclean cooking fuels	Women living in households that use unhealthy cooking fuels, such as kerosene, charcoal, wood, straw/shrubs/grass, agricultural crops, or animal dung
Independent variables (also called predictors)	Day land surface temperature	Mean annual daytime land surface temperature (skin temperature) measured in degrees Celsius
	Drought episodes	Magnitude of monthly precipitation less than or equal to 50 percent of its long-term median value for three or more consecutive months
	Average annual rainfall	Average amount rain per year (in millimeters)
	Aridity index	Average yearly precipitation divided by average yearly potential evapotranspiration
	Probability of riverine flood	Estimated probability of major river basins flooding in 50 years
	Proximity to water bodies	Geodesic distance to either a lake or the coastline, in meters
Control variables	Education	Educational attainment in single years
	Employment	Women's employment status at the time of the survey
	Age	Women's age at the time of the survey

(*Continued*)

Table 11.1   *(Continued)*

Type of variable	Name of variable	Description of variable
	Wealth	Wealth quintiles (based on DHS's wealth index)
	Location	Household location (urban or rural)
	Buildup index	Degree of urbanization at the cluster level
	Proximity to national borders	Geodesic distance to international border, in meters
	Proximity to protected area	Geodesic distance to protected areas, such as national parks, national forests, and national seashores

11.3.4.1 Random forest

Random forest classification has gained attention as a powerful predictive model in recent years, especially in climate change and ecological studies (Gaál et al., 2012). The random forest algorithm uses a collection of decision trees to perform classifications or regression tasks and, in doing so, achieves the identification of key variables (or 'variables of importance') for predicting outcomes. In this sense, the random forest model was used to compute multiple decision trees for classifying the risk of an outcome, such as child marriage, given the independent variables in the model (for example, variations in temperatures, aridity).

Random forest was selected for this analysis as it offers high classification accuracy and can be applied to complex, non-linear associations (Cutler et al., 2007) (Evans et al., 2010). It provides an intuitive method of determining the variables of importance, through the 'mean decrease in accuracy' metric. Among the many popular predictive machine learning techniques available, RF models are found to perform with robustness and higher accuracy compared to support vector machines (Best et al., 2020) and were found to result in lower root mean squared errors when compared to the Xgboost algorithm (Wang, 2014).

11.3.4.2 Multivariate logistic regression

As the gender outcomes under consideration are constructed as binary categorical variables (for example, $0 =$ no child marriage, and $1=$ child marriage), binary logistic regression analysis was used to estimate the effect of multiple predictor variables (that is, climate change related variables) on these outcomes. Common covariates (wealth, education, employment) were controlled for to isolate the effect of the climate-related variables alone.

11.4 FINDINGS: CLIMATE CHANGE HAS GENDERED CONSEQUENCES

The first half of this section focuses on findings from the random forest model, which determine which climate variables are of relevance to explain the risk of gender outcomes. The second half looks at odds ratios from the multivariate binary logistic regression to examine whether these associations are direct or inverse, and how strong. Both models return findings suggesting there are clear connections between climate change variables and gender outcomes.

Findings highlight that the aridity index, mean daylight surface temperatures, distance to the nearest lake, and distance to the nearest marine coastline all contribute substantially to most of the gender equality outcomes considered. Access to clean water and use of clean fuels appear to be the outcomes most affected by climate change across all countries (other factors, including fuel prices and water infrastructure availability, also have a significant effect on these two outcomes).[4] Child marriage is also affected by climate variables quite substantially across countries. The effects on adolescent birth rates and especially on IPV are substantially smaller, although not negligible in some countries.

Due to geo-ecological, social, and economic differences across countries, the directions and strengths of associations between climate variables and gender outcomes vary by location. For instance, Bangladesh is the country most affected by climate variables when it comes to child marriage, adolescent birth rates, and rates of use of clean fuels. When looking at the aridity index and temperatures only, Nepal's child marriage rates are particularly susceptible. Cambodia seems to be the most vulnerable country to climate change when it comes to impacts on access to water, while for IPV, the explanatory power of climate variables is small throughout, with the Philippines and Timor-Leste seeing the most.

Given the multiplicity of factors that may influence these relations, it is likely that the associations between climate variables and gender outcomes aren't linear. As such, some of the findings highlighted by RF were not reflected directly in the logistic regression outputs. Similarly, affected by the localized nature of climate change and any regional factors uncontrolled for, while some variables (for example, increases in the frequency of droughts) lowered the likelihood of a gender outcome in some countries (for example, lacking clean fuels in Cambodia), they increased it in others (Bangladesh, Philippines). The details of all associations and potential contributing factors are examined below.

11.4.1 Random Forest (RF)

RF provides a metric of 'mean decrease in accuracy' for predicting gender outcomes when each of the climate variables is removed from the model. For instance, RF classifies the sample into high or low risk of experiencing child marriage, if the aridity index is removed from the model. By implementing such decision trees, RF provides insights on the most relevant variables to explain gender outcomes. The findings of the RF model suggest that many climate-related factors are important predictors for gender outcomes.[5] The relevance of climate-related variables for each of the outcomes is depicted in Figure 11.1 and discussed subsequently.

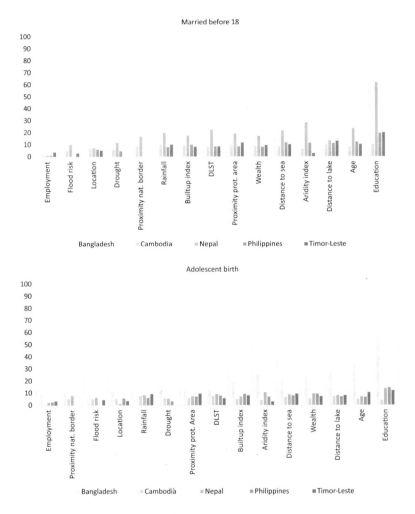

Figure 11.1   *Mean decrease in accuracy (in event of variable removal), by gender outcome (percentage)*

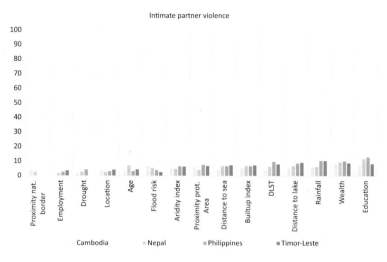

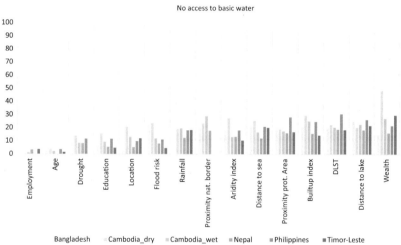

Figure 11.1 (Continued)

11.4.1.1 Child marriage

Across all countries, proximity to water (lakes or coastline, depending on the country) is among the most important climate-related variables for predicting the risk of child marriage. Literature shows that living near water can have positive and detrimental effects on livelihoods and, consequently, child marriage (Asadullah et al., 2021). For instance, increases in sea level rise may have a detrimental effect on the livelihoods of populations living near

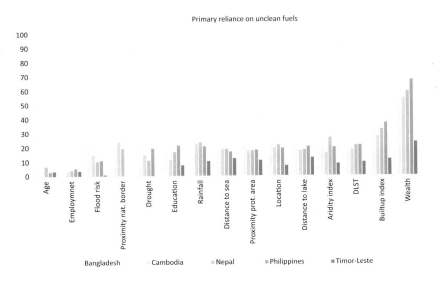

Primary reliance on unclean fuels

Figure 11.1   (Continued)

coastlines, but overall proximity to coasts may be advantageous for accessing fishery-related livelihoods. Random forest does not explain the direction of the associations.

The aridity index was also highlighted as a key variable for classifying the risk of child marriage in Bangladesh, Nepal, and the Philippines. This is in line with findings from the logistic regression model (see below), as well as with the literature, which highlights that changes in relative aridity affect water sources, crop production, food security, and other poverty-related indicators (Hu et al., 2021) that are known drivers of child marriage.

11.4.1.2   Adolescent births

Average annual rainfall appears to be the most important variable in explaining the risk of adolescent births in Cambodia (even more than non-climate factors such as educational attainment). The country relies heavily on agriculture, and yield is strongly dependent on the monsoon rain and natural floods/recession of the Tonle Sap Lake and Mekong River (WWF Greater Mekong, 2016). As a result, rainfall in Cambodia conditions livelihoods, access to education, age at first marriage, and many other factors that may result in adolescent birth rates. As the frequency and intensity of droughts and floods in the country continue to increase (The World Bank Group and Asian Development Bank, 2021), their effects on people's livelihoods, and thus adolescent births, are intensifying. Since 2007, Cambodia's adolescent birth rates have shifted from 47 to 52 births per 1000 women (United Nations Population Division, World Population Prospects, 2022). The findings from RF indicate that the shift may be more pronounced in areas more exposed to changes in rainfall and is thus likely to worsen over time, ceteris paribus.

As with child marriage, distance to water (nearest lake or marine coastline) is also important for describing the risk of adolescent births across all countries, an unsurprising finding given the known correlation between child marriage and adolescent births (Godha et al., 2013). Average day land surface temperature is a good predictor for adolescent births as well, especially in Cambodia, Nepal, and the Philippines. Sustained increases in land surface temperatures are known to correlate with forest transition, biodiversity loss, reduced agricultural yield (Olsson et al., 2019), and many other livelihood-related indicators. These are known to affect the likelihood of girls falling victim to child marriage (Asadullah et al., 2021), dropping out of school, and lacking agency and access to information – all known drivers of adolescent births. Finally, RF flagged the importance of relative aridity for predicting adolescent births in Bangladesh and Nepal, likely via similar enabling factors.

11.4.1.3   Intimate partner violence

According to RF, climate change variables have the poorest predictive power over IPV. After removing the climate change variables from the model, its accuracy drops by a small margin. This points to the possibility that IPV may be driven by factors not considered in this study, such as social norms, intra-household inequalities, and differentials in the ownership of assets, known to affect IPV rates (WHO, 2012) (Muluneh et al., 2021).

Among the non-climate factors considered, education and wealth were the best predictors in all countries. Although they are less important for explaining the risk of IPV across countries, the role of climate-related variables is not negligible. Average annual rainfall, for instance, is of some relevance in Cambodia, the Philippines, and Timor-Leste. Proximity to lakes, coastlines, and protected areas also had some, although limited, predictive power. Further analysis is necessary to ascertain the driving factors behind these findings, although climate-related economic stressors are likely to play a role.

11.4.1.4   Access to basic water sources

Across all five countries, climate-related variables are key in predicting women's access to basic water sources (climate variables have higher classification power than any other factor, except for wealth in some countries). Proximity to coastlines, and particularly to lakes, is among the most important contributors to the model's accuracy. The literature shows that freshwater lakes are valuable resources for travel, trade, fishing, and irrigation, but cyanobacterial blooms have increasingly become a challenge accelerated by rising temperatures, the use of pesticides, and pollution (National Geographic, 2020). If cyanobacteria reach wetlands and groundwater reservoirs near lakes, they may have severe consequences on the quality of the water in nearby areas (Gkelis, 2017). People who would otherwise drink from open water or groundwater sources may thus be pushed to rely on rainwater, bottled water, or other improved sources. In Cambodia, although distance to nearest lake is highly relevant during the wet season (when open water source contamination is higher due to runoff and bacteria, and when people can rely on rainwater), distance to nearest coastline has higher importance during the dry season. In the absence of rains, people in coastal areas substantially depend on open water sources and unprotected wells for drinking water, while away from the coasts, the availability of piped water is higher. Further research, however, is necessary to ascertain additional reasons behind this dichotomy.

Riverine flooding (probability of floods in a 50-year period) also explains substantially the risk of lacking basic drinking water in Cambodia (during the dry season) and especially in Bangladesh. Given the cyclical nature of severe flooding in Bangladesh, it is well documented that drinking water sources are contaminated during floods, as water sources are infiltrated by fecal matter and other debris (Islam et al., 2007). This may push people who would otherwise drink from open sources to drink bottled or other forms of improved water, to prevent water-borne disease. The same is true in Cambodia, where 19 percent of the population drinks from rivers, streams, and other open surface water sources during the dry season (when rainwater is unavailable). As climate change intensifies the likelihood of flooding in both countries (The World Bank Group, 2021) (The World Bank Group and Asian Development Bank, 2021), access to basic water sources may be at stake for many, with consequent impacts on women's time and health.

As expected, given their connections with aridification, land degradation, and extreme weather, day land surface temperatures also explain the risk of lacking basic water sources in all countries, particularly in the Philippines, where the predictive power of the model would decrease by as much as 31 percent if the variable was removed. Similarly, in Bangladesh, Cambodia, Nepal, and Timor-Leste it would decrease by 19 percent or more. In Cambodia, furthermore, relative aridity accounts for almost 28 percent of the model's accuracy during the wet season.

Other non-climate related variables such as wealth and built-up index (degree of urbanization) also have high classification power, as it is widely documented that urban areas and wealthier households have better access to piping and other water infrastructure (WHO & UNICEF, 2017).

11.4.1.5   Use of clean cooking fuels

Along with access to water, using clean cooking fuels is the outcome best explained by climate change–related factors. Environmental variables such as temperatures, aridity, and rainfall play a major role in determining whether women use these fuels, although RF shows that non-climate variables such as wealth and built-up index (for example, fuel prices and infrastructure) also matter substantially.

Average day land surface temperature is of high relevance across all countries considered. In Bangladesh, where model accuracy would decrease by as much as 34 percent if the temperature variable was removed, this may be due to a multiplicity of factors. First, warmer temperatures triggering erratic precipitation patterns (the flood variable is also very relevant for fuels in Bangladesh) may lower the reliance on woodfire and other unclean fuels, prompting people to pay for electricity or gas. Second, the existence of urban heat islands in Dhaka and Chittagong (where fuel infrastructure is more widely available) may be affecting this relationship (see Figures 11.2a and 11.2b). Additional analysis also indicates that fuel infrastructure in Bangladesh conditions a direct association between temperatures and the use of clean fuels. In the country, the location of clusters cooking with natural gas (an improved fuel) overlaps largely with the distribution of major gas condensate fields and wells (Curiale et al., 2002), many of which are hot areas. Worryingly, oil drilling itself may be contributing to the warming of these areas (the literature shows that areas subject to fossil fuel extraction experience relatively high rates of temperature rise overall) (Nawaz & Sharif, 2019). Despite their positive effect on promoting the use of clean cooking fuels in Bangladesh, as extraction operations go on, temperature rises in such areas may continue to increase, with consequent negative effects on biodiversity loss, land degradation, and thus gender outcomes (Barbir & Veziroğlu, 1990) (Bertrand, 2021).

The aridity index, rainfall, and distance to lakes and coastlines also appear relevant in all countries. For aridity and rainfall, similar results are shown by the regression analysis (arid conditions worsen the use of clean fuels). A multiplicity of factors may be at play, such as rainfall contributing to the curbing of electricity prices, maintaining livelihoods, and enabling access to clean cooking fuels despite higher prices. Further research, however, is necessary to understand the complex set of variables that may be affecting clean fuel availability and prices and thus to isolate the effect of climate variables on fuel use.

11.4.2   Logistic Regression Analysis

Logistic regression models identified the largest positive or negative associations between gender outcomes and drought, relative aridity, and temperature. Figure 11.3 presents these results through adjusted odds ratios (AOR)

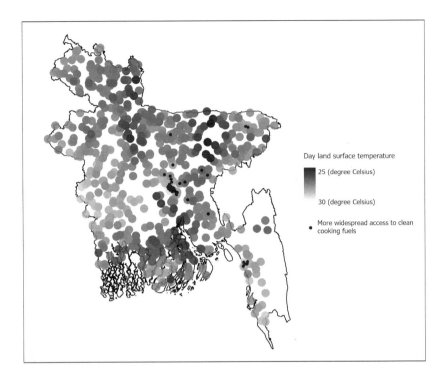

Note: The black circular markers represent clusters with better access to clean cooking fuels (25 percent of clusters with the lowest clean cooking fuels usage). The map indicates a higher prevalence of access to clean fuels across warmer clusters

Figure 11.2   *(a) Geographical distribution of clusters where women have better access to clean cooking fuels, by average day land surface temperature (degree Celsius), Bangladesh*

(for example, the likelihood that an outcome, such as child marriage, occurs given a particular exposure, such as increases in the frequency of droughts, compared to the odds of the outcome occurring in the absence of that exposure, holding the effect of all control variables constant to their central tendency) (Szumilas, 2015). AORs greater than one indicate a positive correlation between the independent variable and dependent variables (for example, child marriage increasing if droughts become more frequent), those lower than 1 indicate a negative correlation (for example, child marriage decreases when droughts become more frequent), while those equal to 1 indicate no effect (child marriage rates don't change). Each of the climate variables showed different positive or negative effects depending on the location and its socio-demographic and geographical characteristics.

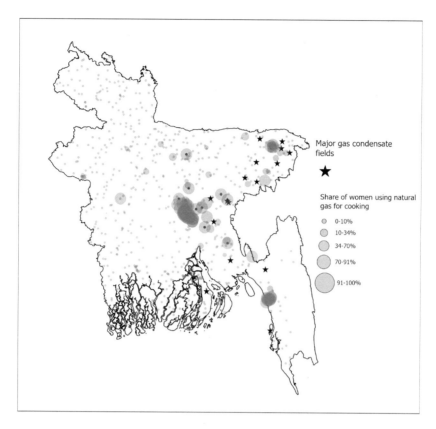

Note: The map shows that natural gas use is more widespread in clusters near gas fields
Source: Data on major gas condensate fields is based on Curiale et al., 2002

Figure 11.2   *(b) Major gas fields and share of women using natural gas*
as a cooking fuel, by cluster, Bangladesh

11.4.2.1 Drought episodes

The size and intensity of the effects of droughts on different gender outcomes
vary across countries, as the impact of drought depends on whether the region
is arid or semi-arid, whether drought episodes are short-term or long-term,
and whether the effects are localized or widespread (Kulkarni & Rao, 2008).
Each country's dependence on agriculture, a sector that absorbs a large part of
the direct shocks associated with droughts, is also likely to determine the
extent of the impacts (FAO, 2022). Importantly, people's capacity to cope with
droughts (and therefore the effect of drought on gender outcomes) is also determined by their socio-economic characteristics (for example, wealth, location,

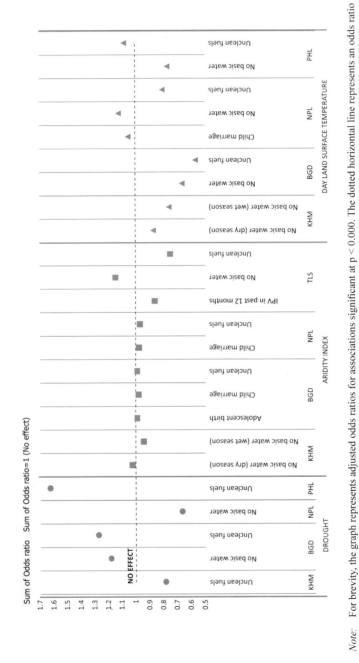

Note: For brevity, the graph represents adjusted odds ratios for associations significant at p < 0.000. The dotted horizontal line represents an odds ratio of 1 (no association). The three-digit country codes can be interpreted as: KHM (Cambodia), BGD (Bangladesh), NPL (Nepal), PHL (the Philippines), and TLS (Timor-Leste)

Figure 11.3   Adjusted odds ratios (p < 0.000) for the effect of drought, aridity index, and day land surface temperature on gender outcomes

asset ownership, access to credit) and how rare or unexpected the drought event is. Although this analysis controlled for some socio-economic characteristics, data was not available for many others (for example, asset ownership, access to credit) that may contribute to the gender effects observed.

Findings show that when droughts are frequent, women are more likely to encounter barriers to accessing basic water sources, which may lengthen the time they spend collecting water, cooking, and providing hygiene for the household. Similarly, in line with existing literature, frequent drought episodes are also strongly associated with limited access to clean cooking fuels in Bangladesh and especially the Philippines, where the effects are some of the largest in this study (Bangladesh AOR 1.28***; Philippines AOR 1.63***). Fuel cost, among other factors, may also contribute to this association. Although fuel price data was not considered for this analysis, the literature shows that water scarcity limits energy production by hydropower and coal plants (International Energy Agency, 2016), which are highly dependent on water for cooling, thus increasing energy prices. Further, drought-driven economic stresses from reduced agricultural yields may push households to rely on cheaper cooking fuels, such as wood, charcoal, or kerosene (Poch & Tuy, 2012).

11.4.2.2 Relative aridity

Relative aridity (as measured by the aridity index) is significantly connected with gender-related outcomes, although the magnitude of the connections is small in most countries. These effects are felt the most in Timor-Leste, where clear associations exist with the prevalence of IPV, access to basic water sources, and the use of clean cooking fuels.

With a prolonged history of conflict, Timor-Leste suffers from widespread poverty and safety concerns. The prevalence of IPV is the highest among the five countries considered (an estimated 35 percent of women experienced physical and/or sexual violence at the hands of their partner in the 12 months preceding the survey). Analysis shows that increases in relative aridity correlate with rises in IPV (Figure 11.3). Although multiple factors are likely to contribute, aridity-related economic stresses, which worsen poverty, may increase insecurity and pressures to meet bride price commitments and thus IPV (stress associated with bride price is known to worsen IPV in the country (Rees et al., 2017)). Given the projected effects of climate change in Timor-Leste (temperatures are expected to increase by 0.3–1.2 degrees Celsius by 2030, which will alter rainfall patterns, relative aridity, the onset of seasons, sea level rise, and the intensity and frequency of extreme weather events (Green Climate Fund, 2019)) and the heavy dependence of its population on agriculture (it is the main source of income for more than 80 percent of the population (Green Climate Fund, 2019)), these changes are expected to worsen agricultural yield, poverty, and thus the risk of IPV in the future.

Changes in relative aridity were also found to be associated (although less so) with the availability of basic water sources in Cambodia, where increases in humidity enhance the likelihood of women lacking basic water sources during the dry season but lower it during the wet season (AOR=1.03*** and AOR=0.95***, respectively). This is largely due to the different water sources utilized in humid vs. dry environments in the country. Although women living in arid clusters mostly rely on tube wells (an improved source) throughout the year, many in humid clusters rely on rainfall (an improved source) during the wet season but shift to unprotected wells and open surface water during dry seasons. This highlights the risks that climate change brings about, as shifts in relative humidity are likely to further alter the predictability of water availability, lower water quality, and increase water fetching and treatment burdens on women.

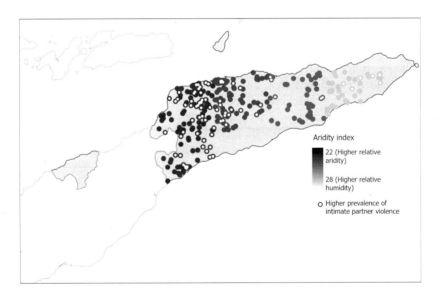

Note: The white circular markers represent clusters with a higher prevalence of intimate partner violence (top 25 percent of cluster values). The map indicates that arid clusters are more likely to see higher rates of intimate partner violence in the past 12 months

Figure 11.4   Geographical distribution of clusters with high rates of intimate partner violence in the past 12 months, by level of relative aridity, Timor-Leste

11.4.2.3 Day land surface temperature

Increases in day land surface temperature reflect global warming, urban heat islands, and extended hot and cold waves, while contributing to other issues such as land degradation (Olsson et al., 2019), sea level rise, reduced agricultural yield, forest transition, biodiversity loss, and human disease (IPCC, 2019). Thus, unsurprisingly, findings show that temperatures are strongly connected with gender-related outcomes across almost every country, and in many of the countries the effects are large.

In Cambodia and Nepal, increases in day land surface temperature enhance the odds of child marriage. This is likely linked to their effects on agricultural yield and other natural resources, which contribute to economic insecurity and the use of child marriage as a coping strategy (Rumble et al., 2018) (World Bank & ICRW, 2016). In Nepal, this association is stronger (AOR=1.05***) and heavily concentrated across warm clusters in the south-eastern Terai region, where prevailing social norms and traditions are overall supportive of child marriage practices (Sajeda & Bajracharya, 2020).

In Bangladesh, Cambodia, and the Philippines, increases in temperatures correlate with better access to basic drinking water sources. In areas where improved water infrastructure is not available, the effects of temperatures on freshwater availability and contamination may contribute to these associations. Temperature rises typically present simultaneously with fresh water source depletion (for example, wetland drying, conversion of freshwater wetlands to agricultural land) and land degradation (for example, dry forest clearing, salinization) (Olsson et al., 2019) which may result in poor rain absorption and thus runoff draining into waterways and polluting the water supply (National Geographic Society, 2022). Consequently, populations living in high temperature clusters without access to piped water may shift from drinking river and stream water to improved sources such as bottled or rainwater. In the Philippines, for instance, women living in hot clusters depend on bottled water disproportionately (66.7 percent, compared to 28.7 in cooler clusters). Despite being improved sources, bottled and rainwater consumption still require fetching efforts and thus contribute to women's burdens, unlike other improved sources such as piped water. Conversely, in Nepal, increases in temperatures correlate with increased difficulty accessing basic water sources, but disparities in the availability of water infrastructure appear to be affecting this association.

In the Philippines, as expected, increases in day land surface temperatures are associated with a higher risk of using unhealthy fuels. Besides major cities such as Metro Manila and Cebu (which have better fuel infrastructure and LPG availability), clusters reliant on clean cooking fuels are more likely to be located in cooler areas. Economic strains associated with heat-driven reductions in agricultural yield and biodiversity loss, coupled with increased electricity and gas prices as a result of heat (Cian et al., 2007), may be prompting people in hot clusters to shift to cheaper but dirtier fuels. Unexpectedly, this association is inverse in Bangladesh and Nepal. In Bangladesh, it is affected by fuel infrastructure and availability (women living in areas with natural gas fields are more likely to use it, and these are warmer areas, as natural gas extraction increases day land surface temperature) (see Figures 11.2a and 11.2b). In Nepal, the use of cleaner cooking fuels, such as LPG and biogas, is mostly concentrated in the Central (Kathmandu valley) and Western regions. As clean fuel infrastructure is not available in the coldest and more remote mountain regions, the analysis shows an inverse correlation, but further analysis controlling for fuel infrastructure and prices could provide further insights on whether the association with climate factors alone is indeed inverse in these two countries.

11.5   CONCLUSION

The purpose of the study was to test the association between climate change factors and gender-related outcomes, which was achieved by analyzing DHS data integrated with geospatial data. Random forest machine learning was used to ascertain the importance of climate change variables in classifying women into groups at high or low risk of experiencing select gender outcomes. A multivariate binary logistic regression model was then used to measure the degree and direction of these associations. Findings proved the hypothesis that climate change–related factors are associated with gender outcomes in all countries considered for the study. This remained true even after controlling for several socio-demographic variables.

Droughts, temperatures, relative aridity, proximity to lakes, proximity to coastlines, and rainfall were all found to be important variables in explaining gender outcomes. Across all countries, proximity to lakes and/or coastlines appears to be particularly important in determining the risk of lacking basic water sources, utilizing unhealthy cooking fuels, and experiencing child marriage and adolescent births. Temperatures and rainfall also contribute to these outcomes substantially. Not surprisingly, the analysis also revealed that, of all outcomes considered, climate change–related variables had the largest effects on the risk of lacking access to basic drinking water sources and clean cooking fuels (proximity to lakes and coastlines, flood risk, temperature, and aridity all enhanced substantially the classification power of water and fuel models). Conversely, climate change–related variables had the lowest classification power over intimate partner violence, the risk of which appears more closely associated with education and wealth across most countries (although rainfall did matter in Timor-Leste and the Philippines).

Logistic regression showed that increases in drought episodes, relative aridity, and temperatures are associated with worsening gender outcomes overall. In particular, more frequent drought episodes are linked with a lack of access to basic drinking water sources (Bangladesh and Cambodia) and less use of clean fuels for cooking (Bangladesh and the Philippines). Increases in relative aridity (low aridity index) correlate with worsening child marriage and adolescent birth rates (Bangladesh and Nepal), although these effects are smaller in size. The largest aridity effects appear in Timor-Leste, where IPV and the use of unclean fuels both increase substantially with arid conditions, while access to basic water sources worsens with humid conditions. Temperature rises show detrimental effects on the availability of basic water sources (Nepal), clean cooking fuels (the Philippines), and child marriage rates (Nepal). In Cambodia and Bangladesh the relation between temperatures and availability of water and fuels is inverse, likely due to infrastructure and the prices of these goods.

These findings hold key implications that should be taken into consideration for policy making. They are evidence that climate change–related effects, particularly those associated with changes in the amounts and patterns of rainfall, temperatures, and quality of water bodies, may hinder the achievement of not only SDG5, but also the rest of the SDGs in Asia. They provide empirical evidence on the importance of addressing climate change and gender equality in tandem to ensure transformative results.

Due to limitations associated with data availability, the localized nature of climate-related phenomena, and the multiplicity of factors at play, further analysis is needed to ascertain the causes of these connections and their effects across different population groups. For instance, additional controls for key variables such as prices of goods and available infrastructure are necessary to better understand these connections. As existing literature highlights that disadvantaged groups may suffer from climate change disproportionately (Sevoyan & Hugo, 2014), further analysis with multiple disaggregation by sex and age, or sex and ethnicity, for instance, could provide additional insights. Additionally, future studies could build on the same methodology to explore other potential gendered impacts of climate change on health and nutritional status, food security, asset ownership, migration patterns, and educational attainment to name a few.

NOTES

1. This paper was written by Sara Duerto Valero and Sneha Kaul, with support from Tsz Yu Chang and Cecilia Tinonin. The paper builds on previous analysis developed by Daniel Clarke and Yichun Wang. The authors would like to acknowledge the valuable guidance, comments, and contributions provided by Ginette Azcona,

Antra Bhatt, Christophe Bontemps, Anthony Dean Burgard, Prim Devakula, Sangita Dubey, Jessamyn Encarnacion, Maria Holtsberg, Inkar Kadyrzhanova, Eunkoo Lee, Yongyi Min, Papa Seck, Sharita Serrao, Yichun Wang, and Frank Yrle. The views expressed in this publication are those of the authors and do not necessarily represent the views of UN Women, the United Nations, or any of its affiliated organizations. The designations employed and the presentation of the material in this publication do not imply the expression of any opinion whatsoever on the part of UN Women concerning the legal status of any country, territory, city, or area or of its authorities, or concerning the delimitation of its frontiers or boundaries.
2. Bangladesh's DHS did not include information on IPV, so the country was not considered for IPV analysis.
3. A 12-month reference period was deemed preferable over lifetime experiences given the increasing variability in weather patterns in recent years.
4. See results of random forest model (Figure 11.1), where built up index (degree of urbanization) has high classification power for water results, and wealth has it for both water and use of clean fuels.
5. This is in addition to some of the socio-economic control variables, such as wealth and education.

REFERENCES

Alston, M., Whittenburg, K., Haynes, A., & Godden, N. (2014). Are climate challenges reinforcing child and forced marriage and dowry as adaptation strategies in the context of Bangladesh? *Women's Studies in International Forum*. Retrieved from https://www.sciencedirect.com/science/article/abs/pii/S0277539514001381

Aryanti, T., & Muhlis, A. (2020). Disaster, gender, and space: Spatial vulnerability in post-disaster shelters. *Earth and Environmental Science*. Retrieved from https://iopscience.iop.org/article/10.1088/1755-1315/447/1/012012/pdf

Asadullah, M., Islam, K., & Wahhaj, Z. (2021). Child marriage, climate vulnerability and natural disasters in coastal Bangladesh. *Journal of Biosocial Science*, 948–967. https://doi.org/10.1017/S0021932020000644

Barbir, F., & Veziroğlu, T. (1990). Environmental damage due to fossil fuels use. *International Journal of Hydrogen Energy*. Retrieved from https://www.sciencedirect.com/science/article/abs/pii/036031999090005J

Bartlett, S. (2008). Climate change and urban children: Impacts and implications for adaptation in low and middle-income countries. International Institute for Environment and Development. Retrieved from https://www.iied.org/

Bertrand, S. (2021). Climate, environmental, and health impacts of fossil fuels. Environmental and Energy Study Institute. Retrieved from https://www.eesi.org/papers/view/fact-sheet-climate-environmental-and-health-impacts-of-fossil-fuels-2021

Best, K., Gilligan, J., Baroud, H., Carrico, A., Donato, K., & Ackerly, B. (2020). Random forest analysis of two household surveys can identify important predictors of migration in Bangladesh. *Journal of Computational Social Science*. Retrieved from https://link.springer.com/article/10.1007/s42001-020-00066-9

Chinwendu, O., Sadiku, S., Okhimamhe, A., & Eichie, J. (2017). Households vulnerability and adaptation to climate variability induced water stress on downstream Kaduna River Basin. *American Journal of Climate Change*. Retrieved from https://www.scirp.org/html/3-2360441_76112.htm?pagespeed=noscript

Corno, L., Hildebrandt, N., & Voena, A. (2017). Age of marriage, weather shocks, and the direction of marriage payments. NBER. Retrieved from https://www.nber.org/system/files/working_papers/w23604/w23604.pdf

Couronné, R., Probst, P., & Boulesteix, A. (2018). Random forest versus logistic regression: A large-scale benchmark experiment. *BMC Bioinformatics*. Retrieved from https://bmcbioinformatics.biomedcentral.com/articles/10.1186/s12859-018-2264-5

Crate, S. A., & Nuttall, M. (2009). Introduction: Anthropology and climate change. Retrieved from https://www.taylorfrancis.com/chapters/edit/10.4324/9781315434773-5/introduction-anthropology-climate-change-susan-crate-mark-nuttall

Curiale, J., Covington, G., Shamsuddin, A., & Morelos, J. (2002). Origin of petroleum in Bangladesh. *AAPG Bulletin*. Retrieved from https://pubs.geoscienceworld.org/aapgbull/article-abstract/86/4/625/39983/Origin-of-Petroleum-in-Bangladesh

Cutler, R., Edwards Jr., T., Beard, K., Cutler, A., Hess, K., Gibson, J., & Lawler, J. (2007). Random forest for classification in ecology. *Ecology*. Retrieved from https://esajournals.onlinelibrary.wiley.com/doi/abs/10.1890/07-0539.1

Das, I., Jagger, P., & Yeatts, K. (2017). Biomass cooking fuels and health outcomes for women in Malawi. *Ecohealth*. Retrieved from https://www.ncbi.nlm.nih.gov/pmc/articles/PMC5357447/

De Cian, E., Lanzi, E., & Roson, R. (2007). The impact of temperature change on energy demand: A dynamic panel analysis. FEEM Working Paper No. 46.2007, University Ca' Foscari of Venice, Dept. of Economics Research Paper Series No. 0. Retrieved from https://papers.ssrn.com/sol3/papers.cfm?abstract_id=984237

Delpla, I., Jung, A. V., Baures, E., Clement, M., & Thomas, O. (2009). Impacts of climate change on surface water quality in relation to drinking water production. *Environment International*, 35(8), 1225–1233. Retrieved from https://www.researchgate.net/profile/Arif-Reza/post/What_is_the_relationship_between_surface_water_quality_and_climate_change/attachment/59d63820c49f478072ea5388/AS%3A273695707205633%401442265550316/download/2009_Impacts+of+climate+change+on+surface+water

DHS. (n.d.). Spatial data repository. Retrieved from spatialdata.dhsprogram.com: https://spatialdata.dhsprogram.com/covariates/

ELIAMEP. (2008). Gender, climate change and human security: Lessons from Bangladesh, Ghana and Senegal. Retrieved from https://repository.ubn.ru.nl/bitstream/handle/2066/72456/72456.pdf

Epstein, A., Bendavid, E., Nash, D., Charlebois, E., & Weiser, S. (2020). Drought and intimate partner violence towards women in 19 countries in sub-Saharan Africa during 2011–2018: A population-based study. *PLOS Medicine*. Retrieved from https://journals.plos.org/plosmedicine/article?id=10.1371/journal.pmed.1003064

Evans, J., Murphy, M., Holden, Z., & Cushman, S. (2010). Modeling species distribution and change. *Predictive Species and Habitat Modeling in Landscape Ecology*. Retrieved from https://link.springer.com/chapter/10.1007/978-1-4419-7390-0_8#citeas

FAO. (2022). Drought and agriculture. Retrieved from fao.org: https://www.fao.org/land-water/water/drought/droughtandag/en/

Fernando, M., & Jose Ignacio, R. (2020). Variable importance plot (mean decrease accuracy and mean decrease Gini). *PLOS One*. Retrieved from https://plos.figshare.com/articles/figure/Variable_importance_plot_mean_decrease_accuracy_and_mean_decrease_Gini_/12060105/1

Gaál, M., Moriondo, M., & Bindi, M. (2012). Modelling the impact of climate change on the Hungarian wine regions using random forest. *Applied Economics.* Retrieved from https://www.researchgate.net/profile/Marco-Moriondo/publication /236107259_Modelling_the_impact_of_climate_change_on_the_Hungarian_wine _regions_using_Random_Forest/links/00463515f5b9ed96f9000000/Modelling -the-impact-of-climate-change-on-the-Hungarian-wine-

Germanwatch. (2021). Global climate risk index 2021: Who suffers most from extreme weather events? Weather-related loss events in 2019 and 2000–2019. Retrieved from https://germanwatch.org/sites/default/files/Global%20Climate%20Risk%20Index %202021_2.pdf

Gevers, A., Musuya, T., & Bukuluki, P. (2019). Why climate change fuels violence against women. Apolitical. Retrieved from https://apolitical.co/solution-articles/en /why-climate-change-fuels-violence-against-women

Gkelis, S. (2017). Can cyanobacteria infect underground water sources? Indications from small scale monitoring of a natural drinking water source. *Advances in Oceanography and Limnology.* Retrieved from https://pagepressjournals.org/index .php/aiol/article/view/6280/6895

Godha, D., Hotchkiss, D., & Gage, A. (2013). Association between child marriage and reproductive health outcomes and service utilization: A multi-country study from South Asia. *Journal of Adolescence Health.* Retrieved from https://pubmed.ncbi .nlm.nih.gov/23608719/

Goh, A. (2012). A literature review of the gender differentiated impacts of climate change on women's and men's assets and well-being in developing countries. Retrieved from https://www.worldagroforestry.org/sites/default/files/4.pdf

Green Climate Fund. (2019). Democratic republic of Timor-Leste. Retrieved from https://www.greenclimate.fund/sites/default/files/document/timor-leste-country -programme.pdf

Hamdy, A., & Aly, A. (2014). Land degradation, agriculture productivity and food security. Fifth International Scientific Agricultural Symposium. Retrieved from http://www2.agrosym.rs.ba/agrosym/agrosym_2014/documents/4epnm/epnm9.pdf

Hsiang, S., Burke, M., & Miguel, E. (2013). Quantifying the influence of climate on human conflict. Retrieved from https://science.sciencemag.org/content/341/6151 /1235367

Hu, W., Ran, J., Dong, L., Du, Q., Ji, M., & Yao, S. (2021). Aridity-driven shift in biodiversity-soil multifunctionality relationships. *Nature Communication.* Retrieved from https://www.nature.com/articles/s41467-021-25641-0

IEA, IRENA, UNSD, Bank, W., & WHO. (2020). Tracking the SDG 7: The energy progress report. Retrieved from https://trackingsdg7.esmap.org/data/files/download -documents/tracking_sdg_7_2020-full_report_-_web_0.pdf

ILO. (2018). Women and men in the informal economy: A statistical picture. Retrieved from https://www.ilo.org/wcmsp5/groups/public/---dgreports/---dcomm /documents/publication/wcms_626831.pdf

International Energy Agency. (2016). Water energy nexus: Excerpt from the world energy outlook 2016. Retrieved from https://iea.blob.core.windows.net/assets/ e4a7e1a5-b6ed-4f36-911f-b0111e49aab9/WorldEnergyOutlook2016ExcerptWaterE nergyNexus.pdf

IPCC. (2001). Summary for policymakers. Climate change 2001: Impacts, adaptation and vulnerability. Retrieved from http://www.ipcc.ch/

IPCC. (2007). Retrieved from https://www.ipcc.ch/site/assets/uploads/2018/02/ar4 _syr_full_report.pdf

IPCC. (2014). Climate change 2014: Impacts, adaptation, and vulnerability. Retrieved from https://www.ipcc.ch/site/assets/uploads/2018/02/WGIIAR5-PartA_FINAL.pdf

IPCC. (2019). Climate change and land: An IPCC special report on climate change, desertification, land degradation, sustainable land. In P. Shukla, J. Skea, E. C. Buendia, V. Masson-Delmotte, H.-O. Pörtner, D. C. Roberts ... J. Petzold. Retrieved from https://www.ipcc.ch/site/assets/uploads/sites/4/2021/07/210714-IPCCJ7230 -SRCCL-Complete-BOOK-HRES.pdf

Islam, M., Brooks, A., Kabir, M., Jahid, I., Islam, M., Goswami, D., ... Yukiko, W. (2007). Faecal contamination of drinking water sources of Dhaka city during the 2004 flood in Bangladesh and use of disinfectants for water treatment. *Journal of Applied Microbiology*. Retrieved from https://pubmed.ncbi.nlm.nih.gov/17584454/

IUCN. (2020). Environment and Gender Information (EGI). Retrieved from genderandenvironment.org: https://genderandenvironment.org/egi/#:~:text=IUCN's%20new%20data%20reveals%20incremental,compared%20to%2012%25%20in%202015.&text=environmental%20decision%20making-,IUCN's%20new%20data%20reveals%20incremental%20change%3A%20in%202020%2C%20women%20held,comp

IUCN. (n.d.). Gender and climate change. Retrieved from https://www.iucn.org/resources/issues-briefs/gender-and-climate-change

Kennedy, E., Gray, N., Azzopardi, P., & Creati, M. (2011). Adolescent fertility and family planning in East Asia and the Pacific: A review of DHS reports. *Reproductive Health*. Retrieved from https://reproductive-health-journal.biomedcentral.com/articles/10.1186/1742-4755-8-11

Kohno, A., Techasrivichien, T., Suguimoto, S., Dahlui, M., Farid, N., & Nakayama, T. (2020). Investigation of the key factors that influence the girls to enter into child marriage: A meta-synthesis of qualitative evidence. *PLOS One*. Retrieved from https://journals.plos.org/plosone/article/metrics?id=10.1371/journal.pone.0235959 #citedHeader

Kuhla, K., Willner, S., Otto, C., Wenz, L., & Leverman, A. (2021). Future heat stress to reduce people's purchasing power. *PLOS One*. Retrieved from https://www.ncbi .nlm.nih.gov/pmc/articles/PMC8191966/

Kulkarni, S., & Rao, N. (2008). Gender and drought in South Asia: Dominant constructions and alternate propositions. In *Drought and Integrated Water Resource Management in South Asia*. Retrieved from https://books.google.co.in/books?hl =en&lr=&id=OYHEbasIeR0C&oi=fnd&pg=PA70&dq=drought+episodes+AND +asia+&ots=zaq-NGB1UJ&sig=9yLYYzZe8k3dykCSnUOhqHu5BPY&redir_esc =y#v=onepage&q=drought%20episodes%20AND%20asia&f=false

Lee-Rife, S., Malhotra, A., Warner, A., & Glinski, A. (2012). What works to prevent child marriage: A review of the evidence. *Studies in Family Planning*. Retrieved from https://onlinelibrary.wiley.com/doi/10.1111/j.1728-4465.2012.00327.x

Malhotra, A., Warner, A., McGonagle, A., & Lee-Rife, S. (2011). Solutions to end child marriage. Retrieved from https://www.healthynewbornnetwork.org/hnn -content/uploads/Solutions-to-End-Child-Marriage1.pdf

Muluneh, M., Alemu, Y., & Meazaw, M. (2021). Geographic variation and determinants of help seeking behaviour among married women subjected to intimate partner violence: Evidence from national population survey. *International Journal for Equity in Health*. Retrieved from https://link.springer.com/article/10.1186/s12939 -020-01355-5#citeas

National Geographic. (2020). Lake. Retrieved from education.nationalgeographic.org: https://education.nationalgeographic.org/resource/lake

National Geographic Society. (2022). How climate change impacts water access. Retrieved from https://education.nationalgeographic.org/resource/how-climate-change-impacts-water-access

Nawaz, R., & Sharif, A. (2019). Earth thermal emissions and global warming. *Journal of Scientific Research and Reports*. Retrieved from https://journaljsrr.com/index.php/JSRR/article/view/30117

Nguyen, M. C., & Wodon, Q. (2014). Impact of child marriage on literacy and education attainment in Africa. Retrieved from http://ais.volumesquared.com/wp-content/uploads/2015/02/OOSC-2014-QW-Child-Marriage-final.pdf

O'Brien, G., O'Keefe, P., Meena, H., Rose, J., & Wilson, L. (2008). Climate adaptation from a poverty perspective. *Climate Policy*, 194–201. Retrieved from https://www.tandfonline.com/doi/abs/10.3763/cpol.2007.0430

Olsson, L., Barbosa, H., Bhadwal, S., Cowie, A., Delusca, K., Flores-Renteria, D., ... Li, D. (2019). Land degradation. In P. Shukla, J. Skea, E. C. Buendia, V. Masson-Delmotte, H.-O. Pörtner, and D. C. Zhai (Eds.), *Climate Change and Land: An IPCC Special Report on Climate*. Retrieved from https://www.ipcc.ch/site/assets/uploads/sites/4/2019/11/07_Chapter-4.pdf

Oluwatayo, I. (2011). Climate change and adaptive capacity of women to water stress in urban centers of Nigeria: Emerging concerns and reactions. In K. Otto-Zimmermann (Ed.), *Resilient Cities*. Springer. Retrieved from https://link.springer.com/chapter/10.1007/978-94-007-0785-6_7#citeas

Oxfam. (2002). Gender, development and climate change. Retrieved from https://oxfamilibrary.openrepository.com/bitstream/handle/10546/121149/bk-gender-development-climate-change-010102-en.pdf?sequence=1#page=12

Peterman, A., Potts, A., O'Donnell, M., Thompson, K., Shah, N., Oertelt-Prigione, S., & van Gelder, N. (2020). Pandemics and violence against women and children. Center for Global Development. Retrieved from https://www.cgdev.org/sites/default/files/pandemics-and-vawg-april2.pdf

Poch, K., & Tuy, S. (2012). Cambodia's electricity sector in the context of. In Y. Wu, X. Shi, and F. Kimura (Ed.), *Energy Market Integration in East Asia: Theories, Electricity Sector and Subsidies* (pp. 141–172). Jakarta: ERIA. Retrieved from https://www.eria.org/Chapter%207-Cambodia%27s%20Electricity%20Sector%20in%20the%20Context%20of%20Regional%20Electricity%20Market%20Integration.pdf

Rees, S., Mohsin, M., Tay, A., Soares, E., Tam, N., Costa, Z., & Tol, W. (2017). Associations between bride price stress and intimate partner violence amongst pregnant women in Timor-Leste. *Globalization and Health*. Retrieved from https://globalizationandhealth.biomedcentral.com/articles/10.1186/s12992-017-0291-z#citeas

Rumble, L., Peterman, A., Irdiana, N., Triyana, M., & Minnick, E. (2018). An empirical exploration of female child marriage determinants in Indonesia. *BMC Public Health*. Retrieved from https://bmcpublichealth.biomedcentral.com/articles/10.1186/s12889-018-5313-0#citeas

Sajeda, A., & Bajracharya, A. (2020). Costs of marriage—Marriage transactions in the developing world. Retrieved from https://knowledgecommons.popcouncil.org/departments_sbsr-pgy/833/

Sevoyan, A., & Hugo, G. (2014). Vulnerability to climate change among disadvantaged groups: The role of social exclusion. In J. P. Palutikof, S. L. Noulter, J. Barnett, & D. Rissik (Eds.), *Applied Studies in Climate Adaptation*. Australia: Wiley-Blackwell, pp. 258–265.

Siles, J., Prebble, M., Wen, J., Hart, C., & Schuttenberg, H. (2019). Advancing gender in the environment: Gender in fisheries - A sea of opportunities. IUCN and USAID. Retrieved from https://portals.iucn.org/library/sites/library/files/documents/2019 -040-En.pdf

Singh, S. (1998). Adolescent childbearing in developing countries: A global review. *Studies in Family Planning.* Retrieved from https://www.jstor.org/stable/172154 ?seq=1

Szumilas, M. (2015). Explaining odds ratios. *Journal of the Canadian Academy of Child and Adolescent Psychiatry.* 2010 Aug 19(3), 227–229. Erratum in Journal of the Canadian Academy of Child and Adolescent Psychiatry. Retrieved from https:// www.ncbi.nlm.nih.gov/pmc/articles/PMC2938757/

Tsaneva, M. (2020). The effect of weather variability on child marriage in Bangladesh. Retrieved from https://onlinelibrary.wiley.com/doi/abs/10.1002/jid.3507

U.S. Energy Information Administration. (n.d.). EIA expects U.S. hydropower generation to decline 14% in 2021 amid drought. *Today in Energy.* Retrieved from https://www.eia.gov/todayinenergy/detail.php?id=49676#

UN General Assembly. (2015). Transforming our world: The 2030 agenda for sustainable development. Retrieved from https://documents-dds-ny.un.org/doc/ UNDOC/GEN/N15/291/89/PDF/N1529189.pdf?OpenElement

UN Women. (n.d.). Retrieved from https://www.unwomen.org/en/what-we-do/ economic-empowerment/facts-and-figures

UN Women. (n.d.). Retrieved from https://www.unwomen.org/en/news/in-focus/ women-and-the-sdgs/sdg-6-clean-water-sanitation

UN Women. (n.d.). Retrieved from https://www.unwomen.org/en/news/in-focus/ women-and-the-sdgs/sdg-7-affordable-clean-energy

UN Women. (2015). The Beijing declaration and platform for action turns 20. Retrieved from Available from: https://www.unwomen.org/-/media/headquarters /attachments/sections/library/publications/2015/sg%20report_synthesis-en_web .pdf?la=en&vs=5547

UN Women. (2018). Turning promises into action: Gender equality in the 2030 agenda for sustainable development. Retrieved from https://www.unwomen.org/sites/ default/files/Headquarters/Attachments/Sections/Library/Publications/2018/SDG -report-Gender-equality-in-the-2030-Agenda-for-Sustainable-Development-2018 -en.pdf

UN Women. (2020). From insights to action: Gender equality in the wake of COVID-19. Retrieved from https://www.unwomen.org/sites/default/files/Headquarters/ Attachments/Sections/Library/Publications/2020/Gender-equality-in-the-wake-of -COVID-19-en.pdf

UNDESA. (n.d.). Transforming our world: The 2030 agenda for sustainable development. Retrieved from sdgs.un.org: https://sdgs.un.org/2030agenda

UNDRR. (2017). GAR 2017 Atlas risk data and software download facility. Retrieved from risk.preventionweb.net: https://risk.preventionweb.net/index.html

UNFPA. (2020). In climate change-affected Lesotho, self-injected contraceptives empower women to choose their own future. Retrieved from https://www.unfpa .org/news/climate-change-affected-lesotho-self-injected-contraceptives-empower -women-choose-their-own

UNICEF. (n.d.). Retrieved from https://www.unicef.org/protection/child-marriage#:~ :text=Child%20marriage%20refers%20to%20any,an%20adult%20or%20another %20child.&text=Child%20marriage%20robs%20girls%20of,threatens%20their% 20lives%20and%20health

UNICEF. (2014). Ending child marriage: Progress and prospects. Retrieved from https://data.unicef.org/resources/ending-child-marriage-progress-and-prospects/

UNICEF. (n.d.). Joint Monitoring programme. Drinking water. Retrieved from https://washdata.org/monitoring/drinking-water

United Nations. (2019). Producing statistics on asset ownership from a gender perspective. Retrieved from https://unstats.un.org/edge/publications/docs/Guidelines_final.pdf

United Nations Population Division, World Population Prospects. (2022). Retrieved August 2022, from https://genderdata.worldbank.org/countries/cambodia/#:~:text =52%20of%20every%201%2C000%20girls,roughly%20the%20same%20since %202010

Valero, S., Emandi, R., Encarnacion, J., Kaul, S., & Seck, P. (2022). Utilizing big data to measure key connections between gender and climate change. *Statistical Journal of the IAOS*, 38(3), 973–994. https://doi.org/10.3233/SJI-220964

Wang, Y. (2014). DHS and Geo-covariates data integration case study on Bangladesh survey 2014: Report. Retrieved from https://repository.unescap.org/bitstream/ handle/20.500.12870/831/ESCAP-2014-PB-DHS-geo-covariates-data-integration -case-study-Bangladesh-survey.pdf?sequence=1

Wessel, P., & Smith, W. (2017). A global self-consistent, hierarchical, high-resolution shoreline database. Retrieved from soest.hawaii.edu: http://www.soest.hawaii.edu /pwessel/gshhg/

WHO. (2012). Understanding and addressing violence against women. Retrieved from https://apps.who.int/iris/bitstream/handle/10665/77432/WHO_RHR_12.36_eng .pdf;sequence=1

WHO. (2014). Adolescent pregnancy: Situation in South-East Asia Region. Retrieved from https://apps.who.int/iris/bitstream/handle/10665/204765/B5164.pdf

WHO. (2020). Adolescent pregnancy. Retrieved from https://www.who.int/news -room/fact-sheets/detail/adolescent-pregnancy

WHO and UNICEF. (2017). Progress on drinking water, sanitation, and hygiene. Retrieved from https://www.unwater.org/app/uploads/2020/04/WHOUNICEF -Joint-Monitoring-Program-for-Water-Supply-Sanitation-and-Hygiene-JMP-%E2 %80%93-2017_ENG.pdf

World Bank Group. (2021). Climate risk country profile: Bangladesh (2021). Retrieved from https://climateknowledgeportal.worldbank.org/sites/default/files/country -profiles/15502-WB_Bangladesh%20Country%20Profile-WEB.pdf

World Bank Group and Asian Development Bank. (2021). Climate risk profile: Cambodia. Retrieved from https://climateknowledgeportal.worldbank.org/sites/ default/files/2021-08/15849-WB_Cambodia%20Country%20Profile-WEB.pdf

World Bank and ICRW. (2016). Basic profile of child marriage in Nepal. Retrieved from https://openknowledge.worldbank.org/bitstream/handle/10986/24546/Bas ic0profile0of0child0marriage0in0Nepal.pdf?sequence=1&isAllowed=y

WWF Greater Mekong. (2016). Mekong river in the economy. Retrieved from http:// d2ouvy59p0dg6k.cloudfront.net/downloads/mekong_river_in_the_economy _final.pdf

Yadav, S., & Lal, R. (2018). Vulnerability of women to climate change in arid and semi-arid regions: The case of India and South Asia. *Journal of Arid Environments*. Retrieved from https://www.sciencedirect.com/science/article/abs/ pii/S0140196317301532

12. SDG interactions from a regional perspective: a case study from Sweden

Anja Eliasson and Erik Grönlund

12.1 INTRODUCTION

Achieving sustainability can be found as a policy goal at all levels of society; internationally as well as nationally, regionally, and locally. The Sustainable Development Goals (SDGs) are described by the United Nations (UN) as indivisible (UN, 2015), meaning that none of the goals can be achieved at the expense of another and that success is required within all areas to achieve sustainable development. While advocates describe it as an indivisible whole, studies aimed at examining the interlinkages of the SDGs provide a more complex image with the occurrence of both synergies and trade-offs (Bali Swain & Ranganathan, 2021; Cling & Delecourt, 2022; ICSU, 2017; Lyytimäki et al., 2020; McCollum et al., 2018; Nilsson et al., 2016; Pradhan et al., 2017; Warchold et al., 2021; Weitz et al., 2018). Generally speaking, synergies arise when progress in one goal favours progress in another, while trade-offs are signified by progress in one goal that hinders progress in another (Pradhan et al., 2017). The inability to overcome persistent trade-offs has been found to seriously threaten the achievement of Agenda 2030 (Kostetckaia & Hametner, 2022; Kroll et al., 2019). However, there have been several attempts at using the knowledge on synergies and trade-offs as a means for policy support to enhance progress across all 17 SDGs and their 169 targets (Allen et al., 2018; Miola et al., 2019; Weitz et al., 2018). Disentangling interactions among the SDGs can support the effective and coherent implementation of policies across sectors (Weitz et al., 2018).

The work of Nilsson et al. (2016) highlights the importance of context when it comes to working with the SDGs. How the goals or targets interact with each other will be different when taking key contextual determinants such as geographical conditions and governance into consideration (Nilsson et al., 2018). There have been a small number of studies investigating the topic in a Swedish context, such as Engström et al. (2019) who looked at interactions between water- and land-related SDGs (goal 2, 6, 7, 11, 13, 15) and Weitz et al. (2018) who examined the interactions among 34 targets relevant for Sweden.

There are also examples of how regions and municipalities have taken on the work with the Agenda (SKR, 2019), but information regarding what conflicts might exist within the Agenda and how these affect regional actors in Sweden is limited. The work of Nilsson et al. (2016) indicates a need for investigating the SDGs from a local or regional perspective to gain useful information on how to approach Agenda 2030. Kostetckaia and Hametner (2022) have found that trade-offs seem to have a bigger influence on the pace of progress towards the SDGs than synergies, making it an important issue to prioritise in order to reach the goals in time. This study focuses on the interlinkages between selected SDG targets through a case study of the region Jämtland Härjedalen, located in the middle of Sweden.

Using the SDG interaction framework developed by Nilsson et al. (2016), the purpose of the study is to identify interactions between 15 SDG targets relevant to Jämtland Härjedalen. Furthermore it aims to contribute to an understanding of how knowledge of synergies and trade-offs within Agenda 2030 can be used to view the SDGs as an integrated whole and to assess and prioritise targets in the work within sustainable development on a regional level. The objectives are to assess where synergies and trade-offs can be found between the selected SDG targets and to identify which targets require specific attention from a policy perspective based on identified synergies and trade-offs.

12.2   BACKGROUND

Municipalities and regions are central actors in the implementation of the 2030 Agenda. This has been highlighted by the European Union (EU) (European Commission, 2018) as well as on a national level. In proposition 2019/20:188 regarding the implementation of Agenda 2030, the Swedish government emphasises the importance of the regional/local level as Sweden's decentralised model of society means that responsibility for many of the basic welfare assignments lies with regions and municipalities (Swedish Government, 2019c). The 21 regions in Sweden are self-governing and are run by elected political assemblies. Their work is directly or indirectly linked to the implementation of the SDGs and areas of responsibility and entails regional development and growth, public transport, and healthcare, among others (Kullander, 2021).

The work with the 2030 Agenda has had a breakthrough in Swedish municipalities and regions. A report conducted by the State Office (2019) shows that 70 per cent of municipalities and almost all regions are using the Agenda as a tool in their work with sustainable development. Despite this, their investigation concluded that the work with the 2030 Agenda so far has had little effect on the overall work on sustainability. The actors' way of working and their priorities have not shifted in any significant way within most of the regions or municipalities, and the concrete operational changes that the actors have implemented are in many cases superficial. Performed activities have instead been characterised by single efforts and smaller, time-limited side projects such as seminars, shorter trainings, and the mapping of operations (State Office, 2019). In their final report to the government, one of the key factors that the State Office brings forward is that the directives need to come from the highest level of management (both the political and official leadership) to give sustainability a greater space in the actors' operations (State Office, 2020). The joint organisation for Sweden's municipalities and regions (SKR, 2020) makes a similar analysis and emphasises the importance of integrating Agenda 2030 and the goals into the steering and management of municipalities and regions to achieve the goals on a national level.

However, the report from the State Office describes how the implementation of the 2030 Agenda in steering and action has proven difficult for regions and municipalities. Uncertainties in how the work should be performed to fulfil the national commitment of the Agenda have resulted in requests for further support on how to work with and prioritise the goals in relation to other national objectives (State Office, 2019).

Being responsible for regional development and growth, Region Jämtland Härejdalen is obliged to develop a Regional Development Strategy (RDS) according to Swedish law (Swedish Parliament, 2017). This is an important steering tool that is the foundation for other regional strategies and programmes, and sustainability should be an integral part of it (ibid.). As a step towards strengthening the implementation of aspects of sustainability and global goals according to Agenda 2030, Region Jämtland Härjedalen had their old RDS analysed to clarify its connection to the SDGs (Oxford Research, 2019). They assessed that a majority of the goals found in the RDS were in line with the SDGs. Goals concerning education, work and economic growth, sustainable industry, infrastructure, and sustainable cities along with health and well-being were the focus of the RDS. They also concluded that goals concerning equality as well as environment and climate needed to be more directly implemented. Goal number 10 on reduced inequality was completely missing from the strategy.

12.3   METHODS

The key method used in the study was the SDG interactions framework developed by Nilsson et al. (2016). One important factor in the methodology is the emphasis given to key contextual determinants (Nilsson et al., 2018). Finding relevant literature in terms of geographical context, time horizon, and governance was therefore an important first step.

The interactions between the SDG targets were assessed in a cross-impact matrix based on two systematically selected literature sources per target. In addition, a screening for relevant policy documents in Region Jämtland Härjedalen with regard to the chosen targets was performed. Documents were chosen based on how well they matched the description of the target in question and their relevance from a Swedish perspective, with preference given to specific information on the northern regions or Jämtland. Mostly grey literature in terms of published reports was included; however, journal articles and books were also part of the review. Recently published information was prioritised to ensure updated information and data (oldest article from 2013). The sample of literature did not aim to be exhaustive but to give guidance for scoring based on context-specific data.

The target level of the SDGs was chosen for the analysis instead of the goal level since targets are more specific, and this is where substantive interactions are more easily discerned (ICSU, 2017). A total of 15 targets were included in the analysis, resulting in a total of 210 interactions to be analysed, as shown in Table 12.1. The selection was guided by key performance indicators that the Council for the Promotion of Municipal Analyses has put forward to support the regional and local implementation of Agenda 2030 (RKA, 2020). Previous research on SDG interactions relevant from a Swedish perspective was also used as guidance (Weitz et al., 2018). The selection was further supported by looking into grey literature, such as regional plans and strategic documents, to highlight especially important targets for Jämtland Härjedalen. Considering the geographic location of Jämtland Härjedalen, with no coastline, goal 14 (life below land) was excluded, as well as goal 17 (partnerships for the goals) since it focuses on the means of implementing goals.

The cross-impact matrix analysis was guided by the SDG interactions framework. The core of the framework is a typology that characterises the nature of binary relationships between SDGs at target level and involves the scoring of interactions on a seven-point scale. The scoring ranges between indivisible (+3) and cancelling (−3), where positive scores represent synergies, while negative scores represent trade-offs. The framework has been used in its original form in several studies (Allen et al., 2018; ICSU, 2017; Lyytimäki et al., 2020; Weitz et al., 2018) and with certain adaptations (Boman, 2018). This study uses an adapted version, following the lines of Boman (2018), where a degree of uncertainty is part of the evaluation, see Table 12.2.

Table 12.1   *The 15 SDG targets chosen for Region Jämtland Härjedalen with official descriptions*

Target	Short description	Official description
1.2	Poverty	By 2030, reduce at least by half the proportion of men, women and children of all ages living in poverty in all its dimensions according to national definitions
2.4	Food production/agriculture	By 2030, ensure sustainable food production systems and implement resilient agricultural practices that increase productivity and production, that help maintain ecosystems, that strengthen capacity for adaptation to climate change, extreme weather, drought, flooding and other disasters and that progressively improve land and soil quality
3.4	Non-communicable diseases	By 2030, reduce by one-third premature mortality from non-communicable diseases through prevention and treatment and promote mental health and well-being
4.4	Technical/vocational skills	By 2030, substantially increase the number of youth and adults who have relevant skills, including technical and vocational skills, for employment, decent jobs and entrepreneurship
5.5	Women's participation	Ensure women's full and effective participation and equal opportunities for leadership at all levels of decision-making in political, economic and public life
6.6	Water-related ecosystems	By 2020, protect and restore water-related ecosystems, including mountains, forests, wetlands, rivers, aquifers and lakes
7.2	Renewable energy	By 2030, increase substantially the share of renewable energy in the global energy mix
8.9	Sustainable tourism	By 2030, devise and implement policies to promote sustainable tourism that creates jobs and promotes local culture and products

(Continued)

Table 12.1   *(Continued)*

Target	Short description	Official description
9.1	Infrastructure	Develop quality, reliable, sustainable and resilient infrastructure, including regional and transborder infrastructure, to support economic development and human well-being, with a focus on affordable and equitable access for all
10.1	Economic equality	By 2030, progressively achieve and sustain income growth of the bottom 40 per cent of the population at a rate higher than the national average
11.2	Transport	By 2030, provide access to safe, affordable, accessible and sustainable transport systems for all, improving road safety, notably by expanding public transport, with special attention to the needs of those in vulnerable situations, women, children, persons with disabilities and older persons
12.5	Waste	By 2030, substantially reduce waste generation through prevention, reduction, recycling and reuse
13.2	Climate change/policy planning	Integrate climate change measures into national policies, strategies and planning
15.2	Biodiversity	Take urgent and significant action to reduce the degradation of natural habitats, halt the loss of biodiversity and, by 2020, protect and prevent the extinction of threatened species
16.7	Decision-making	Ensure responsive, inclusive, participatory and representative decision-making at all levels

The scoring was based on the literature review where the key concepts were scrutinised and information about positive or negative connections was highlighted. This information was then collected and compiled in a table to build the base for the scoring. To ensure that the scoring was performed in a consistent way, it was based on the criteria found in Table 12.2. An example of the scoring is provided in Box 12.1.

Table 12.2   Criteria used for scoring interactions, ranging from –3 to +3

Score	Meaning
+3	Progress on one target creates very good conditions for achieving progress on another target. The literature describes a positive connection between progress of the analysed target and target X and explains the connection (*sure prognosis*).
+2	Progress on one target leads to a synergy between that and another target. The literature describes a positive connection between progress of the analysed target and target X and explains the connection (*sure prognosis*).
+1	Progress on one target leads to a possible synergy between that and another target. The literature is limited or contradictory (*unsure prognoses*).
0	There is no significant link between two targets' progress found in the literature
–1	Progress on one target leads to a possible trade-off between that and another target but the literature is limited or contradictory (*unsure prognosis*).
–2	Progress on one target leads to a trade-off between that and another target. The literature describes a negative connection between progress of the analysed target and target X and explains the connection (*sure prognosis*).
–3	Progress on one target makes it very difficult to achieve progress on another target. The literature describes a negative connection between progress of the analysed target and target X and explains the connection (*sure prognosis*).

Source: Adapted from Nilsson et al. (2016) and Boman (2018)

BOX 12.1   ASSESSMENT EXAMPLE OF THE SCORING OF INTERACTION

Assessment example:

Target 6.6 (*water-related ecosystems*) → Target 15.5 (*biodiversity*)

Combating impoverishment and restoring affected ecosystems are of the utmost importance for the work of conserving biodiversity (Ebenhard et al., 2021). Among unique, red-listed species in Norrland, felling is classified as the most common impact factor (Eide et al., 2020).

Comment: The protection of water-related ecosystems such as forests or wetlands will create good conditions for halting the loss of biodiversity, which gives a score of +3.

Target 7.2 (*renewable energy*) → Target 8.9 (*sustainable tourism*)

The tourism industry's contribution to carbon dioxide emissions comes mainly from travelling. As tourism is not predicted to decline there is a great need to develop energy sources, rather than change the means of transport (Jonsson & Pettersson, 2020). An increased expansion of wind-power in the north may mean that formally protected mountain areas with good wind conditions will be exploited which may negatively affect active outdoor life (Energimyndigheten, 2019). The hospitality industry in Jämtland Härjedalen has a conflict of aims concerning land use between wind-power and tourism (Jonsson & Pettersson, 2020).

Comment: The expansion of renewable energy can have both positive and negative effects on tourism. The contradiction suggests a possible trade-off which gives a score of –1.

12.3.1   Method Discussion

Using the SDG interaction framework as a method to analyse synergies and trade-offs between the SDGs entails both stronger and weaker aspects. Since it was created, the framework has been used in a number of studies and is therefore a proven concept (Allen et al., 2018; ICSU, 2017; Lyytimäki et al., 2020; McCollum et al., 2018; Nilsson et al., 2016; Weitz et al., 2018). However, the scoring process in previous studies has been based on the judgement of different expert groups. This was not possible within this study due to practical limitations and time restrictions, which is why an adaptation of the original typology was seen as necessary. The ambiguity of the goals resulted in sometimes contradictory statements in the literature which made it difficult to assess the connections according to the original seven-point scale. The degree of uncertainty is therefore a part of the evaluation in this study. Because of this the method gives an indication both of the strength of interaction and also of how certain the scoring is. This has different consequences for the results. It can be argued that the results are not as clearly conveyed as in the previously mentioned studies or that the results are not as reliable. That the results are not as clearly conveyed cannot be overlooked, but presenting the uncertainties this way gives a fair picture of reality since many of the goals are complex. This has however had some positive effects on the methodology, as one potential weakness with the judgement-based exercise is that the identification of connections is highly dependent on the assumptions made by the evaluator (Lyytimäki et al. 2020). This was partly avoided by using a literature base for the scoring which can be seen as a strength in the study.

Another limitation of the study is that the initial decision on which targets to include could introduce bias into the analysis. A relatively small number of targets was included which is why this study should be seen as an initial step. Further investigations would benefit from including more targets to give a more comprehensive mapping of interactions across the SDGs.

One obvious difficulty that occurs when working with the SDGs is that of scale. The SDGs are global goals, and it can be difficult to interpret them at a regional or local level. Looking at the target level is helpful as the targets are more specific, and it makes it easier to clarify how they relate to the regional/ local context. This method highlights the importance of contextualisation of the global targets to regional priorities and circumstances and can serve as an important first step in the implementation of the goals.

12.4   RESULTS

The cross-impact matrix is the result of the analysis of 210 interactions and shows the influence that targets exert on each other (Figure 12.1). The analysis

	1.2	2.4	3.4	4.4	5.5	6.6	7.2	8.9	9.1	10.1	11.2	12.5	13.2	15.5	16.7	Sum
1.2		1	3	3	3	0	0	0	0	3	-1	-1	-1	-1	2	*11*
2.4	0		2	0	0	1	1	1	0	1	0	3	3	1	0	*12*
3.4	2	0		1	2	0	0	0	0	2	0	0	1	0	0	*8*
4.4	3	1	3		2	1	0	2	0	3	1	1	2	1	3	*23*
5.5	2	0	3	2		1	0	0	1	2	1	1	2	1	3	*19*
6.6	0	2	2	0	0		-2	1	-1	1	-2	0	1	3	0	*5*
7.2	0	1	2	0	0	-2		-1	2	0	2	2	3	-2	0	*7*
8.9	0	2	0	1	0	1	-1		1	0	3	1	2	1	1	*12*
9.1	1	-1	2	2	0	-1	2	2		1	3	0	3	-1	2	*15*
10.1	3	1	3	3	3	0	0	0	0		-1	-1	-1	-1	1	*10*
11.2	1	0	3	1	2	-1	2	3	3	1		2	3	-1	0	*19*
12.5	1	2	1	0	0	3	1	1	0	1	0		3	3	0	*16*
13.2	1	3	3	0	0	-1	3	2	3	1	3	2		1	0	*21*
15.5	0	3	2	0	0	3	-2	2	-1	1	-2	0	-1		0	*5*
16.7	1	1	2	1	3	1	0	2	1	1	1	0	2	1		*17*
Sum	*15*	*16*	*31*	*14*	*15*	*6*	*4*	*15*	*8*	*18*	*8*	*10*	*22*	*6*	*12*	

Figure 12.1   · *Cross-impact matrix. Visualisation of the 15 targets and their interactions. The row-sum represents the net influence from a target on all other targets, and the column-sum represents how the target is influenced*

will give further examples of what information can be drawn from the cross-impact matrix and how this can be used for policy making. Mainly positive or neutral connections have been identified, which means that targets in general exert more positive than negative influence on each other. This also means that progress in one area often makes it easier to fulfil other targets simultaneously. Only eight per cent of the connections have negative scores, but they mark important exceptions as this indicates conflicts of aims.

The matrix can be examined from different perspectives, where the numerical row-sum indicates the net influence of a target on other targets. A target with a high row-sum can be seen as a synergetic one as this implies that the successful implementation of a target makes the realisation of other targets easier. A negative or low row-sum suggests that the implementation of a target generally makes it more difficult to achieve other targets. The column-sum shows us how a target is influenced by the progress of other targets. Here, a high number suggests a predominant positive influence from other targets, while a negative or low column-sum implies that the successful implementation of other targets makes it more difficult to reach the target. However, the numerical sums (row and column) in isolation do not show if the net influence is due to a large number of weak or contradictory influences on several targets or a few strong ones, nor does it show the distribution between positive and negative connections.

12.4.1   Summary of Row and Column Sums

Several targets only exert a positive influence, such as 4.4 (*technical/vocational skills*), 5.5 (*women's participation*), 16.7 (*decision-making*), 12.5 (*waste*), and 3.4 (*non-communicable diseases*). Some of these targets also have the highest row-sum. At the top we find target 4.4 (sum 23) followed by target 13.2 (*climate change policy/planning*) (sum 21) and thereafter targets 5.5 and 11.2 (*transport*) (sum 19). Both targets 13.2 and 11.2 exert a negative influence on other targets despite the high row-sum.

The other end of the spectrum shows targets with the least amount of positive net influence on other targets. The lowest row-sum is held by targets 6.6 (*water-related ecosystems*) and 15.5 (*biodiversity*), which both have a sum of five. Following that are targets 7.2 (*renewable energy*) (sum 7) and 3.4 (*non-communicable diseases*) (sum 8). There are however important differences between these results. Target 15.5 exerts a negative influence of –6, making it the target with the least positive influence on other targets. Targets 6.6 and 7.2 both have a negative influence of –5, while target 3.4 has no negative influence but is given a low number due to its many neutral connections.

Looking at the column-sums, which indicate how a specific target is influenced by other targets, we find targets 3.4 (*non-communicable diseases*) (sum

31), 13.2 (*climate change policy/planning*) (sum 22), and 10.1 (*economic equality)* (sum 18) at the top. This indicates that these targets will be helped when progress is made on other targets. Again it is important to not only look at the final sum, as target 13.2, for example, is negatively influenced by other targets as well (–3 in total). At the bottom end we find target 7.2 (*renewable energy*) (sum 4), followed by target 15.5 (*biodiversity)* (sum 6) and target 6.6 (*water-related ecosystems*) (sum 6). However, looking specifically at the negative influence from other targets, the matrix shows that both targets 15.5 and 11.2 (*transport*) receive the same amount of negative influence from other targets (–6), followed by targets 6.6 and 7.2 that both receive a negative influence of –5.

12.4.2 Policy Implications

The analysis performed by Oxford Research on the old version of Jämtland Härjedalens RDS can be used to demonstrate the implications of using the SDG interaction framework for policy. Target 10.1 on economic equality is not found in the former RDS. Taking a closer look at the analysis of how this target is connected to the network, we find that targets that the Region are already prioritising such as health, education, infrastructure, and sustainable transport will have a positive influence on economic equality. This indicates that progress will be made in this target even if it is not a priority, but it also suggests that a potential negative influence might take place as well whether measures are aimed at making progress in target 10.1 or not. It also shows the potential of positive reinforcement that target 10.1 can have on other areas of the SDGs which might be lost if measures aimed specifically at this target are not pursued.

An analysis of this kind can also provide useful information when it comes to policies in which departments would benefit from deeper cooperation. Figure 12.2a shows which other targets affect the ability to make progress on target 10.1 and whom the people in charge need to foster good collaboration with. Figure 12.2b shows how target 10.1 affects other targets and where it might meet resistance or where the need for negotiation might be greater.

12.5 DISCUSSION

The findings are in line with earlier studies performed in the same contextual area, which suggests that most of the relationships within the SDGs are synergistic ones (Lyytimäki et al., 2020; Weitz et al., 2018). This means that activities aimed at reaching one goal or target generally improve opportunities to reach other goals or targets as well. None of the interactions were seen to make it very difficult to make progress in another target. The analysis

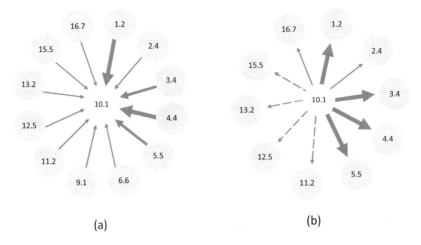

(a)   (b)

Figure 12.2   Analysis of target 10.1. (a) Network of interactions based on target 10.1: influence from other targets; (b) network of interactions based on target 10.1: influence on other targets. The thickness of arrows represents the level of influence (–3 to +3). Negative influence dashed lines, positive solid lines

shows that progress in targets 4.4 (*technical/vocational skills*), 13.2 (*climate change policy/planning*), 5.5 (*women's participation*), and 11.2 (*transportation*) generates the most positive influence on other targets which suggests that efforts to make progress here should be prioritised as it will have positive ripple effects that drive progress on the 15 SDG targets overall. These can be good starting points to achieve maximum synergistic effects.

Targets with the least positive influence on other targets are target 15.5 (*biodiversity*) and target 6.6 (*water-related ecosystems*), followed by 7.2 (*renewable energy*). This means that making progress in these targets will make it more difficult to achieve other targets, and therefore special attention needs to be directed here to mitigate the problem. This result highlights the ongoing debate about how we should use the forest which is related to its differing benefits for climate (Bergström et al., 2020).

Targets 3.4 (*non-communicable diseases*), 13.2 (*climate change policy/ planning*), and 10.1 (*economic equality*) receive the most positive influence from progress in other targets. At first sight it might look like these targets would not need as much targeted support or that they might not need to be made priorities in strategies such as the RDS. However, Weitz et al. (2018) point out that progress in other goals should not be assumed. If anything, this result indicates a high dependency on other targets which may make these targets' progress more uncertain as they are highly influenced by what happens in other areas. It indicates that close collaboration is needed with the actors that hold the key to their development. It should however be noted that several of the scores connected to target 10.1 (*economic equality*) are +1 and that additional information is needed to confirm the total score. Target 15.5 (*biodiversity*) receives the most negative influence from other targets followed by targets 6.6 (*water-related ecosystems*) and 7.2 (*renewable energy*). This means that progress in other areas will make it harder to achieve these goals. For the people in charge of these goals it could be of special interest to collaborate with actors that have the potential to make progress in their areas more difficult.

Both low and high row- and column-sums suggest that special attention should be directed to the implementation of the target in question (Lyytimäki et al., 2020). It is, however, important to note that synergies or trade-offs between targets may exist despite the total sum being high or low. It is therefore important to use Figure 12.1 as a starting point for further analysis and discussions on policy implications. Looking in detail at the connections in Figure 12.2 can be a useful way to move further with the sustainability work and to highlight where cooperation is most needed to facilitate it. Although only eight per cent of the interactions indicate trade-offs, they call for careful consideration, especially since some of these trade-offs risk leading to irreversible problems. The targets concerning climate change (13.2) and transportation (11.2) are a good example of this, where the net influence of the targets is positive but without careful consideration the use of more biofuels could have a negative effect on the restoration and protection of forests as well as biodiversity connected to forests.

Many of the identified connections are paired with an uncertainty (scores of −1 and +1) that stems from limited or contradicting information from the literature. One example is the effect of the protection of biodiversity (15.5) on climate measures (13.2). There are several synergetic effects, such as how the protection of natural environments can help increase carbon storage and mitigate climate change. On the other hand, this can interfere with climate measures aimed at replacing fossil energy with bioenergy. These types of uncertainties are not just a result of a lack of literature; rather they are connected to the complexity of many of the targets and show how important it is to have a systems perspective when implementing measures. The risk is otherwise that certain efforts will backfire unexpectedly in another part of the system. Some targets are paired with more uncertainties than others. Target 16.7 stands out as having the most uncertain scoring (nine connections are marked +1). This is related to limited information on the connections rather than any contradictions. Higher participation seems to have an overall positive effect on other targets, but more information is needed on the matter before any definite conclusions can be drawn. It should also be mentioned that in order to draw more certain conclusions overall it would be beneficial to test and validate these initial results and to include more targets in a further analysis.

One of the main principles of Agenda 2030 is that of indivisibility, meaning that none of the goals can be achieved at the expense of another (State Office, 2019). As mentioned earlier, the Agenda has received critique for inconsistencies, particularly between the socio-economic development and the environmental sustainability goals (ICSU and ISSC, 2015). The fact that trade-offs exist within the SDGs is established, and this study is yet more proof of that. The results and analysis show that there is a risk of losing the principle of indivisibility if careful consideration is not given to the impact on other goals. This leads to dilemmas when it comes to simultaneously fulfilling all targets.

12.5.1   Measures to Reduce Trade-Offs and Enhance Synergies

The seven-point typology is useful for detecting potential synergies and trade-offs, but it does not offer any guidance on how to deal with these findings. This must be dealt with on a case-by-case basis. Looking elsewhere there are different views on how trade-offs can be mitigated. Ekener et al. (2019b) describe how the negative connections in many cases can be avoided if there is a sustainability-creating policy framework in place that can reduce the risks of progress in one area of society taking place at the expense of progress in another. One example from this investigation is how the development of tourism (8.9) is seen as a way to increase the possibilities of local food production (target 2.4), although this can only be seen as a synergy if the increased level of agriculture is performed in a sustainable matter. What measures are put in place is important for the overall outcome.

Bergström et al. (2020) instead find it unrealistic to expect full goal fulfilment for different competing goals. They conclude that synergetic effects are not something that will come automatically; they need to be planned. Related to this is the finding that questions regarding sustainability need to be given more space at the highest level of management and that Agenda 2030, and for the goals to achieved they need to be integrated into the steering and management (SKR, 2020; State Office, 2019).

Investing in interdisciplinary research, strengthening knowledge and competence regarding Agenda 2030 and its connections, and providing support to all actors at all levels of society to absorb this information are other key parts in reaching the goals (Ekener et al., 2019a). Another important factor in avoiding trade-offs and enhancing synergies is cooperation. In the final report from the Swedish Agenda 2030 delegation (Swedish Government, 2019a), they present suggestions for the continued implementation of Agenda 2030.

The need for cooperation between different sectors and authorities as well as between different levels (local, regional, national) is emphasised as key to being able to achieve the targets. The need for leadership that acts long-term is also highlighted.

Regardless of one's belief concerning the possibilities of reaching full goal fulfilment there is agreement that awareness is needed of how different goals relate to each other to be able to manage conflicts and to enhance synergies (Bergström et al., 2020; Ekener et al., 2019b).

12.5.2   Implications for Region Jämtland Härjedalen

The analysis of Jämtland Härjedalens Regional Development Strategy (RDS) concluded that the current steering document did not include all the aspects of the SDGs which suggests there is a need for something further to be implemented. Some questions can be hard to affect at a regional level as they are decided at the national level through legislation and funds, but there are aspects of the framework that could be helpful in organising the work. Using this framework could provide decision-makers with an understanding of where there are arguments for focusing specific attention on implementing certain goals or targets and where there are risks of significant harmful effects that need to be taken into account. The framework can also serve as an important piece in understanding the integrated nature of the SDGs.

Goals concerning equality and the environment were missing from the region's old RDS. Apart from the inherent value of these questions, this study also shows that it could be wise from a policy perspective to focus on these aspects. Target 5.5 on women's participation and target 13.2 on climate policy are found to be highly synergetic. Among the environmental targets (6.6 and 15.5) there are some important trade-offs to handle, and these might be given more attention if the goals are prioritised in the new RDS.

The negative aspects of using this method can be summarised as time and money. The framework is time consuming, and to achieve the best effect, officials from different departments would have to be involved which would also result in high costs. The time spent could however result in great possibilities. Using the framework would give a better overview of the region's work with sustainability and could increase cooperation between different sectors, which in itself is seen as an important factor for achieving the goals. It would also increase the chances of using the possible synergies and be a way of acknowledging trade-offs which is a first step towards dealing with them. Overall, it is likely to lead to better informed decision-making.

This chapter focuses on what potential progress across the investigated SDGs would lead to and less on what would happen if progress is not achieved.

This scenario could bring even bigger conflicts and lead to increased costs for society as a whole. One example of this is lack of education which can cause a downward spiral leading to unemployment (Kvist, 2020) and poverty (Mood & Jonsson, 2019). The consequences of climate change risk far-reaching negative consequences for ecosystems around the world, as well as for human societies and livelihoods (IPCC, 2014). The risks for serious and irreversible effects are expected to increase the longer we wait to take action, and so are the costs for society (ibid.). Another example relates to inequality, where it has been shown that economic inequality tends to lead to increased social tension and anxiety and increased criminality as well as growing intolerance and extremism (Swedish Government, 2019b). This needs to be taken into account when working with the SDGs and is a reminder to not let potential conflicts slow down the work towards the goals, all while the risk of conflicting aims cannot be overlooked.

12.6   CONCLUSIONS

The interactions found reveal mostly synergetic effects between the SDG targets; only eight per cent of the connections are associated with trade-offs. Several targets only exert a positive or neutral influence on others. Out of these, targets 4.4 (*technical/vocational skills*) and 5.5 (*women's participation*) stand out as having the most positive influence on other targets, which implies that efforts to make progress here will maximise synergistic effects. In this category we also find targets 13.2 (*climate change policy/planning*) and 11.2 (*transportation*), although they have some negative influence that needs to be considered. Target 13.2 also stands out as being highly dependent on other targets which means that close collaboration with actors in charge of the targets that hold the key to its progress should be developed. The positive ripple effects that come with progress in these targets can however provide guidance on where to focus specific attention. Target 15.5 (*biodiversity*) has the least positive influence on other targets followed by target 6.6 (*water-related ecosystems*) and target 7.2 (*renewable energy*). Progress in these targets is associated with difficulties in making progress in other areas, and the risk of harmful effects calls for careful consideration from a policy perspective.

Taking on the SDGs on a regional level of a nation can prove difficult due to the scale and complexity of the goals. Looking at the target level is helpful as the targets are more specific which makes it easier to clarify how they relate to the regional/local context. An important part of the implementation is to start with contextualising the global targets in regional circumstances. The SDG interaction framework brings insight and knowledge on the Agenda and how the targets and goals connect to one another. It can also be used as a tool for prioritisation and gives knowledge on how different decisions will influence other aspects of sustainability.

An important first step is making sure that questions regarding sustainability have a natural place in the highest level of management and that Agenda 2030 and the goals are integrated into the steering and management to achieve the goals. Based on this investigation a suggestion to the region would be to have a special committee under the regional council to ensure that the SDGs are a part of the decisions being made. In addition to this it should be said that the need for structural change involves all levels of society and that national support and prioritisation are needed as well.

Having knowledge on potential trade-offs does not make the obstacles of solving them any easier, and there is no blueprint on how to achieve full goal fulfilment in all areas of the SDGs. It can however be concluded that awareness of how different targets relate to each other is an important step in being able to manage conflicts and to enhance synergies and can lead to better informed decision-making.

REFERENCES

Allen, C., Metternicht, G., & Wiedmann, T. (2018). Prioritising SDG targets: Assessing baselines, gaps and interlinkages. *Sustainability Science*, 14(2), 421–438. https://doi.org/10.1007/s11625-018-0596-8

Bali Swain, R., & Ranganathan, S. (2021). Modeling interlinkages between sustainable development goals using network analysis. *World Development*, 138, 105136. https://doi.org/10.1016/j.worlddev.2020.105136

Bergström, L., Borgström, P., Smith, H. G., Bergek, S., Caplat, P., Casini, M., Ekroos, J., Gårdmark, A., Halling, C., Huss, M., Jönsson, A. M., Limburg, K., Miller, P., Nilsson, L., & Sandin, L. (2020). *Klimatförändringar och biologisk mångfald – Slutsatser från IPCC och IPBES i ett svenskt perspektiv [Climate Change and Biodiversity – Conclusions from IPCC and IPBES in a Swedish Perspective]*. Klimatologi Nr 56. SMHI and Naturvårdsverket, Norrköping and Stockholm, Sweden.

Boman, I. (2018). *Synergier och målkonflikter mellan klimatmålet om noll nettoutsläpp av växthusgaser år 2045 och Sveriges Nationella Miljömål [Synergies and Trade-Offs Between the Climate Goal of Zero Net-Emissions of GHG Emissions Year 2045 and the Swedish National Environmental Objectives]*. [Master thesis], Department of physical geography, Stockholm University, Stockholm.

Cling, J.-P., & Delecourt, C. (2022). Interlinkages between the sustainable development goals. *World Development Perspective*, 25, 100398. https://doi.org/10.1016/j.wdp.2022.100398

Ebenhard, T,. Bergström, L., Hägerhäll, C., Johansson, M., Lenartsson, T., Sandström, C., Tunón, H., & Öberg Ben Ammar, L. (2021). *Utarmning och restaurering av landekosystem – Ett svensk perspektiv på IPBES-rapporten Land Degradation and restoration [Depletion and Restoration of Terrestrial Ecosystems – A Swedish Perspective on the IPBES Report Land Degradation and Restoration]*. Report 6948. Naturvårdsverket, Stockholm.

Eide, W., Ahrné, K., Bjelke, U., Nordström, S., Ottosson, E., Sandström, J., & Sundberg, S. (2020) *Tillstånd och trender för arter och deras livsmiljöer – rödlistade arter i Sverige 2020 [Conditions and Trends for Species and Their Habitats – Red-listed Species in Sweden 2020]*. Artdatabanken rapporterar nr 24. Sveriges Lantbruksuniversitete (SLU), Uppsala.

Ekener, E., Katzeff, C., Gunnarsson-Östling, U., & Skånberg, K. (2019a). *Ömsesidiga beroenden mellan olika hållbarhetsperspektiv: Möjligheter att genom kunskaper om synergier och trade-offs mellan olika globala hållbarhetsmål förbättra förutsättningarna att nå Agenda 2030 i sin helhet [Mutual Dependencies Between Different Sustainability Perspectives: Opportunities to Improve the Conditions for Achieving Agenda 2030 in Its Entirety Through Knowledge of Synergies and Trade-Offs Between Different Global Sustainability Goals]*. Report 6903. Naturvårdsverket, Stockholm.

Ekener, E., Katzeff, C., Gunnarsson-Östling, U., & Skånberg, K. (2019b). *Så hänger jämställdhet och jämlikhet ihop med miljömålen: En analys av ömsesidiga beroenden mellan olika hållbarhetsmål [How gender equality and equality are linked to environmental goals: An analysis of interdependencies between different sustainability goals]*. Report 6856. Naturvårdsverket, Stockholm.

Energimyndigheten. (2019). *100 procent förnybar el: Delrapport 2 – Scenarier, vägval och utmaningar [100 Percent Renewable Electricity: Interim Report 2 – Scenarios, Choices and Challenges]*. ER 2019:06. Energimyndigheten, Eskilstuna.

Engström, R., Destouni, G., Howells, M., Ramaswamy, V., Rogner, H., & Bazilian, M. (2019). Cross-scale water and land impacts of local climate and energy policy—A local Swedish analysis of selected SDG interactions. *Sustainability*, 11(7), 1847. 10.3390/su11071847

ICSU. (2017). *A Guide To SDG Interactions: From Science to Implementation*. Paris: International Council for Science.

ICSU & ISSC. (2015). *Review of Targets for The Sustainable Development Goals: The Science Perspective*. Paris: International Council for Science & International Social Science Council.

IPCC. (2014). *Climate Change 2014: Synthesis Report. Contribution of Working Groups I, II and III to the Fifth Assessment Report of the Intergovernmental Panel on Climate Change*. Geneva: IPCC.

Jonsson, A., & Pettersson, R. (2020). *Besöksnäringens roll för regional utveckling – Ett nedslag i Jämtland Härjedalen [The Role of the Hospitality Industry for Regional Development – An example in Jämtland Härjedalen]*. ETOUR Report 2020. Mid Sweden University, Sundsvall.

Kostetckaia, M., & Hametner, M. (2022). How sustainable development goals interlinkages influence European countries' progress towards the 2030 agenda. *Sustainable Development*, 30(5), 916–926. https://doi.org/10.1002/sd.2290

Kroll, C., Warchold, A., & Pradhan, P. (2019). Sustainable Development Goals (SDGs): Are we successful in turning trade-offs into synergies? *Palgrave Communications*, 5, 140. https://doi.org/10.1057/s41599-019-0335-5

Kullander, B. (2021). *Regionernas åtaganden [Committments of the Regions]*. Sveriges Kommuner Och Regioner. Regionernas åtaganden | SKR (Accessed: 29 November 2022).

Kvist, M. (2020). *Varken resurs eller problem, om lågutbildade ungas etablerings- och försörjnings-möjligheter [Neither a Resource nor a Problem, About the Establishment and Support Opportunities of Low-Educated Young People]*. [Doctoral dissertation], Malmö University, Malmö, Sweden.

Lyytimäki, J., Lonkila, K. M., Furman, E., Korhonen-Kurki, K., & Lähteenoja, S. (2020). Untangling the interactions of sustainability targets: Synergies and trade-offs in the Northern European context. *Environment, Development and Sustainability*, 23(3), 3458–3473. https://doi.org/10.1007/s10668-020-00726-w

McCollum, D. L., Gomez Echeverri, L., Busch, S., Pachauri, S., Parkinson, S., Rogelj, J., Krey, V., Minx, J. C., Nilsson, M., Stevance, A.-S., & Riahi, K. (2018). Connecting the sustainable development goals by their energy inter-linkages. *Environmental Research Letters*, 13(3), 033006. http://doi.org/10.1088/1748-9326/aaafe3

Miola, A., Borchardt, S., Neher, F., & Buscaglia, D. (2019). *Interlinkages and Policy Coherence for the Sustainable Development Goals Implementation: An Operational Method to Identify Trade-Offs and Co-Benefits in a Systemic Way.* Luxembourg: Publications Office of the European Union.

Mood, C., & Jonsson, J. (2019). Välfärden - den nya fattigdomen [Welfare - the new poverty]. In J. Björkman & P. Hadenius (Eds.), *Det nya Sverige - Riksbankens Jubileumsfonds årsbok 2019* (pp. 9–50). Göteborg, Sweden: Makadam förlag.

Nilsson, M., Chisholm, E., Griggs, D., Howden-Chapman, P., McCollum, D., Messerli, P., Neumann, B., Stevance, A.-S., Visbeck, M., & Stafford-Smith, M. (2018). Mapping interactions between the sustainable development goals: Lessons learned and ways forward. *Sustainability Science*, 13(6), 1489–1503. https://doi.org/10.1007/s11625-018-0604-z

Nilsson, M., Griggs, D., Visbeck, M., & Ringler, C. (2016). *A Draft Framework for Understanding SDG Interactions.* Paris: International Council for Science.

Oxford Research. (2019). *Processtöd för att implementera hållbarhets-aspekter och Agenda 2030 i strategiarbetet [Process Support for Implementing Sustainability Aspects and Agenda 2030 in the Strategy Work].* Oxford Research, Stockholm.

Pradhan, P., Costa, L., Rybski, D., Lucht, W., & Kropp, J. P. (2017). A systematic study of Sustainable Development Goal (SDG) interactions. *Earth's Future*, 5(11), 1169–1179. http://doi.org/10.1002/2017ef000632

RKA. (2020). *Agenda 2030- Nyckeltal för kommuner och regioner [Agenda 2030- Key Figures for Municipalities and Regions].* Rådet för främjande av kommunala analyser [The Council for the Promotion of Municipal Analyses], Stockholm.

SKR. (2019). *Regionala initiativ inom Agenda 2030 i Sverige [Regional Initiatives Within Agenda 2030 in Sweden].* Sveriges Kommuner och Regioner [The joint organization for Sweden's municipalities and regions], Stockholm.

SKR. (2020). *Öppna Jämförelser - Agenda 2030 [Open Comparisons - Agenda 2030].* Sveriges Kommuner och Regioner [The joint organization for Sweden's municipalities and regions], Stockholm.

Swedish Government. (2019a). *Agenda 2030 och Sverige: Världens utmaning – världens möjlighet [Agenda 2030 and Sweden: The World's Challenge - the World's Opportunity].* SOU 2019:13 [Swedish Government Official Reports, reports by Government commissions of inquiry (SOU series)], Stockholm.

Swedish Government. (2019b). *Låt fler forma framtiden [Allow More People to Shape the Future].* SOU 2016:5 [Swedish Government Official Reports, reports by Government commissions of inquiry (SOU series)], Stockholm.

Swedish Government. (2019c). *Sveriges genomförande av Agenda 2030 [Sweden's Implementation of Agenda 2030].* Prop. 2019/20:188 [Government bill to the Swedish Parliament], Stockholm.

Swedish Parliament. (2017). *Förordning om reginalt tillväxtarbete [Ordinance on Regional Growth Work].* SFS 2017:583 [Ordinance from the Ministry of Economic Affairs], Stockholm.

State Office. (2019). *Agenda 2030 i myndigheter, kommuner och regioner: Delrapport.* *[Agenda 2030 in Authorities, Municipalities and Regions: Progress Report].* 2019:15. State Office, Stockholm.

State Office. (2020). *Agenda 2030 i myndigheter, kommuner och regioner: Slutrapport.* *[Agenda 2030 in Authorities, Municipalities and Regions: Final Report].* 2020:15. State Office, Stockholm.

UN. (2015). *Resolution Adopted by the General Assembly on 25th September 2015: Transforming Our World: The 2030 Agenda for Sustainable Development.* UN.

Warchold, A., Pradhan, P., & Kropp, J. P. (2021). Variations in sustainable development goal interactions: Population, regional, and income disaggregation. *Sustainable Development*, 29(2), 285–299. http://doi.org/10.1002/sd.2145

Weitz, N., Carlsen, H., Nilsson, M., & Skånberg, K. (2018). Towards systemic and contextual priority setting for implementing the 2030 agenda. *Sustainability Science*, 13(2), 531–548. https://doi.org/10.1007/s11625-017-0470-0

Index